Toxicity of Pure Foods

Toxicity of
Pure Foods

Author:

E. M. Boyd (deceased)

Professor Emeritus of Pharmacology
Queen's University
Kingston, Ontario, Canada

Edited by:

Carl E. Boyd, M.D.
Chief, Drug Information Bulletin Division
Health Protection Branch
Health and Welfare Canada
Ottawa, Ontario, Canada

published by:

18901 Cranwood Parkway, Cleveland, Ohio 44128
Formerly The Chemical Rubber Co.

International Standard Book Number 0-87819-035-x

Library of Congress Card Number 73-83414

PREFACE

The studies described in this volume demonstrate that there is a dose or amount of all pure foods which can produce a lethal toxicity syndrome in laboratory animals. Pure foods are usually regarded as nontoxic apart from an occasional stomach upset from eating too much of certain foods, especially in children, and the continued overeating of pure foods, which may produce obesity.

The concept that pure foods can produce death, if administered in a sufficiently large dose, arose a number of years ago in studies by the author and his associates. In 1963, following the thalidomide disaster, the government of Canada introduced new legislation that before a new drug could be sold in Canada, the manufacturer had to provide, among other things, proof of the safety of the new drug under the conditions of use. Evidence of safety, therefore, became a necessary part of any application for acceptance of a new drug by the government of Canada. It then became necessary to define what was meant by safety. Safety obviously meant the absence of toxic effects, especially death. Toxic effects, in turn, are related to dosage so that the required evidence should include a study of toxic effects of doses ranging up to those which produced death. Such studies obviously had to be performed largely on laboratory animals and the science of Predictive Toxicometrics came to maturity as a result.

Predictive Toxicometrics is concerned with predicting toxicity in man from studies on laboratory animals. The subject is divided into three main phases. The first of these is Factorial or Etiological Toxicometrics, which is concerned with the various factors that affect the response of laboratory animals to toxic doses of drugs and other agents. Acute or single dose toxicity is discussed under the heading of Uniposal Toxicometrics. Subacute and chronic toxicity is described under the heading of Multiposal Toxicometrics. These topics have been discussed by the author in a volume entitled *Predictive Toxicometrics,* Scientechnica Publishers Ltd., Bristol, England, 1972.

In the course of these studies it was noted that skin reactions to drugs rarely appeared in laboratory animals but are frequent in man. Since skin reactions are common manifestations of certain vitamin deficiencies, it was postulated that they might occur in persons with a marginal vitamin deficiency. To test this hypothesis, laboratory animals were placed on various vitamin-deficient diets and then given toxic doses of drugs such as benzylpenicillin. It was found that the vitamin deficiency augmented susceptibility to drug toxicity but that the augmentation was not due to the absence of vitamins in the diet.

To make a long story short, it was finally discovered that augmentation of drug toxicity in vitamin deficient animals was due to the presence of large amounts of certain pure foods, such as sucrose, in the vitamin deficient diet fed to the animals. This observation prompted a study of the uniposal and multiposal toxicity of pure foods.

The results demonstrated that there are toxic and lethal doses of all pure foods. The amount or dose required to produce a lethal syndrome is within the limits of possible human consumption for some pure foods and beyond these limits for others. Since toxic doses vary with body weight, a child is more likely to consume a lethal dose of pure foods than is an adult. For example, based on animal data, a child of 22 lb eating and retaining half a pound of candy would receive the equivalent of a dose of sucrose of 25 g/kg, which is a fatal dose in albino rats.

Data on lethal doses of other pure foods in laboratory animals suggest that death in man from single doses would be extremely unlikely due to the large lethal dose. For example, in a single meal a man would have to eat half his body weight of starch before getting doses that killed albino rats in terms of g/kg body weight. On the other hand, it is possible that sublethal doses could produce signs of sublethal toxicity, such as gastrolith from large amounts of starch.

The chronic toxicity of pure foods is such that large fractions of the $LD_{50\ (1\ dose)}$ have to be given daily to produce severe toxicity and death.

The $LD_{50\ (100\ days)}$, or dose which kills 50% of animals over a period of 100 days of daily administration, is about 90% of the $LD_{50\ (1\ dose)}$ in the instance of sucrose. The $LD_{50\ (100\ days)}$ expressed as a percentage of the $LD_{50\ (1\ dose)}$ is termed the 100-day LD_{50} index. The higher the 100-day LD_{50} index, the relatively more safe is a substance for chronic use. Pure foods, therefore, are relatively safe for repeated daily use, which is a well-known fact.

The survey of the toxicity of pure foods described in this book has been confined of necessity largely to clinicopathological syndromes at lethal doses. Time did not permit extensive studies on the toxicity of sublethal doses. Such studies obviously should be conducted and could yield valuable information. For example, the author and his associates found that phenacetin given daily for two thirds of a year to albino rats in amounts that produced no other obvious toxic effect caused a complete inhibition of spermatogenesis in the animals. There remains a great deal to be done in the science of predictive toxicometrics.

Finally, the author wishes to acknowledge the receipt of many grants in aid of research on the toxicity of pure foods in his laboratory. In particular should be mentioned generous financial assistance from the Department of National Health and Welfare of Canada and the Medical Research Council of Canada.

Eldon M. Boyd
Kingston, Ontario, Canada

TABLE OF CONTENTS

Chapter 1

FOOD INTAKE AND LIPID METABOLISM

Scope of the Book

This volume will *not* deal with aspects of food toxicity due to food additives and contaminants. It will not be concerned with toxicity from substances in food such as coloring agents, antioxidants, pH modifiers, and synthetic flavoring agents which have been discussed by authors such as Furia.[1] Nor will it consider topics such as anticaking and bleaching agents, emulsifiers and stabilizers, preservatives, glazers, polishers, and sequestering agents, which have been reviewed by Chapman and Pugsley.[2] The toxicity of "food chemicals," as noted by the National Academy of Sciences,[3] will likewise not be described. "Food chemicals" are defined as substances added directly or indirectly to food for a functional purpose without intending that they remain in the final product.[3] Finally, this book will not deal with food contaminants which have been extensively reviewed, for example, at a Symposium of the Food and Drug Directorate at Ottawa.[4]

Rather, this book will present recent evidence on the toxicity of pure foods, carbohydrates, fats, proteins, salts, water, vitamins, and food adjuvants such as caffeine. Most of the evidence to be described was obtained by the author and his associates in studies which defined the range of lethal doses of pure foods and the clinicopathological syndrome of toxicity. Pure foods are popularly believed to be largely free of poisonous effects to most persons. It will be shown that while the lethal dose of some pure foods is so high as to be unlikely of consumption by man, that of others is within the range of possible human intake. It will also be shown that animals fed large amounts of certain pure foods, in diets upon which they grow and appear normal, become highly susceptible to stresses such as to toxic doses of drugs and other agents, including pesticides.[5]

The basic concept that arises from these studies is that there is probably a toxic dose or amount of everything. This dose is an amount which overwhelms the body mechanisms for dealing with the substance in question. The toxic amount is small for substances popularly known as poisons and large for those called pure foods. Conversely, in amounts that can be satisfactorily dealt with by body mechanisms, no substance is toxic or poisonous. This is not a new concept. It was proposed over 400 years ago by Paracelsus, who stated:[6] "All things are poisons, for there is nothing without poisonous qualities. It is only the dose which makes a thing a poison."

Fasting and Blood Lipids

A piece of knowledge becomes personally significant only when it may be used to solve a personal problem. The earliest impression of the author was that while diet was undoubtedly important, it had little influence on body functions as long as it was adequate. This impression arose during studies on lipid metabolism. Following graduate studies under Professor W. R. Bloor at Rochester, N.Y.,[7] the author transferred to a department of obstetrics and gynecology for a postdoctoral research program. A method for the differential lipid analysis of blood plasma was developed[8] and applied to the study of a series of problems in obstetrics and gynecology.[9-14] The author was then appointed to the staff of the Department of Pharmacology at Queen's University in 1934 and had a research laboratory in the Kingston General Hospital. This arrangement was ideal for studies of blood lipids in patients with various diseases.[15,16]

At that time it was believed that samples of blood for lipid analysis should be collected from patients in a fasting state, i.e., in the morning before breakfast. To obtain such prebreakfast samples of blood meant that the wards of the hospital had to be visited very early in the morning. The author reviewed the evidence indicating that blood should be collected with the patient in a fasting condition and reached the conclusion that such evidence was not too conclusive.[17] He therefore collected samples of blood from eight unfasted persons at intervals over a

TABLE 1

The Constancy of Lipid Levels in the Blood Plasma of Nonfasted Human Subjects*

Composition of total lipid

Hour of sampling	Total lipid	Neutral fat	Fatty acids				Cholesterol			Phospholipid
			Total	Phospholipid	Cholesterol ester	Neutral fat	Total	Ester	Free	
8 a.m.	595	150	349	123	83	143	177	124	53	185
11 a.m.	591	146	345	122	84	139	178	126	52	183
2 p.m.	591	156	340	120	82	148	174	123	51	179
5 p.m.	570	114	323	132	83	108	175	124	51	198
8 p.m.	581	128	334	128	84	122	177	126	51	192
12 p.m.	563	131	324	121	79	124	171	118	53	182
4 a.m.	586	140	337	118	86	133	183	129	54	177

*The results are expressed as mean mg/100 ml of plasma. (From Boyd[7] with the permission of *The Journal of Biological Chemistry.*)

period of 24 hr from 8 a.m. one morning until 4 a.m. the next morning.

Blood plasma of these samples was analyzed for its lipid composition and the results are summarized in Table 1. It was found that the mean values of the various lipids noted in Table 1 did not change significantly over a period of 24 hr in persons who ate regular meals. Subsequent studies disclosed that conditions such as toxic goiter,[18] nephritis,[19] and parenchymatous hepatic diseases[20] produced greater alterations in the concentration of plasma lipids than did fasting.

Regeneration of Blood Lipids

Other evidence of the stability of concentrations of lipids in blood plasma was obtained by Boyd and Stevenson.[21] One quarter of the blood volume of rabbits was removed via the marginal ear veins and the lipids of blood plasma and of the red blood cells determined at subsequent periods of 0, 3, 6, 12, 24, and 48 hr. The removal of blood produced no significant changes in the lipid content of the erythrocytes. Changes in the levels of lipids in blood plasma are summarized in Table 2. It will be noted that the concentration of blood hemoglobin was reduced by about one quarter of the value before hemorrhage and that hemoglobin was not regenerated in significant amounts over the period of 48 hr of measurement.

The level of plasma phospholipid was reduced by a mean of 39% following the hemorrhage. Plasma phospholipid levels were restored to

normal over a period of 24 hr. The pattern followed by the plasma cholesterol fractions was similar to that of phospholipid. The concentration of plasma triglyceride (neutral) fat was not affected by hemorrhage until 48 hr, when it was significantly increased to values above those initially present in the animals. Boyd and Stevenson[21] reviewed evidence suggesting that the slight lipemia at 48 hr may have been a response to oxygen deficit.

Prolonged Fasting

It is well known that prolonged fasting at normal body temperature produces a loss of body fat due to the need for calories to maintain body temperature. Baker et al.[22] investigated changes produced by prolonged starvation in a form of life which could exist at a low temperature and under conditions in which there was little or no need to maintain body temperature. They measured the water, lipids, glycogen, and iodine content of Nova Scotia oysters stored at 4°C. Representative values are noted in Table 3.

Without the need for calories to maintain body temperature, prolonged starvation had little effect on the constituents of oyster flesh. There was some loss of water after two months of storage. The concentration of neutral fat and free sterol was unaffected by storage. The level of sterol esters slowly declined and of phospholipid slowly increased in the second and third months. The concentration of glycogen and of iodine also

TABLE 2

The Regeneration of Lipids in the Blood Plasma of Rabbits Following a Single Massive Hemorrhage*

Time after bleeding (hr)	Hemoglobin	Total lipid	Neutral fat	Total fatty acids	Cholesterol Total	Ester	Free	Phospholipid
3	−25	−14	+18	− 4	−37	−39	−26	−39
6	−26	− 4	+21	+ 1	−30	−40	−10	−20
12	−26	− 7	−15	−10	+15	+ 7	+16	− 6
24	−29	+ 1	+ 8	+ 4	− 6	− 7	+12	− 1
48	−26	+34	+88	+45	+ 9	+ 5	+14	+13

*(From Boyd and Stevenson[21] with permission of *The Journal of Biological Chemistry*.)

TABLE 3

Mean Changes in the Composition of the Flesh of Nova Scotia Oysters Stored at 4°C

Measurement	Weeks of storage 3−5	7−9	13−15
Body water (g/100 g dry wt)	486	428	428
Total lipid (mg/100 g dry wt)	6,292	6,940	7,012
Neutral fat (mg/100 g dry wt)	4,225	4,420	4,383
Total fatty acids (mg/100 g dry wt)	4,985	5,539	5,662
Free sterol (mg/100 g dry wt)	430	352	434
Sterol ester (mg/100 g dry wt)	274	254	194
Phospholipid (mg/100 g dry wt)	1,193	1,744	1,971
Glycogen (mg/100 g dry wt)	−	10,900	6,910
Iodine (μg/100 g dry wt)	440	393	340

slowly fell. These various results indicated that prolonged fasting had little effect when there was no need for calories to maintain body temperature.

Obesity

Obesity is popularly believed to be due to overeating, although there are many examples of overeating producing obesity in one person but not in another. Obesity occurs in albino rats as they grow older and providing they have food available ad libitum. The amount of food that albino rats eat actually declines with age if food intake is calculated as g/kg body weight/day. Is obesity in the albino rat due to overeating, in the sense of total g intake of food, or to some other factor?

To investigate the cause of obesity in albino rats, a series of studies was made upon the activity of the genital,[23] perirenal,[24] mesenteric,[25] skinfold,[26] and omental[27] fat depots. It was first confirmed that as the total neutral fat content of the body increases, the amount of neutral fat in the fat depots also increases. This is exemplified in Figure 1, in which the amount of neutral fat in the genital fat depots of albino rats, expressed as g/kg body weight, is plotted against total body neutral fat in animals weighing from 200 to over 500 g. It may be seen that as the total amount of body neutral fat increased, per kg body weight, the amount of neutral fat stored in the genital fat depots also increased.

While concentrations of neutral fat are usually expressed as shown in Figure 1, this method has the disadvantage that the substance being compared − neutral fat − is part of the denominator −

3

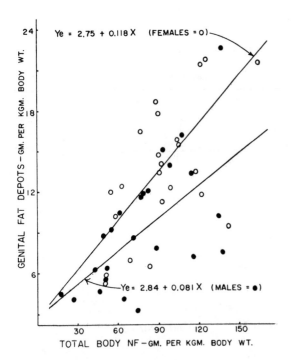

FIGURE 1. The correlation between the amount of neutral fat in the genital fat depots of male and female albino rats and the amount of neutral fat in their entire bodies. (From Boyd and Lower[23] with the permission of the *International Review of Vitamin-Research,* copyright © 1957, Hans Huber, Medical Publishers, Berne, Switzerland.)

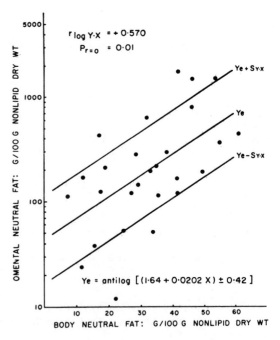

FIGURE 2. The correlation between concentrations of neutral fat in the omentum of albino rats and neutral fat in the animal's body. (From Boyd[27] with the permission of the *Giornale dell'Arteriosclerosi,* copyright © 1967, Centro Editoriale Pubblicitario Italiano, Rome, Italy.)

body weight — as well as of the numerator. The disadvantage may be overcome by expressing concentrations of neutral fat as g/100 g of nonlipid dry weight, as exemplified in Figure 2. Nonlipid dry weight of the tissues illustrated in Figure 2 is practically synonymous with tissue protein. There was positive correlation, significant at P = 0.01, between concentration of neutral fat in the omentum of albino rats and concentration of body neutral fat, as shown in Figure 2.

If storage of neutral fat is an active rather than passive function of the fat depots, one might anticipate that with storage of increasing amounts of neutral fat there would be evidence of increased physiological activity in the depots. Many years ago Professor W. R. Bloor established that increase in physiological activity of tissues is associated with an increase in the concentration of phospholipid and of free cholesterol in such tissues. The Bloor hypothesis was applied to a study of the postoperative activity of the blood leukocytes by Boyd.[12]

The concentration of neutral fat in the fat depots was, therefore, compared with the concentration of phospholipid in the same depots. This was done by plotting concentration of neutral fat, as g/100 g nonlipid dry weight, against concentration of phospholipid, similarly expressed, in five body fat depots and in the total body. The correlations were mostly positive and correlation coefficients are assembled in Table 4. Correlation coefficients in Table 4 of 0.200 or higher were statistically significant at P = 0.05 or less, with the available value of N. By this criterion, it may be concluded that a primary active function of the mesentery, omentum, and skin is to store neutral fat. Similar active storage would appear to be a possible secondary function of the genital and perirenal depots.

When concentrations of neutral fat were plotted against concentrations of free cholesterol in a similar manner, correlation coefficients in all five fat depots were significantly positive, as shown by data in Table 5. The author had previously obtained evidence that with increase in the physiological activity of a tissue there is an increase in the concentration of water per unit of

TABLE 4

Correlation Coefficients Obtained from the Regression of Concentration of Neutral Fat on Concentrations of Phospholipid in the Fat Depots of Albino Rats*

Fat depot	Males (N=22 to 63)	Females (N=24 to 47)	References
Genital fat depot	+0.100	+0.211	23
Mesenteric fat depot	+0.365	+0.374	25
Omental fat depot	+0.465	+0.423	27
Perirenal fat depot	+0.003	+0.175	24
Skinfold fat depot	+0.688	+0.806	26
Total body	+0.275	−0.009	23−27

*Concentrations were calculated as g/100 g nonlipid dry weight. Correlation coefficients of 0.200 or greater were significant at P = 0.05 or less.

TABLE 5

Correlation Coefficients Obtained by Plotting the Regression of Concentrations of Neutral Fat on Concentration of Free Cholesterol in the Fat Depots of Albino Rats*

Fat depot	Males (N=22 to 63)	Females (N=24 to 47)	References
Genital fat depot	+0.696	+0.259	23
Mesenteric fat depot	+0.847	+0.658	25
Omental fat depot	+0.914	+0.816	27
Perirenal fat depot	+0.882	+0.575	24
Skinfold fat depot	+0.554	+0.648	26
Total body	−0.107	+0.204	23−27

*Concentrations were calculated as g/100 g nonlipid dry weight. Correlation coefficients of 0.200 or greater were significant at P = 0.05 or less.

protein. Concentrations of neutral fat were, therefore, plotted against concentrations of water in the same five fat depots and the correlation coefficients are listed in Table 6. It may be seen that by the criteria tested in Tables 5 and 6, storage of neutral fat appears to be an active, rather than a passive physiological function of the body fat depots.

When the composition of adipose tissue is expressed as g/100 g wet or dry weight, results indicate that it contains neutral fat and very little of other ingredients. A different picture is obtained when concentration is calculated as g/100 g nonlipid (or protein) dry weight. The mean concentrations of phospholipid, free cholesterol, and water, as g/100 g nonlipid dry weight, have been listed in Table 7 and compared with corresponding values in a variety of other tissues. It may be seen that appreciable amounts of these three indicators of physiological activity are present in the fat depots when concentration is expressed as g/100 g nonlipid dry weight. From the values listed in Table 7, it would be estimated that the level of physiological activity in the fat depots is not as high as that in brain, liver, and testicles, although activity of the omentum was similar to activity in tissues such as lung, heart, and kidneys.

These various results indicate that obesity in the albino rat is not a passive response to overeating. As the animal grows toward adult weight, it eats less food/kg body weight, presumably because less nutrient is required for the formation of body proteins and related essential growth elements. As the needs for growth decline, adipose tissue becomes increasingly active and a greater proportion of the food intake is actively stored as neutral fat. The earliest function of the body appears to be growth and when that is satisfied, food is eaten and much of it stored as

TABLE 6

Correlation Coefficients Obtained by Plotting the Concentration of Neutral Fat, in g/100 g Nonlipid Dry Weight, Against Concentrations of Water, in g/100 g Nonlipid Dry Weight, in the Fat Depots of Albino Rats*

Fat depot	Males (N=22 to 63)	Females (N=24 to 47)	References
Genital fat depot	+0.853	+0.901	23
Mesenteric fat depot	+0.929	+0.392	25
Omental fat depot	+0.559	+0.923	27
Perirenal fat depot	+0.944	+0.892	24
Skinfold fat depot	+0.894	+0.904	26
Total body	+0.498	+0.111	23—27

*Concentrations were calculated as g/100 g nonlipid dry weight. Correlation coefficients of 0.200 or greater were significant at P = 0.05 or less.

TABLE 7

Mean Concentrations of Phospholipid, Free Cholesterol, and Water, Expressed as g/100 g Nonlipid Dry Weight, in the Tissues and Organs of Albino Rats

Organ	Reference	Phospholipid	Free cholesterol	Water	Organ	Reference	Phospholipid	Free cholesterol	Water
Brain	28	40.4	9.81	702	Spleen	32	5.9	1.28	370
Liver	28	13.6	0.82	326	Thymus	33	5.7	1.00	472
Testicle	29	12.5	1.35	770	Leg muscle	29	5.5	0.35	353
Testicle	29	12.2	1.23	787	Thymus	30	5.2	1.06	430
Lung	28	11.6	2.17	510	Leg muscle	29	5.1	0.41	383
Heart	28	11.4	0.79	449	Diaphragm	30	4.6	0.53	343
Testicle	29	11.0	1.32	743	Leg muscle	29	4.4	0.40	341
Duodenum	28	10.8	1.69	581	Mesentery	25	4.0	0.67	241
Rat tumor	28	10.0	1.56	666	Belly muscle	34	3.6	0.36	330
Omentum	27	9.2	1.77	568	Trachea	30	3.4	0.86	364
Salivary gland	30	8.5	1.41	395	Skin	28	3.3	0.88	249
Kidney	31	8.3	1.35	390	Perirenal depot	24	2.2	0.54	72
Lymph nodes	30	6.6	1.14	445	Genital depot	23	2.2	0.71	94

fat, presumably for possible use in periods of famine.

Conclusions

Evidence obtained in early studies on lipid metabolism in the author's laboratory, between 1930 and 1960, suggested that diet, providing it was adequate, had minor influence on body function. This evidence was as follows:

1. Levels of lipids in human blood plasma are not affected by ordinary meals.

2. Amounts of blood lipids removed by a single massive hemorrhage are replaced within 24 hr.

3. Prolonged fasting does not affect levels of tissue lipids, providing there is no need to produce calories in order to maintain body temperature.

4. Obesity is not due to overeating but to the active storage of neutral fat, in adipose tissue, from food that is no longer needed for body growth.

REFERENCES

1. Furia, T. E. Ed., *CRC Handbook of Food Additives,* The Chemical Rubber Company, Cleveland, Ohio, 1968.
2. **Chapman, D. G. and Pugsley, L. I.,** Food additives, *Mod. Med. Can.,* 26, 7, 1971.
3. *Evaluating the Safety of Food Chemicals,* National Academy of Sciences, Washington, D.C., 1970.
4. FDD Symposium, Chemical Contaminants in Food — Hazard or Not? *Food Cosmet. Toxicol.,* 9, 65, 1971.
5. **Boyd, E. M.,** *Protein Deficiency and Pesticide Toxicity,* Charles C Thomas, Springfield, Ill., 1972.
6. Paracelsus, cited by Sigerist, H. E., in *The Great Doctors,* Doubleday and Company, New York, 1958.
7. **Boyd, E. M.,** Low phospholipid values in dog plasma, *J. Biol. Chem.,* 91, 1, 1931.
8. **Boyd, E. M.,** A differential lipid analysis of blood plasma in normal young women by micro-oxidative methods, *J. Biol. Chem.,* 101, 323, 1933.
9. **Boyd, E. M.,** The lipid content of the white blood cells in normal young women, *J. Biol. Chem.,* 101, 623, 1933.
10. **Boyd, E. M.,** The lipemia of pregnancy, *J. Clin. Invest.,* 13, 347, 1934.
11. **Boyd, E. M.,** The lipid composition of the white blood cells in women during pregnancy, lactation, and the puerperium, *Surg. Gynecol. Obstet.,* 59, 744, 1934.
12. **Boyd, E. M.,** The post-operative activity of the white blood cells as measured by their lipid content, *Can. Med. Assoc. J.,* 31, 626, 1934.
13. **Boyd, E. M. and Wilson, K. M.,** The exchange of lipids in the umbilical circulation at birth, *J. Clin. Invest.,* 14, 7, 1935.
14. **Boyd, E. M.,** Blood lipids in the puerperium, *Am. J. Obstet. Gynecol.,* 29, 797, 1935.
15. **Boyd, E. M.,** The lipopenia of fever, *Can. Med. Assoc. J.,* 32, 500, 1935.
16. **Boyd, E. M. and Tweddell, H. J.,** The lipids of human blood, *Trans. R. Soc. Can., Third Series, Section V,* 29, 113, 1935.
17. **Boyd, E. M.,** Diurnal variations in plasma lipids, *J. Biol. Chem.,* 110, 61, 1935.
18. **Boyd, E. M. and Connell, W. F.,** Further studies of plasma lipids in toxic goitre: Evidence of a bimodal distribution, *Quart. J. Med.,* 8, 41, 1939.
19. **Boyd, E. M.,** Nephritic lipaemia, *Can. Med. Assoc. J.,* 36, 18, 1937.
20. **Boyd, E. M. and Connell, W. F.,** Lipopenia associated with cholesterol estersturz in parenchymatous hepatic disease, *Arch. Intern. Med.,* 61, 755, 1938.
21. **Boyd, E. M. and Stevenson, J. W.,** The regeneration of blood lipids following a single massive hemorrhage in rabbits, *J. Biol. Chem.,* 122, 147, 1937.
22. **Baker, M. E. T., Boyd, E. M., Clarke, E. L., and Ronan, A. K.,** Variations in the water, fat, glycogen and iodine of the flesh of oysters (*Ostrea virginica*) during hibernation and storage at 4°C, *J. Physiol.,* 101, 36, 1942.
23. **Boyd, E. M. and Lower, A. H.,** Studies on obesity: the genital fat depots, *Int. Rev. Vit. Res.,* 27, 253, 1957.
24. **Boyd, E. M. and Lower, A. H.,** Neutral fat of the perirenal fat depots, *Can. J. Biochem. Physiol.,* 35, 157, 1957.
25. **Boyd, E. M. and Crandell, E. M.,** Mesenteric neutral fat in obese rats, *Can. J. Biochem. Physiol.,* 36, 913, 1958.
26. **Boyd, E. M.,** Skinfold neutral fat in obese rats, *Can. J. Biochem. Physiol.,* 39, 321, 1961.
27. **Boyd, E. M.,** Storage of neutral fat in the fat depots of obese rats, *G. Arterioscler.,* 5, 607, 1967.
28. **Boyd, E. M., McEwen, H. D., and Shanas, M. N.,** The lipid composition and water content of brain, heart, lung, liver, gut, and skin in the host component of the albino rat-Walker carcinoma 256 dual organism, *Can. J. Med. Sci.,* 31, 493, 1953.
29. **Boyd, E. M., Boyd, C. E., Hill, J. G., and Ravinsky, E.,** The lipid and water content of carcass, skeletal muscle, and testicle in the host component of the albino rat-Walker carcinoma 256 dual organism at progressive stages of tumor growth, *Can. J. Biochem. Physiol.,* 32, 359, 1954.
30. **Boyd, E. M., Kelly, E. M., Murdoch, M. E., and Boyd, C. E.,** Lipid and water levels in five organs of albino rats bearing Walker carcinosarcoma 256, *Cancer Res.,* 16, 535, 1956.
31. **Boyd, E. M. and Tikkala, A. O.,** Lipid and water levels in the kidneys of albino rats bearing Walker carcinoma 256, *Can. J. Biochem. Physiol.,* 34, 259, 1956.
32. **Boyd, E. M., McEwen, H. D., and Murdoch, M. E.,** Unusual hydrolipotropic shifts in the spleen of albino rats bearing Walker carcinosarcoma 256, *J. Natl. Cancer Inst.,* 16, 913, 1956.
33. **Boyd, E. M., Fontaine, V., and Hill, J. G.,** Significant changes in the lipid and water content of the thymus gland in albino rats bearing Walker carcinoma 256, *Can. J. Biochem. Physiol.,* 33, 69, 1955.
34. **Boyd, E. M. and Crandell, E. M.,** The concentration of lipids and water in skeletal muscle of albino rats bearing Walker carcinoma 256, *Cancer Res.,* 16, 198, 1956.

Chapter 2

STUDIES ON VITAMIN DEFICIENT DIETS

Vitamin A Deficient Diet

An area of toxicology in which the author and his associates have been active for many years is that of predicting toxicity in man from studies on laboratory animals, a discipline which is termed "Predictive Toxicometrics."[1] In a series of studies on the acute oral toxicity of benzylpenicillin in albino mice,[2,3] albino rats,[2,3] guinea pigs,[4] rabbits,[5] cats and dogs,[6] and on the chronic oral toxicity in albino mice[7] and albino rats,[8] signs of toxicity recorded in man were duplicated in animals with certain exceptions. A common exception in these animal studies was the absence of skin reactions to penicillin, reactions which are relatively common in man. Boyd et al.[9] noted that animals used in the studies cited above had been fed diets more than adequate in vitamin A. Evidence was reviewed which indicated that the incidence of signs of toxicity to various agents may be lowered by increasing the daily intake of vitamins.[9]

Boyd et al.[9] therefore proceeded to determine the clinicopathological syndrome of toxicity to benzylpenicillin given to animals fed a diet deficient in vitamin A. The diet was prepared after instructions in the U.S.P. XIV (1950) and contained 18% casein (vitamin-free), 65% cornstarch, 5% cottonseed oil, 4% salt mix U.S.P. XIV, and 8% dried brewer's yeast. Initially, the diet was fed to some 300 adult albino mice for up to 12 weeks. At approximately weekly intervals, 15 to 40 mice were given an estimated acute, oral LD_{50} of benzylpenicillin potassium. The relation of percent mortality to this acute dose of benzylpenicillin is shown in Figure 3. It is apparent that death rates to the challenging dose increased the longer the mice were fed the vitamin A deficient diet. The coefficient of correlation of the regression shown in Figure 3 was +0.779; with P = 0.01 that correlation was zero.[10] Death rates in an equal number of control mice fed Purina ® Fox Chow Checkers did not change during the 12 weeks of feeding. Feeding the diet deficient in vitamin A

had augmented the susceptibility of mice to an acute lethal dose of benzylpenicillin.

The chronic oral toxicity of benzylpenicillin was studied in young adult albino rats which were fed the same vitamin A deficient diet for one month and then were given a daily challenging dose of benzylpenicillin potassium. The dose selected was the oral LD_{50} (100 days) or daily dose which will kill 50% of animals over a period of 100 days of daily administration. Administration of benzylpenicillin was terminated after six weeks, when survivors were autopsied and organ weights and water content measured.

Control rats fed the vitamin A deficient diet but given no daily benzylpenicillin grew as well as controls fed a standard laboratory chow. Their

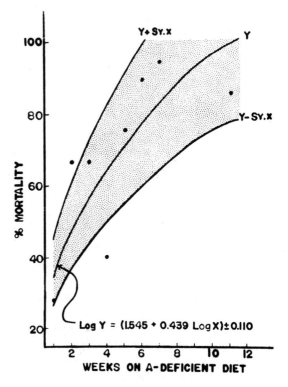

FIGURE 3. The regression of percentage mortality in mice to an oral median lethal dose of benzylpenicillin potassium given after progressive weeks the animals were fed a diet deficient in vitamin A. (From Boyd et al.[9] with the permission of the National Research Council of Canada, publishers of the *Canadian Journal of Biochemistry and Physiology.*)

TABLE 8

The Clinical Signs of Toxicity to Benzylpenicillin Given Daily for Six Weeks in a Dose Equal to the Oral $LD_{50 (100 \text{ days})}$ to Albino Rats Fed a Diet Deficient in Vitamin A and to Controls Fed a Standard Laboratory (Fox) Chow[a]

Measurement	Vitamin A deficient diet	Fox chow
Death rate		
(% of animals)	58.0 ± 19.6*	10.7 ± 3.3
Body weight (g)	217 ± 16	221 ± 15
Food intake		
(g/kg in 24 hr)	51 ± 16*	112 ± 17
Water intake		
(ml/kg in 24 hr)	188 ± 28*	236 ± 24
Colonic temperature (°F)	100.5 ± 0.6*	99.8 ± 0.7
Urine volume (ml/kg in 24 hr)	24.8 ± 20.6*	14.2 ± 10.5
Urine pH	6.2 ± 0.1*	6.6 ± 0.5
Urine protein		
(mg/100 ml)	167 ± 166	126 ± 195
Urinary glucose (g/100 ml)	0.04 ± 0.11*	0.19 ± 0.30
Blood hemoglobin		
(g/100 ml)	15.2 ± 0.9*	16.1 ± 0.8
Blood W.B.C. $(10^3/mm^3)$	12.5 ± 1.7	11.4 ± 2.6
Diarrhea (1+ to 4+)	3.3 ± 0.6	3.7 ± 0.8
Soiling of skin		
(% of skin surface)	65 ± 15*	43 ± 10
Loss of hair		
(% of total)	25 ± 15*	3 ± 5
Cyanosis (1+ to 4+)	0.4 ± 0.4*	0.1 ± 0.1

[a]The results are expressed as mean ± standard deviation of weekly measurements. Means for animals on a diet deficient in vitamin A that differed at $P \leqslant 0.05$ from corresponding means for animals on a diet of fox chow are indicated by an asterisk.
(From Boyd et al.[9] with the permission of the National Research Council of Canada, publishers of the *Canadian Journal of Biochemistry and Physiology.*)

urine was slightly acidic and they drank less water than chow-fed rats due to a lower gram intake of the concentrated synthetic diet which contained no roughage, as is present in standard laboratory chows. The calorie intake in rats eating a vitamin A deficient diet was the same as that of rats eating chow and both groups of animals looked grossly the same.

Rats fed the vitamin A deficient diet were more susceptible to benzylpenicillin toxicity than were rats fed fox chow, as is indicated by clinical signs of toxicity summarized in Table 8. The death rate was significantly higher in the vitamin A deficient animals, which exhibited anorexia, oligodipsia, fever, diuresis, aciduria, anemia, and cyanosis. The only evidence of skin disorders in the vitamin A deficient rats was alopecia associated with soiling of the skin. Histological examination disclosed

that the skin of the vitamin A deficient group contained many immature hair follicles and the epithelium lining the ducts of the submaxillary salivary glands had undergone some metaplasia to a stratified squamous type.

Autopsy on survivors at six weeks revealed loss of weight in the tissues of the gastrointestinal tract of rats fed the vitamin A deficient diet but given no benzylpenicillin, presumably due to some atrophy from the lower bulk of the diet. There was also a tendency toward a mild dehydration in most organs of the control group fed a diet deficient in vitamin A but given no benzylpenicillin. The main effect of daily administration of benzylpenicillin to vitamin A deficient rats was the production of a fairly generalized hydration of body organs and loss of weight in some organs such as muscle, salivary glands, and testes.

Absence of vitamin A was *not* the factor responsible for augmented susceptibility to benzylpenicillin toxicity in animals fed the vitamin A deficient diet. The augmented susceptibility was not prevented by dietary or parenteral supplementation of vitamin A in amounts up to ten times the normal requirement nor by multivitamin supplementation.[9] Susceptibility was increased to benzylpenicillin given subcutaneously as well as orally to animals fed the vitamin A deficient diet so that augmentation of susceptibility to oral benzylpenicillin could not have been due to augmented absorption from the gastrointestinal tract. The only general conclusion from these studies was that something about the vitamin A deficient diet other than vitamin deficiency had made animals somewhat more susceptible to benzylpenicillin toxicity.

Vitamin C Deficient Diet

Boyd[11] reported a similar study of benzylpenicillin toxicity in albino rats fed a standard vitamin C deficient diet. The diet was composed of 30% skim milk powder (heated for 2 hr at $100°C$), 39% rolled oats (fortified), 20% wheat bran, 8% cottonseed oil, and 3% salts, plus vitamins other than ascorbic acid. The diet was essentially a mixture of natural, unpurified, and unconcentrated carbohydrates, fats, and proteins with the necessary salts and vitamins other than ascorbic acid. Fed to young adult albino rats, the diet alone did not affect the growth rate nor gross appearance of the animals. The only clinical effects of the diet were a mild pallor, mild diarrhea, and a slight leukocytosis.

When benzylpenicillin potassium was given daily in a dose at the range of the $LD_{50 \ (100 \ days)}$ for a period of eight weeks, mortality rates were the same in animals fed the vitamin C deficient diet as in controls fed laboratory chow. In the vitamin C deficient animals, daily benzylpenicillin administration produced a mild hypothermia, alopecia, and skin soiling which was not affected by supplements of ascorbic acid.

The vitamin C deficient diet alone produced few significant changes in organ weights and water levels in survivors. Daily benzylpenicillin administration to vitamin C deficient rats caused changes in organ weights and water levels of survivors which, for the most part, were similar to those produced in rats fed a standard laboratory chow and given daily benzylpenicillin. The mild

effects of the vitamin C deficient diet were found not due to absence of ascorbic acid in the diet.

Vitamin D Deficiency

Studies similar to those on diets deficient in vitamin A and vitamin C were performed on young adult rats fed a diet deficient in vitamin D prepared as indicated in U.S.P. XIV.[9] The diet contained 76% ground yellow corn, 20% ground gluten, 3% calcium carbonate, and 1% sodium chloride. The animals were given benzylpenicillin potassium at a daily dose equal to the oral $LD_{50 \ (100 \ days)}$ and toxicity compared with that in controls fed a standard laboratory chow. It has been the author's experience that toxicity of an agent in animals fed one type of commercially available laboratory chow is similar to that in animals fed other standard chows. Verrusio et al.[12] reported that the teratogenic effect of 6-aminonicotinamide was augmented in one strain of pregnant mice, but not in a second strain, when the animals were transferred from Purina Laboratory Chow to Breeder Chow.

The vitamin D deficient diet produced a slight alkalinuria and diuresis, presumably due to its content of calcium carbonate. Daily administration of benzylpenicillin caused some alopecia, skin soiling, and cyanosis, but death rates were identical to those in controls fed a standard laboratory chow and given the same daily dose of benzylpenicillin.

Results to this point indicated that the toxicity of benzylpenicillin was not augmented by feeding young adult albino rats diets containing skim milk powder, rolled oats, wheat bran, ground corn, and ground gluten. Toxicity was augmented somewhat in animals fed casein and cornstarch. The incidence of benzylpenicillin-induced alopecia was augmented in animals fed all three purified diets.

Biotin Deficient Diet

The first indication that purified diets can markedly affect drug toxicity was obtained in studies in which rats were fed a biotin deficient diet. Biotin deficiency can be produced in weanling rats by (a) feeding them a diet high in raw egg white which contains a protein, avidin, that binds with biotin in the gastrointestinal tract,[13-15] (b) by feeding a biotin deficient diet to germ-free rats in which biotin cannot be synthesized by intestinal organisms,[16] and (c) by feeding a biotin deficient diet plus an antiinfective agent to prevent growth of intestinal organsims.[17-19] Method (a) is the oldest means of producing biotin deficiency, having been reported in 1916 by Bateman.[20] Biotin was termed factor X by Boas[21] in 1927 and vitamin H by György[22] in 1939.

A powdered raw egg white diet was used to produce biotin deficiency in studies conducted in the author's laboratory. The diet contained 30% dried egg white, 48% cornstarch, 14% cottonseed oil, 3% cod liver oil, 5% salt mix, and supplements of all vitamins except biotin. This formula was proposed by Rubin et al.[23] and its origin has been traced by Peters.[24]

The biotin deficient diet alone produced, over a period of eight weeks in young adult female rats, some slight inhibition of growth with no change in calorie intake, an alkalinuria, slight anemia, and some leukocytosis.[25] The animals appeared grossly normal, there was some dehydration in certain organs such as stomach, small bowel, cecum, and liver, hydration in others such as skeletal muscle and ovaries, and few significant changes in organ weights. The animals were, however, highly susceptible to the toxic effects of benzylpenicillin[25,26] and of caffeine[27-32] and died within a few days of oral administration of the drugs in a dose equal to the $LD_{50\ (100\ days)}$.

This result was not anticipated. Dr. E. J. Sargeant began the studies by giving benzylpenicillin to 60 rats fed a biotin deficient diet.[25] Expecting no deaths for a week or two, this author left the laboratory to attend a medical meeting on the day his associate, Dr. Sargeant, started giving benzylpenicillin. On return to the laboratory in one week, this author found that Dr. Sargeant had had to work day and night to complete autopsies on rats which had died! Death rates are illustrated in Figure 4. Administration of benzylpenicillin to biotin deficient rats produced a marked loss of body weight, anorexia, hypothermia, aciduria, leukocytosis, diarrhea, skin soiling, abdominal bloating, alopecia, dermatitis, cyanosis, anogenital inflammation, abducted gait, and an arched back. In rats fed the biotin deficient diet, benzylpenicillin also produced a marked stress reaction in the adrenal glands, spleen, and thymus gland, a marked local inflammatory reaction in the tissues of the gastrointestinal tract, and degenerative changes in the kidneys and liver. There was a marked loss of weight in practically all body

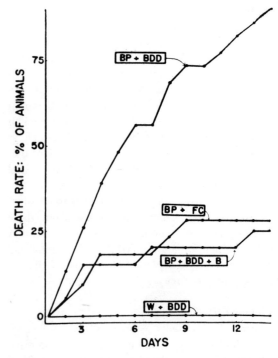

FIGURE 4. Death rates in albino rats given a daily challenging dose of benzylpenicillin (BP) or water (W) on a biotin deficient diet (BDD) or fox chow (FC) with and without daily subcutaneous injection of biotin (B) in doses of 1 to 125 μg/kg. (From Boyd and Sargeant[25] with the permission of the *Journal of New Drugs*, copyright © 1962, Revere Publishing Co., New York.)

organs without much change in organ water levels, possibly because water intake was not affected.

There were three types of skin lesions in rats fed the biotin deficient diet and given benzylpenicillin and none in benzylpenicillin-treated rats fed a standard chow. There was first an atrophic lesion with excessive conversion of stratum corneum to stratum disjunctum plus atrophy of the hair follicles. A second erythematous lesion consisted of capillary-venous congestion, thrombosis, and leukocytic infiltration of the dermis and subcutaneous tissue. The third lesion was a papular one which was similar to the second but exhibited in addition necrosis of the epidermis and atrophy of the stratum malpighi. The simultaneous subcutaneous administration of large daily doses of biotin prevented development of the skin lesions and reduced mortality (see Figure 4) but did not influence the neurological signs of benzylpenicillin poisoning in rats fed the biotin deficient diet.

Peters[24,33] reported that young adult albino

rats fed a high egg white diet, which induced signs of biotin deficiency in weanlings, become markedly susceptible to caffeine toxicity. Caffeine was given daily in a dose similar to the oral $LD_{50\ (100\ days)}$ and which, in 30 days, killed some 10% of control rats fed laboratory chow. Death rates in rats fed the biotin deficient diet are shown in Figure 5. It will be noted that subcutaneous biotin supplementation did not prevent death, although in later studies mortality was slightly reduced by high doses of supplementary biotin.[24] The clinical and pathological signs of toxicity were similar to those noted from administration of benzyl-penicillin except that the erythematous and papular skin lesions did not appear. Alopecia was present in 6% of rats fed the biotin deficient diet alone and this increased to 43% when caffeine was given. Alopecia of the lower body is illustrated in Figure 6. Signs of chronic caffeine intoxication such as stimulation of the central nervous system and intussusception were augmented by the biotin deficient diet. A photograph of the small bowel invaginated into the colon is shown in Figure 7.

The general conclusions from these studies are that biotin deficiency induced by a diet containing large amounts of raw egg white powder may be responsible for some of the increased susceptibility to drug toxicity of albino rats fed such a diet.

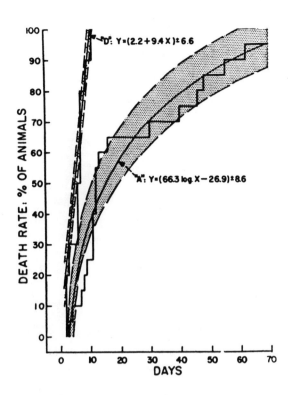

FIGURE 5. The percent mortality to caffeine in doses at the range of the oral $LD_{50\ (100\ days)}$ in albino rats fed a biotin deficient diet with ("D") and without ("A") subcutaneous biotin supplementation. (From Peters[24] with the permission of the author.)

FIGURE 6. A photograph of a rat fed a biotin deficient diet and given caffeine daily in doses at the range of the oral $LD_{50\ (100\ days)}$ showing loss of hair over the lower part of the body. (From Peters[24] with the permission of the author.)

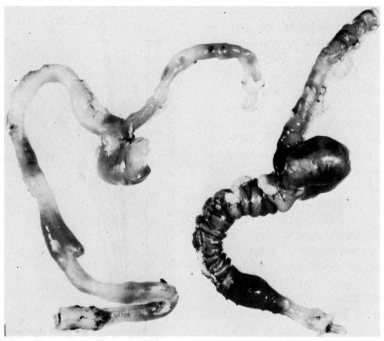

FIGURE 7. A photograph of the posterior end of the small bowel, the cecum, and the colon of a normal rat (left) and of a rat (right) fed a biotin deficient diet in which intussusception of the cecum and colon had been produced by daily administration of caffeine in an oral dose of 185 mg/kg/day. (From Peters[33] with the permission of the author.)

Most of the augmented susceptibility appears to be due to other factors in the diet. Peters and Boyd[32] proved that lack of cellulose bulk was not one of these other factors.

Pantothenic Acid Deficient Diet

The influence on benzylpenicillin toxicity in mice and rats of feeding the animals a diet deficient in pantothenic acid was reported by Boyd et al.[34] The diet was that of Nelson and Evans,[35] containing 24% vitamin-free casein, 64% sucrose, 8% cottonseed oil, 4% salt mix (Phillips-Hart IV), and vitamin supplements except pantothenic acid. Fed to male albino rats of an initial body weight from 130 to 200 g, this diet produced some decline in the growth rate after a fortnight's feeding, a slight anemia, and leukocytosis, but the gross appearance of the animals was normal. After eight weeks of feeding, the experiment was terminated. Signs of deficiency of pantothenic acid which appear in weanling rats fed this diet, such as dermatitis and spastic gait,[36] were not present in these young adult animals. There was some loss of weight and water content in body organs of survivors at eight weeks.

The death rates to benzylpenicillin potassium given to mice orally in a dose of 8.8 g/kg and subcutaneously in a dose of 5.4 g/kg were the same during the initial two weeks of feeding the pantothenic acid deficient diet as in controls fed a standard laboratory chow. After two and up to eight weeks of feeding, the mortality to benzylpenicillin given orally averaged 64% in mice fed the pantothenic acid deficient diet and 14% in mice fed chow with $P < 0.001$ that the difference in mortality was zero.

When albino rats were fed the pantothenic acid deficient diet and given benzylpenicillin daily in a dose equivalent to the oral $LD_{50 \ (100 \ days)}$ there followed a fulminating toxic reaction, the clinical signs of which are illustrated in Figure 8. Death rates were markedly higher in rats fed the pantothenic acid deficient diet than in controls fed fox chow, as shown in Figure 9. At death, autopsy disclosed marked loss of weight, dehydration, and capillary-venous congestion in the organs of rats fed the synthetic diet and degenerative changes in some organs such as the thymus gland and testes.

The augmented susceptibility to benzylpenicillin toxicity was not due to absence of pantothenic

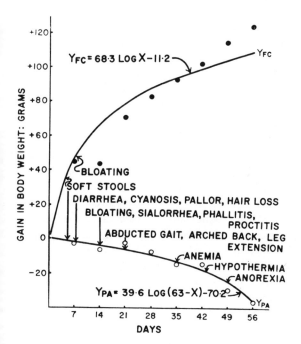

FIGURE 8. The regression of changes in body weight upon days of oral administration of benzylpenicillin at the LD_{50} (100 days) and the order of appearance of clinical signs of toxicity in young adult male albino rats fed a standard laboratory chow (Y_{fc} = Purina Fox Chow) or a synthetic pantothenic acid deficient diet (Y_{pa}). (From Boyd et al.[34] with the permission of the National Research Council of Canada, publishers of the *Canadian Journal of Physiology and Pharmacology*.)

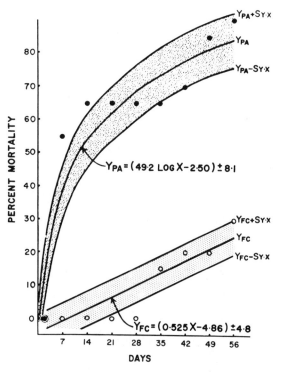

FIGURE 9. The regression of death rates upon days of daily oral administration of benzylpenicillin potassium in a dose equal to the LD_{50} (100 days) to albino rats fed a synthetic diet deficient in pantothenic acid (Y_{pa}) and in controls fed Purina Fox Chow Checkers (Y_{fc}). (From Boyd et al.[34] with the permission of the National Research Council of Canada, publishers of the *Canadian Journal of Physiology and Pharmacology*.)

acid in the synthetic diet. Neither the acute syndrome in mice nor the chronic toxic reaction in rats was affected by daily supplements of calcium d-pantothenate in a range of doses up to 100 mg/kg orally and parenterally. Augmented susceptibility was not due to production of toxic substances on aging of the pantothenic acid deficient diet — death rates in mice fed a sample of diet which had been stored unsealed for three years were similar to those in mice fed a fresh synthetic diet when benzylpenicillin was given as a single challenging lethal dose. The addition of inert cellulose to the synthetic diet, in amounts from 2.5 to 20.0% of the diet, did not affect mortality rates to benzylpenicillin in mice.

Feeding the synthethic pantothenic acid deficient diet to rats for one month prior to daily administration of benzylpenicillin augmented the susceptibility of the animals to the drug. Daily administration of benzylpenicillin potassium in a dose of 5.34 g/kg/day for four weeks to chow-fed

rats produced no deaths; changing the animals to the pantothenic acid deficient diet and continuing daily benzylpenicillin administration produced toxicity no greater than would have been expected in chow-fed rats during weeks 5 to 7, after which augmented susceptibility again appeared. The death rates in these studies are illustrated in Figure 10. Dubos et al.[37] had suggested that changes in the intestinal flora produced by benzylpenicillin in animals on a synthetic diet may vary from those in chow-fed animals. The results indicated that benzylpenicillin-induced changes in the intestinal flora were a factor of probably minor importance and emphasized that some other factor in the synthetic diet was chiefly responsible for augmented susceptibility to benzylpenicillin toxicity.

Feeding synthetic diets enhances the activity of certain drugs such as stibophen and sulfadiazine[38] and the toxicity of others such as isoproterenol[39] and antioxidants.[40] The substance present in the

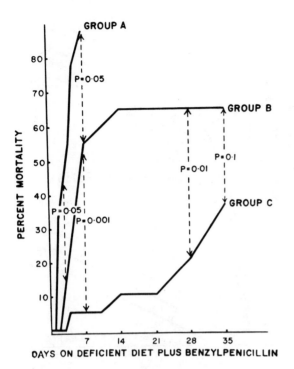

PERCENT MORTALITY

DAYS ON DEFICIENT DIET PLUS BENZYLPENICILLIN

FIGURE 10. Death rates in three groups of albino rats given benzylpenicillin daily and maintained on a synthetic pantothenic acid deficient diet. Group A received the synthetic diet for one month before administration of benzylpenicillin was started. Group B received the synthetic diet at the same time as benzylpenicillin administration was started. Group C received benzylpenicillin daily for one month before being placed upon the synthetic diet. P values refer to the significance of differences between death rates indicated by arrows and interrupted lines. (From Boyd et al.[34] with the permission of the National Research Council of Canada, publishers of the *Canadian Journal of Physiology and Pharmacology*.)

greatest amount in the pantothenic acid deficient diet was sucrose, of which the diet contained 64%. Harper and Worden[41] reported that diets containing 80% sucrose become toxic to rats after several weeks of feeding, while Shore and Shore[42] found a diet of 100% sucrose (plus vitamins) produced loss of body weight in a week or two. Boyd et al.[34] calculated that albino rats eating the pantothenic acid deficient diet consumed an average of 40 g of sucrose per day. When they gave this dose of sucrose by a single intragastric administration, it killed over 50% of the animals. The conclusion from these studies was that the high sucrose content of the synthetic pantothenic acid deficient diet was the main factor accounting for augmented susceptibility to benzylpenicillin toxicity in albino rats fed the synthetic diet.[34]

Pyridoxine Deficient Diet

Boyd et al.[43] measured the toxicity of benzylpenicillin in albino rats fed a pyridoxine deficient diet. The diet was that of Clarke and Lechycka[44] and contained 22% vitamin-free casein, 69.4% sucrose, 4% salt mix (Phillips-Hart IV), 2% cottonseed oil, 2% cod liver oil, 0.5% wheat germ oil, and vitamin supplements excluding pyridoxine. Female albino rats of 150 to 200 g body weight fed this diet appeared grossly normal but slowly lost weight and at three weeks had loss of weight and water content in some body organs.[43]

When young adult female rats were fed the pyridoxine deficient diet and given benzylpenicillin potassium orally in a dose of 5.34 g/kg/day for six days a week, 72% of them were dead within three days when they were aggregated and 64% in three weeks when they were segregated, one animal per cage. In albino rats fed Purina Laboratory Chow and given the same daily dose of benzylpenicillin, the mortality at three weeks was 7%.

Statistically significant differences in the clinicopathological syndrome of toxicity to benzylpenicillin-treated rats fed the pyridoxine deficient diet and in controls given only the synthetic diet are listed in Table 9. Corresponding differences between benzylpenicillin-treated rats fed laboratory chow and chow-fed controls given no benzylpenicillin are listed in Table 10. It may be seen that there were differences in the clinicopathological syndrome of toxicity to benzylpenicillin between the two dietary groups. To quantitate these differences, the syndrome in rats fed a pyridoxine deficient diet was compared with that in rats fed laboratory chow. Statistically significant differences are assembled in Table 11.

Of 42 rats fed laboratory chow and given benzylpenicillin daily, 39 survived to 3 weeks. Of 54 animals fed the pyridoxine deficient diet and given the same daily dose of benzylpenicillin, 19 survived to 3 weeks. A comparison of the syndrome of toxicity in these two groups (see Table 11) disclosed that rats fed the synthetic diet ate less food (as calories) and lost body and organ weight. They drank less water and dehydration appeared in many body organs. Hematuria, alopecia, hair soiling, diarrhea, gastric ulcers, pneumonia, and a stress reaction were all more marked in animals fed the pyridoxine deficient diet.

The augmented susceptibility of albino rats fed

TABLE 9

A Summary of Significant Clinical and Pathological Differences in Albino Rats Given Daily Doses of Benzylpenicillin and Fed a Pyridoxine Deficient Diet[1]

Clinical measurements (N = 54 + 20 controls)	1 week	2 weeks	3 weeks
Food intake: cal/kg/24 hr	−19.6*	+ 2.9	− 24.0
Water intake: ml/kg/24 hr	+60.3**	+172.0**	+253.6**
Colonic temperature: °C	− 0.5	− 0.5	− 1.3**
Urinary volume: ml/kg/24 hr	−22.1	+231.7*	+ 79.4*
Urinary pH: 24 hr sample	−15.5*	− 1.6	− 6.3
Urinary occult blood:[2] 1+ to 4+	+ 0.3	+ 0.6*	+ 0.3
Hair soiling:[2] 1+ to 4+	+ 1.8**	+ 1.0*	+ 1.3**
Diarrhea:[2] 1+ to 4+	+ 4.0**	+ 4.0**	+ 4.0**
Alopecia:[2] 1+ to 4+	+ 1.5**	+ 2.7**	+ 2.0**

Measurements at autopsy (N = 10 plus 10 controls)	3 weeks
Adrenal gland water level: g/100 g dry wt	+ 36.6**
Cecum dry weight: g	+ 48.2**
Heart water level: g/100 g dry wt	− 5.1*
Liver dry weight: g	− 28.1**
Muscle (abdominal) dry weight: g	− 22.7*
Pyloric stomach ulcers:[2] % incidence	+ 40.0**
Salivary (submaxillary) gland dry weight: g	− 19.4**
Salivary (submaxillary) gland water level: g/100 g dry wt	−113**
Spleen dry weight: g	− 56.2**
Thymus gland dry weight: g	− 31.8**
Thymus gland water level: g/100 g dry wt	− 19.7**
Residual carcass dry weight: g	− 10.2*

[1] The results, except those indicated by footnote 2, are expressed as mean percent change from controls given daily doses of distilled water and fed a pyridoxine deficient diet, specifically as $[(\overline{X}_d - \overline{X}_c)/\overline{X}_c]$ x 100, where $\overline{X}_d$ is the mean in the benzylpenicillin-treated group and $\overline{X}_c$ in the controls. Mean differences significant at P = 0.05 to 0.02 are indicated by one asterisk and at P = 0.01 or less by two asterisks.

[2] The results are expressed as mean difference from control $(\overline{X}_d - \overline{X}_c)$, not as mean percent difference because $\overline{X}_c$ was zero.

(From Boyd et al.[43] With permission of *Chemotherapia*, copyright © 1966, S. Karger, Basel.)

the pyridoxine deficient diet was not due to absence of pyridoxine in the diet. Daily supplementation with pyridoxine hydrochloride in doses up to 5 mg/kg/day given subcutaneously did not influence the augmented susceptibility to benzylpenicillin toxicity of rats fed the pyridoxine deficient diet. Pretreatment of rats by feeding the pyridoxine deficient diet for one month before starting daily administration of benzylpenicillin likewise did not influence the fulminating syndrome of toxicity of the drug in this dietary group.

On the other hand, when rats were fed labora-tory chow, given the same daily dose of benzylpenicillin for one month and then survivors transferred to the pyridoxine deficient diet and daily benzylpenicillin continued, diet-induced augmentation of benzylpenicillin toxicity completely disappeared during the subsequent three weeks, after which the experiment was terminated. It is possible that, had the study been extended beyond three weeks, augmentation of benzylpenicillin toxicity might have reappeared in rats pretreated with the antibiotic and then fed the pyridoxine deficient diet. As noted above, augmentation of toxicity in a similar pretreatment

TABLE 10

A Summary of Significant Clinical and Pathological Differences in Albino Rats Given Daily Doses of Benzylpenicillin and Fed Laboratory Chow[1]

Clinical measurements (N = 42 + 20 controls)	1 week	2 weeks	3 weeks
Water intake: ml/kg/24 hr	+ 56.9**	+ 92.7**	+ 80.8**
Urinary volume: ml/kg/24 hr	+189*	+192*	+361**
Urinary glucose output: mg/kg/24 hr	+720*	+325*	+350*
Urinary protein output: mg/kg/24 hr	+ 98	+ 5	+833*
Urinary pH: 24 hr sample	− 6.0	− 10.6*	0.0
Urinary occult blood: 1+ to 4+	+200	+450*	+500**
Hair soiling: 1+ to 4+ (mean diff.)	+ 0.2	+ 0.34	+ 0.46**
Diarrhea: 1+ to 4+ (mean diff.)	+ 0.37	+ 1.67**	+ 0.46

Measurements at autopsy (N = 10 + 10 controls)	3 weeks
Adrenal gland dry weight: g	+ 21.6*
Cecum dry weight: g	+ 54.2**
Cecum water level: g/100 g dry wt	+ 26.2**
Heart dry weight: g	− 16.6**
Kidney dry weight: g	− 11.0*
Ovaries dry weight: g	− 16.9*
Skin dry weight: g	− 13.1*

[1] The results are expressed as mean percent changes from controls fed laboratory chow and given daily doses of distilled water, specifically as $[(\overline{X}_d - \overline{X}_c)/\overline{X}_c] \times 100$, where $\overline{X}_d$ is the mean in the benzylpenicillin-treated group and $\overline{X}_c$ in the controls. Results for hair soiling and diarrhea are expressed as mean differences, not mean percent changes since these signs did not appear in the controls. Mean differences significant at $P = 0.05$ to 0.02 are indicated by one asterisk and at $P = 0.01$ or less by two asterisks. (From Boyd et al.[43] With the permission of *Chemotherapia,* copyright © 1966, S. Karger, Basel.)

experiment using a diet deficient in pantothenic acid did not reappear until after about three weeks on the purified diet.

There is evidence that changes in the intestinal flora produced by dietary administration of antibiotics may lead to intestinal synthesis of pyridoxine which may stimulate growth in weanling rats fed diets deficient in pyridoxine.[45-47] This would not appear to have been a factor in the benzylpenicillin-pretreated rats and their subsequent lack of susceptibility to transfer to the diet deficient in pyridoxine since lack of susceptibility was not produced by pyridoxine supplementation alone. It is possible that pretreatment with benzylpenicillin altered the intestinal flora and that this alteration temporarily lessened susceptibility to the combination of benzylpenicillin plus a diet deficient in pyridoxine. When compared with results of studies on the diet deficient in pantothenic acid, the common factor,

however, appeared to be the high sucrose content of both diets.

Choline Deficient Diet

Boyd et al.[43] reported a similar augmentation of benzylpenicillin toxicity in young adult male rats fed a diet deficient in choline. The diet contained 64.8% glucose, 20% alcohol extracted peanut meal (which supplied most of the protein), 6% vitamin-free casein, 4% salt mix, 3% corn oil, 2% cod liver oil, and vitamin supplements except choline.

Of 62 rats fed the choline deficient diet and given benzylpeniçillin in an oral dose of 5.34 g/kg/day for 6 days a week, 47 or 76% were dead at 10 days. After the same interval the death rate in rats fed a laboratory chow and given the same daily dose of benzylpenicillin was only 15%. There were no deaths in controls fed either diet and given no benzylpenicillin. The clinicopathological

TABLE 11

A Summary of Significant Clinical and Pathological Differences in Albino Rats Given Daily Doses of Benzylpenicillin and Fed a Pyridoxine Deficient Diet[1]

Clinical measurements (N = 54 plus 42 controls)	1 week	2 weeks	3 weeks
Body weight: g	− 5.1	− 10.4*	− 23.1**
Food intake: cal/kg/24 hr	− 34.7**	− 29.6**	− 19.2*
Water intake: ml/kg/24 hr	− 48.9*	− 37.9**	− 37.3**
Urinary occult blood: 1+ to 4+	+ 48.3*	+ 50.0*	+ 77.3**
Hair soiling: 1+ to 4+	+ 889**	+ 112*	+ 183**
Diarrhea: 1+ to 4+	+ 983**	+ 609**	+ 896**
Alopecia: 1+ to 4+	+1400**	+2600**	+1900**

Measurements at autopsy (N = 10 plus 10 controls)	3 weeks
Adrenal gland water level: g/100 g dry wt	+ 24.2**
Gastrointestinal tract	
Pyloric stomach dry weight: g	− 25.9**
Pyloric stomach ulcers: % incidence	+ 300*
Small bowel dry weight: g	− 20.9**
Cecum dry weight: g	− 27.8**
Cecum water level: g/100 g dry wt	− 28.6**
Colon dry weight: g	− 29.3**
Colon water level: g/100 g dry wt	− 17.1**
Heart water level: g/100 g dry wt	− 6.1*
Liver dry weight: g	− 25.0**
Lung water level: g/100 g dry wt	− 10.4**
Lung infection: % incidence	+ 300*
Skin water level: g/100 g dry wt	− 21.1**
Spleen dry weight: g	− 53.7**
Submaxillary salivary gland water level: g/100 g dry wt	− 14.3**
Thymus gland dry weight: g	− 57.2**
Thymus gland water level: g/100 g dry wt	− 20.2**

[1] The results are expressed as mean percent change from controls given daily doses of benzylpenicillin and fed laboratory chow, specifically as $[(\overline{X}_p - \overline{X}_c)/\overline{X}_c] \times 100$, where $\overline{X}_p$ is the mean in rats fed a pyridoxine deficient diet and $\overline{X}_c$ those fed laboratory chow. A mean difference significant at P = 0.05 to 0.02 is indicated by one asterisk and at P = 0.01 or less by two asterisks. (From Boyd et al.[43] with the permission of *Chemotherapia*, copyright © 1966, S. Karger, Basel.)

syndrome of toxicity in rats fed the choline deficient diet and given benzylpenicillin was similar to that noted above in rats fed a pyridoxine deficient diet.

The common feature of diets deficient in pantothenic acid, pyridoxine, and choline is the high sugar content of these diets. The biotin deficient diet had a high percentage of another common food, egg white. Most of the diets contained food oils such as cottonseed oil. These various observations drew attention to the possibility that natural pure foods were being fed in amounts which approached toxic levels and led to a study of the toxicity of pure foods.[48-50]

Conclusions

In a series of studies designed to find the effect of vitamin deficiencies on drug toxicity in albino rats, it was noted that many vitamin deficient diets augmented drug toxicity. Augmentation was not due to deficiency of vitamins, however, since it was not prevented by vitamin supplementation.

There appeared to be features of each deficient diet that could account for augmentation of drug toxicity. The only common feature was the presence (or absence) of large amounts of purified or semipurified foodstuffs. Thus: (a) drug toxicity was unaffected or influenced to a minor degree by diets containing large amounts of natural or relatively unpurified foods such as cornstarch, milk powder, rolled oats, and ground corn; and (b) drug toxicity was markedly augmented by diets containing large amounts of purified foods such as dried egg white, sucrose, and glucose.

These observations suggested that augmentation of drug toxicity noted in animals fed certain diets was due to a combination of sublethal toxicity from a pure food and from a drug producing a fulminating lethal reaction. The suggestion led to a study of the acute and chronic toxicity of pure foods.

REFERENCES

1. Boyd, E. M., *Predictive Toxicometrics,* Scientechnica (Publishers) Ltd., Bristol, England, 1971.
2. Boyd, E. M., Broughton, R. J., and James, J., The acute oral toxicity of benzylpenicillin ammonium, *Antibiot. Chemother.,* 9, 739, 1959.
3. Boyd, E. M., Broughton, R. J., and James, J., The acute oral toxicity of benzylpenicillin potassium, *Arch. Int. Pharmacodyn. Ther.,* 123, 295, 1960.
4. Boyd, E. M. and Fulford, R. A., The acute oral toxicity of benzylpenicillin potassium in guinea pigs, *Antibiot. Chemother.,* 11, 276, 1961.
5. Boyd, C. E., The acute oral toxicity of benzylpenicillin potassium in the rabbit, *Antibiot. Chemother.,* 10, 376, 1960.
6. Boyd, C. E., Boyd, E. M., and Brown, M. D., Penicillin vomiting, *Can. Med. Assoc. J.,* 82, 195, 1960.
7. Mills, D. W., Studies on the chronic oral toxicity of potassium penicillin G, *Arch. Int. Pharmacodyn. Thér.,* 125, 83, 1960.
8. Boyd, E. M. and Selby, M. J., The chronic oral toxicity of benzylpenicillin, *Antibiot. Chemother.,* 12, 249, 1962.
9. Boyd, E. M., Mulrooney, D. A., and Sargeant, E. J., The toxicity of benzylpenicillin in animals on vitamin A deficient test diet, U.S.P. XIV, *Can. J. Biochem. Physiol.,* 40, 1685, 1962.
10. Waugh, A. E., *Elements of Statistical Method,* 3rd edition, McGraw-Hill, New York, 1952.
11. Boyd, E. M., Ascorbic acid and benzylpenicillin toxicity, *Clin. Med.,* 70, 2223, 1963.
12. Verrusio, A. C., Pollard, D. R., and Fraser, F. C., A cytoplasmically transmitted diet–dependent difference in response to the teratogenic effects of 6-aminonicotinamide, *Science,* 160, 206, 1968.
13. Green, N. M., Avidin. 1. The use of ^{14}C biotin for kinetic studies and for assay, *Biochem. J.,* 89, 585, 1963.
14. Melamed, M. D. and Green, N. M., Avidin. 2. Purification and composition, *Biochem. J.,* 89, 591, 1963.
15. Green, N. M., Avidin. 3. The nature of the biotin-binding site, *Biochem. J.,* 89, 599, 1963.
16. Luckey, T. D., Pleasants, J. R., Wagner, M., Gordon, H. A., and Reyniers, J. A., Some observations on vitamin metabolism in germ-free rats, *J. Nutr.,* 57, 169, 1955.
17. Welch, A. D. and Wright, L. D., The role of "folic acid" and biotin in the nutrition of the rat, *J. Nutr.,* 25, 555, 1943.
18. Nielsen, E. and Black, A., Biotin and folic acid deficiencies in the mouse, *J. Nutr.,* 28, 203, 1944.
19. Ham, W. E. and Scott, K. W., Intestinal synthesis of biotin in the rat, *J. Nutr.,* 51, 423, 1953.
20. Bateman, W. G., The digestibility and utilization of egg proteins, *J. Biol. Chem.,* 26, 263, 1916.
21. Boas, M. A., The effect of dessication upon the nutritive properties of egg white, *Biochem. J.,* 21, 712, 1927.
22. György, P., The curative factor (vit. H) for egg white injury, with particular reference to its presence in different foodstuffs and in yeast, *J. Biol.,* 131, 733, 1939.
23. Rubin, S. H., Diekter, L., and Moyer, E. H., Biological activity of synthetic d,1-desthiobiotin, *Proc. Soc. Exp. Biol. Med.,* 58, 352, 1945.
24. Peters, J. M., Caffeine Toxicity in Rats on a Biotin Deficient Diet, Thesis for an M.Sc. (Med.) in Pharmacology, Douglas Library, Queen's University, Kingston, Ontario, Canada, 1964.
25. Boyd, E. M. and Sargeant, E. J., The prediction of skin reactions to benzylpenicillin in animals on a biotin-deficient diet, *J. New Drugs,* 2, 283, 1962.
26. Sargeant, E. J. and Boyd, E. M., The toxicity of benzylpenicillin in animals on a biotin deficient diet, *Proc. Can. Fed. Biol. Soc.,* 5, 70, 1962.
27. Peters, J. M., A fulminating toxic reaction to daily administration of caffeine in albino rats on a biotin deficient diet, Am. Ind. Hyg. Conference Abstracts, 1963, 18.
28. Peters, J. M., Toxicity due to other than biotin deficiency in adult albino rats on a biotin deficient, dried egg white, diet, *Fed. Proc.,* 22, 311, 1963.

29. **Peters, J. M. and Boyd, E. M.,** Clinical and pathological signs of winter toxicity from biotin deficient raw egg white diet in albino rats, *Pharmacologist,* 5, 232, 1963.
30. **Peters, J. M. and Boyd, E. M.,** Secondary factors in caffeine toxicity, *Proc. Can. Fed. Biol. Soc.,* 7, 37, 1964.
31. **Peters, J. M. and Krijnen, C. J.,** Organ weights and water contents of rats fed purified diets, *Growth,* 30, 99, 1966.
32. **Peters, J. M. and Boyd, E. M.,** Diet and susceptibility to caffeine, *Environ. Physiol.,* 1, 12, 1971.
33. **Peters, J. M.,** Factors in Caffeine Toxicity, Thesis for a Ph.D. in Pharmacology, Douglas Library, Queen's University, Kingston, Ontario, Canada, 1966.
34. **Boyd, E. M., Mulrooney, D. A., Pitman, C. A., and Abel, M.,** Benzylpenicillin toxicity in animals on a synthetic high sucrose diet, *Can. J. Physiol. Pharmacol.,* 43, 47, 1965.
35. **Nelson, M. M. and Evans, H. M.,** Sparing action of protein on pantothenic acid requirement of rat; fibrin as protein component, *Proc. Soc. Exp. Biol. Med.,* 66, 299, 1947.
36. **Sebrell, W. H., Jr. and Harris, R. S.,** *The Vitamins,* Vol. 2, Academic Press, New York, 1954, 589.
37. **Dubos, R., Schaedler, R. W., and Costello, R.,** Composition, alteration, and effects of the intestinal flora, *Fed. Proc.,* 22, 1322, 1963.
38. Review, Diet and drug response, *Nutr. Rev.,* 20, 187, 1962.
39. **Balazs, T., Sahasrabudhe, M. R., and Grice, H. C.,** The influence of excess body fat on the cardiotoxicity of isoproterenol in rats, *Toxicol. Appl. Pharmacol.,* 4, 613, 1962.
40. **Ershoff, B. J.,** Comparative effects of a purified and stock diet on DBH (2,5-di-tert-butylhydroquinone) toxicity in the rat, *Proc. Soc. Exp. Biol. Med.,* 112, 362, 1963.
41. **Harper, K. H. and Worden, A. N.,** Comparative toxicity studies on glucose, fructose, and sucrose, Abstracts: Third Annual Meeting, Society of Toxicology, Williamsburg, Va., 1964, 365.
42. **Shore, V. and Shore, B.,** Effect of mercuric chloride on some kidney enzymes in chow-fed and sucrose-fed rats, *Am. J. Physiol.,* 198, 187, 1960.
43. **Boyd, E. M., Covert, E. L., and Pitman, C. A.,** Benzylpenicillin toxicity in albino rats fed synthetic high sugar diets, *Chemotherapia,* 11, 320, 1966.
44. **Clarke, M. F. and Lechycka, M.,** The biological assay of pyridoxine (Vitamin B_6), *J. Nutr.,* 25, 571, 1943.
45. **Linkswiler, H., Baumann, C. A., and Snell, E. E.,** Effect of aureomycin on the response of rats to various forms of vitamin B_6, *J. Nutr.,* 43, 565, 1951.
46. **Sauberlich, H. E.,** Effect of aureomycin and penicillin upon the vitamin requirements of the rat, *J. Nutr.,* 46, 99, 1952.
47. **Guzman-Garcia, J., Sarles, W. B., and Baumann, C. A.,** Microorganisms in the intestines of rats fed penicillin, *J. Nutr.,* 49, 647, 1953.
48. **Boyd, E. M.,** Food and drug toxicity. A summary of recent studies, *J. Clin. Pharmacol.,* 8, 281, 1968.
49. **Boyd, E. M.,** Dietary protein and pesticide toxicity in male weanling rats, *Bull. WHO,* 40, 801, 1969.
50. **Boyd, E. M.,** Diet and drug toxicity, *Clin. Toxicol.,* 2, 423, 1969.

Chapter 3

SUCROSE

Sucrose was first used as sugar cane in the islands of the South Pacific Ocean as early as 10,000 B.C. The juice was boiled to concentrate it, but pure sugar was not prepared until the early Christian era, probably originally in India. It was called 'shakar' by the Persians, 'sukkar' by the Arabs, and 'zucchero' by the early Italians. The fascinating story of the history of sugar has been reviewed by several authors such as Rolph,[1] Boyd,[2] Tacke et al.,[3] Baikow,[4] and Constantopoulos.[5]

Sucrose has been estimated to comprise one quarter of the dietary carbohydrate of the U.S.[6] It may be present in various forms such as in fruits, vegetables, molasses, and syrup. The International Sugar Council[3] estimated that the world sugar consumption more than doubled between 1930 and 1960. Cleave et al.[7] have reviewed evidence indicating that the incidence of diabetes mellitus increases with increase in sugar consumption, although they admit that this does not necessarily indicate a causative relationship.

The Acute Oral Toxicity of Sucrose

Boyd et al.[8] reported a study of the clinicopathological syndrome of toxicity to sucrose in doses at the range of the acute, oral LD_{50} given to male and female rats. The animals were starved for 10 hr (overnight) to empty the stomach prior to administration of sucrose. Sucrose was given by intragastric cannula in doses of from 5 to 80 g/kg dissolved in distilled water to a volume of 60 ml/kg. Clinical signs of toxicity were recorded hourly during the first day, daily for six days, and then casually in survivors for one month. Clinical measurements were quantitated daily. Autopsies were performed upon animals that died, provided the autopsy could be made within 1 hr of death to avoid postmortem changes described by Boyd and Knight.[9] At autopsy were recorded gross and microscopic pathology and the weight and water content of body organs. Similar autopsies were performed upon survivors at a

fortnight and at one month. The results were compared with those in controls given the vehicle (distilled water) but no sucrose.

Acute Lethal Doses

No animals died following oral doses of 5 to 24 g/kg. As the dose was progressively raised above these levels, the interval to death progressively declined. The regression of mean hours to death on dose was best fitted by a quadratic equation, $Y = a - bX + cX^2$, as shown in Figure 11. Doses of 60 to 80 g/kg produced death in all animals within 5 hr.

Lesser doses produced death at two intervals, an early death at less than 9 to 10 hr and a delayed death. Most of the delayed deaths occurred at 10 to 48 hr but a few occurred at 2 to 11 days after giving sucrose. It was possible to calculate an

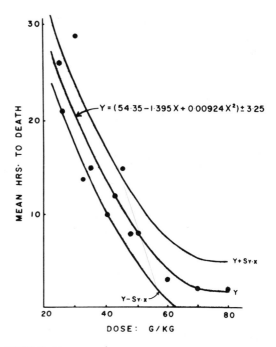

FIGURE 11. The regression of mean interval to death upon dose of sucrose given orally to adult male albino rats. (From Boyd et al.[8] with the permission of *Toxicology and Applied Pharmacology,* copyright © 1965, Academic Press, New York.)

LD$_{50}$ ± S.E. for early deaths in all animals and for delayed deaths in survivors. The results are assembled in Table 12. It may be seen that females were much more susceptible than males to early death from sucrose. The difference between the sexes was much less for delayed deaths. The acute oral LD$_{50}$ varied from 27.9 g/kg to 42.2 g/kg.

During the early twentieth century, 'osmotherapy' was a popular procedure.[10] It consisted of giving sucrose parenterally. Kuriyama[11] reported in 1917 that sucrose produced no deaths in dogs with intravenous doses between 2 and 10 g/kg. Hausmann[10] found that doses of 30 to 40 g/kg given subcutaneously produced death in about 6 hr in mice. The median lethal dose of sucrose given intravenously to rabbits was reported as of the order of 30 to 40 g/kg by Helmholtz and Bollman.[12] A similar range was reported for the intravenous LD$_{50}$ of glucose by Spector.[13] It would appear, therefore, that the acute oral LD$_{50}$ of sucrose is similar to the acute parenteral LD$_{50}$. This may be due to the fact, noted below, that sucrose produced a violent gastroenteritis in doses at the range of the acute oral LD$_{50}$. Gastrointestinal inflammation may have made absorption of sucrose given by mouth as rapid as absorption given parenterally. Delak and Adamič[14] reported that 40, but not 20, g/kg produced death in sheep.

Boyd et al.[8] calculated that the acute oral LD$_{50}$ of sucrose in albino rats was of the order of 103 ± 20 mM per kg body weight. Corresponding estimates of the acute oral LD$_{50}$ of sodium chloride are 64.1 ± 7.4 mM per kg and of potassium chloride 40.5 ± 1.9.[15] Calculated as g/kg, the acute oral toxicity of sodium and potassium chlorides is 10 to 15 times that of sucrose, i.e., the LD$_{50}$ of the salts is one tenth to one fifteenth that of sucrose. Calculated as millimoles per kg, however, the spread is only twofold. These comparisons indicate that acute toxicity is related primarily to number of molecules of the three agents rather than to grams. The lethal dose is that equivalent to a child of 25 lb swallowing—and retaining—less than a pound of candy.

Clinical Signs of Acute Toxicity

The controls given only distilled water in a dose of 60 ml/kg exhibited signs of toxicity during the first 6 hr after administration. These consisted of hypokinesia, prostration, abdominal bloating, and diarrhea. These signs disappeared in the water-treated controls after the sixth hour.

In animals given sucrose dissolved in distilled water, the same signs were present but to a more marked degree during the first few hours. In addition, sucrose-treated rats exhibited cyanosis. The various clinical signs persisted to 24 hr in rats given sucrose. The premortem signs in animals that died within 9 to 10 hr were tonoclonic convulsions followed by stupor and respiratory failure. An early convulsive death was also reported from intravenous administration of sucrose to rabbits by MacKay and MacKay.[16] Hausmann[10] found that sucrose given as a 50% solution subcutaneously or intraperitoneally to mice produced a hypothermic "osmonarkose" and death in about 6 hr. Hypothermic narcosis appeared in rats with delayed deaths in the study of Boyd et al.[8]

Measurements of food and water intake and colonic temperature at 24 hr after oral administration of a range of doses of sucrose to surviving albino rats are summarized in Figure 12. Values for all three measurements rose slightly following administration of increasing sublethal doses of sucrose and fell as increasing lethal doses were given. Lethal doses also produced loss of body weight at 24 hr in survivors. Loss of weight was due, at least in part, to anorexia and diarrhea. Bavetta and Ershoff[17] reported loss of body weight from large amounts of dietary sucrose in female rats. Peraino et al.[18] found that large amounts of dietary sucrose inhibited the passage of casein out of the stomach. Anorexia from large

TABLE 12

The Acute Oral LD$_{50}$ of Sucrose, in g/kg, and Interval to Death in Male and Female Albino Rats

Sex	Interval to death (hr)	Acute oral LD$_{50}$ ± S.E. (g/kg)
Male	All intervals	35.4 ± 7.0
Female	All intervals	29.7 ± 3.7
Male	< 9-10 hr	42.2 ± 4.5
Female	< 9-10 hr	35.9 ± 1.3
Male	> 10 hr	29.8 ± 1.4
Female	> 10 hr	27.9 ± 1.6

(From Boyd et al.[8] with the permission of *Toxicology and Applied Pharmacology*, copyright © 1965, Academic Press, New York.)

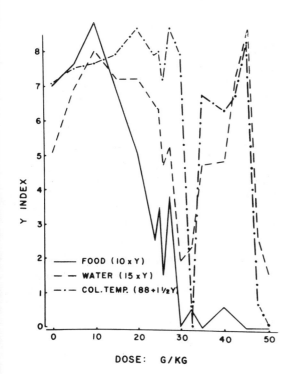

FIGURE 12. The effect at 24 hr of increasing oral doses of sucrose on food intake (g/kg/24 hr), water intake (ml/kg/24 hr), and colonic temperature (°F) of male albino rats. The Y index must be multiplied by factors indicated in parenthesis to obtain mean values for the three parameters. (From Boyd et al.[8] with the permission of *Toxicology and Applied Pharmacology*, copyright © 1965, Academic Press, New York.)

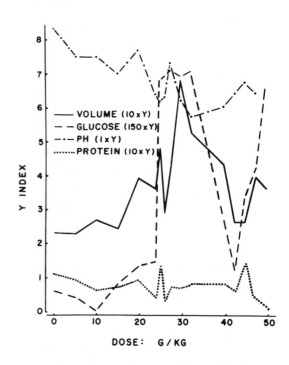

FIGURE 13. The influence of increasing oral doses of sucrose on urinary volume (ml/kg/24 hr), glucose, and protein output (mg/kg/24 hr) and pH of the first 24-hr samples of urine collected after administration of the agent. The Y index must be multiplied by factors indicated in parenthesis to obtain mean measured amounts of the four parameters. (From Boyd et al.[8] with the permission of *Toxicology and Applied Pharmacology*, copyright © 1965, Academic Press, New York.)

amounts of sucrose has been reported by many authors.[19-22]

Measurements on the first 24-hr samples of urine are indicated in Figure 13. Increasing sublethal doses progressively increased the volume output of increasingly acidic urine. Lethal oral doses produced a further aciduria and, in addition, a glycosuria. Urinary protein output was not affected significantly at any dose of sucrose. Diuresis from sucrose has been noted by several authors.[23,24] MacDonald and Braithwaite[25] reported that a high intake of sucrose in man produced epigastric discomfort, muscular aches, sweating, anorexia, and an increase in serum neutral fat, mainly in glycerides of oleic and palmitic acids.

Gross and Microscopic Pathology in Acute Toxicity

On gross observation of animals that died, sucrose was found to have produced an irritant gastroenteritis consisting of vascular congestion, gastric ulcers, loss of muscle tone, and a lumen dilated with gas and a yellowish syrupy fluid. There was congestion of the brain and meninges, heart, lungs, and testes. The adrenal glands, liver, kidneys, and spleen frequently exhibited areas of discoloration.

On microscopic examination of the gastro-intestinal tract, there were found a capillary, venous, and arteriolar vasodilatation of the lamina propria and submucosa of cardiac stomach with areas of lysis of the inner surface layers of the stratified squamous epithelium. There was a similar vasodilatation in pyloric stomach with marked lysis of the lining surface columnar cells and mucous neck cells. The parietal cells of pyloric stomach were somewhat less involved, the zymogens were shrunken, and the lamina propria at the base of the pyloric glands were edematous. In animals that died after 24 hr, the acute irritant gastritis had disappeared leaving some hyperemia of the submucosa. In animals that died at four days, there was some edema of the arteriolar walls.

In the small bowel, the villi were congested, the lamina propria edematous, and the columnar epithelium lining the villi completely lysed away in many areas. There was a little hemorrhage into the lumen of the small bowel. The cecum was mildly inflamed and there was some hyperemia of the colon. The inflammatory reaction had disappeared in animals that died 24 hr or longer after sucrose administration.

Several body organs were congested by large doses of sucrose as part of the early reaction to the agent. The coronary arteries were dilated and the arterial wall was swollen and pale-stained in animals that died as early as 3 hr after sucrose administration. The capillaries of the myocardium were dilated and there were some areas of capillary hemorrhage. There was also early congestion of other organs such as the adrenal glands, liver, and thymus gland. Organ congestion had disappeared in late deaths and was replaced by degenerative changes. In the heart, for example, the delayed reaction was accompanied by small areas of focal necrosis with leukocyte and fibroblast infiltration. In late deaths, the adrenal glands were hypertrophied and there was loss of thymocytes in the thymus gland as part of a stressor reaction.

Apparently due to the presence in blood of large amounts of sucrose absorbed through the denuded intestinal lining, toxic damage was recorded as early as 1 hr in the arterioles. It consisted of periarteriolar edema in the lung, edema and pale-staining of the intima and media in the splenic arterioles, and edema of the tunica externa as well in arterioles of the heart and mesentery. Large numbers of leukocytes were observed in the blood vessels.

The early lethal reaction was characterized by toxic changes in some organs such as the liver, kidneys, testes, and muscle. At 3 hr, the hepatic cells were shrunken and the Kupffer's cells were often lysed away from the lining of the sinusoids. At 24 hr the liver appeared histologically normal. At 1 hr, the renal glomeruli were shrunken and distorted and granules were prominent at the base of the brush border. By 3 hr, the proximal renal tubular cells had become edematous and obliterated the lumen. At this time the loop cells were also edematous and cells of the distal convoluted tubules were shrunken with casts in the lumen. At 1 hr the seminiferous tubules of the testes were shrunken and the M discs of striated muscle were prominent.

As the interval to death was prolonged, degenerative changes became more prominent particularly in the kidney. At and after 24 hr, vacuolar degeneration appeared in the proximal renal tubular cells and bits of tubular debris could be noted in the space beneath Bowman's capsule. The descending limb of Henle's loop had become edematous and the cuboidal epithelium lining the ascending limb was frequently necrosed. Areas of focal necrosis appeared in the myocardium. In the testes, the spermatogenic cells had separated from the tubular wall, the sperm were small, and the interstitial tissue was infiltrated with leukocytes.

Similar lesions from large doses of sucrose have been noted in the kidney of rabbits,[26] dogs,[27] and man[28,29] with various suggested mechanisms of action.[30] Studies have been reported on the effect of large doses of sucrose on the liver,[31-33] heart,[34,35] placenta,[36] gastrointestinal tract,[37,38] teeth,[39,40] and skin.[41]

Organ Weights and Water Content in Acute Toxicity

A summary of measurements of organ weights of albino rats at death from oral administration of sucrose and in survivors at two weeks and one month is presented in Table 13. At death, there was a considerable loss of body weight due to losses in organs such as the heart, liver, testes, and residual carcass. At death, the weight of the stomach and small bowel was increased and there was hypertrophy of the adrenal glands. These changes persisted to a greater or lesser degree in survivors at two weeks after giving a lethal dose of sucrose as may be seen by data assembled in Table 13. In survivors at one month, all measurements of organ weights, except that of liver, were within the limits of controls given no sucrose, as shown in Table 13.

Corresponding shifts in the water content of the same body organs are summarized in Table 14. At death due to oral administration of sucrose, practically all body organs were markedly dehydrated. Loss of water at death was particularly marked in pyloric stomach, small bowel, cecum, colon, lungs, skeletal muscle, skin, testes, and residual carcass. Dehydration became progressively less marked at two weeks and one month after sucrose administration in survivors, as indicated in Table 14.

TABLE 13

Shifts in the Fresh Wet Weight of Body Organs in Albino Rats Given Sucrose in Doses at the Range of the Acute, Oral LD$_{50}$[a]

Organ	Nonsurvivors	Survivors at 2 weeks	Survivors at 1 month
Adrenal glands	+30.9 (0.05)	+35.5 (0.005)	– 1.8 (0.9)
Brain	+ 4.3 (0.3)	– 3.2 (0.2)	– 5.8 (0.2)
Gastrointestinal tract			
Cardiac stomach	+18.4 (0.05)	+29.4 (0.001)	– 0.4 (1.0)
Pyloric stomach	+ 0.1 (0.9)	+25.9 (0.005)	– 1.5 (0.8)
Small bowel	+16.4 (< 0.001)	+52.7 (< 0.001)	– 2.5 (1.0)
Cecum	+16.0 (0.1)	+66.3 (< 0.001)	– 5.4 (0.6)
Colon	– 7.5 (0.2)	– 3.2 (0.7)	0.0 (1.0)
Heart	–11.2 (0.05)	–14.6 (0.01)	0.0 (1.0)
Kidneys	– 5.4 (0.3)	–12.8 (0.01)	– 1.9 (0.7)
Liver	–42.6 (< 0.001)	–14.4 (0.02)	–26.1 (< 0.001)
Lungs	+ 5.9 (0.5)	+ 1.7 (0.9)	– 9.1 (0.3)
Muscle[b]	+ 1.7 (0.9)	+27.8 (< 0.001)	– 3.1 (0.7)
Skin	– 8.3 (0.5)	– 3.6 (0.7)	+ 3.0 (0.4)
Spleen	– 5.0 (0.7)	–20.5 (0.02)	– 7.8 (0.5)
Testes	– 7.2 (0.02)	– 0.3 (0.8)	– 3.3 (0.5)
Thymus gland	+ 7.5 (0.5)	+18.2 (0.3)	–15.3 (0.3)
Residual carcass	–13.9 (< 0.001)	– 3.2 (0.7)	+ 1.7 (0.8)

[a]The results are expressed as $[(\overline{X}_s - \overline{X}_c)/\overline{X}_c]$ x 100 (P that $\overline{X}_s$ equals $\overline{X}_c$), where $\overline{X}_s$ is the mean weight in grams in animals given sucrose and $\overline{X}_c$ in control animals given distilled water only.
[b]Abdominal wall
(From Boyd et al.[8] with the permission of *Toxicology and Applied Pharmacology*, copyright © 1965, Academic Press, New York.)

In summary, therefore, sucrose produced death when given orally to albino rats in doses of some 25 g/kg and over. There were two types of toxic reactions to oral sucrose. There was (a) an early reaction characterized by hypokinesia, prostration, cyanosis, abdominal bloating, and diarrhea with death within 10 hr of administration of sucrose following tonoclonic convulsions, stupor, and respiratory failure. Autopsy on animals with early deaths disclosed the presence of a violent local irritant gastroenteritis, an inflammatory reaction in various organs such as the liver, kidneys, heart, and adrenal glands, a loss of organ weight and water content in most structures and early degenerative changes in organs such as the liver, kidneys, testes, and muscle.

The type (b) or delayed reaction produced deaths at 10 hr to 11 days with a broad plateau at 12 to 48 hr. The initial signs were similar to those noted for the early, type (a), reaction. At 24 hr and continuing until death, food intake and water intake were reduced, there was a diuresis with glycosuria and aciduria, the irritant local gastro-

enteritis gradually disappeared, and the microscopic appearance of the liver returned to normal. The delayed reaction was associated with a marked tubular nephritis, myocardial focal necrosis, a stressor adrenal hypertrophy, testicular atrophy, dehydration, and loss of body and organ weights. Recovery was essentially complete in survivors at one month after giving a toxic dose of sucrose.

Sucrose Toxicity at the Oral LD$_{50}$ (100 days)

The oral LD$_{50}$ (100 days) is that dose per kg body weight which, given once daily by gavage, kills 50% of animals by the end of 100 days of administration. It is a measure of multiposal toxicity described in some detail by Boyd.[42] The clinicopathological syndrome of toxicity to sucrose given to young, male albino rats in doses at the range of the oral LD$_{50}$ (100 days) has been described by Constantopoulos[5,43] and by Constantopoulos and Boyd.[44,45]

Sucrose was given once daily by gavage to 280 unstarved young, male albino rats initially weighing 150 to 175 g. Sucrose was dissolved in

TABLE 14

Shifts in the Water Levels of Body Organs of Albino Rats Following Oral Administration of Sucrose in Doses at the Range of the LD_{50}[a]

Organ	Nonsurvivors	Survivors at 2 weeks	Survivors at 1 month
Adrenal glands	+ 8.1 (0.4)	–12.7 (0.1)	+ 7.8 (0.3)
Brain	– 5.3 (0.1)	– 3.7 (0.005)	+ 1.8 (0.5)
Gastrointestinal tract			
Cardiac stomach	+17.6 (0.1)	– 3.8 (0.2)	– 0.3 (0.9)
Pyloric stomach	–39.6 (< 0.001)	– 7.2 (0.05)	– 0.5 (0.8)
Small bowel	–25.7 (< 0.001)	– 4.5 (0.3)	– 4.3 (0.3)
Cecum	–43.5 (< 0.001)	+ 1.3 (0.9)	0.0 (1.0)
Colon	–27.2 (< 0.001)	+ 0.5 (0.9)	– 1.7 (0.7)
Heart	– 2.2 (0.8)	– 4.8 (0.5)	– 2.8 (0.4)
Kidneys	– 4.3 (0.1)	– 3.2 (0.3)	0.0 (1.0)
Liver	– 6.3 (0.3)	– 5.4 (0.2)	– 0.9 (0.9)
Lungs	–22.5 (< 0.001)	– 0.6 (1.0)	– 5.1 (0.2)
Muscle[b]	–19.6 (< 0.001)	+ 3.7 (0.4)	0.0 (1.0)
Skin	–24.2 (< 0.001)	– 2.1 (0.8)	– 7.8 (0.4)
Spleen	– 1.5 (0.8)	–10.8 (0.05)	– 3.5 (0.05)
Testes	–15.8 (< 0.001)	– 4.6 (0.3)	+ 4.1 (0.5)
Thymus gland	+57.1 (0.1)	0.0 (1.0)	–28.0 (0.01)
Residual carcass	–28.9 (< 0.001)	–10.0 (0.1)	– 4.1 (0.4)

[a]Water levels are calculated as grams water per 100 g dry weight of organ. The results are expressed as $[(\overline{X}_s - \overline{X}_c)/\overline{X}_c] \times 100$ (P that $\overline{X}_s$ equals $\overline{X}_c$), where $\overline{X}_s$ is the mean in animals given sucrose and $\overline{X}_c$ in control animals given distilled water only.
[b]Abdominal wall
(From Boyd et al.[8] with the permission of *Toxicology and Applied Pharmacology*, copyright © 1965, Academic Press, New York.)

distilled water and administered through an intragastric cannula in daily doses of from 20.0 to 45.0 g/kg in a total volume of 50 ml/kg of aqueous solution. The sugar was given five days a week after preliminary trials indicated that mortality from a total weekly dose divided into five equal parts each given daily for five days a week was the same as that from division of the total weekly dose into seven equal parts each part given daily for seven days a week.[46,47] Each dose was given for 100 days or until a majority of the animals had died, whichever occurred first. Clinical signs were measured weekly, or at shorter intervals if changing rapidly, and gross and microscopic pathology were recorded on animals which died. The weight and water content of body organs were determined in survivors.

The LD_{50} was calculated at weekly intervals and plotted against days of administration. The regression was best fitted by the equation $Y = (52.1 - 11.8 \log X) \pm 1.32$, where Y is the daily dose of sucrose and X the number of days of oral administration. By substituting 2 for log X,

the LD_{50} (100 days) $\pm$ S.E. was found to be 28.5 ± 1.3 g/kg/day. The regression is shown in Figure 14. Using the acute oral LD_{50} of 35.4 ± 7.0

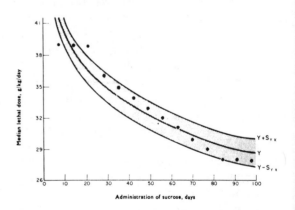

FIGURE 14. The regression, on days of oral administration of sucrose to albino rats (X), of the single daily dose that killed 50% of animals (Y). The shaded area is the calculated value of Y ± its standard error. (From Constantopoulos and Boyd[45] with the permission of the authors and of *Food and Cosmetics Toxicology*, copyright © 1968, Pergamon Press, England.)

noted in Table 12, the 100-day LD_{50} index was calculated as $(28.5/35.4) \times 100$ or 80.6 ± 3.7. Most deaths were of the delayed type (see Table 12) and using its acute oral LD_{50} of 29.8 ± 1.4, the 100-day LD_{50} index may be calculated to be 95.8 ± 4.4. Calculated in a similar manner, the maximal $LD_{0 \, (100 \, days)}$ was found to be 19.8 ± 1.9 g/kg/day and the minimal $LD_{100 \, (100 \, days)}$ 35.5 ± 0.5 g/kg/day. The latter values are practically synonymous with the $LD_{1 \, (100 \, days)}$ and $LD_{99 \, (100 \, days)}$, respectively.

Clinical Signs at the $LD_{50 \, (100 \, days)}$

The clinical signs of toxicity were quantitated in clinical units of 1+ to 4+. The percentage of animals with clinical signs of 2+ or over (a statistically significant value) was plotted against daily dose of sucrose and the results are shown in Figure 15. All regressions were linear and were fitted by the following equations:

a. for drowsiness: $Y = 3.45X - 62.6$
b. for pallor: $Y = 3.29X - 68.3$
c. for prostration: $Y = 3.45X - 73.9$
d. for hyporeflexia: $Y = 1.58X - 28.5$
e. for ataxia: $Y = 1.78X - 40.2$
f. for diarrhea: $Y = 1.36X - 29.4$
g. for fur soiling: $Y = 0.52X - 11.0$

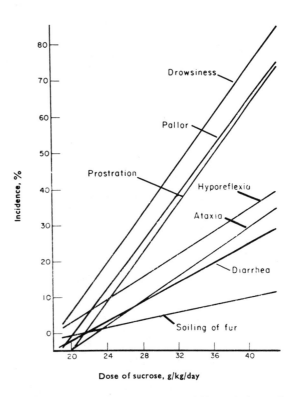

FIGURE 15. The regression, on daily oral dose of sucrose, of the percentage of albino rats exhibiting clinical signs of 2+ or higher clinical units. (From Constantopoulos and Boyd[45] with the permission of the authors and of *Food and Cosmetics Toxicology,* copyright © 1968, Pergamon Press England.)

Krogh[48] reported that a sucrose diet killed sheep and produced a sour, whey-like, rumen content. Several other clinical signs of toxicity to sucrose appeared in some animals but were not dose dependent. These included piloerection, irritability, dyspnea, epistaxis, cyanosis, convulsions, hemodacryorrhea, and hematuria. Death from large daily doses was due to respiratory failure following convulsions and frequently accompanied by a high fever. Smaller daily doses produced death in hypokinetic hypothermic cachexia.

Changes in body weight and in food (Purina laboratory chow checkers) and total calorie intake (calories in food plus calories in dose of sucrose) are illustrated in Figure 16. Growth rate was increasingly inhibited by increasing daily doses of sucrose and at the end of 100 days, sucrose-treated albino rats weighed 9.5 to 24.7% less than the water-treated controls. The intake of laboratory chow progressively declined with increasing daily dose of sucrose but there was no significant change

in the caloric intake calculated as the sum of calories in food plus calories in administered sucrose. Richter[50] reported a reduction in chow intake but no change in caloric intake in rats given other sugars such as glucose and fructose. Loss of body weight, therefore, was not due to starvation, although it could have been due to decreased protein intake. Shore and Shore[51] reported that rats fed sucrose lost 30% of their weight by four weeks.

Significant changes in water intake and urinary volume and pH are shown in Figure 17. Sucrose administration produced a diuresis, polydipsia, and aciduria which increased in intensity with increasing daily dose of sucrose until a dose approximately equivalent to the $LD_{50 \, (100 \, days)}$ was reached. Higher oral doses of sucrose caused a progressive diminution in the values of these three parameters resulting in quadratic regressions as indicated in Figure 17. Glycosuria occurred in most animals but was not dose dependent over the range of doses of sucrose used. Urinary protein

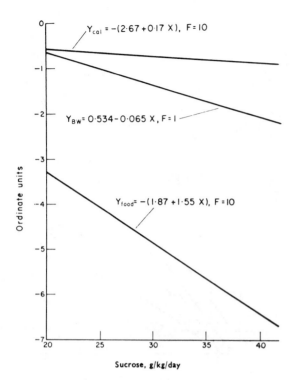

$Y_{cal} = -(2.67 + 0.17 \, X), \; F = 10$

$Y_{BW} = 0.534 - 0.065 \, X, \; F = 1$

$Y_{food} = -(1.87 + 1.55 \, X), \; F = 10$

Sucrose, g/kg/day

FIGURE 16. The regression, on daily oral dose of sucrose, of the mean percent change from controls given no sucrose in (a) calorie intake calculated as kcal/kg body weight/24 hr, (b) body weight in g, and (c) food (chow) intake calculated as g/kg/24 hr. Ordinate units must be multiplied by the factors (F) shown after each equation to obtain the mean percent change from controls. (From Constantopoulos and Boyd[45] with the permission of the authors and of *Food and Cosmetics Toxicology,* copyright © 1968, Pergamon Press, England.)

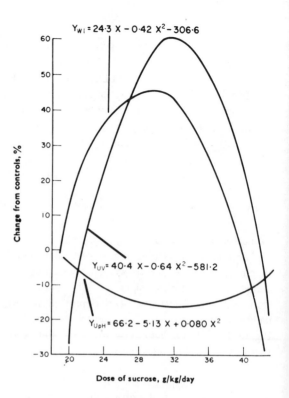

$Y_{WI} = 24.3 \, X - 0.42 \, X^2 - 306.6$

$Y_{UV} = 40.4 \, X - 0.64 \, X^2 - 581.2$

$Y_{UpH} = 66.2 - 5.13 \, X + 0.080 \, X^2$

Dose of sucrose, g/kg/day

FIGURE 17. The regression, on daily oral dose of sucrose given to albino rats, of mean percent changes from controls in water intake, calculated as ml/kg body weight/day and shown as "WI," urinary volume, (UV) calculated as ml/kg/24 hr, and the pH of urine (UpH) measured on 24-hr samples. (From Constantopoulos and Boyd[45] with the permission of the authors and of *Food and Cosmetics Toxicology,* copyright © 1968, Pergamon Press, England.)

levels were not significantly affected by daily administration of sucrose in the doses indicated in Figures 16 and 17. There were also no significant changes in body (colonic) temperature except premortally when it frequently fell.

Gross and Microscopic Pathology at the LD₅₀ (100 days)

Gross examination of the body organs of albino rats that died following daily oral administration of sucrose disclosed congestion of the brain, gastrointestinal tract, lungs, and testes. The liver and kidneys were discolored and there was a stress reaction in the adrenal glands, thymus gland, and spleen.

Histopathological findings at death are summarized in Table 15. When death occurred within the first week of daily sucrose administration, there was found a violent local gastroenteritis associated with inflammation in body organs such

as the aorta, brain, meninges, heart, kidneys, and lungs; degenerative changes in organs such as kidneys, liver, and pancreas; and a stress reaction in the adrenal and thymus glands. Cohen et al.[49] reported that a high intake of dietary sucrose produced ischemic heart disease in Yemenite Jews.

The local reaction of the gastrointestinal tract to daily administration for 9 to 100 days of large volumes of sucrose solution was hypertrophy of the mucosa, smooth muscle, and supporting connective tissue, as indicated in Table 15. This was associated with degenerative changes in many structures such as the arterioles, brain, meninges, kidneys, liver, skeletal muscle, pancreas, salivary glands, testes, and thymus gland.

Organ Weights and Water Contents at the LD₅₀ (100 days)

Shifts in the fresh wet weight of body organs at death due to oral administration of sucrose in

TABLE 15

Histopathological Findings at Autopsy on Albino Rats that Died from Daily Oral Administration of Lethal Doses of Sucrose

Organ	Deaths after treatment of	
	Less than 1 week	9 to 100 days
Adrenal glands	Lipoid vacuoles prominent	Cortical hypertrophy, sinusoidal congestion and occasional hemorrhages
Aorta (thoracic)	Minor capillary-venous congestion of tunica adventitia	Occasional vacuolation of tunica media; occasional small aneurysm
Arterioles (splenic)	Normal appearance	Occasional vacuolation of tunica media
Brain	Capillary-venous congestion of brain and meninges	Capillary-venous congestion and occasional hemorrhage of brain and meninges; infiltration of meninges with granulocytes; occasional brain abscess
Gastrointestinal tract		
Cardiac stomach	Capillary-venous congestion of lamina propria and submucosa	Hypertrophy of stratified squamous epithelium, muscularis mucosae and muscularis externa; hyperemia of lamina propria and submucosa
Pyloric stomach	Capillary-venous congestion of lamina propria and submucosa, occasionally with hemorrhage, lysis of gastric glands and granulocyte infiltration	Mostly normal appearance; occasional capillary hemorrhage and granulocyte infiltration
Small bowel	Capillary-venous congestion of lamina propria and submucosa	Hypertrophy of villi, muscularis mucosae, and muscularis externa; hyperemia
Cecum	Capillary-venous congestion of lamina propria and submucosa	Hypertrophy of Lieberkühn's glands, muscularis mucosae, and muscularis externa; hyperemia
Colon	Capillary-venous congestion of lamina propria and submucosa	Normal appearance to slight hypertrophy
Heart	Minor capillary congestion of myocardium	Occasionally capillary congestion with hemorrhage and thrombosis
Kidneys	Glomeruli shrunken; capillary-venous congestion occasionally with hemorrhage; fine vacuolation of tubules	Capillary-venous congestion, occasional hemorrhage and thrombosis; tubular cloudy swelling, vacuolation and necrosis; occasional shrinkage of glomerular tuft

TABLE 15 (Continued)

Deaths after treatment of

Organ	Less than 1 week	9 to 100 days
Liver	Areas of granulation and vacuolation of hepatic cells	Normal appearance or sinusoidal congestion with areas of centri-lobular vacuolation and necrosis
Lungs	Capillary-venous congestion and areas of venous thrombosis	Areas of capillary-venous congestion and venous thrombosis
Muscle (ventral abdominal wall)	Normal appearance	Occasional weak cross-striation
Pancreas	Acinar glands shrunken with loss of zymogenic granules and areas of necrosis	Acinar glands shrunken with loss of zymogenic granules and areas of necrosis
Salivary (submaxillary) glands	Normal appearance	Occasional atrophy of serous glands and loss of zymogenic granules
Skin	Normal appearance	Normal appearance
Spleen	Normal appearance	Contracted red pulp
Testes	Normal appearance	Varying degrees of deficiency of sperm and inhibition of spermatogenesis
Thymus gland	Minor loss of thymocytes	Varying degrees of loss of thymocytes and of capillary-venous congestion

(From Constantopoulos and Boyd[45] with the permission of the authors and of *Food and Cosmetics Toxicology*, copyright © 1968, Pergamon Press, England.)

doses at the range of the minimal $LD_{100 (100 days)}$ and in survivors at the range of the $LD_{50 (100 days)}$ and maximal $LD_{0 (100 days)}$ are summarized in Table 16. It will be noted that the changes were related primarily to death and not to daily dose of sucrose. Hypertrophy of the gastrointestinal tract had produced an increase in the weight of its several parts, as indicated in Table 16. There was a stressor gain in weight of the adrenal glands and loss of weight in the spleen and thymus gland. Loss of weight was least marked in brain. Loss of weight occurred in most other body organs at one or more daily doses of sucrose.

Shifts in organ water levels are summarized in Table 17. Part of the increase in weight of the gastrointestinal tissues may be seen to have been due to an increase in water content. Changes in the water levels of other organs were mostly insignificant with a few exceptions noted in Table 17.

Withdrawal Syndrome

Abrupt withdrawal of sucrose administration at 100 days was followed by no evidence of a withdrawal syndrome indicative of physical dependence upon sucrose. The animals ate more laboratory chow and gradually regained their lost weight. There was a slight increase in locomotor activity accompanied by disappearance of the signs shown in Figures 15 and 17.

The animals were autopsied after ten days of withdrawal of sucrose administration. There were no gross pathological lesions at ten days and the only microscopic lesion was some residual inhibition of spermatogenesis. At four weeks after cessation of sucrose administration, the weight and water contents of body organs were insignificantly different from those of the controls.

The 100-day LD_{50} Index

Calculated values of the 100-day LD_{50} index of

TABLE 16

Shifts in the Fresh Wet Weight of Body Organs of Albino Rats at Death Due to Daily Oral Administration of Sucrose[†]

Organ	No. of controls / No. of treated rats	Minimal LD_{100} (100 days)	LD_{50} (100 days)	Maximal LD_0 (100 days)
	No. of controls	28	22	5
	No. of treated rats	28	25	10
Adrenal glands		+ 4.0	+11.2*	+15.1**
Brain		− 0.9	− 3.4*	− 1.3
Gastrointestinal tract				
Cardiac stomach		+33.2**	+24.1**	+10.8*
Pyloric stomach		+ 9.7*	+ 7.2*	+14.2**
Small bowel		+ 5.4	+10.4*	+13.4*
Cecum		+ 5.7	+28.4**	+40.1**
Colon		− 0.1	− 0.7	+14.3*
Heart		− 7.3*	−13.5**	− 9.1*
Kidneys		−10.4**	−16.2**	−16.1**
Liver		− 8.2*	−12.8**	− 9.5*
Lungs		+ 9.2	− 9.8*	− 3.5
Muscle (ventral abdominal wall)		− 9.2*	−12.9*	− 4.8
Salivary (submaxillary) glands		+ 4.3	−17.7**	− 1.6
Skin		− 9.7*	−21.8**	−14.8**
Spleen		−20.8**	−23.9**	−16.5*
Testes		− 7.5*	− 4.7*	− 0.7
Thymus gland		−22.7**	− 8.7	−26.9**
Residual carcass		− 7.1**	−15.6**	−12.7**
Total body weight		− 6.6**	−14.9**	−10.4**

Header note: *Fresh weight (g) for doses in range of*

[†]Results are expressed as mean percent change from controls, specifically as $[(\bar{X}_d - \bar{X}_c)/\bar{X}_c] \times 100$, where $\bar{X}_d$ is the mean in the sucrose-treated rats and $\bar{X}_c$ in their controls. Asterisks indicate that $\bar{X}_d - \bar{X}_c$ was significant.
*P = 0.05 to 0.02; **P = 0.01 or less.
(From Constantopoulos and Boyd[45] with the permission of the authors and of *Food and Cosmetics Toxicology*, copyright © 1968, Pergamon Press, England.)

sucrose have been compared in Table 18 with corresponding indices of other chemical agents. The lower the value of the 100-day LD_{50} index, the relatively more toxic is a substance for repeated daily ingestion in the sense that death can be produced by a smaller fraction of the acute LD_{50} (1 dose).

The lowest available value for the 100-day LD_{50} index is (± S.E.) 2.0 ± 0.3 for the pesticide captan given orally to albino rats fed a diet containing 9% casein which is one third the optimal protein intake for these animals. In other words, 2% of the acute oral LD_{50} of captan given daily by gavage to young albino rats fed one third

the optimal amount of protein killed 50% of the animals over a period of 100 days.

It will be noticed that there is a distinct break in Table 18 between the 100-day LD_{50} index of phenacetin given orally to male albino rats and benzylpenicillin given the same way. All substances from benzylpenicillin to sucrose had high values for the 100-day LD_{50} index. These results indicate that such substances are relatively nontoxic for chronic use in the sense that they require a high percentage of the acute LD_{50} (1 dose) to kill the animals. It is of interest that substances which are part of the daily diet of man, such as sodium chloride, caffeine, and sucrose, fall into this category. The relatively high

TABLE 17

Changes in the Water Levels of Body Organs of Albino Rats due to Daily Oral Administration of Sucrose[†]

		Water content (g/100 g dry weight) for doses in range of		
		Minimal LD_{100} (100 days)	LD_{50} (100 days)	Maximal LD_0 (100 days)
Organ	No. of controls	28	22	5
	No. of treated rats	28	25	10
Adrenal glands		+2.6	+ 1.3	+ 4.2
Brain		−0.3	0.0	− 0.6
Gastrointestinal tract				
Cardiac stomach		+8.6*	+ 5.8*	+ 3.7
Pyloric stomach		+5.6*	+ 5.4*	+ 3.7
Small bowel		+3.3	+ 5.5	+17.8**
Cecum		−6.0*	+11.4*	+ 9.3*
Colon		−1.0	+ 0.1	+10.2*
Heart		+0.7	− 0.5	+ 3.3**
Kidneys		+2.8	+ 1.5	− 0.5
Liver		+5.5**	+ 2.7	+ 7.2**
Lungs		−0.6	− 0.6	− 1.8
Muscle (ventral abdominal wall)		−1.7	− 3.3	+ 2.5
Salivary (submaxillary) glands		+1.4	− 3.1	− 2.9
Skin		+6.3*	+ 3.7	− 1.7
Spleen		−0.7	− 0.7	− 0.8
Testes		+0.5	+ 0.1	− 0.7
Thymus gland		−4.1	− 0.6	+ 5.8
Residual carcass		−1.9	+ 1.5	+ 4.1

[†]The results are expressed as mean percent change from controls, specifically as $[(\bar{X}_d - \bar{X}_c)/\bar{X}_c] \times 100$, where $\bar{X}_d$ is the mean in the sucrose-treated rats and $\bar{X}_c$ in their controls. Asterisks indicate that $\bar{X}_d - \bar{X}_c$ was significant.
*P = 0.05 to 0.02; **P = 0.01 or less.
(From Constantopoulos and Boyd[45] with the permission of the authors and of *Food and Cosmetics Toxicology*, copyright © 1968, Pergamon Press, England.)

indices for mixtures of acetylsalicylic acid and caffeine with (APC mixture) and without (AC mixture) phenacetin seem to be due to the caffeine content of the mixture.

Conclusions Regarding Sucrose
Acute Oral Toxicity

1. The acute oral $LD_{50} \pm$ S.E. of sucrose given to albino rats varies from 27.9 ± 1.6 g/kg to 42.2 ± 4.5 g/kg, being lowest in females with a delayed death and highest in males with an early death.

2. Clinical signs of toxicity in early (less than 10 hr) deaths consisted of diarrhea and signs of depression of the central nervous system. Death

was due to respiratory failure following convulsions.

3. Clinical signs in delayed deaths included anorexia, diarrhea, loss of body weight, aciduria, glycosuria, and death in hypothermic cachexia.

4. At autopsy there was found a fulminating gastroenteritis in early but not in late deaths. In early deaths many organs were inflamed; in late deaths inflammation tended to be replaced by degenerative changes.

5. Most organs were dehydrated and had lost weight at death. The adrenal glands and the gastrointestinal tissues had gained weight.

Toxicity at the Oral LD_{50} (100 days)

1. The oral LD_{50} (100 days) $\pm$ S.E. was

TABLE 18

The 100-day LD_{50} Index of a Group of Foods, Pesticides, and Drugs

Agent	Diet	100-day LD_{50} index	Reference
Captan	9% casein	2.0 ± 0.3	52,53
Spiramycin[a]	Dog chow	5.0	54
Captan	Lab chow	7.3 ± 2.3	55,56
Phenacetin[b]	Guinea pig chow	8.6 ± 3.1	57
Atropine[c]	Rabbit chow	13.2 ± 0.8	58,59
Dicophane (DDT)	3% casein	14.5 ± 1.8	60,61
Cottonseed oil	3% casein	15.1 ± 2.4	60
Acetylsalicylic acid	Lab chow	16.4 ± 4.5	62–64
Pilocarpine	Lab chow	17.1 ± 0.2	65,66
Dicophane (DDT)	Lab chow	17.6 ± 0.2	61,67,68
Dicophane (DDT)	9% casein	18.6 ± 0.3	61,69
Paracetamol	Lab chow	20.6 ± 0.6	70,71
Phenacetin	Lab chow	27.1 ± 0.3	72,73
Benzylpenicillin	Lab chow	61.8 ± 3.0	74,75
Sodium chloride	Lab chow	71.7 ± 3.2	15,76
Caffeine[d]	Lab chow	78.2 ± 1.6	77,78
Aspirin–caffeine mixture	Lab chow	79.6	79
Sucrose	Lab chow	80.6 ± 3.7	8,45
APC mixture	Lab chow	84.7 ± 7.1	80,81
Sucrose	Lab chow	95.8 ± 4.4	This chapter

[a]Given orally to dogs and produced vomiting.
[b]Given orally to guinea pigs.
[c]Given intramuscularly to rabbits.
[d]Given orally to female rats.

The estimates were based upon studies on male albino rats except as otherwise indicated.

28.5 ± 1.3 g/kg/day in male albino rats. The 100-day LD_{50} index ± S.E. lay between 80.6 ± 3.7 and 95.8 ± 4.4.

2. The clinical signs of toxicity were those of depression alternating with stimulation of the central nervous system plus diarrhea, pallor, and bleeding. Deaths within the first week were due to respiratory failure following convulsions, later deaths to hypothermic cachexia.

3. Weekly clinical measurements revealed a gradual loss of body weight without any change in caloric intake. At the $LD_{50 \ (100 \ days)}$ there was a diuresis accompanied by polydipsia and aciduria.

4. Early deaths were characterized by a violent local gastroenteritis associated with inflammation of many body organs, degenerative changes in some organs, and a stress reaction. Delayed deaths were characterized by gastrointestinal hypertrophy and widespread organ degeneration.

5. The value of the oral 100-day LD_{50} index is among the highest reported to date.

REFERENCES

1. **Rolph, G. M.,** *Something About Sugar. Its History, Growth, Manufacture and Distribution,* John J. Newbegin, San Francisco, 1917.
2. **Boyd, E. M.,** The cough syrup, *Br. Med. J.,* 2, 735, 1946.
3. **Tacke, E. F., Stepanov, A. S., Ali, L., and Hallmans, M. G. W.,** *The World Sugar Economy, Structure and Policies,* Vol. 2, International Sugar Council, London, 1963, 3.
4. **Baikow, V. E.,** *Manufacture and Refining of Raw Cane Sugar,* Elsevier Publishing Company, New York, 1967.
5. **Constantopoulos, G.,** The Chronic Oral Toxicity of Sucrose in Albino Rats, Ph.D. Thesis, Douglas Library, Queen's University, Kingston, Ontario, Canada, 1968.
6. **Hockett, R. C.,** *Sugars in Human Nutrition. Use of Sugars and Other Carbohydrates in the Food Industry,* Advances in Chemistry, Series No. 12, American Chemical Society, Washington, D.C., 1955.
7. **Cleave, T. L., Campbell, G. D., Painter, N. S., and Doll, R.,** *Diabetes, Coronary Thrombosis, and the Saccharine Disease,* John Wright and Sons, Bristol, England, 1969.
8. **Boyd, E. M., Godi, I., and Abel, M.,** Acute oral toxicity of sucrose, *Toxicol. Appl. Pharmacol.,* 7, 609, 1965.
9. **Boyd, E. M. and Knight, L. M.,** Postmortem shifts in the weight and water levels of body organs, *Toxicol. Appl. Pharmacol.,* 5, 119, 1963.
10. **Hausmann, W.,** Zur Kenntnis der Toxischen Wirkung konzentrierter Zuckerlösungen, *Wien. Klin. Wochenschr.,* 38, 332, 1925.
11. **Kuriyama, S.,** The fate of sucrose parenterally administered, *Am. J. Physiol.,* 43, 343, 1917.
12. **Helmholtz, H. F. and Bollman, J. L.,** The diuretic action of sucrose and other solutions, *Proc. Staff Meet. Mayo Clin.,* 14, 567, 1939.
13. **Spector, W. S.,** *Handbook of Toxicology,* Vol. 1, Acute Toxicities, W. B. Saunders Company, Philadelphia, 1956, 150.
14. **Delak, M. and Adamič, S.,** Intoxication in sheep produced by sucrose, *Nutr. Abstr. Rev.,* 30, 503, 1960.
15. **Boyd, E. M. and Shanas, M. N.,** The acute oral toxicity of sodium chloride, *Arch. Int. Pharmacodyn. Ther.,* 144, 86, 1963.
16. **MacKay, L. L. and MacKay, E. M.,** Convulsions resulting from fluid administration following sucrose injections and water abstinence, *Proc. Soc. Exp. Biol. Med.,* 21, 286, 1924.
17. **Bavetta, L. A. and Ershoff, B. H.,** Comparative effects of dietary sucrose and corn starch on tryptophan requirement of the rat, *Proc. Soc. Exp. Biol. Med.,* 90, 349, 1955.
18. **Peraino, C., Rogers, Q. R., Yoshida, M., Chen, M.-L., and Harper, A. E.,** Observations on protein digestion in vivo. II. Dietary factors affecting the rate of disappearance of casein from the gastrointestinal tract, *Can. J. Biochem.,* 37, 1475, 1959.
19. **Stare, F. J.,** *Blood Sugar, Appetite and Obesity. Ten Years of Research, 1943–1953,* Project 84, Sugar Research Foundation, Inc., New York, 1955.
20. **Hays, R. L., Hahn, E. W., and Kendall, K. A.,** Evidence for decreased steroidogenesis in pregnant rats fed a sucrose diet, *Endocrinology,* 76, 771, 1965.
21. **Harper, K. H. and Worden, A. N.,** Comparative toxicity studies on glucose, fructose, and sucrose, *Toxicol. Appl. Pharmacol.,* 6, 365, 1964.
22. **Allen, R. J. L. and Leahy, J. S.,** Some effects of dietary dextrose, fructose, liquid glucose and sucrose in the adult male rat, *Br. J. Nutr.,* 20, 339, 1966.
23. **Carr, C. J.,** *Intravenous Sucrose Administration in Clinical Practice,* Scientific Report Series No. 2, Sugar Research Foundation, Inc., New York, 1945.
24. **Hoffman, W. S.,** *The Biochemistry of Clinical Medicine,* 3rd ed., Year Book Medical Publishers, Chicago, 1964.
25. **MacDonald, I. and Braithwaite, D. M.,** The influence of dietary carbohydrates on the lipid pattern in serum and in adipose tissue, *Clin. Sci.,* 27, 23, 1964.
26. **Helmholz, H. F.,** Renal changes in the rabbit resulting from intravenous injection of hypertonic solution of sucrose, *J. Pediatr.,* 3, 144, 1933.
27. **Lindberg, H. A., Wald, M. H., and Barker, M. H.,** Renal changes following administration of hypertonic solutions, *Arch. Intern. Med.,* 63, 907, 1939.
28. **Cutler, H. H.,** Effect of sucrose on the kidney, *Proc. Staff Meet. Mayo Clin.,* 14, 318, 1939.
29. **Anderson, W. A. D. and Bethea, W. R., Jr.,** Renal lesions following administration of hypertonic solution of sucrose (report of six cases), *J.A.M.A.,* 114, 1983, 1940.
30. **Janigan, D. T. and Santamaria, A.,** A histochemical study of swelling and vacuolation of proximal tubular cells in sucrose nephrosis in the rat, *Am. J. Pathol.,* 39, 175, 1961.
31. **Wattiaux, B., Wattiaux-De Coninck, S., Rutgeerts, M.-J., and Tulhens, P.,** Influence of the injection of a sucrose solution on the properties of rat-liver lysosomes, *Nature,* 203, 757, 1964.
32. **MacDonald, I.,** Some influences of dietary carbohydrate on liver and depot lipids, *J. Physiol.,* 162, 334, 1962.
33. **Zuckerman, A. J. and MacDonald, I.,** The role of dietary carbohydrates and infection on liver lipids and collagen, *Br. J. Exp. Pathol.,* 45, 589, 1964.
34. **Yudkin, J.,** Nutrition and palatability with special reference to obesity, myocardial infarction, and other diseases of civilization, *Lancet,* 1, 1335, 1963.

35. **Yudkin, J. and Roddy, J.,** Levels of dietary sucrose in patients with occlusive atherosclerotic disease, *Lancet*, 2, 6, 1964.

36. **Moore, W. M. O., Hellegers, A. E., and Battaglia, F. C.,** In vitro permeability of different layers of the human placenta to carbohydrates and urea, *Am. J. Obstet. Gynecol.*, 96, 951, 1966.

37. **Neale, G., Clark, M., and Levin, B.,** Intestinal sucrase deficiency presenting as sucrose intolerance in adult life, *Br. Med. J.*, 2, 1223, 1965.

38. **Matsuoka, H.,** Pathological changes in the gastric mucous membrane due to orally administered sucrose and their etiological persuance, *Nutr. Abstr. Rev.*, 30, 126, 1960.

39. **Wood, J. M. and Critchley, P.,** The extracellular polysaccharide produced from sucrose by a cariogenic streptococcus, *Arch. Oral Biol.*, 11, 1039, 1966.

40. **Green, R. M. and Hartles, R. L.,** The effect of uncooked and roll-dried wheat starch, alone and mixed in equal quantity with sucrose, on dental caries in the albino rat, *Br. J. Nutr.*, 21, 921, 1967.

41. **Bett, D. G., Morland, J., and Yudkin, J.,** Sugar consumption in acne vulgaris and seborrheic dermatitis, *Br. Med. J.*, 2, 153, 1967.

42. **Boyd, E. M.,** *Predictive Toxicometrics,* Scientechnica (Publishers) Ltd., Bristol, England, 1971.

43. **Constantopoulos, G.,** The chronic oral toxicity of sucrose, *Proc. Can. Fed. Biol. Soc.*, 10, 50, 1967.

44. **Constantopoulos, G. and Boyd, E. M.,** Encephalitis and meningitis from repeated large daily doses of sucrose, *Fed. Proc.*, 27, 598, 1968.

45. **Constantopoulos, G. and Boyd, E. M.,** Maximal tolerated amounts of sucrose given by daily intragastric administration to albino rats, *Food Cosmet. Toxicol.*, 6, 717, 1968.

46. **Constantopoulos, G. and Boyd, E. M.,** Factors affecting sucrose toxicity, Paper presented at the Fourth Annual Meeting of the Canadian Society of Chemotherapy, Montreal, Quebec, January 29–30, 1968.

47. **Constantopoulos, G. and Boyd, E. M.,** Factors affecting sucrose toxicity, *Int. J. Clin. Pharmacol. Ther. Toxicol.*, 1, 539, 1968.

48. **Krogh, N.,** Studies on alterations in the rumen fluid of sheep, especially concerning the microbial composition, when readily available carbohydrates are added to the food. I. Sucrose, *Nutr. Abstr. Rev.*, 30, 986, 1960.

49. **Cohen, A. M., Bavly, S., and Poznanski, R.,** Changes in the diet of Yemenite Jews in relation to diabetes and ischaemic heart disease, *Lancet*, 2, 1399, 1961.

50. **Richter, C. P.,** Self-regulatory functions during gestation and lactation, in *Gestation,* Viller, C. A., Ed., Josiah Macy, Jr. Foundation, Madison Printing Co., Madison, N.J., 1956.

51. **Shore, V. and Shore, B.,** Effect of mercuric chloride on some kidney enzymes in chow-fed and sucrose-fed rats, *Am. J. Physiol.*, 198, 187, 1960.

52. **Boyd, E. M. and Horne, C. J.,** The toxicity of captan at the oral $LD_{50\ (100\ days)}$ in albino rats fed one third the optimal amount of dietary protein, unpublished data, 1972.

53. **Krijnen, C. J. and Boyd, E. M.,** Susceptibility to captan pesticide of albino rats fed from weaning on diets containing various levels of protein, *Food Cosmet. Toxicol.*, 8, 35, 1970.

54. **Boyd, E. M., Jarzylo, S., Boyd, C. E., and Cassell, W. A.,** The chronic oral toxicity of spiramycin in dogs, *Arch. Int. Pharmacodyn. Thér.*, 115, 360, 1958.

55. **Boyd, E. M. and Krijnen, C. J.,** Toxicity of captan and protein-deficient diet, *J. Clin. Pharmacol.*, 8, 225, 1968.

56. **Boyd, E. M. and Carsky, E.,** The 100-day LD_{50} index of captan, *Acta Pharmacol. Toxicol.*, 29, 226, 1971.

57. **Boyd, E. M. and Carro-Ciampi, G.,** The oral 100-day LD_{50} index of phenacetin in guinea pigs, *Toxicol. Appl. Pharmacol.*, 16, 232, 1970.

58. **Boyd, C. E. and Boyd, E. M.,** The acute toxicity of atropine sulfate, *Can. Med. Assoc. J.*, 85, 1241, 1961.

59. **Boyd, C. E. and Boyd, E. M.,** The chronic toxicity of atropine administered intramuscularly to rabbits, *Toxicol. Appl. Pharmacol.*, 4, 457, 1962.

60. **Boyd, E. M. and Krijnen, C. J.,** The toxicity of dicophane and cottonseed oil at the $LD_{50\ (100\ days)}$ in albino rats fed from weaning on a diet containing 3% protein as casein, Lecture presented at the Second International Congress of Pesticide Chemistry, Tel Aviv, Israel, February 21–27, 1971.

61. **Boyd, E. M. and Krijnen, C. J.,** Dietary protein and DDT toxicity, *Bull. Environ. Contam. Toxicol.*, 4, 256, 1969.

62. **Boyd, E. M.,** The acute oral toxicity of acetylsalicylic acid, *Toxicol. Appl. Pharmacol.*, 1, 229, 1959.

63. **Coldwell, B. B. and Boyd, E. M.,** The acute rectal toxicity of acetylsalicylic acid, *Can. J. Physiol. Pharmacol.*, 44, 909, 1966.

64. **Boyd, E. M.,** Analgesic abuse: Maximal tolerated daily doses of acetylsalicylic acid, *Can. Med. Assoc. J.*, 99, 790, 1968.

65. **Boyd, E. M., Covert, E. L., and Jarzylo, S.,** The acute oral toxicity of pilocarpine, Third International Meeting in Forensic Immunology, Medicine, Pathology and Toxicology, Plenary Session VII A, London, April 16–24, 1963.

66. **Boyd, E. M. and Jarzylo, S. V.,** Daily oral doses of pilocarpine tolerated by albino rats, *Arch. Int. Pharmacodyn. Thér.*, 175, 84, 1968.

67. **Boyd, E. M. and De Castro, E. S.,** Protein-deficient diet and DDT toxicity, *Bull. WHO*, 38, 141, 1968.

68. **Boyd, E. M. and Lin, F. M.,** Maximal tolerated daily doses of dicophane, *Acta Pharmacol. Toxicol.*, 28, 149, 1970.

69. **Boyd, E. M. and Horne, C. J.,** The toxicity of dicophane at the range of the oral $LD_{50\ (100\ days)}$ in albino rats fed from weaning on a diet containing one-third the optimal amount of protein, unpublished data, 1972.

70.   **Boyd, E. M. and Bereczky, G. M.,** Liver necrosis from paracetamol, *Br. J. Pharmacol. Chemother.*, 26, 606, 1966.
71.   **Boyd, E. M. and Hogan, S. E.,** The chronic toxicity of paracetamol at the range of the LD_{50} $_{(100\ days)}$ in albino rats, *Can. J. Physiol. Pharmacol.*, 46, 239, 1968.
72.   **Boyd, E. M.,** The acute oral toxicity of phenacetin, *Toxicol. Appl. Pharmacol.*, 1, 240, 1959.
73.   **Boyd, E. M. and Hottenroth, S. M. H.,** The toxicity of phenacetin at the range of the oral LD_{50} $_{(100\ days)}$ in albino rats, *Toxicol. Appl. Pharmacol.*, 12, 80, 1968.
74.   **Boyd, E. M., Broughton, R. J., and James, J.,** The acute oral toxicity of benzylpenicillin potassium, *Arch. Int. Pharmacodyn. Thér.*, 123, 295, 1960.
75.   **Boyd, E. M. and Selby, M. J.,** The chronic oral toxicity of benzylpenicillin, *Antibiot. Chemother.*, 12, 249, 1962.
76.   **Boyd, E. M., Abel, M. M., and Knight, L. M.,** The chronic oral toxicity of sodium chloride at the range of the LD_{50} $_{(0.1\ L)}$, *Can. J. Physiol. Pharmacol.*, 44, 157, 1966.
77.   **Boyd, E. M.,** The acute oral toxicity of caffeine, *Toxicol. Appl. Pharmacol.*, 1, 250, 1959.
78.   **Boyd, E. M., Dolman, M., Knight, L. M., and Sheppard, E. P.,** The chronic oral toxicity of caffeine, *Can. J. Physiol. Pharmacol.*, 43, 995, 1965.
79.   **Boyd, E. M. and Shanas, B. D.,** The oral 100-day LD_{50} index of a mixture of aspirin and caffeine, unpublished data, 1972.
80.   **Boyd, E. M.,** The acute oral toxicity of a mixture of acetylsalicylic acid, phenacetin, and caffeine, *Toxicol. Appl. Pharmacol.*, 1, 258, 1959.
81.   **Boyd, E. M., Shanas, B. D., and Shanas, M. N.,** The toxicity of a mixture of acetylsalicylic acid, phenacetin and caffeine at the range of the oral LD_{50} $_{(100\ days)}$ in male albino rats, unpublished data, 1972.

GLUCOSE

Albino rats can tolerate large amounts of glucose in their diet without showing obvious ill effects. In 1939 Meyer[1,2] fed young rats weighing 60 to 70 g a diet containing 71% glucose with adequate amounts of protein (casein), fats, minerals, and vitamins. At the end of two weeks they weighed as much as controls fed a standard stock diet. Similar results were reported in 1966 by Boyd, Covert, and Pitman,[3] who recorded a slight loss of body weight due to tissue dehydration. The susceptibility of such animals to drug toxicity may or may not be altered. Mortality from subcutaneous injection of an approximate LD_{50} of phenol, cyanide,[1] and diphtheria toxin[2] was not affected by the previous feeding of a diet high in glucose, but the animals were very susceptible to death from orally administered benzylpenicillin.[3]

Fitch and Chaikoff[4] found that the activity of certain hepatic enzymes, such as phosphoglucomutase, was increased in rats fed diets high in glucose. Womak and Marshall[5] reported that diets high in sucrose produced fatty livers in rats; liver fat was reduced by substituting glucose for sucrose but not by substituting fructose for sucrose. Fructose stimulates certain hepatic enzymes such as aldolase,[4] which is deficient in children with hereditary fructose intolerance.[6] Rats fed a diet containing 70% galactose develop eye defects.[14]

The Acute Oral Toxicity of Glucose

The finding that substitution of starch for glucose in high glucose diets lowered the susceptibility of rats to the lethal effects of orally administered benzylpenicillin[7] prompted Boyd and Carsky[8] to measure the syndrome of acute oral toxicity to glucose in albino rats. Spector[9] had reported that oral doses of the order of 20 g/kg were lethal to rabbits and 8 to 12 g/kg to dogs when given at one time on an empty stomach. Glucose was freshly dissolved in distilled water and given through an intragastric cannula in a volume of 60 ml/kg to overnight-fasted albino rats in doses from 15 to 35 g/kg.

The oral $LD_{50} \pm$ S.E. was found to be 25.8 ± 2.0 g/kg. The maximal LD_0 was 21.6 g/kg and the minimal LD_{100} 30.1 g/kg. The greater the dose of glucose, the shorter the interval to death. Ninety percent of the deaths occurred from two to six hours following administration of glucose.

Clinical Signs

Within a few minutes after the oral administration of glucose, an evacuation of a loose stool occurred. As shown in Figure 18, diarrhea persisted for 1 hr and had disappeared at the end of the second hour. Most of the animals were listless and died in hypothermic coma. Some were excited, went into generalized clonic convulsions,

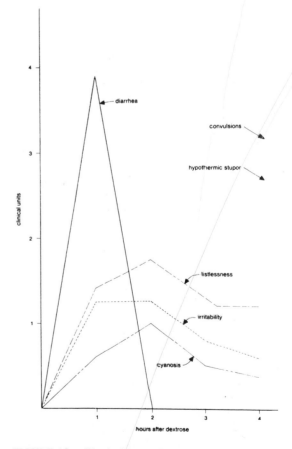

FIGURE 18.   The incidence, in clinical units, of clinical signs of intoxication to lethal oral doses of glucose in albino rats. (From Boyd and Carsky[8] with the permission of *Acta Diabetologica Latina.*)

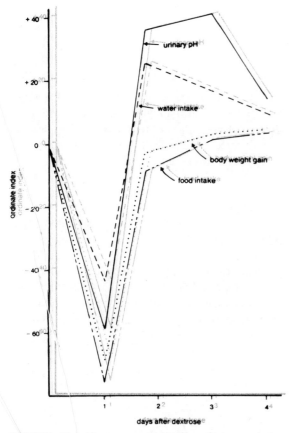

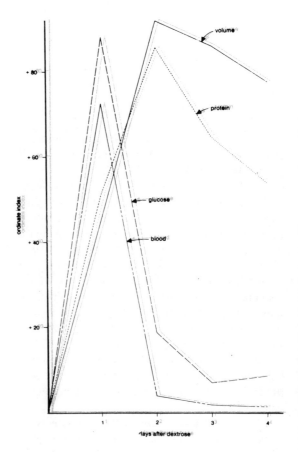

FIGURE 19. Mean percentage changes from controls given no glucose in daily body weight gain (F = 10), daily food intake in g/kg/24 hr (F = 1.0), daily water intake in ml/kg/24 hr (F = 1.0), and the pH of 24-hr samples of urine (F = 0.2) of albino rats given glucose in doses at the range of the acute oral LD_{50}. The ordinate index must be multiplied by the indicated factors (F) to obtain the actual mean percentage change. (From Boyd and Carsky[8] with the permission of *Acta Diabetologica Latina*.)

FIGURE 20. Changes in the urine of albino rats following oral administration of glucose in doses at the range of the LD_{50}. Urinary volume was calculated as ml/kg/24 hr (F = 1.0) and urinary protein output as mg/kg/24 hr (F = 2.0); both are entered as a mean percentage change from controls given no glucose. Urinary glucose (F = 14) and occult blood (F = 5.0) are entered as mean mg/kg/24 hr since they were not present in the controls. The ordinate index must be multiplied by the indicated factors (F) to obtain the recorded changes. (From Boyd and Carsky[8] with the permission of *Acta Diabetologica Latina*.)

and died in postconvulsive respiratory failure. Most rats had a degree of cyanosis.

Measurements at intervals of 24 hr after administering glucose are illustrated in Figures 19 and 20. In animals that survived to 24 hr, body weight had declined about five times as much as the controls had gained. Loss of weight was associated with marked anorexia and oligodipsia. Urinary volume was increased (Figure 20) and accompanied by proteinuria, glycosuria, hematuria, and aciduria.

By 48 hr, most measurements in survivors were normal. Daily gain in body weight, food intake, and water intake (Figure 19) were within the limits of the controls. The aciduria, glycosuria, and hematuria had disappeared, but there were some

residual diuresis and proteinuria (Figure 20). Colonic temperature was normal in survivors. All clinical signs of toxicity had disappeared in survivors at two weeks and one month.

Autopsy Findings

Gross pathological observations at death due to oral ingestion of glucose consisted of congestion of the brain, lungs, and gastrointestinal tract and a darkening of the liver and muscular tissue.

Microscopic changes are listed in Table 19. When death occurred at 2 to 5 hr after giving

TABLE 19

Histopathological Findings in Albino Rats at Death due to Oral Administration of Glucose in Doses at the Range of the LD_{50}

Organ	Death at 2 to 5 hr	Death at 25 to 30 hr
Adrenal glands	Normal	Fatty degeneration of zona fasciculata
Brain	Marked capillary-venous congestion of meninges and brain	Mild capillary-venous congestion
Gastrointestinal tract		
Cardiac stomach	Moderate capillary-venous congestion of the submucosa	Mild congestion and edema of the submucosa
Pyloric stomach	Marked capillary-venous congestion of the lamina propria and submucosa	Mild capillary-venous congestion of the lamina propria and submucosa
Small bowel	Congestion and lysis of villi	Hyperemic villi
Cecum	Capillary-venous congestion of the lamina propria and submucosa	Congestion and ulcer formation
Colon	Moderate congestion	Mild congestion
Heart	Occasional venous congestion and thrombosis	Normal
Kidneys	Capillary-venous congestion and occasional venous thrombosis	Areas of fatty degeneration and necrosis of the tubules
Liver	Peripheral lobular necrotic-like lysis of hepatic cells	Normal or mild lysis
Lungs	Mild capillary-venous congestion	Venous congestion and thrombosis
Muscle (skeletal)	Normal	Occasional weakening of cross-striation
Salivary glands	Normal	Occasional venous thrombosis
Skin	Hypovascular	Normal
Spleen	Vacuolation of arteriolar intima and media	Leukocytosis in venous blood
Testes	Interstitial congestion	Interstitial congestion
Thymus gland	Mild venous congestion	Loss of thymocytes

(From Boyd and Carsky[8] with the permission of *Acta Diabetologica Latina*.)

glucose, the lamina propria and submucosa of the gastrointestinal tract exhibited an inflammatory reaction and some of the villi were lysed by the local action of concentrated glucose solutions. Absorption of toxic amounts of glucose had produced inflammation of the brain, meninges, heart, kidneys, lungs, testes, and thymus gland. Venous thrombosis was seen in the heart and kidneys. Glucose had produced a peripheral necrosis of the hepatic lobules and degenerative changes in walls of the arterioles of the spleen.

As indicated in Table 19, when death was delayed to the second day, most of the local irritant reaction in the gastrointestinal tract had disappeared, leaving a tendency to ulcer formation in the cecum. The tissue inflammatory reaction had also largely disappeared apart from venous congestion and thrombosis in the lungs. Fatty

TABLE 20

The Effect of Lethal Oral Doses of Glucose on the Weight of Body Organs of Albino Rats [a]

Organ	At death in 2 to 5 hr (N = 16 + 16 controls)	Survivors at 14 days (N = 14 + 16 controls)	Survivors at 28 days (N = 16 + 16 controls)
Adrenal glands	− 8.3	− 8.1	−10.2
Brain	− 5.5**	+ 0.9	− 4.7*
Gastrointestinal tract			
Cardiac stomach	−10.6**	− 4.7	−11.7
Pyloric stomach	−31.4**	+ 4.2	+ 1.0
Small bowel	− 0.4	+24.8**	+10.7
Cecum	−20.3**	+10.1	− 1.6
Colon	− 7.2	+10.9	− 3.2
Heart	+ 0.7	− 6.1	− 7.6*
Kidneys	+ 0.7	− 3.8	−11.6*
Liver	−20.1**	− 0.9	+ 1.2
Lungs	− 7.9**	+ 3.1	− 9.5
Muscle (ventral abdominal wall)	− 4.4	− 4.9	+ 1.4
Salivary glands (submaxillary)	+ 2.1	− 0.8	+ 8.5
Skin	− 3.7	− 3.5	− 1.9
Spleen	−30.3**	+ 1.1	− 8.9*
Testes	− 4.9	− 4.7	− 5.7*
Thymus gland	−10.0	+ 5.4	−13.3
Residual carcass	− 7.6**	− 3.9	+ 5.8
Total body weight	− 2.0	− 4.8	+ 3.0

[a]Organ weight was measured in grams. The results are expressed as a mean percent change from values in controls given no glucose, specifically as $[(\bar{X}_g - \bar{X}_c)/\bar{X}_c] \times 100$, where $\bar{X}_g$ is the mean in glucose-treated rats and X_c in the controls. One asterisk indicates that $\bar{X}_g - \bar{X}_c$ was significant at P = 0.05 to 0.02 and two asterisks at P = 0.01 or less. (From Boyd and Carsky[8] with the permission of *Acta Diabetologica Latina.*)

degeneration was present in the zona fasciculata of the adrenal glands and in the renal tubules. Mild degenerative changes appeared in the liver, skeletal muscle, and thymus gland. On the second day, there was leukocytosis in the blood.

Data on organ weights are summarized in Table 20. The characteristic finding in animals that died 2 to 5 hr after administration of glucose was loss of organ weight. This was particularly evident in the gastrointestinal organs, the liver, and the spleen. In survivors at two weeks and one month, organ weights were mostly within the limits of those in controls given no glucose.

Organ water levels are summarized in Table 21. When the rats died 2 to 5 hr after glucose administration, practically all organs were found to be dehydrated. Loss of water extended to as great as 41.5% of that in controls in the case of one organ (pyloric stomach). In survivors, organ water levels had largely returned to normal limits at 14 and 28 days after glucose administration.

Discussion

Lethal oral amounts of glucose produce a type of death that Boyd[10] has categorized as the general osmotic or dehydration syndrome. A similar type of death is produced by oral administration of concentrated aqueous solutions of substances such as sucrose (see Chapter 3), sodium chloride,[11] water-soluble, spray-dried egg white powder,[12] and water-soluble hydrolyzed casein.[13] The basic mechanism of death from such agents appears to be the osmotic attraction of water into the lumen of the gastrointestinal tract, producing diarrhea, blood and tissue dehydration, and tissue inflammation or degeneration.

TABLE 21

The Effect of Lethal Oral Doses of Glucose on the Water Content of Body Organs Measured Immediately after Death of Albino Rats [a]

Organ	At death in 2 to 5 hr (N = 16 + 16 controls)	Survivors at 14 days (N = 14 + 16 controls)	Survivors at 28 days (N = 16 + 16 controls)
Adrenal glands	− 1.3	+3.9	+ 3.9
Brain	−18.4**	−0.5	+ 0.1
Gastrointestinal tract			
Cardiac stomach	−31.5**	−0.8	− 3.0
Pyloric stomach	−41.5**	−2.4	− 8.9**
Small bowel	−18.4**	−2.2	− 9.3**
Cecum	−34.4**	−9.6*	−12.8**
Colon	−28.2**	−0.6	− 4.1
Heart	−21.0**	+0.6	− 2.0
Kidneys	−12.2**	+1.9	− 4.9
Liver	− 5.9**	−0.8	− 4.7
Lungs	−23.9**	−2.2	− 3.1
Muscle (ventral abdominal wall)	−28.0**	−3.6	− 0.7
Salivary glands (submaxillary)	−15.5**	−3.7	− 8.4*
Skin	−23.4**	−4.2	− 6.9*
Spleen	−10.6**	−7.3	− 2.3
Testes	−17.8**	+1.2	− 3.1
Thymus gland	−23.4**	−0.2	− 2.2
Residual carcass	−18.7**	−1.7	− 9.1*

[a]Water content was calculated as g water per 100 g dry weight of organ. The results are expressed as a mean percentage change from controls given no glucose, specifically as $[(\bar{X}_g - \bar{X}_c)/\bar{X}_c] \times 100$, where $\bar{X}_g$ is the mean in glucose-treated rats and $\bar{X}_c$ in controls. One asterisk indicates that $\bar{X}_g - \bar{X}_c$ was significant at P = 0.05 to 0.02 and two asterisks at P = 0.01 or less. (From Boyd and Carsky[8] with the permission of *Acta Diabetologica Latina.*)

This reaction was produced by doses of the order of 10 g/kg and over given on an empty stomach, doses of 25 g/kg killing half the albino rats. It is important to emphasize that these doses were given on an empty stomach. When mixed with the diet and eaten 24 hr of the day, rats can tolerate per day amounts up to three times those which are lethal when dissolved in water and are given on an empty stomach.

Conclusions Regarding Glucose

The $LD_{50} \pm$ S.E. of glucose given intragastrically as hypertonic aqueous solutions to albino rats previously starved overnight to empty the stomach is 25.8 ± 2.0 g/kg. Doses of the order of three times these amounts can be tolerated by rats if the glucose is mixed with the diet and eaten over a period of 24 hr.

The hypertonic glucose solution attracts water into the lumen of the gastrointestinal tract where it produces a gastroenteritis, diarrhea, and dehydration of body organs. Absorption of toxic amounts of glucose produces tissue inflammatory reactions accompanied by either stimulation (convulsions) or depression (hypothermic stupor) of the central nervous system and death usually within 5 hr of administration of glucose.

In animals that survived to 24 hr, there was marked loss of body weight associated with anorexia, oligodipsia, and clinical signs of nephritis. Autopsy disclosed renal degeneration and degenerative changes in other body organs such as the thymus gland. The clinical and pathological signs of glucose intoxication gradually disappeared in survivors at two and four weeks after giving the agent.

REFERENCES

1. **Meyer, A. R.,** Influence of diet on intoxication with phenol and cyanide, *Proc. Soc. Exp. Biol. Med.,* 41, 402, 1939.
2. **Meyer, A. R.,** Influence of diet on resistance to diphtheria toxin, *Proc. Soc. Exp. Biol. Med.,* 41, 404, 1939.
3. **Boyd, E. M., Covert, E. L., and Pitman, C. A.,** Benzylpenicillin toxicity in albino rats fed synthetic high sugar diets, *Chemotherapia,* 11, 320, 1966.
4. **Fitch, W. M. and Chaikoff, I. L.,** Extent and patterns of enzyme activities in livers of normal rats fed diets high in glucose and fructose, *J. Biol. Chem.,* 235, 554, 1960.
5. **Womak, M. and Marshall, M. W.,** Starches, sugars and related factors affecting liver fat and nitrogen balance in adult rats fed low levels of amino acids, *J. Nutr.,* 57, 193, 1955.
6. **Sacrez, R., Juif, J.-G., Metais, P., Sofatzis, J., and Dourof, N.,** Un cas mortel d'intolérance héréditaire au fructose. Etude biochemique et enzymatique, *Pediatrie,* 17, 875, 1962.
7. **Boyd, E. M., Dobos, I., and Taylor, F.,** Benzylpenicillin toxicity in albino rats fed synthetic high starch versus high sugar diets, *Chemotherapy,* 15, 1, 1970.
8. **Boyd, E. M. and Carsky, E.,** Maximal tolerated amounts of dextrose given intragastrically to albino rats, *Acta Diabetol. Lat.,* 4, 538, 1967.
9. **Spector, W. S.,** Acute toxicities of solids, liquids and gases to laboratory animals, *Handbook of Toxicology,* Vol. 1, W. B. Saunders Company, Philadelphia, 1956, 150.
10. **Boyd, E. M.,** *Predictive Toxicometrics,* Scientechnica (Publishers) Ltd., Bristol, England, 1971.
11. **Boyd, E. M. and Shanas, M. N.,** The acute oral toxicity of sodium chloride, *Arch. Int. Pharmacodyn. Ther.,* 144, 86, 1963.
12. **Boyd, E. M., Peters, J. M., and Krijnen, C. J.,** The acute oral toxicity of reconstituted spray-dried egg white, *Ind. Med. Surg.,* 35, 782, 1966.
13. **Boyd, E. M., Krijnen, C. J., and Peters, J. M.,** Lethal amounts of casein, casein salts and hydrolyzed casein given orally to albino rats, *J. Nutr.,* 93, 429, 1967.
14. **Craig, J. M. and Maddock, C. E.,** Observations on the nature of galactose toxicity in rats, *Arch. Pathol.,* 55, 118, 1953.

Chapter 5

GUM TRAGACANTH

Gum tragacanth has been extensively employed to stabilize aqueous suspensions of relatively insoluble substances in toxicity studies on orally administered products such as phenacetin,[1] kaolin,[2] barium sulfate,[3] and paracetamol.[4] It is an off-white powder obtained from the white gavan or *Astralagus gummifer* Labillardiere and other species of *Astralagus,* found in Iran, Syria, and Asia Minor.[5]

Tragacanth consists of high molecular weight polysaccharides composed of galacto-arabans and acid polysaccharides containing galacturonic acid groups.[6],[7] Mixed with water, 70% of tragacanth forms a gel, bassorin, of molecular weight $(C_{22}H_{20}O_{10})_n$, and the remainder forms a sol called tragacanthin. Tragacanthin is said to consist of 3 mol glycuronic acid, 1 mol arabinose, and a side chain of 2 mol arabinose.[5] It breaks down to yield arabinose, xylose, fucose, galactose, and galacturonic acid.[6]

The mucilaginous properties of tragacanth are the basis of its use to suspend heavy insoluble powders, to emulsify other agents, as a thickening agent and stabilizer in foods, in adhesive preparations such as mucilages and pastes, and in the textile, printing, and dyeing industries.[5],[6] FAO/WHO noted in 1970[8] that while tragacanth has been extensively employed for many years, little information is available on its metabolic fate and upon its pharmacological and toxicological properties. Riccardi and Fahrenbach[9] reported that levels of up to 3% plus 3% cholesterol in diets fed to white leghorn cockerels inhibited the development of hypercholesterolemia. This hypocholesterolemic effect was shared by several mucilaginous polysaccharides such as guar gum, carageenan, locust bean gum, tragacanth gum, pectin, and karaya gum, but not by others such as gum acacia. It appeared that the hypocholesterolemic action was not solely related to mucilaginous properties. Riccardi and Fahrenbach[9] recorded no toxic effects in cockerels given mucilaginous gums at 3% of the diet. Boyd, Ciampi, and Krijnen[10] found that use of gum tragacanth as a suspending agent augmented the oral toxicity of aqueous suspensions of phenacetin. The augmentation was no greater from addition of tragacanth to a concentration of 2.0% than from addition of tragacanth to 0.2%. This suggested that augmented toxicity was due to stabilization of the suspension and not to gum tragacanth.

Fujimoto[11] obtained evidence that gum tragacanth may have an action on the liver of mice. Given subcutaneously, intraperitoneally, or by mouth in a dose of 0.1 g/kg, gum tragacanth had no effect on the duration of sleeping time to hexobarbital sodium in a dose of 150 mg/kg given intraperitoneally (average sleeping time 1 to 1½ hr). Stimulation of hepatic detoxification of hexobarbital by oral administration of urethane and phenobarbital (and hence shortening of hexobarbital sleeping time) was nullified by administration of gum tragacanth intraperitoneally or subcutaneously. Fujimoto[11] concluded that the results indicate an hepatotoxic effect of gum tragacanth under the conditions of the experiment, i.e., inhibition of hepatic enzyme induction. As will be noted below, large oral doses of gum tragacanth were found to have initial hepatotoxic effects in albino rats.

The Acute Oral Toxicity of Gum Tragacanth

The acute oral toxicity of gum tragacanth was studied by Boyd, Shanas, and Shanas.[12] Gum tragacanth was used as the powdered form of the British and U.S. pharmacopeias, and administered intragastrically to young male albino rats as a 2% aqueous colloidal solution. Higher concentrations in distilled water turn solid on standing. The 2% solution was given through a stomach tube in a volume of 100 ml/kg, repeated at intervals of 90 min. The interval between dosing was selected from preliminary trials. It was realized that this technique involved administering large volumes of distilled water and that distilled water could be toxic in itself. Boyd and Godi[13] had reported that the acute, oral LD_{50} of distilled water was approximately 60 ml/kg repeated eight times at intervals of 20 min in albino rats. Given at longer intervals, distilled water was absorbed and eliminated through the kidneys as fast as it was administered by mouth.[13]

Following preliminary trials, gum tragacanth was administered in definitive doses of 8, 9, 10, and 12 g/kg/day as the 2% aqueous solution given at the rate of 2 g/kg every 90 min. One set of controls received distilled water orally at the rate of 100 ml/kg every 90 min for four to six administrations per dose of gum tragacanth, respectively. A second set of controls received only the insertion of a stomach tube at intervals of 90 min. This technique was repeated daily for ten days. Clinical signs were recorded as they appeared. Gross and microscopic pathology were noted on any animal that died and that could be autopsied within 1 hr of death to avoid postmortem changes recorded by Boyd and Knight.[14] Organ weights and water levels were measured on survivors at ten days.

Clinical Signs of Intoxication

The clinical syndrome of intoxication was most marked during the first 24 hr of the onset of daily administration of gum tragacanth. The common clinical signs were diarrhea, hypothermia, pallor, dyspnea, and tonoclonic convulsions. Diarrhea, pallor, and hypothermia persisted into the second day when some animals showed hyperreflexia and others soiling of the fur. All of these signs disappeared in survivors on the third day of daily administration of gum tragacanth and remained absent for the remainder of the test, i.e., until the tenth day. The syndrome of intoxication was confined, therefore, to the first two days of administration of gum tragacanth. Following this period, survivors developed tolerance to daily dosing of the gum.

The initial body weight of the animals was 175 ± 19 g (mean ± standard deviation). During the first two days, controls given stomach tube insertions only lost an average of 8 g of body weight and during the subsequent eight days of tolerance gained an average of 2 to 6 g per day. The controls dosed daily with distilled water in the same volumes as received by animals given gum tragacanth lost an average of 12 g in body weight during the first two days. Thereafter during the period of tolerance, these controls gained weight at the average rate of 2 to 5 g per day. Animals given gum tragacanth lost an average of 15 g in body weight during the initial two days of toxicity

and thereafter gained weight at the mean rate of 1 to 15 g per day. Changes in body weight were not dependent upon the daily dose of distilled water or of gum tragacanth within the limits of doses employed.

Data on clinical measurements at 24 hr after giving gum tragacanth are summarized in Table 22. Administration of large volumes of distilled water lowered food intake to about one half that in controls given stomach tube insertions only. Addition of gum tragacanth to the distilled water further lowered food intake and the higher the dose of gum tragacanth the greater the reduction. Changes in water intake tended to parallel those in food intake. Administration of large volumes of distilled water had no effect on colonic temperature. Gum tragacanth lowered body temperature but the effect was not dose dependent within the range of doses employed.

The volume of urine was markedly augmented by administration of distilled water and the extent of the increase was positively dependent on the volume given by mouth. Addition of gum tragacanth to the distilled water produced no further change in the volume of urine. Distilled water produced a hematuria which was less marked in animals given gum tragacanth. Administration of distilled water did not affect the glucose content of urine which was zero in both tube and water controls. Gum tragacanth produced a glycosuria which was dose dependent. The concentration of urinary protein was not markedly affected by administration of distilled water or gum tragacanth: there was a slight increase which was dose dependent on volume of distilled water and g/kg of gum tragacanth. Finally, urinary pH was lowered to about the same extent by both distilled water and gum tragacanth. The aciduria was most evident following the lower doses of distilled water and gum tragacanth.

In summary, the clinical signs of intoxication to gum tragacanth were similar to those of distilled water in some respects and differed in others. Distilled water did not produce signs such as dyspnea, pallor, convulsions, and death. These signs occurred in the study of Boyd and Godi[13] in which distilled water was given at intervals of 20 min rather than 90 min, as in the study on gum tragacanth of Boyd et al.[12] The total amounts of distilled water given daily by Boyd et al.[12] were of the order of those which produced mortality in the study of Boyd and Godi.[13] Lack of toxic signs

TABLE 22

Clinical Measurements (Mean ± Standard Deviation) during the First 24 hr after Oral Administration of Gum Tragacanth to Male Albino Rats[1][2]

Measurement	Stomach tube controls (N = 20)	Distilled water controls (N = 20)	Tragacanth-treated rats (total daily dose)			
			8 g/kg	9 g/kg	10 g/kg	12 g/kg
Food intake: g/kg/day	96 ± 24	44 ± 18	48 ± 19	23 ± 18	31 ± 19	4 ± 8
Water intake: ml/kg/day	171 ± 34	112 ± 32	116 ± 56	44 ± 22	55 ± 25	10 ± 21
Colonic temp.: °F	97.5 ± 1.0	98.4 ± 0.4	94.4 ± 1.5	96.8 ± 0.9	95.9 ± 1.5	96.0 ± 5.9
Urine volume: ml/kg/day	32.9 ± 17.0	396 ± 42*	390 ± 37	268 ± 77	317 ± 41	444 ± 130
Urine blood: units/kg/day	0.0	1.1 ± 0.8		0.1 ± 0.1	0.1 ± 0.2	0.3 ± 0.5
Urine glucose: mg/kg/day	0.0	0.0		0.7 ± 1.2	1.6 ± 1.4	1.8 ± 1.5
Urine protein: mg/kg/day	46 ± 67	77 ± 38*	39 ± 4	43 ± 12	32 ± 4	61 ± 29
Urine pH: 24-hr sample	8.7 ± 0.4	7.1 ± 0.4*	6.1 ± 0.4	6.9 ± 0.5	6.8 ± 0.4	7.1 ± 0.5

*Urine volume, protein content, and pH varied positively with the volume/kg of distilled water administered.

such as convulsions and death from distilled water in the work of Boyd et al.[1][2] was related to the longer interval between oral administrations of distilled water. It is possible that the interval of 90 min used by Boyd et al.[1][2] produced subtoxic signs of intoxication to distilled water and that these subtoxic signs added to signs from gum tragacanth to produce deaths during the first 24 hr after administration of gum tragacanth in large volumes of distilled water. Other signs indicating that gum tragacanth was toxic in itself during the first day or two of oral administration in the doses used were hypothermia and glycosuria. Aciduria was possibly more evident in rats given gum tragacanth than in controls given distilled water. Toxicity to administration of gum tragacanth in 50 vol of distilled water was due, therefore, in part to the distilled water and in part to gum tragacanth during the first two days of oral administration to albino rats.

Death Rates During the Initial Reaction

The common premortem clinical signs were marked hypothermia, anorexia, oligodipsia, oliguria, aciduria, hematuria, convulsions or convulsive movements, prostration, dirty, reddish incrustations about the face, and the mouth filled with regurgitated gum tragacanth solution. The interval to death extended from 8 to 50 hr after the onset of administration of the 2% solution of gum tragacanth with one delayed death at 122 hr. The mean ± standard deviation interval to death was 34 ± 7 hr, excluding the delayed death. The LD_{50} ± S.E. was 16.4 ± 2.0 g of gum tragacanth per kg body weight, with two thirds of the deaths following one day's dosing and one third following two days of dosing.

Gross and Microscopic Pathology at Death

There were no signs of gross pathology in control rats given stomach tube insertions with or without administration of distilled water. Some organs, such as the lungs, were hyperemic but not obviously congested. Pathological lesions seen on gross examination of body organs at death in the initial toxic reaction to gum tragacanth are summarized in Table 23. All animals that died had a congested stomach with hemorrhages, the small bowel and peritoneal cavity were distended with a yellowish fluid, and the cecum was shrunken. The incidences of other lesions are listed in Table 23.

A summary of histopathological lesions seen on the microscopic examination of body organs of albino rats that died from oral administration of a 2% aqueous solution of gum tragacanth during the initial toxic reaction is presented in Table 24. There was a marked local irritant inflammation of the storage or cardiac stomach. An example showing congestion of the submucosa with hemorrhage through the stratified squamous epithelium into the gastric lumen is shown in Figure 21. Following absorption, gum tragacanth produced congestion in many body organs such as the adrenal glands, brain, heart, kidneys, liver, lungs, and thymus gland. Vascular congestion was particularly marked in the kidneys. An example showing capillary congestion of the loop region of the kidney in an albino rat that died at 50 hr

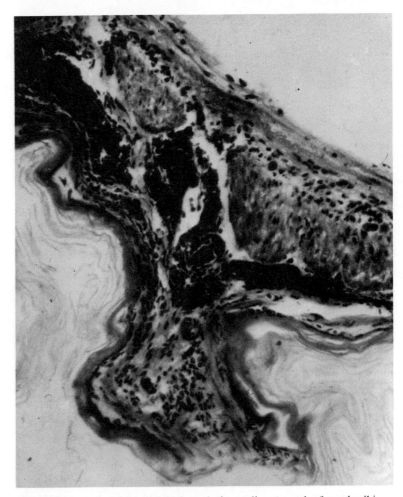

FIGURE 21. A photomicrograph through the cardiac stomach of a male albino rat that died 31 hr after receiving a total dose of 20 g of gum tragacanth per kg body weight, showing marked vascular congestion of the submucosa and hemorrhage through the stratified squamous epithelium into the lumen of the stomach. Hematoxylin-phloxine-saffron, x 100.[1,2]

TABLE 23

Pathological Changes Seen on Gross Examination of Body Organs at Deaths due to Oral Administration of a Lethal Dose of a 2% Aqueous Solution of Gum Tragacanth to Albino Rats*[1,2]

Lesion	% Incidence	Lesion	% Incidence
Congested stomach	100%	Congested mesentery	50%
Gastric hemorrhages	100%	Friable intestines	50%
Yellow fluid in peritoneum	100%	Congested intestine	33%
		Congested lung	33%
Intestines distended with yellowish fluid	100%	Pulmonary hemorrhage	33%
Cecum (shrunken)	100%	Bowel obstruction	33%
Cecum (congested)	67%	Stomach rupture	16%
Lungs spotted	67%	Dark liver	16%
Lungs pale	67%	Congested adrenals	16%
		Pale adrenals	16%

*There were no signs of gross pathology in controls given stomach tube insertions with or without distilled water.

TABLE 24

Histopathological Lesions Seen at Autopsy on Albino Rats that Died from Intragastric Administration of Gum Tragacanth[1][2]

Organ	Histopathology
Adrenal glands	Congestion of the zona glomerulosa and cortical sinusoids; lipoid droplets prominent
Brain	Early deaths: mild meningeal congestion; late deaths: normal appearance
Gastrointestinal tract	
Cardiac stomach	Marked capillary-venous congestion of the lamina propria and submucosa with tissue hemorrhage; occasionally hemorrhage through the stratified squamous epithelium into the gastric lumen or through the muscularis externa to the tunica adventitia (serosa); occasionally leukocytic infiltration
Pyloric stomach	Mild congestion
Small bowel	Moderate congestion
Cecum	Mild congestion
Colon	Occasionally mild congestion
Heart	Mild to moderate capillary-venous congestion of the myocardium, occasionally with venous stasis and thrombosis; occasionally mild hydropic degeneration of the coronary arterioles
Kidneys	Marked congestion occasionally with venous stasis and thrombosis; varying degrees of cloudy swelling, hydropic degeneration and diffuse fatty degeneration
Liver	Varying degrees of sinusoidal congestion occasionally with venous stasis and thrombosis; cloudy swelling and occasionally centrilobular pale-staining and hydropic degeneration
Lungs	Variations from normal to parenchymal congestion to massive congestion with hemorrhage, venous stasis and thrombosis
Muscle (ventral abdominal wall)	Early deaths: normal; late deaths: cross-striation weak
Salivary (submaxillary) glands	Early deaths: normal; late deaths: loss of zymogenic granules in the serous glands, serous ducts empty and hydropic degeneration of glandular epithelium
Skin	Early deaths: normal; late deaths: stratum granulosum very prominent
Spleen	Contracted red pulp
Testes	Early deaths: normal; late deaths: spermatids and sperm shrunken and lysed, nuclei of primary spermatogonium and of spermatocytes shrunken and pyknotic
Thymus gland	Varying degrees of congestion and loss of thymocytes

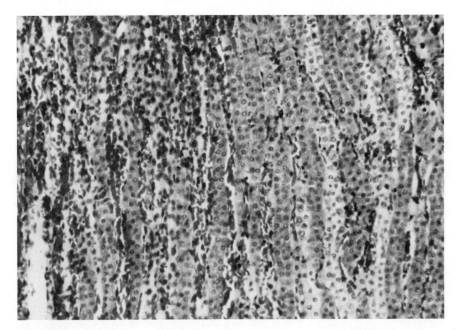

FIGURE 22.   A photomicrograph of the region of Henle's loop in the kidney of an albino rat that died 49 hr following oral administration of a total of 18 g of gum tragacanth per kg body weight showing congestion of the capillaries. Hematoxylin-phloxine-saffron, x 100.[12]

following oral administration of gum tragacanth in a total dose of 18 g/kg is shown in Figure 22.

During the initial lethal reaction, there was a stress reaction in the adrenal glands, spleen, and thymus gland. Degenerative changes appeared in various organs such as the heart, kidneys, liver, skeletal muscle, salivary glands, testes, and thymus gland. An example of necrosis in the acinar cells of the serous salivary glands is shown in Figure 23. When death was delayed, degenerative changes appeared in other organs such as the stratum granulosum of skin, as illustrated in Figure 24.

Post-toxicity Tolerance

Following the initial lethal toxic reaction of the first two days or so of oral administration of gum tragacanth, the animals developed a tolerance to daily administration of the gum. The clinical signs of toxicity disappeared and growth rate was restored to approximately normal in spite of continued daily dosing with gum tragacanth. Clinical measurements made one week after disappearance of the initial toxic reaction are collected in Table 25 in exemplification. Apart from some augmented polydipsia and diuresis, measurements in gum-treated rats were identical to those in water-treated controls.

Organ weights and water contents were measured on albino rats that survived ten days of daily administration of water or gum tragacanth solution. Results in rats given daily water administration are compared with data on controls given daily stomach tube insertions in Table 26. Water administration had produced significant increases in the wet weight of adrenal glands and cardiac stomach and a decrease in the wet weight of the total body and of most other organs. The marked increase in weight of cardiac stomach was due to hypertrophy of the stratified squamous epithelium and muscularis mucosae, as illustrated in Figures 25 and 26. Decrease in body weight was due mainly to loss of weight in muscle and skin. The most marked loss of weight was found in the liver and thymus gland. Loss of weight in water-treated rats was due in part to loss of water as may be seen from data summarized in the last column of Table 26.

Results of measurements of organ weights and water levels in albino rats at the end of ten days of daily administration of aqueous gum tragacanth solution are compared with data on controls given the same volume of daily oral administration of distilled water in Table 27. In addition to the effect of the large volume of water in which it was

FIGURE 24. A section through the skin of an albino rat that died 50 hr after receiving a total oral dose of 21 g of phenacetin per kg body weight, showing granular degeneration of the stratum granulosum. Hematoxylin-phloxine-saffron, x 450.[12]

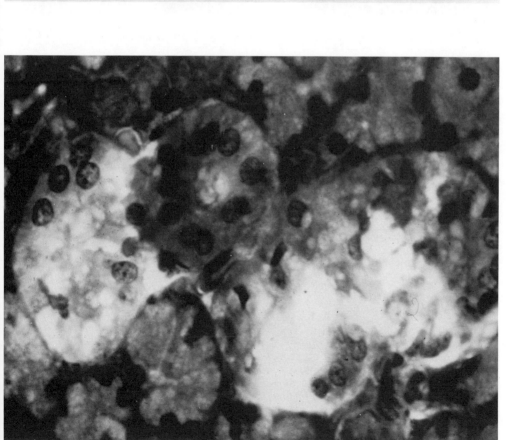

FIGURE 23. A photomicrograph of the serous salivary (submaxillary) glands of a male rat that died 8 hr after receiving a total oral dose of 10 g of gum tragacanth per kg body weight, showing necrosis of the acinar glands. Hematoxylin-phloxine-saffron, x 450.[12]

TABLE 25

Clinical Measurements (Mean ± Standard Deviation) at One Week after the Initial Toxic Reaction to Daily Administration of Gum Tragacanth Solution to Albino Rats[1][2]

Measurement	Stomach tube controls	Distilled water controls	Tragacanth-treated rats (daily dose)			
			8 g/kg	9 g/kg	10 g/kg	12 g/kg
Food intake: g/kg/day	97 ± 13	94 ± 10	97 ± 11	88 ± 16	96 ± 10	84 ± 10
Water intake: ml/kg/day	140 ± 17	139 ± 42	167 ± 43	158 ± 36	208 ± 62	239 ± 48
Colonic temp.: °F	96.9 ± 1.1	98.4 ± 0.4	96.0 ± 0.5	96.3 ± 0.7	97.3 ± 0.3	98.4 ± 0.4
Urine volume: ml/kg/day	35.1 ± 15.4	434 ± 67*	363 ± 23	381 ± 41	457 ± 72	530 ± 27
Urine blood: units/kg/day	0.0 ± 0.0	0.9 ± 0.3		0.8 ± 0.6	0.5 ± 0.1	0.5 ± 0.6
Urine glucose: mg/kg/day	0.0 ± 0.0	0.0 ± 0.0	0.0 ± 0.0	0.0 ± 0.0	0.0 ± 0.0	0.0 ± 0.0
Urine protein: mg/kg/day	67 ± 60	37 ± 11	36 ± 2	30 ± 17	45 ± 17	53 ± 3
Urine pH: 24-hr sample	8.8 ± 0.2	7.9 ± 0.5	7.9 ± 0.6	7.7 ± 0.7	8.0 ± 0.6	7.9 ± 0.5

*Urine volume varied positively with the volume per kg body weight of distilled water administered.

TABLE 26

The Wet Weight and Water Content of Body Organs of Albino Rats Given Distilled Water Orally for 10 days at a Daily Dose of 100 mg/kg every 90 min for 4 Dosings (= 400 ml/kg/day) Compared with Results in Controls Treated only by Gastric Tube Insertions[a][1][2]

Organ	Weight	Water content
Adrenal glands	+18.8*	−11.4*
Brain	− 1.2	− 1.4
Gastrointestinal tract		
Cardiac stomach	+62.6**	0.0
Pyloric stomach	+ 3.4	+ 4.4
Small bowel	− 4.5	− 2.3
Cecum	−10.5	− 0.9
Colon	− 7.4	− 2.1
Heart	− 6.5	− 2.9
Kidneys	−15.8**	− 8.6**
Liver	−26.1**	+ 2.8
Lungs	+ 3.4	− 5.7*
Muscle (ventral abdominal wall)	−17.0**	− 1.3
Salivary (submaxillary) glands	− 3.2	− 5.9
Skin	−17.9**	−10.2*
Spleen	−16.6**	− 1.4
Testes	− 1.9	− 1.3
Thymus gland	−35.9**	− 1.6
Residual carcass	−14.3**	− 0.8
Autopsy body weight	−14.1**	

[a]N = 5 plus 5 controls. Wet weight was measured in grams and water content in grams water per 100 g dry weight of tissue. The results are expressed as a mean percent change from tube-inserted controls, specifically as $[(\overline{X}_w - \overline{X}_c)/\overline{X}_c] \times 100$, where $\overline{X}_w$ is the mean in water-treated rats and $\overline{X}_c$ in controls.
*$\overline{X}_w - \overline{X}_c$ was significant at P = 0.05 to 0.02.
**$\overline{X}_w - \overline{X}_c$ was significant at P = 0.01 or less.

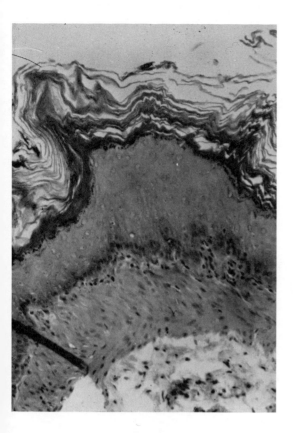

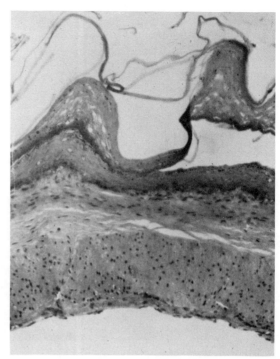

FIGURE 26. A section through the cardiac stomach of a control rat given only daily stomach tube insertions, illustrating the normal diameter of the layers of the stomach wall for comparison with Figure 25. Hematoxylin-phloxine-saffron, x 100.[1][2]

FIGURE 25. A section through the cardiac stomach of a control rat given daily administration of large volumes of distilled water for ten days. When compared with Figure 26, it may be seen that daily administration of distilled water in a large volume (400 ml/kg/day) had produced hypertrophy of the stratified squamous epithelium and the muscularis mucosae. The muscularis externa, not shown in Figure 25, was also hypertrophied. Hematoxylin-phloxine-saffron, x 100.[1][2]

dissolved, gum tragacanth produced a significant increase in the wet weight of small bowel, cecum, and liver. The considerable increase in weight of the cecum was found to be due to hypertrophy of smooth muscle, particularly of the inner layer of the muscularis externa, as shown in Figures 27 and 28. Loss of organ weight was augmented in a few instances such as in the testes, thymus gland, and residual carcass. Organ water levels tended to be higher than those in water-treated controls.

The effects of daily administration of distilled water, in a dose of 400 ml/kg/day for ten days, on the microscopic appearance of body organs are summarized in Table 28. The local effects on the gastrointestinal tract consisted of hypertrophy of cardiac stomach and mild congestion of other

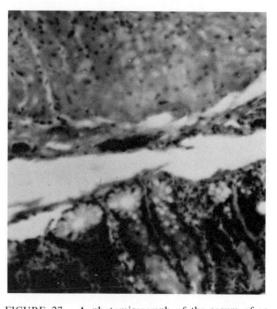

FIGURE 27. A photomicrograph of the cecum of an albino rat at the end of ten days of daily oral administration of a 2% aqueous solution of gum tragacanth in a dose of 400 ml/kg/day, showing hypertrophy of the inner layer of the muscularis externa (compare with Figure 28). Hematoxylin-phloxine-saffron, x 40.[1][2]

TABLE 27

The Wet Weight and Water Content of Body Organs of Albino Rats Given Gum Tragacanth in a Dose of 8 g/kg/day for 10 Days[a,1,2]

Organ	Weight	Water content
Adrenal glands	+ 2.6	+1.5
Brain	– 0.7	–0.3
Gastrointestinal tract		
Cardiac stomach	+ 5.1	+1.2
Pyloric stomach	– 0.8	+0.2
Small bowel	+25.5***	+5.3*
Cecum	+35.1**	+4.4**
Colon	+ 9.1	+1.3
Heart	– 5.7	+0.4
Kidneys	– 3.2	–2.0
Liver	+ 9.6*	–5.6
Lungs	– 3.2	+1.7
Muscle (ventral abdominal wall)	+ 1.7	–1.4
Salivary (submaxillary) glands	+ 1.2	0.0
Skin	– 2.8	+9.5*
Spleen	– 6.2	–0.2
Testes	– 6.2*	–1.4
Thymus gland	–13.2*	–3.1
Residual carcass	– 8.2**	+2.2
Autopsy body weight	– 2.7	

[a]N = 9 plus 5 controls. Wet weight was measured in grams and water content in grams water per 100 g dry weight of tissue. The results are expressed as a mean percent change from controls given water only (400 ml/kg/day), specifically as $[(\bar{X}_g - \bar{X}_w)/\bar{X}_w] \times 100$, where $\bar{X}_g$ is the mean in animals given gum tragacanth and $\bar{X}_w$ in water-treated controls.

*$\bar{X}_g - \bar{X}_w$ was significant at P = 0.05 to 0.02.
**$\bar{X}_g - \bar{X}_w$ was significant at P = 0.01 or less.

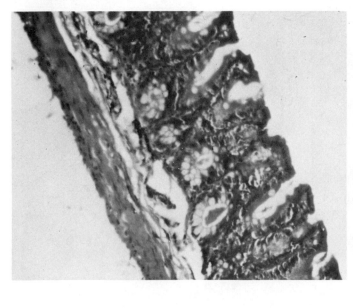

FIGURE 28. A photomicrograph of the cecum of a control albino rat, at the end of ten days of daily insertions of a stomach tube only, showing the normal diameter of the muscularis externa. Hematoxylin-phloxine-saffron, x 40.[1,2]

TABLE 28

Histopathological Lesions in Albino Rats Given Distilled Water at a Dose of 100 ml/kg Four Times a Day for Ten Days[1][2]

Organ	Histopathology
Adrenal glands	Lipoid droplets prominent in the cortex
Brain	Normal appearance
Gastrointestinal tract	
Cardiac stomach	Hypertrophy of stratified squamous epithelium, muscularis mucosae and muscularis externa
Pyloric stomach	Hyperemia to mild congestion
Small bowel	Hyperemia
Cecum	Mild congestion
Colon	Normal appearance
Heart	Occasionally hyperemia and mild capillary congestion
Kidneys	Capillary-venous congestion of Henle's loop, occasionally tubular cloudy swelling
Liver	Sinusoidal congestion
Lungs	Occasionally areas of parenchymal congestion
Muscle (ventral abdominal wall)	Myofibrils shrunken
Salivary (submaxillary) glands	Normal or occasionally some loss of zymogenic granules in the serous glands
Skin	Normal appearance
Spleen	Red pulp contracted
Testes	Occasionally edema of interstitial tissue
Thymus gland	Some congestion and minor loss of thymocytes

TABLE 29

Histopathological Lesions in Albino Rats that Survived Daily Oral Administration of Gum Tragacanth and Were Necropsied at Ten Days[1][2]

Organ	Histopathology
Adrenal glands	Lipoid droplets prominent in the cortex
Brain	Minor meningeal congestion
Gastrointestinal tract	
Cardiac stomach	Hypertrophy of mucosal and muscular layers
Pyloric stomach	Occasionally minor congestion
Small bowel	Hypertrophy
Cecum	Hypertrophy
Colon	Normal appearance
Heart	Occasionally areas of mild capillary congestion
Kidneys	Capillary-venous congestion of Henle's loop; occasionally tubular cloudy swelling
Liver	Granular appearance with areas of hemorrhage and necrosis
Lungs	Occasionally mild congestion
Muscle (ventral abdominal wall)	Myofibrils shrunken
Salivary (submaxillary) glands	Occasionally a deficiency of zymogenic granules in the serous glands
Skin	Normal appearance
Spleen	Red pulp contracted
Testes	Interstitial edema; varying degrees of inhibition of spermatogenesis
Thymus gland	Loss of thymocytes marked

parts of the alimentary canal. Following absorption, the large volumes of distilled water had produced a mild congestion of several body organs such as the heart, kidneys, liver, lungs, and thymus gland. There was a stress reaction in the adrenal glands, spleen, and thymus gland. Very minor degrees of degeneration appeared in the kidneys, salivary glands, testes, and thymus gland.

The addition of gum tragacanth to the distilled water had minor histopathological effects during the period of tolerance, as indicated by data summarized in Table 29. Local effects on the gastrointestinal tract were similar to those produced by distilled water plus the addition of hypertrophy of the small bowel and cecum. The systemic stress reaction, organ inflammation, and degenerative changes were, in general, similar to, or slightly more marked than, those produced by daily oral administration of large volumes of distilled water.

Conclusions Regarding Gum Tragacanth

Oral administration of aqueous colloidal solutions of gum tragacanth to albino rats in doses of from 8 to 12 g/kg/day produces an initial toxic and lethal reaction during the first two days or so, followed by adaptation and development of tolerance to lethal doses of gum tragacanth.

The initial lethal reaction followed doses at the range of the acute oral $LD_{50} \pm$ S.E. of 16.4 ± 2.0 g/kg given over a period of one to two days. The mean ± standard deviation interval to death was 34 ± 7 hr from the start of administration of gum tragacanth. Signs of toxicity which did not appear in controls given the same large volumes of distilled water included dyspnea, pallor, convulsions, marked loss of body weight, hypothermia, glycosuria, aciduria, and death. At autopsy, signs peculiar to gum tragacanth included a marked, local inflammation of cardiac stomach, congestion and degeneration of many body organs, and a stress reaction.

During the period of tolerance following the initial toxic reaction, most of the signs of toxicity to gum tragacanth disappeared. Measurements upon such animals were similar to, or slightly more marked than, those in controls given the same large volumes of distilled water.

REFERENCES

1. **Boyd, E. M.,** The acute oral toxicity of phenacetin, *Toxicol. Appl. Pharmacol.,* 1, 240, 1959.
2. **Boyd, E. M., Covert, E. L., and Shanas, M. N.,** Death from bowel obstruction due to intragastrically administered kaolin, *Ind. Med. Surg.,* 34, 874, 1965.
3. **Boyd, E. M. and Abel, M.,** The acute toxicity of barium sulfate administered intragastrically, *Can. Med. Assoc. J.,* 94, 849, 1966.
4. **Boyd, E. M. and Bereczky, G. M.,** Liver necrosis from paracetamol, *Br. J. Pharmacol. Chemother.,* 26, 606, 1966.
5. **Stecher, P. G., Windholz, M., Leahy, D., Bolton, D. M., and Eaton, L. G.,** *The Merck Index. An Encyclopedia of Chemicals and Drugs,* 8th ed., Merck and Company, Inc., Rahway, N.J., 1968.
6. **FAO/WHO,** Specifications for the Identity and Purity of Some Food Colours, Emulsifiers, Stabilizers, Anti-caking Agents and Certain Other Food Additives, FAO Nutrition Meetings Report Series No. 46B, WHO/Food Add./70.37, Food and Agriculture Organization and World Health Organization, Geneva, 1970.
7. **Smith, F. and Montgomery, R.,** *The Chemistry of Plant Gums and Mucilages,* Reinhold, N. Y., 1969.
8. **FAO/WHO,** Toxicological Evaluation of Some Food Colours, Emulsifiers, Stabilizers, Anti-caking Agents and Certain Other Substances, FAO Nutrition Meetings Report Series No. 46A, WHO/Food Add./70.36, Food and Agriculture Organization and World Health Organization, Geneva, 1970.
9. **Riccardi, B. A. and Fahrenbach, J. M.,** Hypocholesterolemic activity of mucilaginous polysaccharides in white leghorn cockerels, *Fed. Proc.,* 24, 265, 1965.
10. **Boyd, E. M., Ciampi, G. C., and Krijnen, C. J.,** Intragastric versus dietary administration of phenacetin, *Pharmacol. Res. Commun.,* 1, 259, 1969.
11. **Fujimoto, J. M.,** Effect of gum tragacanth, urethan, and phenobarbital on hexobarbital narcosis in mice, *Toxicol. Appl. Pharmacol.,* 7, 287, 1965.
12. **Boyd, E. M., Shanas, M. N., and Shanas, D. B.,** The acute oral toxicity of gum tragacanth in albino rats, unpublished data, 1972.
13. **Boyd, E. M. and Godi, I.,** Acute oral toxicity of distilled water in albino rats, *Ind. Med. Surg.,* 36, 609, 1967.
14. **Boyd, E. M. and Knight, L. M.,** Postmortem shifts in the weight and water levels of body organs, *Toxicol. Appl. Pharmacol.,* 5, 119, 1963.

Chapter 6

STARCH

Studies reviewed in Chapter 5 indicated that the oral LD_{50} of gum tragacanth is of the same order as that of sucrose, noted in Chapter 3, and glucose, noted in Chapter 4. The interval to death is longer for gum tragacanth than for the two sugars. These results suggest the possibility that death from gum tragacanth is due to the digestive conversion of the polysaccharide to mono-saccharides which are absorbed and produce a lethal syndrome similar to that produced by oral lethal doses of sugars. Tolerance to toxic effects on repeated oral administration of gum tragacanth, noted in Chapter 5, also occurred from repeated oral administration of large doses of sucrose, noted in Chapter 3. The toxicity of these three carbo-hydrates, therefore, had much in common. The oral toxicity of starch differed markedly. It produced what Boyd[1] has termed the 'bulk syndrome of toxicity,' which is characteristic of certain other substances such as oral kaolin[2] and barium sulfate.[3] The oral toxicity of starch has been described by Liu,[4] by Liu and Boyd,[5,6] and by Boyd and Liu.[7]

Starch was first prepared by the partial fermentation of grain during the second century A.D., according to Herstein.[8] It was used as a cosmetic, in medicines, and in laundering. In the early 19th century (1811) sugar was produced from starch by treating it with dilute sulfuric acid. Production from corn was discovered in the latter part of the 19th century and corn is now the main source of starch. Starch may be regarded as a mixed polymer of glucose[9] consisting of about one quarter linear polymers (amyloses) and three quarters branched polymers (amylopectins or waxy starches). Amyloses adsorb other com-pounds, such as iodine with which it produces a blue color; amylopectins yield a reddish-violet color with iodine. Amyloses are digested by man somewhat less readily than amylopectins, but when gelatinized by cooking the difference is minor.[10]

The properties of starch are variously modified by physical and chemical treatments. Heating a starch solution produces partial breakdown to smaller molecules, called dextrins, which are more readily digested. Filtering off the insoluble material from the hot mixture and evaporating the filtrate produces 'soluble starch,' which was used in the studies of Liu.[4] Other treatments include acid or alkaline hydrolysis, bleaching, oxidation (produces carboxy groups), esterification (esters usually in the 2, 3, or 6 positions), etherization, and cross-bonding to forms of the general formula, starch-O-R-O-starch.[11] FAO/WHO[10] notes that very little toxicological data are available on these modified starches; the oral LD_{50} of some derivatives was found to be over 7 g/kg; the main effect of dietary administration was hypertrophy of the cecum which is characteristic of oral ingestion of large amounts of indigestible material. Other aspects of the chemistry of starch have been extensively reviewed, for example by Whistler and Paschall.[12]

Natural, uncooked starch is poorly digested by man and animals due to the resistant coating of individual starch grains. The coating is destroyed by boiling and cooking which improves digestion.[13] Digestion occurs within the lumen of the bowel and on its inner surface by means of enzymes fixed on the cell surface, the so-called "membrane digestion."[14] Starches occur abundantly in grains, tubers, seeds, and fruits which, with sucrose, are the main sources of calories in the human diet.

If all dietary calories are provided as protein or as fat, the diet is toxic, especially during post-weaning. The basic action of dietary starches appears to be to provide calories in a nontoxic form, at the daily amount needed. The minimal amount of starch necessary to prevent toxicity from proteins or fats appears to be some 50 to 65% of the diet. Amounts slightly in excess of calorie requirements are converted to fat and stored in the body. Intake of huge amounts of starches produces the toxicity described in this chapter.

There is some information, in earlier studies, on the pharmacological and toxicological actions of starches. Raw starches appear to contain a heat-labile fraction that resists digestion, produces diarrhea, and impedes utilization of protein.[15-20]

The uncooked starch produces gas in the lower bowel and cecum that results in hypertrophy of the cecum. Immature female rats fed low tryptophane diets grow better when carbohydrates are provided as cornstarch rather than as sucrose.[21] Starch solution is an antidote for iodine and bromine poisoning,[22] and is used as a dusting powder, usually with 5% boric acid to inhibit development of rancidity.[23]

Earlier reports on the toxicity of starch in man were confined to several conditions apparently associated with a high intake of starch. In 1909, Czerny and Keller[24] reported a condition in German infants called "Mehlnährschaden" that they believed was due to excessive intake of cereal flour but which was later shown associated with low protein in the diet of such infants.[7] Another condition in which large amounts of starch are eaten has been termed "starch addiction" or "Argo addiction."[25] Argo refers to Argo® Gloss Starch, a form of cornstarch eaten in large amounts, especially by pregnant Negro women in the U.S. Up to 5 lb/day may be consumed and the satisfaction derived from it is akin to that of chewing gum or smoking cigarettes.[26] The practice evolved from clay-eating by pregnant women which, in the folklore of the 16th to 19th centuries, was believed to produce beautiful babies.[7] Pathology associated with eating large amounts of starch includes iron deficiency anemia due to insufficient intake of iron,[27-32] hypertrophy of the parotid gland,[29] hypersensitivity reactions,[33-35] and gastric obstruction due to a starch gastrolith or bezoar.[30]

Celiac disease is associated with a deficiency of duodenal amylase; removal of starches from the diet of such patients generally leads to rapid clinical improvement.[36,37] The use of cornstarch as a surgical glove powder may produce cornstarch granulomatous peritonitis[38-42] and inhalation of starch may yield a chemical pneumonitis.[43] Daily ingestion of 5 to 8 g of dietary starch per kg body weight produces flatus, borborygmi, cramps, and minor loss of body weight in man.[44-46]

Less information is available on the toxicity of starches to animals. In 1945, Schweigert et al.[47] reported that a diet of 67% soluble starch killed rats in 3 weeks, but in 1946[48] stated that the animals were alive and well after feeding the diet for 14 weeks. Beaton and Sangster[49] found that a diet of 79% starch (and 5% casein) was of nutritional value to the rat for only about 15 days.

Feeding uncooked starches to rats resulted in accumulation of undigested starch and gas in a distended cecum.[19,50] Lindblad[51] investigated the use of hydroxyethyl starch as a blood plasma expander and found that the agent, given intravenously to a variety of species of animals in a dose of 3 to 5 g/kg/day, produced damage to the liver, kidneys, spleen, lymph nodes, adrenal glands, and ovaries with no effect on the lungs, heart, gastrointestinal tract, pancreas, urinary bladder, brain, and muscle. Liu[4-7] gave starch orally to albino rats in increasing doses until lethal toxicity occurred.

The Studies of Liu

Liu[4-7] used Soluble Starch (Fisher Scientific Company Limited, Don Mills, Ontario, Canada) prepared from potatoes. In pilot tests, suspensions in distilled water given to overnight-starved albino rats by stomach tube in doses up to 225 g/kg as 45 g/kg every 4 to 6 hr produced no deaths. It became apparent that large doses of starch would have to be given daily to (unstarved) rats. Starch was administered as a warmed 60% paste in distilled water; 50 ml/kg of this paste could be given every 2.5 hr for four administrations per day without producing gastric rupture. Gastric rupture occurred when larger volumes were given. After the first day, larger doses could be gradually used without producing gastric rupture as the stomach adapted quickly to the large bulk of starch paste. The general technique, therefore, was to give increasing daily volumes of the 60% warmed starch paste intragastrically until death occurred. Three sets of controls were employed, one given daily the same volumes of distilled water, a second stomach tube insertions only, and a third no treatment.

Clinical signs were measured daily and all animals that died were autopsied. Six types of toxicity were encountered, namely:(a) the gastric distension syndrome; (b) regurgitation, aspiration, and asphyxia; (c) stomach rupture; (d) bowel obstruction; (e) the fermentation (green skin) syndrome; and (f) pneumonia.

Utilization of Bulk Starch

Most dietary starches are digested, absorbed by rats, and contribute to gain in their body weight.[18,50] Liu[4] found that as the dose of administered starch was increased to toxic levels, less starch was digested and absorbed, but some part of every dose was utilized. To estimate utilization, Liu[4] measured the total dry weight of starch given intragastrically, subtracted the total dry weight of starch pellets in the feces, and expressed the difference or utilized starch as a percentage of starch given orally. He found that the mean ± standard deviation percentage utilization was 9.28 ± 3.32 with little or no relationship to the toxic dose administered. The mean ± standard deviation absorption of starch was 23.2 ± 9.17 g/kg/day or about 90 kcal/kg/day. The reduction in food (laboratory chow) intake of these animals was approximately equivalent in kilocalories to the amount of starch utilized.

The Initial Gastric Distension Syndrome

The gastric distension syndrome was similar to that of gastric rupture, but rupture did not occur.[4] During administration of the bulk volume of starch suspension, the animal went through motions like those of gagging and retching. Toward the end of starch administrations, tenseness developed and was followed by muscular fasciculations. The weight of starch suspension in the stomach and intestines made it difficult for the rat to right itself when placed on its back and to raise its abdomen when walking. Diarrhea often followed the first administration of starch suspension but did not occur after the first 3 or 4 hr. Other signs are noted in Table 30.

It may be seen from data summarized in Table 30 that the clinical signs of gastric distension, apart from abdominal bloating, were confined to the first two days of daily oral administration of starch suspension. Signs confined to the first two days included pallor, drowsiness, hypokinesia, hyporeflexia, and epistaxis. Abdominal bloating became increasingly more marked with each administration per day of starch suspension. Most of the starch was excreted or absorbed 4 to 6 hr after the last dose of the day and at this point abdominal bloating disappeared. Starch was excreted as large, mucus-covered pellets. The first stool appeared at 6 to 7 hr after the first oral administration of starch and fecal elimination continued for the next 10 to 12 hr.

Dose Dependence of Clinical Signs

The means, over 14 days, of clinical measurements on albino rats, given starch in four divided doses totaling from 36 to 288 g/kg/24 hr and in which no deaths occurred, are listed in Table 31 as percent changes from corresponding means in controls given four insertions of the gastric cannula per day. Insertions of the gastric cannula produced a slight inhibition of growth and a slight decrease in water intake, urinary volume, and urinary pH compared with data on rats given no treatment whatsoever. The animals adjusted to daily stomach tube insertions and soon offered no resistance. The mild effects of daily tube insertion were probably due to mild psychic trauma or to interference with sleep patterns. There were, however, significant effects of daily water administration in controls given the same volume of distilled water as was received by animals given

TABLE 30

Clinical Signs (in Clinical Units) of the Gastric Distension Syndrome in Albino Rats Given Large Volumes of Starch Suspension by Stomach Tube[a]

Clinical signs	Days of daily starch administration						
	1	2	4	6	8	10	12
Pallor	+0.8	+0.2	0	0	0	0	0
Drowsiness	+0.6	+0.2	0	0	0	0	0
Hypokinesia	+0.6	+0.3	0	0	0	0	0
Hyporeflexia	+0.4	+0.1	0	0	0	0	0
Epistaxis	0.0	+0.2	0	0	0	0	0
Abdominal bloating	+2.0	+1.4	+1.7	+2.0	+2.2	+2.5	+2.5

[a]The results are entered as mean differences from controls given gastric cannula insertions only, specifically as $\bar{X}_s - \bar{X}_c$, where $\bar{X}_s$ is the mean in starch-treated animals and $\bar{X}_c$ in the controls, $\bar{X}_c$ usually being zero. (From Liu[4] with the permission of the author.)

TABLE 31

Daily Clinical Measurements and Observations in Albino Rats Given Starch as a 60% Paste by Stomach Tube and in Controls Given Distilled Water Daily for 14 days[a]

	Group	36 N = 10 + 10 controls	72 – 120 N = 20 + 10 controls	168 – 204 N = 20 + 10 controls	240 – 288 N = 20 + 10 controls
Starch: g/kg/24 hr					
Water: ml/kg/24 hr		60 N = 10 + 10 controls	120 – 200 N = 20 + 10 controls	280 – 340 N = 20 + 10 controls	400 – 840 N = 20 + 10 controls
Body weight	Starch	+ 0.5	– 8.2*	– 14.6**	– 14.9**
Body weight	Water	– 3.9[††]	– 4.9[††]	– 7.6[††]	– 10.2[††]
Food (chow) intake	Starch	– 14.3**	– 21.4[††]	– 31.0**	– 27.5**
Food (chow) intake	Water	– 3.8[†]	– 6.0[††]	– 4.8[†]	– 5.4[†]
Water intake	Starch	+ 8.2**	– 12.6*	– 2.8**	– 9.3**
Water intake	Water	– 4.2	– 17.6[††]	– 17.3[††]	– 17.3[††]
Body temperature	Starch	– 0.4	– 1.0	– 0.8	– 0.7
Body temperature	Water	– 1.1	– 1.0	– 0.8	– 0.9
Urinary volume	Starch	+ 23**	+ 11**	+103**	+142**
Urinary volume	Water	+111[††]	+362[††]	+712[††]	+963[††]
Urinary pH	Starch	+ 14.8*	+ 15.1**	+ 15.3**	+ 6.3
Urinary pH	Water	+ 22.2[††]	+ 10.2[††]	+ 10.8[††]	+ 4.0[†]
Urinary blood	Starch	absent	absent	absent	absent
Urinary blood	Water	absent	absent	present	present
Irritability on days 1 and 2	Starch	absent	absent	present	present
Drowsiness on days 1 and 2	Starch	absent	absent	present	present
Pallor on days 1 and 2	Starch	absent	absent	present	present
Hyporeflexia on days 1 and 2	Starch	absent	absent	present	present
Epistaxis on days 1 and 2	Starch	absent	absent	present	present
Abdominal bloating on days 1 and 2	Starch	absent	absent	present	present
Gastric rupture (days 1 and 2)	Starch	absent	absent	present	present
Death from pneumonia	Starch	absent	absent	present	absent
Death from gastrointestinal obstruction	Starch	absent	absent	present	present

[a]Numerical results are expressed as mean percent change from controls given gastric tube insertion only, specifically as $[(\bar{X}_d - \bar{X}_c)/\bar{X}_c] \times 100$, where $\bar{X}_d$ is the mean of 14 days of readings in rats given starch paste or distilled water and $\bar{X}_c$ the corresponding mean in rats given gastric tube insertions only. In animals given starch, * indicates that the mean percent change was significantly different from that in rats given water at P = 0.05 to 0.02 and ** at P = 0.01 or less. In rats given distilled water, † indicates that $\bar{X}_d - \bar{X}_c$ differed from zero at P = 0.05 to 0.02 and †† at P = 0.01 or less. Clinical signs entered as present or absent in all rats given distilled water except as noted. (From Boyd and Liu[7] with the permission of the *Canadian Medical Association Journal.*)

starch paste. Results in water-treated controls, calculated as for starch-treated animals, are included in Table 31.

With increasing daily doses of starch, body weight progressively declined, about half the loss being due to the large daily volumes of water administered. Food intake was reduced much more so in the starch-treated rats than in water-treated controls. Decrease in chow intake was largely compensated by utilization of starch and calorie intake was affected very little. It appeared

that loss of body weight was due mainly to factors other than decrease in calorie intake. Water intake was lowered in both starch- and water-treated rats and there was a tendency toward a slight hypothermia. Urinary volume was increased, particularly in the water-treated controls. The smaller daily volumes of water tended to produce an alkaline urine. The large daily volumes of distilled water produced a hematuria and the larger daily doses of starch produced deaths as noted in Table 31.

The Regurgitation Syndrome

Deaths due to regurgitation of starch paste into the upper esophagus and mouth and aspiration into the lungs producing asphyxia occurred in some 8% of the animals given a 60% starch paste by mouth.[4] Preliminary trials indicated that the incidence of this type of death was more frequent when less concentrated suspensions of starch were given, presumably because the thinner pastes were more readily regurgitated. Death occurred at intervals varying from a few minutes to 10 hr from the onset of administration of starch paste. Ninety percent of the asphyxial deaths followed administration of starch in a dose of 200 g/kg or over.

Gastric Rupture

Gastric rupture occurred during the first 48 hr when the daily dose of starch reached 168 g/kg and over.[4] Of 163 rats given such doses, 94, or 58%, died of stomach rupture, in spite of precautions to avoid this reaction, which was purely mechanical and not due specifically to starch. The initial clinical signs of gastric rupture were similar to those of gastric distension. Following rupture, the animals became extremely sluggish in their movements. They reacted indifferently to stimuli such as proddings, tapping on their cage, or ruffling their fur by blowing it against the grain. They ate no food, drank no water, and were oliguric or anuric. Premortally they became extremely drowsy, all movements stopped, pallor developed, and they died of respiratory failure in deep depression of the central nervous system a few hours after the rupture.

At autopsy, starch paste was found distributed throughout the peritoneal cavity. The stomach was dilated by starch paste which had thickened to a hard mass. Small and variable amounts of starch had left the stomach and were found in the small bowel, but none had entered the large bowel. The stomach was usually ruptured at the junction of the cardiac and pyloric parts and opposite the entrance of the esophagus. No rupture occurred in the intestines. The sequence of events appeared to be first rupture of the muscularis mucosae and muscularis externa with hemorrhage and finally rupture of the stratified squamous epithelium. The lining epithelium appeared to be able to distend more than could the layers of smooth muscle. A photomicrograph illustrating the early events in rupture is presented in Figure 29. Other organs of the body appeared normal histologically.

Animals that survived early death due to regurgitation, aspiration of starch paste into the lungs, and asphyxia or to gastric rupture were able

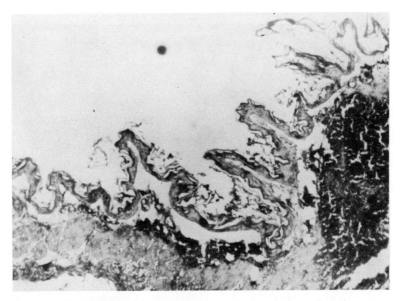

FIGURE 29. A photomicrograph illustrating the initial phase of gastric rupture in rats following oral administration of large doses of starch paste, showing rupture of the muscularis mucosae and muscularis externa at 2 to 5 o'clock position with hemorrhage into the area. (From Liu[4] with the permission of the author.)

to tolerate increasing daily doses of starch paste. This was due to enlargement and hypertrophy of tissues lining the gastrointestinal tract to accommodate the large volumes of starch paste given by stomach tube. Enlargement of the stomach was due mainly to the large volume of administered distilled water. On leaving the stomach, the starch was converted into mucus-covered pellets, as illustrated in Figure 30, and the work involved in forcing this large volume along the intestines produced a considerable hypertrophy. As illustrated in Figure 31, hypertrophy of the cecum was marked and of the small bowel and colon somewhat less.

Starch was given to survivors of early mechanical death in doses that were increased every three days by 24 g/kg/24 hr until death occurred. The causes of death in these rats are collected in Table 32. The most common cause of death was obstruction in the gastrointestinal tract which accounted for 77% of the deaths. The lowest daily dose of starch that produced obstruction was 168 g/kg/24 hr and the largest was 456 g/kg/24 hr. One rat survived until the daily dose reached 456 g/kg/24 hr on day 49 when the animal died of bowel obstruction.

Bowel Obstruction

The clinical signs of bowel obstruction were restricted to a few days before death. Following the early gastric distension syndrome, the animals recovered their healthy appearance and continued to look normal until two or three days before death. During this premortem interval, the animal looked sick, was pale, had difficulty in breathing, ate no food and drank no water. Other clinical signs are listed in Table 33. At autopsy, the main pathological signs were related to the bowel obstruction as noted in Table 33. An example showing the microscopic appearance of a starch calculus in the colon appears in Figure 32. Starch globules occasionally were forced into the tissues of the gastrointestinal tract and even into adjacent structures such as the pancreas, as illustrated in Figure 33.

Death from Pneumonia

While varying degrees of pulmonary congestion were found at autopsy on albino rats that died of bowel obstruction, pneumonia was the sole cause of death in some 15% of survivors of early mechanical death, as noted in Table 32. Death from pneumonia occurred as early as the 4th day of daily oral starch administration and as late as the 32nd day. Death was preceded by anorexia, adipsia, oliguria, and some loss of body weight. The main finding at autopsy was infection of the lung, varying from congestion to marked abscess formation.

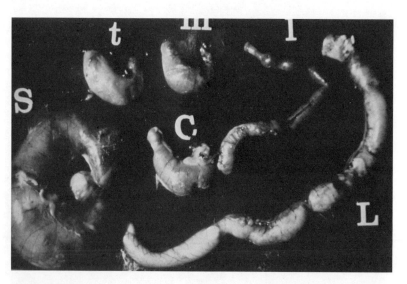

FIGURE 30.   A photograph of the excised stomach (C), cecum (S), and colon (L) of a rat that died from bowel obstruction due to oral administration of large doses of starch compared with the appearance of the stomach (m), cecum (t), and colon (l) of a control rat of the same body weight. (From Liu[4] with the permission of the author.)

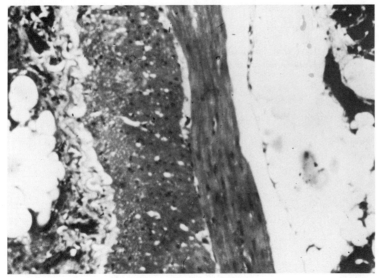

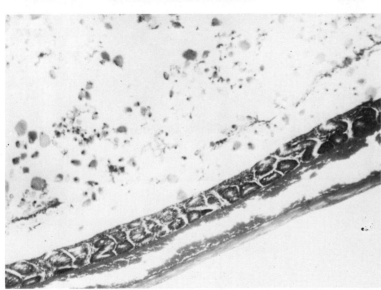

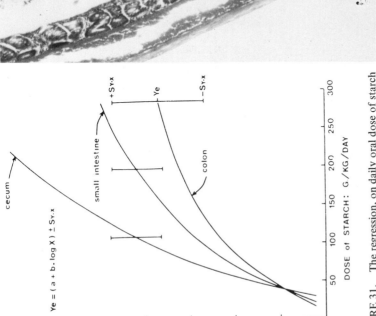

FIGURE 31. The regression, on daily oral dose of starch administered to rats, of mean percent increase in the weight of cecum, small bowel, and colon. Mean percent increase was calculated as the mean percent change over the weight in controls given corresponding volumes of distilled water. The regression equation for each line was $Y_e = (a + b \log X) \pm S_{y.x}$. Values of "a" for cecum, small bowel, and colon were, respectively, $-122, -69,$ and -44, of "b," 80.8, 48.3, and 32.8, and of "$S_{y.x}$," or the standard error of the regression line, 5.7, 5.9, and 9.9, respectively. (From Boyd and Liu[7] with the permission of the *Canadian Medical Association Journal*.)

FIGURE 32. A photomicrograph through a starch calculus in the colon of an albino rat given large oral daily doses of starch paste showing dilatation of the lumen by the calculus, flattening of the Lieberkühn glands, submucosal congestion, and hemorrhage and stretching of the muscularis externa. (From Liu[4] with the permission of the author.)

FIGURE 33. A low power microscopic view of the small bowel of an albino rat that died of a bowel obstruction on the 39th day of daily oral administration of increasing volumes of starch paste showing hypertrophy of the muscularis externa and globules of starch in the submucosa and adjacent pancreas (bottom of photograph). (From Liu[4] with the permission of the author.)

TABLE 32

The Causes of Death in Albino Rats that Survived Early Gastric Rupture or Regurgitative Asphyxia and that Were Given Increasing Daily Doses of Starch Paste

Cause of death	Percentage incidence	Final daily doses of starch (g/kg/24 hr)
Gastrolith	8	168
Gastrolith plus small bowel obstruction	15	168
Small bowel obstruction	46	168–456
Obstruction of the cecum and colon	8	408
Pneumonia	15	192–408
Fermentation (green skin) death	8	384

(From Liu[4] with the permission of the author.)

TABLE 33

Clinical and Pathological Signs of the Bowel Obstruction Syndrome in Albino Rats Given Large Daily Oral Doses of Starch Paste

Clinical signs

1. Adipsia
2. Anorexia
3. Bloating of the abdomen
4. Constipation
5. Drowsiness
6. Dyspnea
7. Epistaxis
8. Fever
9. Head shaking
10. Hyporeflexia
11. Loss of body weight
12. Mouth vibrations
13. Oliguria
14. Pallor
15. Pulmonary rales
16. Respiratory failure

Signs at autopsy

1. Gastrointestinal hypertrophy, congestion, ulceration, and hemorrhage.
2. Impaction of hard starch calculi in various areas of the gastrointestinal tract.
3. Peritoneal fluid occasionally blood-tinged.
4. Stress reaction in the adrenal glands, spleen, and thymus gland.
5. Occasionally pulmonary congestion.
6. Occasionally renal congestion and hemorrhage.
7. Occasionally fatty degeneration and necrosis of the liver.
8. Occasionally testicular congestion.

The Green Skin Syndrome

The diagnostic features of this syndrome were green skin and green skeletal muscle. There was some loss of body weight associated with anorexia and adipsia during the day before death. At autopsy, the peritoneal cavity was found full of fluid and the gastrointestinal tract contained crescent-shaped masses of hard starch, gas, and yellowish fluid. The lung was moderately congested. Skin and muscle were tinged green, especially in those parts over the ventral abdominal wall. The histological appearance of the green areas was that of venous dilatation and congestion. An example of the microscopic appearance of green skin is shown in Figure 34. There is some indication in Figure 34 of gas collecting in the subcutaneous tissue, suggesting that the green skin syndrome may have been a fermentative reaction.

Organ Weights

Organ weights were recorded in survivors after 14 days of daily oral administration of starch. The total daily doses initially ranged from 36 to 168 g/kg/24 hr and in animals that did not die from gastric rupture or regurgitation asphyxia, the daily dose was gradually increased to the highest dose of 288 g/kg/24 hr. Starch was given as a warmed 60% aqueous paste in volumes ranging from 60 to 480 ml/kg/24 hr. Controls for each dose of starch received the same daily volume of distilled water; other controls were given four stomach tube insertions per day; a third group of controls received no treatment. Gastric tube insertions daily had minor effects such as a slight oliguria, aciduria, and decrease in water intake.

Data on organ weights in survivors at 14 days are assembled in Table 34 as mean percent changes from values in controls given daily stomach tube insertions. Tabulation has been confined to two dosage ranges; data on individual doses are listed by Liu.[4] In the last column of Table 34 are entered notations indicating what part, if any, of the changes in starch-treated rats was due to distilled water of the starch paste.

It may be seen from Table 34 that daily oral administration of starch paste produced an increase in the wet weight of all parts of the gastrointestinal tract except pyloric stomach. The larger daily volumes of distilled water produced an increase in the wet weight of pyloric stomach, no change or a decrease in the weight of cecum and colon, a more marked increase in the weight of cardiac stomach, and a less marked increase in the weight of small bowel.

The stressor gain in weight of the adrenal glands

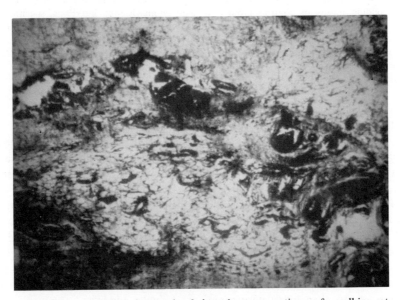

FIGURE 34.   A photomicrograph of the subcutaneous tissue of an albino rat that died of the green skin syndrome on the 30th day of daily oral administration of increasing doses of starch paste, showing venous dilatation and congestion and possibly small amounts of gas in the tissues. (From Liu[4] with the permission of the author.)

TABLE 34

The Wet Weight of Body Organs of Albino Rats that Survived 14 Days of Daily Oral Administration of Starch Paste in Doses of from 36 to 288 g of Starch per kg Body Weight per Day[a]

Organ	Daily dose of starch (in brackets daily volume of water)		Effect due to distilled water vehicle?
	36–120 g/kg (60–200 ml/kg)	168–288 g/kg (280–480 ml/kg)	
Adrenal glands	+ 5.4	+11.1	Yes
Brain	– 1.2	– 5.5*	Partly
Gastrointestinal tract			
Cardiac stomach	+ 1.5	+68.7**	Yes
Pyloric stomach	–23.0**	–13.8**	No
Small bowel	+26.2**	+73.5**	Partly
Cecum	+19.6**	+61.9**	No
Colon	+ 2.5	+22.3**	No
Heart	– 2.6	–21.6**	In small part
Kidneys	– 5.8	–24.5**	In part
Liver	– 4.6	–21.2**	In part
Lungs	– 7.3*	–10.8*	In part
Muscle (ventral abdominal wall)	–12.4	–24.9**	In part
Salivary (submaxillary) glands	+ 3.0	–15.3**	No
Skin	– 8.6*	–32.1**	In part
Spleen	– 2.9	–35.8**	In part
Testes	– 1.7	–10.0**	In part
Thymus gland	–11.9*	–42.2**	In small part
Residual carcass	– 5.7	–22.8**	In small part

[a]Weight was measured in grams. The results are expressed as a mean percent change from corresponding means in controls given only daily stomach tube insertions, specifically as $[(\bar{X}_s - \bar{X}_c)/\bar{X}_c] \times 100$, where $\bar{X}_s$ is the mean in animals given starch paste and $\bar{X}_c$ in stomach tube controls. One asterisk indicates that $\bar{X}_s - \bar{X}_c$ was significant at $P = 0.05$ to 0.02 and two asterisks at $P = 0.01$ or less. (From Boyd and Liu[7] with the permission of the *Canadian Medical Association Journal.*)

was equal to that in water-treated controls and significant only following the larger doses of starch paste. The brain tended to lose more weight in animals given starch paste than in controls given distilled water. Loss of weight in the heart, kidneys, liver, lungs, skeletal muscle, skin, spleen, testes, thymus gland, and residual carcass was also more marked in starch-treated rats than in water-treated controls. The salivary glands lost no weight in water-treated animals.

In brief, loss of wet weight was greater in most organs of starch-treated than of water-treated animals. Gain in weight was more marked in the stomach of water- than of starch-treated animals but less marked in the intestines.

Organ Water Contents

Data on water levels of the organs on which wet weight was recorded are summarized in Table 35. The water content of the intestines tended to be elevated, but that of most other tissues was insignificantly altered in fortnight survivors of large daily doses of starch paste. In most organs of water-treated controls, changes in water levels were similar to those in rats given starch paste. Distilled water alone produced a slight decrease in the water content of the small bowel, colon, kidneys, and liver.

Conclusions Regarding Starch

Starch was found to be relatively nontoxic on

TABLE 35

The Water Content of Body Organs of Albino Rats that Survived 14 Days of Daily Oral Administration of Starch in Doses of from 36 to 288 g/kg/24 hr[a]

Organ	Daily dose of starch (in brackets daily volume of water)		Effect due to distilled water vehicle?
	36–120 g/kg (60–200 ml/kg)	168–288 g/kg (280–480 ml/kg)	
Adrenal glands	− 0.2	− 4.4	Yes
Brain	+ 0.4	− 1.6	Yes
Gastrointestinal tract			
Cardiac stomach	+ 1.7	+ 9.1	Yes
Pyloric stomach	− 1.6	+ 5.1	Yes
Small bowel	+ 3.4	+ 5.4*	No
Cecum	+10.5*	+19.6**	In part
Colon	+ 1.5	+ 5.4*	No
Heart	− 2.0	− 2.0	Yes
Kidneys	− 1.2	− 1.4	No
Liver	+ 1.6	+ 5.1*	No
Lungs	− 0.5	− 2.9	Yes
Muscle (ventral abdominal wall)	− 3.5	− 0.4	Yes
Salivary (submaxillary) glands	− 1.0	− 3.3	Yes
Skin	− 2.0	+ 2.5	Yes
Spleen	+ 0.5	− 1.1	Yes
Testes	− 0.8	− 1.8	Yes
Thymus gland	− 2.0	− 2.7	Yes
Residual carcass	+ 0.9	+ 0.2	Yes

[a]Water content was measured as g water per 100 g dry weight of tissue. The results are expressed as a mean percent change from corresponding values in controls given only daily stomach tube insertions, specifically as $[(\bar{X}_S - \bar{X}_C)/\bar{X}_C] \times 100$, where $\bar{X}_S$ is the mean in rats given starch paste and $\bar{X}_C$ in the controls. One asterisk indicates that $\bar{X}_S - \bar{X}_C$ was significant at P = 0.05 to 0.02 and two asterisks at P = 0.01 or less. (From Boyd and Liu[7] with the permission of the *Canadian Medical Association Journal.*)

oral administration. To produce lethal toxicity in albino rats, starch had to be given as a paste at four intervals during the day and in increasing daily doses. About one tenth of the administered starch was digested and absorbed and the remainder excreted in the feces. The large doses of starch paste produced signs of gastric distension during the first two days. In the first two days, doses of starch of the order of 200 g/kg/24 hr and over produced regurgitation, aspiration into the lungs and asphyxial deaths in some 8% of rats, and gastric rupture in 58%.

In animals that survived initial death due to these mechanical causes, the gastrointestinal tract hypertrophied and was able to accommodate increasing daily doses of starch up to almost half of body weight. The common cause of death at one to two months of daily oral administration of increasing doses of starch paste was bowel obstruction when the intestines could not evacuate large numbers of starch pellets. Pneumonia and a fermentation-like "green skin" reaction were minor causes of death.

Increasing daily doses of starch produced a loss of wet weight with little change in water content of most organs except those of the gastrointestinal tract. Survivors of initial mechanical deaths looked normal but increasing daily doses of starch produced increasing loss of body weight with no change in food intake. There were other signs of systemic toxicity such as minor degrees of pneumonitis, nephritis, and hepatitis. In view of the necessary large doses, it does not appear likely that these types of starch toxicity would occur with any degree of frequency in man.

REFERENCES

1. **Boyd, E. M.,** *Predictive Toxicometrics,* Scientechnica (Publishers) Ltd., Bristol, England, 1972.
2. **Boyd, E. M., Covert, E. L., and Shanas, M. N.,** Death from bowel obstruction due to intragastrically administered kaolin, *Ind. Med. Surg.,* 34, 874, 1965.
3. **Boyd, E. M. and Abel, M.,** The acute toxicity of barium sulfate administered intragastrically, *Can. Med. Assoc. J.,* 94, 849, 1966.
4. **Liu, S.-J.,** The Toxicity of Starch Administered By Mouth, M. Sc. Thesis, Queen's University Library, Queen's University, Kingston, Ontario, Canada, 1968.
5. **Liu, S.-J. and Boyd E. M.,** The toxicity of starch given orally to albino rats, *Proc. Can. Fed. Biol. Soc.,* 10, 49, 1967.
6. **Liu, S.-J. and Boyd, E. M.,** Adaptation of the gastrointestinal tract to increasing bulk of starch administered orally, *Proc. Can. Fed. Biol. Soc.,* 11, 134, 1968.
7. **Boyd, E. M. and Liu, S.-J.,** Toxicity of starch administered by mouth, *Can. Med. Assoc. J.,* 98, 492, 1968.
8. **Herstein, B.,** The centenary of glucose and the early history of starch, *J. Ind. Eng. Chem.,* 3, 158, 1911.
9. **Stecher, P. G., Windholz, M., Leahy, D. S., Bolton, D. M., and Eaton, L. G.,** *The Merck Index. An Encyclopedia of Chemicals and Drugs,* 8th ed., Merck and Company, Inc., Rahway, N. J., 1968.
10. **FAO/WHO,** Toxicological Evaluation of Some Food Colours, Emulsifiers, Stabilizers, Anti-caking Agents, and Certain Other Substances, FAO Nutrition Meetings Report Series No. 46A, WHO/Food Add./70.36, Food and Agriculture Organization and World Health Organization, Geneva, 1970.
11. **FAO/WHO,** Specifications for the Identity and Purity of Some Food Colours, Emulsifiers, Stabilizers, Anti-caking Agents and Certain Other Food Additives, FAO Nutrition Meetings Report Series 46B, WHO/Food Add./70.37, Food and Agriculture Organization and World Health Organization, Geneva, 1970.
12. **Whistler, R. L. and Paschall, E. F.,** Eds., *Starch Chemistry and Technology,* Academic Press, New York, 1965.
13. **Applebaum, S. W.,** Digestion of potato starch by larvae of the flour beetle, *Tribolium castaneum, J. Nutr.,* 90, 235, 1966.
14. **Ugolev, A. N.,** On the existence of membranous (contact) digestion, *Bull. Exp. Biol. Med.,* 49, 12, 1960.
15. **Yoshida, M. and Morimoto, H.,** Utilization of sweet potato starch by rats and its effect on the digestion of dietary protein, *J. Nutr.,* 57, 565, 1955.
16. **Womack, M. and Marshall, M. W.,** Starches, sugars and related factors affecting liver fat and nitrogen balances in adult albino rats fed low levels of amino acids, *J. Nutr.,* 57, 193, 1955.
17. **Harper, A. E., Katayama, M. C., and Jelinek, B.,** The influence of dietary carbohydrates on levels of amino acids in the feces of white rats, *Can. J. Med. Sci.,* 30, 578, 1952.
18. **Booher, L. E., Behan, I., McMeans, E., and Boyd, H. M.,** Biologic utilizations of unmodified and modified food starches, *J. Nutr.,* 45, 75, 1951.
19. **Jelinek, B., Katayama, M. C., and Harper, A. E.,** The inadequacy of unmodified potato starch as dietary carbohydrate for the albino rat, *Can. J. Med. Sci.,* 30, 447, 1952.
20. **Chang, V. O.,** Effect of carbohydrates on utilization of protein and lysine by rats, *J. Nutr.,* 78, 21, 1962.
21. **Bavetta, L. A. and Ershoff, B. H.,** Comparative effects of dietary sucrose and corn starch on tryptophan requirements of the rat, *Proc. Soc. Exp. Biol. Med.,* 90, 349, 1955.
22. **Arena, J. M.,** *Poisoning — Chemistry, Symptoms, Treatments,* Charles C Thomas, Springfield, Ill., 1963.
23. **DiPalma, J. R.,** Ed., *Drill's Pharmacology in Medicine,* 6th ed., McGraw-Hill, New York, 1971.
24. **Czerny, A. D. and Keller, A.,** *Des Kindes Ernährung, Ernährungsstörungen und Ernährungstherapie,* Vol. 2, Franz Deutiche, Leipzig, 1909.
25. News Release, An urge for Argo, *Time* (Canadian ed.), 90, 810, 1967.
26. **Hertz, H.,** Notes on clay and starch eating among Negroes in a southern urban community, *Soc. Forces,* 25, 343, 1947.
27. **Ferguson, J. H. and Keaton, A. G.,** Studies on the diets of pregnant women in Mississippi; the ingestion of clay and laundry starch, *N. Orleans Med. Surg. J.,* 102, 460, 1950.
28. **Edwards, C. H., McDonald, S., Mitchell, J. R., Jones, L., Mason, L., Kemp, A. M., Laing, D., and Trigg, L.,** Clay- and cornstarch-eating women, *J. Am. Diet. Assoc.,* 35, 810, 1959.
29. **Merkatz, I. R.,** Parotid enlargement resulting from excessive ingestion of starch, *N. Engl. J. Med.,* 265, 1304, 1961.
30. **Allan, J. D. and Woodruff, J.,** Starch gastroliths, *N. Engl. J. Med.,* 268, 776, 1963.
31. **Sage, J. C.,** The Practice, Incidence and Effect of Starch Eating in Negro Women at Temple University Medical Center, M. Sc. Thesis, Temple University School of Medicine, Philadelphia, 1962.
32. **Warshauer, S. E.,** Starch eater's anemia, *South. Med. J.,* 59, 538, 1966.
33. **Loveless, M. H.,** Allergy for corn and its derivatives: Experiments with a marked ingestion test for its diagnosis, *J. Allergy,* 21, 500, 1950.
34. **Spielman, A. D.,** Sensitivity to cornstarch, *J. Allergy,* 24, 522, 1953.
35. **Cazort, A. G.,** Clinical experience with objective diagnostic tests on corn sensitivity, *J. Allergy,* 21, 512, 1950.
36. **Anderson, D. H.,** Celiac syndrome. VI. The relation of celiac disease, starch intolerance and steatorrhea, *J. Pediatr.,* 30, 564, 1947.

37. Anderson, C. M., Frazer, A. C., French, J. M., Gerrard, J. W., Sammons, H. G., and Smellie, J. M., Celiac disease: Gastrointestinal studies and the effect of dietary wheat flour, *Lancet,* 1, 836, 1952.
38. McAdams, G. B., Granulomata caused by absorbable starch glove powder, *Surgery,* 39, 329, 1956.
39. Lehman, W. B. and Wilder, J. R., Corn starch granulomatous peritonitis, *J. Abdom. Surg.,* 4, 77, 1962.
40. Fagan, W. G., A case of starch granuloma, *Ir. J. Med. Sci.,* 6, 335, 1965.
41. Howard, P. M. and Maxwell, J. G., Cornstarch granulomatous peritonitis, *Rocky Mt. Med. J.,* 62, 46, 1965.
42. Paine, C. G. and Smith, P., Starch granulomata, *J. Clin. Pathol.,* 10, 51, 1957.
43. Dreisbach, R. H., *Handbook of Poisoning,* 5th ed., Lange Medical Publications, Los Altos, Calif., 1966.
44. Langworthy, C. F. and Deuel, H. J., Digestibility of raw corn, potato and wheat starches, *J. Biol. Chem.,* 42, 27, 1920.
45. Beazell, J. M., Schmidt, C. R., and Ivy, A C., On the digestibility of raw potato starch in man, *J. Nutr.,* 17, 77, 1939.
46. MacDonald, I. and Braithwaite, D. M., The influence of dietary carbohydrates on the lipid pattern in serum and in adipose tissue, *Clin. Sci.,* 27, 23, 1964.
47. Schweigert, B. B., Shaw, J. H., Phillips, P. H., and Elvehjem, C. A., Dental caries in the cotton rat, *J. Nutr.,* 29, 405, 1945.
48. Schweigert, B. B., Potts, E., and Shaw, J. H., Dental caries in the cotton rat, *J. Nutr.,* 32, 405, 1946.
49. Beaton, J. R. and Sangster, J. F., Comparative effects of sucrose and cornstarch in low protein diets fed to rats exposed to cold, *Can. J. Physiol. Pharmacol.,* 43, 241, 1965.
50. Reussner, C., Jr. and Andros, J., Studies on the utilization of various starches and sugars in the rat, *J. Nutr.,* 80, 291, 1963.
51. Lindblad, G., The toxicity of hydroxyethyl starch: investigation in mice, rabbits and dogs, *Proc. Eur. Soc. Stud. Drug Tox.,* 11, 128, 1970.

Chapter 7

CORN OIL

Dietary Fats and Oils

Dietary fats and oils may be selected on the basis of their taste, cost, or fatty acid composition.[1] Fatty acids, in turn, may be classified as saturated, mono-unsaturated and polyunsaturated. Most animal fats are of the saturated variety and most vegetable oils have a large amount of polyunsaturated fatty acids, the latter being indicated in the diet of persons with, or facing the possibility of, coronary heart disease. In Canada, manufacturers are permitted to indicate on the label of vegetable oils the percentage of different types of fatty acids, providing the product contains at least 40% polyunsaturated fatty acids and not more than 20% saturated fatty acids.[1] In the manufacture of margarines, some unsaturated fatty acids are hydrogenated[2,3] and fatty acid composition may be stated on the label if the product contains at least 25% polyunsaturated fatty acids and not more than 20% saturated fatty acids.[1] Shortenings and hydrogenated vegetable oils used as coffee whiteners in general contain very little polyunsaturated fatty acids.[1]

The appearance of arrhythmias in patients with acute myocardial infarction is associated with a rise in the level of free fatty acids in blood.[4,5] Soloff[6] found that the rapid intravenous infusion of long chain saturated, but not of mono-unsaturated or polyunsaturated, fatty acids produced cardiac arrhythmias in dogs.

There have been many studies of the toxic effects of high levels of fats and oils in the diet of animals. Silberberg and Silberberg[7] noted that a high fat diet fed for a life span to mice, beginning during the first year of life, produced earlier than normal deaths. In an earlier publication, Silberberg and Silberberg[30] had found that a high-fat (29%) diet produced an increased incidence of osteoarthritis in mice. Fischer and Kimbel[8] found that about 90% fat fed to rats was absorbed, the balance excreted in the feces as neutral fat, soap, or free fatty acids, and that up to 22.5 g/kg produced no apparent toxic effects. If large amounts of cholesterol are added to a high fat diet, levels of blood cholesterol, but not necessarily of blood phospholipid and neutral fat, are increased in monkeys that develop atherosclerosis.[9] The atherosclerosis was assumed to be due to high dietary cholesterol,[9] but Bruneau, Melik, and Ségal[10] produced atheromatous-like lesions in the aorta of rats fed diets high in fat and protein; there was also a marked fatty degeneration of the liver. Hammerl and Pichler[11] proposed that the presence of vascular lesions predisposes to atherosclerosis in older men who eat diets high in fat.

The toxicity of corn oil was investigated by Boyd, Boulanger, and Carsky[12] and will be discussed later in this chapter. Similar studies were made on cottonseed oil by Boyd and Boulanger[13] and Boyd and Krijnen;[14] these will be described in Chapter 8. Evidence on the toxicity of other dietary fats and oils will be reviewed briefly at this point.

Butter was found to be more toxic than rapeseed oil in studies on male rats conducted by Thomasson.[15] Diets containing butter shortened the life span and produced marked lesions of the liver and kidneys. Orö and Wretlind[16] gave emulsions of fatty acids intravenously to mice and found that the LD_{50} of saturated fatty acids became progressively lower as the length of the carbon chain increased. Stearic acid was ten times more toxic than oleic acid and produced hypotension associated with either hyperpnea or apnea. Orö and Wretlind,[16] therefore, confirmed that saturated fatty acids, particularly long chain fatty acids, were more toxic than unsaturated fatty acids.

Coconut oil is a white, semisolid, lard-like fat that is composed mainly of saturated fatty acids such as those in tripalmitin and tristearin.[17] It has an iodine number of 8 to 10 and is used in making chocolates and candies and in general as a substitute for lard. Pfeifer and Holman[18] reported that feeding rats diets containing large amounts of hydrogenated coconut oil inhibited their growth.

Peanut or arachis oil is composed of 80% or

more of oleic and linoleic acids and has an iodine number of 84 to 102.[19] It is a pale, greenish-yellow oil with a bland taste used commonly as a salad oil.[17] Edgren[20] reported that peanut oil produced fever and other toxic reactions when given intravenously to dogs.

Rapeseed oil is a pale yellow, somewhat viscid liquid, iodine number 97 to 105, which is used in the manufacture of margarines.[17] Thomasson[15] reported that diets containing large amounts of rapeseed oil were tolerated by albino rats better than butter-containing diets. The rapeseed oil, however, produced some slight degeneration of the liver. Beare, Murray, and Campbell[21] found that at 20% of the diet, rapeseed oil inhibited the growth and food intake of weanling rats and sometimes augmented their liver weight. Edgren[20] noted that rapeseed oil given intravenously to dogs produced effects similar to those of peanut oil.

Soybean oil contains 86% unsaturated and 14% saturated fatty acids, with minor amounts of phospholipids and sterols.[17] It is a yellowish substance with a taste that is mildly disagreeable to most persons. It has an iodine number of 127 to 138 and is often mixed with olive oil when used as in foods.[22] Andrews et al.[23] found that oxidation of soybean oil involved formation of peroxides which are readily absorbed from the gastrointestinal tract and tend to inhibit growth at levels of 15 to 20% in the diet.

Corn Oil

Corn oil (maize oil, Mazola® oil) is a by-product in the wet milling of corn for the production of cornstarch, corn syrup, glucose, dextrins, and other substances.[17] It contains about 13% saturated and 83% unsaturated fatty acids, some phospholipids and some sterols, and has an iodine number of 109 to 133.[17] It is used as a salad oil, cooking oil, and as a source of dietary polyunsaturated fatty acids in medicine. Beare, Murray, and Campbell[21] found that corn oil heated to 200°C for 2 hr had no effect on growth when fed to rats at a level of 10% in the diet, but did retard growth at dietary levels of 20%. Caster et al.[24] concluded that the optimal amount of corn oil was 3% in the diet of male albino rats; smaller or larger dietary concentrations (up to 10%) inhibited hepatic detoxification of agents such as hexobarbital and heptachlor. Stohlman[25] found that corn oil produced measurable toxic effects in rabbits given oral doses of 10 to 15 ml/kg. Baron, Casterline, and Fitzhugh[26] reported measurable toxic effects in mice given similar doses intraperitoneally.

The acute oral toxicity of corn oil was studied in young male albino rats by Boyd, Boulanger, and Carsky.[12] In preliminary trials, it was found that single doses in excess of 70 to 80 ml/kg given by intragastric tube were not lethal and were evacuated through the anus shortly after oral administration. A dose of corn oil was, therefore, given once in 24 hr repeated daily for five days, the doses selected being 0, 20, 30, 40, 50, 60, 70, 80, 90, and 100 ml/kg/24 hr or total doses of from 100 to 500 ml/kg. Clinical signs and measurements of toxicity were recorded each day during, and for two weeks and one month after cessation of, administration of corn oil. Gross and microscopic pathology and the weight and water content of body organs were noted at death when an autopsy could be performed within 1 hr of death to avoid postmortem changes reported by Boyd and Knight.[27]

The Acute Oral LD$_{50}$ (5 days)

There were no deaths in control albino rats given no corn oil. In amounts up to 60 ml/kg/24 hr or a total of up to 300 ml/kg over five days, deaths occurred following the fourth and fifth administration with no further deaths during the fortnight following cessation of administration of corn oil. When the daily dose was increased to 70 ml/kg/24 hr and over, delayed deaths occurred over a period of four days following cessation of administration of corn oil.

Corn oil which was evacuated through the anus shortly after oral administration was collected and measured. The volume of immediately evacuated corn oil was 7.1% of doses of 60 ml/kg/24 hr and increased to 15.9% of doses of 100 ml/kg/24 hr. These immediately evacuated amounts were subtracted from the total dose of corn oil administered by stomach tube over five days in arriving at estimates of the acute oral LD$_{50}$ (5 days). The term LD$_{50}$ (5 days) indicates that the oil was given in equal daily amounts for five days in contrast to the usual median lethal dose which is an LD$_{50}$ (1 dose). Since it is possible that some detoxification of corn oil occurred during the five days of administration, the LD$_{50}$ (5 days) may be somewhat higher than the calculated median lethal dose. Other factors in estimates of the median lethal dose have been reviewed by Boyd.[28]

The LD_{50} (5 days) ± S. E. was found to be 279 ± 31 ml/kg or 256 ± 28 g/kg. The maximal LD_0 (5 days), or largest dose given in five equal parts daily for five days that killed no rats, was estimated at 89 g/kg. The maximal LD_0 (5 days) is approximately equivalent to the LD_1 (5 days). The minimal LD_{100} (5 days), or smallest dose given in the same manner which killed all of the animals, was estimated to be 393 g/kg. The minimal LD_{100} is often referred to as the LD_{99}.

Clinical Signs and Measurements

Data on the clinical signs and measurements of toxicity are summarized in Table 36. Doses in the range of the oral LD_{50} (5 days) produced a daily loss of body weight which increased up to the third day and then declined slightly in survivors as the fourth day of oral administration of corn oil. Food (laboratory chow) intake progressively fell to some two fifths of that in controls during the first 24 hr and to 15 to 20% of amounts in controls on the third and fourth days. The controls ate laboratory chow at the rate of some 350 kcal/kg/24 hr. At the oral LD_{50} (5 days), the animals were given some 400 to 500 kcal/kg/24 hr in the form of corn oil, which was obviously not digested, absorbed, and utilized as a source of calories. Loss of body weight, therefore, appeared to be due to inability to utilize the corn oil, to diarrhea, to a slight increase in body temperature (Table 36), and possibly to a relatively increased need for calories in animals with reduced food intake, as noted by Peters.[29]

Inhibition of growth and anorexia from corn oil were associated with an oligodipsia, which was most marked in the first 24 hr as indicated in Table 36. Oliguria became progressively more marked at each succeeding day of administration of corn oil in doses at the range of the oral LD_{50} (5 days). There was also a hematuria during

TABLE 36

The Clinical Signs of Toxicity in Young Male Albino Rats Given Corn Oil in Doses at the Range of the LD_{50} (5 days)[a]

Clinical sign	24 hr	48 hr	72 hr	96 hr
Daily change in body weight: g	−156.1	−167.6	−181.5	−113.4
Food (chow) intake: g/kg/day	− 62.4	− 79.7	− 85.6	− 82.0
Water intake: ml/kg/day	− 60.2	− 39.7	− 44.6	− 47.3
Colonic temperature: °F	+ 0.8	+ 0.8	N.S.	− 1.2
Urinary volume: ml/kg/day	− 62.0	− 62.9	− 71.5	− 76.3
Urinary pH: 24 hr sample	− 18.1	− 24.6	− 19.3	− 19.2
Urinary blood (high doses only): units/kg/day	+223.6	N.S.	N.S.	N.S.
Diarrhea: clinical units	1.3	2.1	2.2	2.3
Soiling of hair: clinical units	1.1	1.8	2.3	2.4
Epistaxis: clinical units	1.6	1.8	1.8	1.3
Listlessness: clinical units	0.9	1.4	2.6	2.7
Pallor: clinical units	1.2	2.1	2.9	3.2
Ataxia: clinical units	1.0	1.6	2.2	2.5
Cyanosis: clinical units	0.1	0.9	1.5	2.0
Prostration: clinical units	0.0	0.8	1.4	1.5

[a]The results, except for those measured in "clinical units," are expressed as mean percent change from controls, specifically as $[(\bar{X}_O - \bar{X}_C)/\bar{X}_C] \times 100$, where $\bar{X}_O$ is the mean in rats given corn oil and $\bar{X}_C$ in the controls given no corn oil. Signs measured in "clinical units" are expressed as $\bar{X}_O - \bar{X}_C$ since $\bar{X}_C$ was zero or very close to zero. For each parameter, $\bar{X}_O - \bar{X}_C$ was significant at $P = 0.02$ or less except when indicated by N.S. (not significant). The measured value of each clinical sign increased significantly with administration of increasing amounts of corn oil. (From Boyd et al.[12] with the permission of *The Journal of Clinical Pharmacology*.)

the first 24 hr and an aciduria during the first four days. These signs were accompanied by diarrhea, hair soiling, epistaxis, listlessness, pallor, ataxia, cyanosis, and prostration, all of which, except epistaxis, became more marked during each succeeding day of administration of corn oil.

The premortem signs included complete anorexia, adipsia, marked oliguria or anuria, and marked loss of body weight. These signs were associated with proteinuria, hemorhinorrhea, and hemodacryorrhea. Death was due to respiratory failure with the animal in a deep hypothermic coma.[12]

Gross and Microscopic Pathology

The main features on gross examination of body organs at autopsy following death of albino rats due to oral administration of corn oil were ulcers in the cardiac stomach, pyloric stomach, and cecum. The brain and lungs were markedly congested and the kidneys were pale. There was a stressor atrophy of the spleen and thymus gland.

Histopathological findings are summarized in Table 37. Lethal oral doses of corn oil produced a local irritant inflammatory reaction in the tissues lining the entire gastrointestinal tract. There were also infiltrative ulcers in cardiac stomach and necrotic ulcers in pyloric stomach and cecum. There was evidence that corn oil was absorbed as droplets through the inflamed mucosa of the gastrointestinal tract and that these droplets became deposited in various tissues such as the brain, kidneys, lungs, and salivary glands. An example of microscopic oil droplets in the base of edematous tubular cells of the kidney is shown in Figure 35. Systemically, corn oil produced capillary-venous congestion, sometimes with hemorrhage, in many body organs such as the brain, meninges, heart, kidneys, liver, lungs, and thymus gland, as indicated in Table 37.

The interval of oral administration of corn oil was sufficiently long to permit development of histologically evident degenerative changes in many body organs. In the kidneys there appeared cloudy swelling of the tubules from all doses and necrosis from large doses. The hepatic cells were edematous and shrunken. There was a deficiency of zymogenic granules in the serous salivary glands. Areas of necrosis appeared in skin, and the testes exhibited inhibition of spermatogenesis. There was a stress reaction in the adrenal glands, spleen, and thymus gland. Thrombosis was noted in some organs, as in the pulmonary arterioles exemplified in Figure 36.

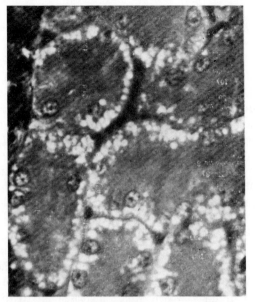

FIGURE 35. A photomicrograph of the kidney of an albino rat that died following oral administration on the fifth day of daily administration of corn oil in a dose of 90 ml/kg/24 hr, showing numerous oil droplets at the base of edematous tubular cells. (From Boyd et al.[12] with the permission of *The Journal of Clinical Pharmacology*.)

FIGURE 36. A photomicrograph of the lung of an albino rat that died on the fourth day of daily oral administration of corn oil in a dose of 80 ml/kg/24 hr, showing thrombosis in a medium-sized artery and marked vascular congestion and hemorrhage of the lung parenchyma. (From Boyd et al.[12] with the permission of *The Journal of Clinical Pharmacology*.)

TABLE 37

Histopathological Observations at Autopsy on Albino Rats that Died from Oral Administration of Corn Oil in Doses at the Range of the LD_{50} (5 days)

Organ	Histopathology
Adrenal glands	Lipoid droplets prominent in zona glomerulosa, zona fasciculata, and zona reticularis
Brain	Capillary-venous congestion of the brain and meninges; oil droplets in many areas of the brain
Gastrointestinal tract	
Cardiac stomach	Capillary-venous congestion of the lamina propria and submucosa with granulocyte infiltration and ulcer formation
Pyloric stomach	Capillary-venous congestion of the lamina propria and submucosa and some necrosis of the gastric gland tips
Small bowel	Varying degrees of capillary-venous congestion of the lamina propria and submucosa with oil droplets in the lamina
Cecum	Capillary-venous congestion of the lamina propria and submucosa with some necrosis of the mucosa
Colon	Capillary-venous congestion of the lamina propria and submucosa; goblet cells mostly empty
Heart	Capillary congestion and occasionally capillary hemorrhage
Kidneys	Capillary-venous congestion, occasionally with hemorrhages and thrombosis; tubular cloudy swelling from small doses and necrosis from large doses; many oil droplets at the base of proximal and distal tubules
Liver	Sinusoidal congestion and cloudy swelling or shrinkage of hepatic cells
Lungs	Capillary-venous congestion and inflammation occasionally with hemorrhage and thromboses in arterioles and veins; oil droplets in blood of some veins
Muscle (ventral abdominal wall)	Normal appearance
Salivary (submaxillary) glands	Serous glands shrunken and zymogenic granules deficient; capillary congestion; oil droplets prominent
Skin	Occasional areas of necrosis of the epidermis
Spleen	Reticulum contained oil droplets, debris and few erythrocytes
Testes	Minor inhibition of spermatogenesis; very few normal sperm present
Thymus gland	Capillary-venous congestion and loss of thymocytes

(From Boyd et al.[12] with the permission of *The Journal of Clinical Pharmacology.*)

Organ Weights and Water Levels

The weight of body organs was measured, in grams, at death, in survivors at two weeks after the start of oral administration of corn oil, and in survivors at one month. Means and standard deviations were calculated; the means were expressed as a percent change from corresponding means in controls given no corn oil and the statistical significance of differences between mean results in survivors and controls determined. The resulting data are collected in Table 38.

The mean loss of body weight at death due to corn oil was 19.3% of body weight in the controls. Loss of body weight was due mostly to loss of weight in skeletal muscle and skin. Loss of weight similar to that in muscle and skin occurred in some organs such as liver, lungs, and salivary glands. Loss of weight was somewhat less in the several parts of the gastrointestinal tract and there was a gain in weight of cardiac stomach due to the presence of large, infiltrated ulcers. Minor or insignificant changes in weight were present in brain, heart, kidneys, and testes. There was a stressor gain in weight of the adrenal glands and marked loss of weight in the spleen and thymus gland.

In survivors at two weeks, there tended to be a rebound gain in weight that was statistically significant in several instances. Most gain in weight was found in the small bowel, cecum, kidneys, liver, salivary glands, and spleen.

In survivors at one month after the beginning of

TABLE 38

Shifts in the Fresh Wet Weight of Body Organs of Young Male Albino Rats Following Oral Administration of Corn Oil in Doses at the Range of the LD_{50} (5 days)[a]

Organ	At death (N = 13 plus 16 controls)	Survivors at two weeks (N = 16 plus 16 controls)	Survivors at one month (N = 16 plus 14 controls)
Adrenal glands	+38.1**	+13.6	+ 6.7
Brain	+ 7.6*	+ 5.5	+ 3.3
Gastrointestinal tract			
Cardiac stomach	+54.2**	+ 7.1	+ 3.2
Pyloric stomach	−11.7*	+ 2.5	+ 3.1
Small bowel	−12.0*	+12.5*	+ 0.8
Cecum	−16.9**	+17.9**	+ 8.2
Colon	−12.0*	+ 4.8	+10.0*
Heart	+ 4.8	+ 5.1	− 0.9
Kidneys	− 4.1	+ 9.5*	+ 3.9
Liver	−25.6**	+14.3**	− 0.7
Lungs	−30.5**	+ 3.1	− 6.2
Muscle (ventral abdominal wall)	−37.9**	+ 3.3	− 2.4
Salivary (submaxillary) glands	−23.3**	+10.2*	+ 2.1
Skin	−17.7**	+ 3.3	+ 0.3
Spleen	−69.1**	+19.4**	− 4.2
Testes	− 7.2*	+ 9.0*	− 4.6
Thymus gland	−75.7**	− 2.0	− 2.1
Residual carcass	−28.8**	+ 5.6	− 2.0
Autopsy body weight	−19.3**	+ 5.4	+ 1.1

[a]Fresh weight was measured in grams. The results are expressed as mean percent change from controls, specifically as $[(\bar{X}_{CO} - \bar{X}_C)/\bar{X}_C] \times 100$, where $\bar{X}_{CO}$ is the mean in animals given corn oil and $\bar{X}_C$ in their corresponding controls. One asterisk indicates that $\bar{X}_{CO} - \bar{X}_C$ was significant at P = 0.05 to 0.02 and two asterisks at P = 0.01 or less. (From Boyd et al.[12] with the permission of *The Journal of Clinical Pharmacology*.)

oral administration of lethal doses of corn oil, the weight of practically all body organs was within the statistical limits of that in controls. Individual results are listed in Table 38.

Shifts in the water levels of the same body organs are indicated in Table 39. The most common change at death was dehydration so that some of the loss of weight noted in Table 38 could have been due to loss of organ water content. Loss of water in residual carcass averaged 13.6% of values in controls given no corn oil. Similar degrees of dehydration occurred in organs such as cardiac stomach, cecum, kidneys, lungs, skeletal muscle, salivary glands, spleen, and testes. The dehydration was somewhat more marked in lungs, skin, and thymus gland. There was a slight hydration of the adrenal glands and insignificant alterations in the

water content of other organs listed in Table 39. The water levels of most organs were within normal limits in survivors at two weeks and of all organs in survivors at one month.

In brief, oral administration of lethal doses of corn oil to albino rats produced dehydration and loss of weight in most body organs at death. Survivors recovered rather quickly, were almost normal at two weeks after the start of oral administration of corn oil, and were quite normal at one month. There were no delayed deaths in survivors.

Conclusions Regarding Corn Oil

The cumulative median lethal dose of corn oil given orally to young male albino rats in equal daily doses over a period of five successive days, or

TABLE 39

Shifts in the Water Levels of Body Organs of Young Male Albino Rats Following Oral Administration of Corn Oil in Doses at the Range of the LD_{50} (5 days)[a]

Organ	At death (N = 13 plus 16 controls)	Survivors at two weeks (N = 16 plus 16 controls)	Survivors at one month (N = 16 plus 14 controls)
Adrenal glands	+ 6.2*	−0.4	−9.1
Brain	− 3.6	+0.5	+3.7
Gastrointestinal tract			
Cardiac stomach	− 7.2*	−3.0	+0.3
Pyloric stomach	− 5.7	+1.2	+1.7
Small bowel	+11.3*	−1.1	+6.0
Cecum	− 8.1*	−1.7	+2.4
Colon	−11.4**	+2.3	+0.7
Heart	− 0.9	+4.1	+2.4
Kidneys	−15.3**	+6.6*	+1.3
Liver	+ 2.4	−1.8	+0.4
Lungs	−23.1**	+2.8	+8.0
Muscle (ventral abdominal wall)	− 8.8*	+1.9	+2.7
Salivary (submaxillary) glands	−10.4*	−0.7	−0.7
Skin	−32.0**	−1.1	−6.5
Spleen	−15.6**	−2.0	−1.4
Testes	− 5.6*	+9.0**	+0.2
Thymus gland	−37.2**	+4.4	+0.4
Residual carcass	−13.6**	+0.8	+0.9

[a]Water content was measured as grams water per 100 g dry weight of tissue. The results are expressed as mean percent change from controls, specifically as $[(\bar{X}_{co} - \bar{X}_c)/\bar{X}_c] \times 100$, where $\bar{X}_{co}$ is the mean in animals given corn oil and $\bar{X}_c$ in their corresponding controls. One asterisk indicates that $\bar{X}_{co} - \bar{X}_c$ was significant at P = 0.05 to 0.02 and two asterisks at P = 0.01 or less.

(From Boyd et al.[12] with the permission of *The Journal of Clinical Pharmacology*.)

LD_{50} (5 days) ± S. E., was 256 ± 28 g/kg. The estimated maximal LD_0 (5 days) was 89 g/kg and the minimal LD_{100} (5 days) was 393 g/kg.

Clinical signs of toxicity included anorexia, loss of body weight, oligodipsia, a slight fever, oliguria, aciduria, hematuria, diarrhea, fur soiling, epistaxis, listlessness, pallor, ataxia, cyanosis, and prostration. Death was due to respiratory failure following a period of deep hypothermic coma.

At autopsy it was found that lethal oral doses of corn oil had produced a violent local irritant gastroenteritis which apparently permitted absorption into the bloodstream of tiny droplets of corn oil. These droplets were seen in many body organs and were apparently responsible for inflammatory reactions, circulatory stasis and thrombosis, hemorrhage, dehydration, loss of organ weight, degenerative changes in many organs, and a stress reaction. Recovery was rapid in survivors.

Many fats and oils have been reported to inhibit growth and to produce a variety of toxic effects in laboratory animals when fed at high levels (about 25% and over) in the diet. This amount of fat or oil, given separately, would approximate the LD_{50} (5 days).

REFERENCES

1. FDD, Labelling of Fats and Oils, FDD Dispatch, No 12, Food and Drug Directorate, Department of National Health and Welfare, Ottawa, 1971.
2. Beare, J. L., Tovell, D., and Murray, T. K., The total cis-methylene-interrupted fatty acids in Canadian margarines, *Can. Med. Assoc. J.*, 93, 1219, 1965.
3. Beare, J. L., Heroux, C., and Murray, T. K., Variation in polyunsaturates of special margarines, *Can. Med. Assoc. J.*, 96, 1575, 1967.
4. Oliver, M. F., Kurien, V. A., and Greenwood, T. W., Relation between serum-free-fatty-acids and arrhythmias and death after acute myocardial infarction, *Lancet,* 1, 710, 1968.
5. Rutenberg, H. L., Pamintuan, J. C., and Soloff, L. A., Serum-free-fatty-acids and their relation to complications after acute myocardial infarction, *Lancet,* 2, 559, 1969.
6. Soloff, L. A., Arrhythmias following infusions of fatty acids, *Am. Heart J.*, 80, 671, 1970.
7. Silberberg, R. and Silberberg, M., Life span of mice fed a high fat diet at various ages, *Can. J. Biochem. Physiol.*, 33, 167, 1955.
8. Fischer, W. and Kimbel, R. H., Die Nahrungsfettbilanz der Ratte, *Z. Gesamte Exp. Med.*, 125, 426, 1955.
9. Cox, G. E., Taylor, B., Cox, L. G., and Counts, M. A., Atherosclerosis in rhesus monkeys. I. Hypercholesterolemia induced by dietary fat and cholesterol, *Arch. Pathol.*, 66, 32, 1958.
10. Bruneau, M., Melik, T., and Ségal, V., Actions d'un régime hyperlipidique sur la biochimie et l'histologie des divers organes du rat blanc, *J. Physiol.* (Paris), 49, 72, 1957.
11. Hammerl, H. and Pichler, O., Verhalten der Serumlipide unter alimentarer Fettbelastung, *Wien. Klin. Wochenschr.*, 71, 351, 1959.
12. Boyd, E. M., Boulanger, M. A., and Carsky, E., The acute oral toxicity of corn oil, *J. Clin. Pharmacol.*, 9, 137, 1969.
13. Boyd, E. M. and Boulanger, M. A., Acute oral toxicity of cottonseed oil, *Toxicol. Appl. Pharmacol.*, 14, 432, 1969.
14. Boyd, E. M. and Krijnen, C. J., Intolerance to cottonseed oil in rats fed a low protein diet, *Food Cosmet. Toxicol.*, 9, 389, 1971.
15. Thomasson, H. J., The biological value of oils and fats. III. The longevity of rats fed rapeseed oil – or butterfat-containing diets, *J. Nutr.*, 57, 17, 1955.
16. Orö, L. and Wretlind, A., Pharmacological effects of fatty acids, triolein and cottonseed oil, *Acta Pharmacol. Toxicol.*, 18, 141, 1961.
17. Stecher, P. G., Windholz, M., Leahy, D. S., Bolton, D. M., and Eaton, L. G., *The Merck Index. An Encyclopedia of Chemicals and Drugs*, 8th ed., Merck and Company, Inc., Rahway, N.J., 1968.
18. Pfeifer, J. J. and Holman, R. T., Effect of saturated fat upon essential fatty acid metabolism of the rat, *J. Nutr.*, 68, 155, 1959.
19. Eckey, E. W., *Vegetable Fats and Oils,* Reinhold, New York, 1954.
20. Edgren, B., Tolerance of the dog to intravenous fat emulsions, *Acta Pharmacol. Toxicol.*, 16, 260, 1960.
21. Beare, J. L., Murray, T. K., and Campbell, J. A., Effects of varying proportions of dietary rapeseed oil on the rat, *Can. J. Biochem. Physiol.*, 35, 1225, 1957.
22. Cowan, J. C., *Encyclopedia of Chemical Technology*, Vol. 12, Interscience, New York, 1954, 689.
23. Andrews, J. S., Griffith, W. H., Mead, J. F., and Stein, R. A., Toxicity of air-oxidized soybean oil, *J. Nutr.*, 70, 198, 1960.

24.   **Caster, W. O., Wade, A. E., Greene, F. E., and Medows, J. S.,** Effect of different levels of corn oil in the diet upon the rate of hexobarbital, heptachlor and aniline metabolism in the liver of the male white rat, *Life Sci.,* 9, 181, 1970.

25.   **Stohlman, E. F.,** The effects of corn oil and olive oil on the blood sugar and rectal temperature of rabbits, *J. Pharmacol. Exp. Ther.,* 93, 346, 1948.

26.   **Baron, R. L., Casterline, J. L., Jr., and Fitzhugh, O. G.,** Specificity of carbamate-induced esterase inhibition in mice, *Toxicol. Appl. Pharmacol.,* 6, 402, 1964.

27.   **Boyd, E. M. and Knight, L. M.,** Postmortem shifts in the weight and water levels of body organs, *Toxicol. Appl. Pharmacol.,* 5, 119, 1963.

28.   **Boyd, E. M.,** *Predictive Toxicometrics,* Scientechnica (Publishers) Ltd., Bristol, England, 1972.

29.   **Peters, J. M.,** Caffeine toxicity in starved rats, *Toxicol. Appl. Pharmacol.,* 9, 390, 1966.

30.   **Silberberg, M. and Silberberg, R.,** Degenerative joint disease in mice fed a high-fat diet at various ages, *Exp. Med. Surg.,* 10, 77, 1952.

Chapter 8

COTTONSEED OIL

Cottonseed oil is obtained from the seeds of *Gossypium herbaceum* L. It is a pale yellow almost odorless oil, with an iodine number of 105 to 114, and is used as a salad oil and medically as a source of polyunsaturated fatty acids.[1] Kaunitz et al.[2] reported that large amounts of fresh oil in the diet were nontoxic to rats but that heat and aeration polymerized the oil and caused death within three weeks at levels of 15 to 20% of the diet. Edgren[3] reported that cottonseed oil given intravenously as an emulsion to dogs produced no toxic effects in doses up to 3 g/kg/day and in some dogs to 6 g/kg/day. Doses over 6 g/kg/day produced lesions in the liver and death. Orö and Wretlind[4] found the intravenous LD_{50} of cottonseed oil to be in excess of 15 g/kg in mice. Munro et al.[5] noted that young male albino rats tolerated daily oral doses of cottonseed oil in the amount of 5 ml/kg. When brominated to produce a density adjusting food additive for use in citrus flavored beverages, cottonseed oil produced a variety of toxic effects.

Boyd and Boulanger[6] reported the lethal toxicity of cottonseed oil given by intragastric cannula to young male albino rats weighing 167 ± 8 g (mean ± standard deviation) and fed Purina laboratory chow checkers. In pilot studies it was found that single oral doses of 100 ml/kg produced signs of toxicity but no deaths. The dose of 100 ml/kg was then repeated at hourly intervals but the bulk of the second and subsequent doses was immediately evacuated through the anus. Further trials indicated that doses repeated at intervals of 24 hr were largely retained or at least not all immediately evacuated through the anus. When repeated at intervals of 24 hr, deaths appeared on the third and fourth days. It was also noted in pilot tests that rats given large doses of cottonseed oil became extremely agitated when aggregated and that many of them died when aggregated but not when segregated, one to a cage.

In definitive tests, therefore, each rat was placed singly in a metabolism cage with food and water available ad libitum. Cottonseed oil was given by stomach tube to unstarved animals in daily doses of from 50 to 110 ml/kg for four days

or in cumulative four-day doses of from 200 to 440 ml/kg. Clinical signs were recorded daily and autopsies were performed on each animal that could be autopsied within 1 hr of death to avoid postmortem changes described by Boyd and Knight.[7] All survivors were chloroformed on day five and the weight and water content of body organs determined. The $LD_{50 \ (4 \ days)}$ was calculated by the linear regression method of Boyd[8] and the statistical significance of differences between means by the technique of Croxton.[9]

The $LD_{50 \ (4 \ days)}$

When cottonseed oil was given as single doses in excess of 60 ml/kg, or as a cumulative four-day dose in excess of 240 ml/kg, appreciable amounts of the oil were evacuated through the anus within a few minutes of intragastric administration. These results are illustrated in Figure 37 together with death rates. The total of cottonseed oil evacuated through the anus immediately following intragastric administration extended from 2 ml/kg following a dose of 50 ml/kg/24 hr repeated once a day for four daily doses to 90 ml/kg at 110 ml/kg/24 hr. Expressed as a percentage of the administered dose, the amount immediately evacuated fell within the ranges of 1 and 20%, as indicated in Figure 37.

In arriving at an estimate of the oral $LD_{50 \ (4 \ days)}$ the total amount immediately evacuated was subtracted from the total dose given by stomach tube over a period of four days. The $LD_{50 \ (4 \ days)}$ ± S.E. was calculated in this manner to be 275 ± 22 ml/kg or 252 ± 20 g/kg. All deaths occurred on days three and four of administration of cottonseed oil, the larger the dose, the shorter the interval to death. Corresponding estimates of the maximal $LD_{0 \ (4 \ days)}$ were 166 g/kg and of the minimal $LD_{100 \ (4 \ days)}$ 284 g/kg. It will be noted that the range of lethal doses of cottonseed oil, from the maximal $LD_{0 \ (4 \ days)}$ to the minimal $LD_{100 \ (4 \ days)}$, was considerably more narrow than that of corn oil described in Chapter 7.

Clinical Signs at the Range of the $LD_{50 \ (4 \ days)}$

The intensity of the clinical signs of toxicity to

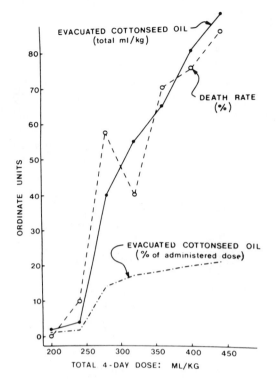

FIGURE 37. The regression, on cumulative four-day dose of cottonseed oil, of death rates and amount of oil immediately evacuated through the anus following oral administration to albino rats. The ordinate units indicate percentage mortality and total ml/kg of cottonseed oil or percent of administered oral dose of cottonseed oil immediately evacuated through the anus. (From Boyd and Boulanger[6] with the permission of *Toxicology and Applied Pharmacology,* copyright © 1969, Academic Press, New York.)

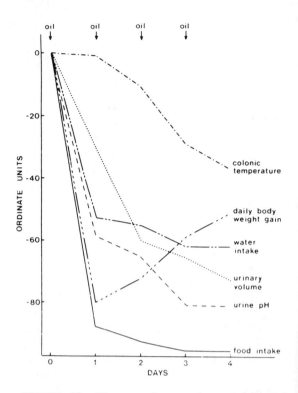

FIGURE 38. The regression, on days of daily oral administration of cottonseed oil in doses at the range of the LD_{50} (4 days) in young albino rats, of **mean** differences in colonic temperature (F = 0.01), daily **grams** change in body weight (F = 4.0), daily water intake as ml/kg/24 hr (F = 1.0), daily urinary volume as ml/kg/24 hr (F = 1.0), daily urinary pH of the 24-hr sample (F = 0.1), and daily food intake as g chow/kg/24 hr (F = 1.0). Mean differences are expressed as a mean percent change from corresponding values in controls, specifically as $[(\bar{X}_O - \bar{X}_c)/\bar{X}_c] \times 100$, where $\bar{X}_O$ is the mean in cottonseed oil-treated rats and $\bar{X}_c$ in controls given no cottonseed oil. The value on the ordinate unit scale is multiplied by the factor indicated in parenthesis after each measurement (F number) to obtain the mean percent change from controls in that measurement. All values of $\bar{X}_O - \bar{X}_c$ in Figure 38 were statistically significant at P = 0.01 or less. (From Boyd and Boulanger[6] with the permission of *Toxicology and Applied Pharmacology,* copyright © 1969, Academic Press, New York.)

cottonseed oil, in doses at the range of the oral LD_{50} (4 days), was dose dependent. The signs were similar to those recorded for corn oil toxicity and described in Chapter 7. They included pallor, listlessness, diarrhea, cyanosis, epistaxis, ataxia, and dyspnea.

Significant effects of cottonseed oil on clinical measurements are indicated in Figure 38. There occurred a hypothermia, oligodipsia, oliguria, aciduria, and anorexia that became progressively more marked on each succeeding day of administration of cottonseed oil. The daily gain in body weight of the controls was replaced by a loss that averaged some three times the gain in the controls at 24 hr. There was less loss of body weight on days three and four, possibly because means on these days included only survivors of cottonseed oil lethality. On the fourth day, colonic temperature had decreased by a mean of 4% from values

in the controls expressed as °F. Urinary volume on the fourth day had decreased by a mean of some 75% and urinary pH by a mean of 8%. There were no significant changes in the urinary output of protein, glucose, or occult blood produced by cottonseed oil.

Autopsy Findings at the Oral LD_{50} (4 days)

Autopsy data are summarized in Table 40. Lethal oral doses of cottonseed oil produced

TABLE 40

Changes in the Wet Weight and Water Content of Body Organs and Histopathologic Observations in Albino Rats Given Amounts of Cottonseed Oil in the Range of the Oral Median Lethal Dose

Organ	Changes in wet weight[a]	Changes in water content[a]	Histopathology
Adrenal glands	+ 0.1	− 4.1	Normal appearance; occasionally oil droplets
Brain	− 0.7	− 0.7	Capillary-venous congestion of meninges and brain; capillary hemorrhages; lysis of erythrocytes; fine oil droplets in areas of brain
Gastrointestinal tract			
Cardiac stomach	+11.8**	−14.9**	Capillary-venous congestion of lamina propria and submucosa; hemorrhage; large ulcers infiltrated with leukocytes
Pyloric stomach	−21.3**	− 7.5**	Capillary-venous congestion of lamina propria and submucosa; small hemorrhages; small degenerative ulcers
Small bowel	− 7.7*	− 5.6*	Hyperemia; columnar epithelium of villi packed with small oil droplets
Cecum	−27.0**	−11.9**	Capillary-venous congestion; Lieberkühn's glands packed with oil droplets
Colon	−25.7**	− 8.5**	Hyperemia; goblet cells prominent
Heart	−12.5**	− 6.1**	Capillary-venous dilatation and stasis; lysis of erythrocytes; capillary hemorrhages
Kidneys	− 9.7**	−6.4*	Capillary-venous congestion; lysis of erythrocytes; capillary hemorrhage; cloudy swelling and fatty degeneration of proximal and distal tubules
Liver	−30.4**	− 3.0	Oil droplets in hepatic cells; lysed erythrocytes
Lungs	−15.2**	−18.3**	Capillary-venous congestion; capillary hemorrhage; lysis of erythrocytes

TABLE 40 (Continued)

Organ	Changes in wet weight[a]	Changes in water content[a]	Histopathology
Mesentery-omentum			Capillary-venous congestion
Muscle (ventral abdominal wall)	−39.0**	− 7.4*	Cross-striation (A discs) weak
Pancreas			Hyperemia; acinar glands shrunken; oil droplets; islets normal
Salivary (submaxillary) glands	−44.4**	− 8.9**	Serous glands shrunken; lysis of erythrocytes
Skin	−14.7**	−28.1**	Normal histology
Spleen	−63.2**	−10.4**	Contracted red pulp; lysed erythrocytes
Testes	−14.2**	− 4.1*	Interstitial hyperemia
Thymus gland	−71.4**	−26.6**	Vascular congestion, lysed erythrocytes; loss of thymocytes
Residual carcass	−22.4**	−16.5**	
Autopsy body weight	−20.4**		

[a]Wet weight was measured in grams and water content in grams of water per 100 g dry weight of tissue. The results are expressed as mean percent change from controls, specifically as $[(\overline{X}_o - \overline{X}_c)/\overline{X}_c]$ x 100, where $\overline{X}_o$ is the mean in the oil-treated rat and $\overline{X}_c$ in the corresponding control. One asterisk indicates that $X_o - \overline{X}_c$ was significant at $P = 0.05$ to 0.02 and two asterisks at $P = 0.01$ or less.

(From Boyd and Boulanger[6] with the permission of *Toxicology and Applied Pharmacology,* copyright © 1969, Academic Press, New York.)

changes which were similar to those produced by corn oil and noted in Chapter 7. There was a marked local irritant inflammatory reaction in the tissues lining the entire gastrointestinal tract. This resulted in dehydration and loss of wet weight in the pyloric stomach, small bowel, cecum, and colon. The weight of cardiac stomach was increased due to the presence of large ulcers heavily infiltrated with white blood cells. There were small necrotic ulcers in the pyloric stomach.

The inflamed intestinal mucosa appeared to allow cottonseed oil to be absorbed as such in the form of tiny microscopic oil droplets. These droplets could be seen in the villi of the small intestine and in Lieberkühn's glands of the cecum. Following absorption into the bloodstream, tiny droplets of cottonseed oil could be noted microscopically in tissues such as the adrenal glands, brain, liver, and pancreas. The presence of oil droplets may have been responsible for a widespread inflammation, with or without capillary

hemorrhage, of body organs such as the brain, meninges, heart, kidneys, lungs, mesentery-omentum, pancreas, and thymus gland. The presence of oil droplets in blood appeared to be responsible for extensive lysis of the erythrocytes seen in organs such as the brain, heart, kidneys, liver, salivary glands, spleen, and thymus gland.

The long duration of oral administration of cottonseed oil permitted the development of histological evidence of degeneration in organs such as the kidneys, skeletal muscle, and the pancreatic acinar glands. There was a stress reaction in the adrenal glands, spleen, and thymus gland.

Loss of weight was most marked in the liver, skeletal muscle, salivary glands, spleen, and thymus gland. There was no significant change in the weight of adrenal glands and brain and small losses in other organs.

All tissues exhibited dehydration at death. Loss of water was not quite statistically significant in adrenal glands, brain, and liver and was most marked in cardiac stomach, cecum, lungs, skin, spleen, thymus gland, and residual carcass.

Cottonseed Oil Toxicity and One Third Optimal Protein Intake

Boyd and Horne[10] studied the influence of daily oral administration of a large dose of cottonseed oil to albino rats fed for 100 days from weaning on a diet containing one third of the optimal daily intake of protein. The work was part of a project designed to measure the toxicity of the fungicide captan which was dissolved in cottonseed oil and given daily in a volume of 20 ml/kg to albino rats for 100 days.[11] The diet itself inhibited growth to an average of about one third that in controls fed optimal amounts of dietary protein.[11]

Albino rats given cottonseed oil daily in a dose of 20 ml/kg/day looked smaller than the controls but otherwise appeared to be in good health. They were markedly susceptible to the toxic effects of daily administration of captan, as noted by Boyd.[11] Clinical measurements are summarized in Table 41 with values at 7 and at 100 days cited in exemplification of the results.

Growth was reduced by about three quarters and at the end of 100 days, cottonseed oil-treated rats had gained only 57 ± 22 g (mean ± S.D.) vs. 240 ± 31 g in the controls given no cottonseed oil. There was a reduction in food (laboratory chow) intake in the oil-treated animals during the first two or three weeks after which there was no further appreciable anorexia. Since the oil-treated rats were receiving a considerable number of calories as cottonseed oil, the total calorie intake of oil-treated rats was actually higher than that of the controls. In spite of this, oil-treated rats had a

TABLE 41

The Influence of Cottonseed Oil Given by Gavage Once Daily for 100 Days in a Dose of 20 ml/kg/day to Male Albino Rats Fed from Weaning on a Diet Containing One Third the Optimal Amount of Protein[10]

Measurement	Value in controls given no cottonseed oil (mean ± standard deviation)	Value in albino rats given cottonseed oil (mean ± standard deviation)
Growth: grams gain in body weight over 100 days	240 ± 31	57 ± 22
Food (chow) intake: g/kg/24 hr		
(a) at 7 days	91 ± 19	70 ± 10
(b) at 100 days	37 ± 9	34 ± 9
Water intake: ml/kg/24 hr		
(a) at 7 days	94 ± 43	111 ± 15
(b) at 100 days	25 ± 10	46 ± 17
Colonic temperature: °F		
(a) at 7 days	96.0 ± 0.6	98.1 ± 0.5
(b) at 100 days	98.6 ± 1.2	97.7 ± 0.5
Urinary volume: ml/kg/24 hr		
(a) at 7 days	30 ± 30	7 ± 4
(b) at 100 days	8 ± 7	9 ± 4
Urinary blood: units/kg/24 hr		
(a) at 7 days	0 ± 0	0 ± 0
(b) at 100 days	0 ± 0	0 ± 0
Urinary glucose: mg/kg/24 hr		
(a) at 7 days	0 ± 0	10 ± 15
(b) at 100 days	0.1 ± 0.3	14 ± 18
Urinary pH: 24-hr sample		
(a) at 7 days	8.1 ± 1.2	7.5 ± 0.5
(b) at 100 days	6.6 ± 0.9	6.2 ± 1.2
Urinary protein: mg/kg/24 hr		
(a) at 7 days	8.2 ± 6.0	2.4 ± 0.9
(b) at 100 days	5.1 ± 2.9	5.7 ± 4.1

marked inhibition of growth, which must be considered a toxic reaction to cottonseed oil at the dose administered. Other evidence of toxicity in these animals included a slight increase in water intake, a slight initial fever, an initial oliguria, a persistent glycosuria, and slight aciduria (see Table 41).

There were no deaths during the period of 100 days of administration of cottonseed oil by gavage at a dose of 20 ml/kg/day. At the end of this period, the animals were autopsied and the wet weight and water content of body organs were measured. The results are summarized in Table 42 as mean percent changes from corresponding values in controls given no cottonseed oil.

At the end of 100 days from weaning, oil-treated rats weighed less than half the weight of their controls not given cottonseed oil. A comparable loss of weight was present in most body organs. Loss of weight was less marked in the several parts of the gastrointestinal tract which

were measured. The entire gastrointestinal tract was slightly hypertrophied. Hypertrophy was most evident in the cardiac stomach. Loss of weight was also less marked in the adrenal glands and brain.

As may be seen from data assembled in Table 42, changes in water content of body organs at 100 days were variable and, for the most part, minor. There was a significant dehydration in the adrenal glands, cardiac stomach, and cecum. Hydration appeared in certain other organs such as the kidneys, lungs, salivary glands, and skin. No significant alteration of water levels occurred in the other body organs listed in Table 42.

The Acute Oral LD_{50} of Cottonseed Oil in Albino Rats Fed a No-growth Protein Deficient Diet

Krijnen and Boyd[12] reported that the acute oral LD_{50} of cottonseed oil in albino rats fed for 28 days from weaning on a diet containing no protein was about one fifth that in rats fed adequate amounts of dietary protein. This

TABLE 42

The Wet Weight and Water Content of Body Organs of Male Albino Rats Fed Diets Containing One Third Optimal Protein, at the end of 100 Days of Daily Administration by Gavage of Cottonseed Oil in a Dose of 20 ml/kg/24 hr[10]

Organ	Weight: g (mean % change from control)	Water: g/100 g dry wt (mean % change from control)
Adrenal glands	−23.3*	−15.2**
Brain	− 9.9*	− 5.7
Gastrointestinal tract		
Cardiac stomach	+ 7.1	−25.2**
Pyloric stomach	−23.6**	+ 4.1
Small bowel	− 4.1	+ 4.4
Cecum	−25.2**	−18.5**
Colon	−24.4**	+ 3.2
Heart	−42.7**	+ 1.5
Kidneys	−41.7**	+ 7.7*
Liver	−46.7**	− 0.6
Lungs	−32.7**	+ 6.9*
Muscle (ventral abdominal wall)	−65.8**	+ 4.6
Salivary (submaxillary) glands	−59.2**	+12.1**
Skin	−64.3**	+ 9.3*
Spleen	−50.0**	− 2.3
Testes	−36.7**	− 3.1
Thymus gland	−52.8**	+ 2.8
Residual carcass	−55.4**	− 0.6
Autopsy body weight	−55.8**	

*Mean percent change significant at P = 0.05 to 0.02.
**Mean percent change significant at P = 0.01 or less.

prompted Boyd and Krijnen[13] to estimate the acute oral LD_{50} of cottonseed oil at intervals of 4 weeks in male albino rats fed for 16 weeks from weaning on a low protein diet on which the weanlings failed to grow whatsoever. The work was performed on 446 rats divided into 5 groups fed the low protein (3% casein) diet for 0, 4, 8, 12, and 16 weeks, respectively. Data on death rates and body weight are summarized in Table 43.

The diet itself did not support growth, and deaths in controls given no cottonseed oil began to appear in the third and fourth months. The acute oral LD_{50} of cottonseed oil fell to 12 to 20% of values in control weanlings given a normal diet with corresponding declines in the estimated LD_1 and LD_{99}. The clinical signs of cottonseed oil toxicity at the range of the acute oral LD_{50} were essentially the same in all groups listed in Table 43 and similar to that noted by Boyd and Boulanger[6] in rats fed laboratory chow.

At autopsy on animals that died from cottonseed oil in doses at the range of the oral LD_{50}, the entire gastrointestinal tract was inflamed and frequently hemorrhagic. Necrosis of the mucous membrane appeared in several areas such as the small bowel exemplified in Figure 39, and cecum, illustrated in Figure 40. Microscopic droplets of oil were absorbed through the inflamed mucosa and

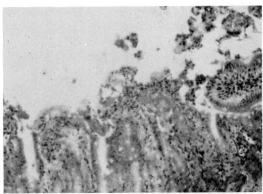

FIGURE 39. A photomicrograph through the wall of the small bowel of a rat, fed a low-protein diet from weaning, that died following oral administration of cottonseed oil in a dose of 60 ml/kg at eight weeks from weaning, showing, in the villi, congestion and hemorrhage, and necrosis of the surface cells. Hematoxylin-phloxine-saffron, x 100. (A previously unpublished figure from the studies of Boyd and Krijnen.[13])

were deposited in organs such as the liver. An exemplification of oil droplets deposited in the hepatic cells adjacent to the portal vein, hepatic artery, and bile duct is shown in Figure 41. The deposition of microscopic oil droplets in the tissues set off an inflammatory reaction, exemplified for the meninges in Figure 42, for the brain in

TABLE 43

Data on the Acute Oral Toxicity of Cottonseed Oil in Male Albino Rats Fed from Weaning on a No-growth Protein Deficient Diet

Index of toxicity	No. of weeks on 3% casein diet				
	0 (control)	4	8	12	16
Body weight (g) at end of feeding period (mean ± S.D.)	55 ± 6	56 ± 6	48 ± 9	53 ± 10	62 ± 12
Incidence of death during feeding (%)	0	1	4	24*	35*
LD_{50} (ml/kg) of cottonseed oil (mean ± S.E.)	281 ± 18	56 ± 10	43 ± 6	33 ± 5	53 ± 13
Estimated LD_1 of cottonseed oil (ml/kg)	179	11	10	6	10
Estimated LD_{99} of cottonseed oil (ml/kg)	385	101	77	60	95
Interval (hr) to death (mean ± S.D.)	72-120†	47 ± 11	30 ± 5	38 ± 6	36 ± 9

*Some deaths were due to cannibalism, especially in the 16-week group.
†These rats were given one quarter of the total dose at intervals of 24 hr for four days.

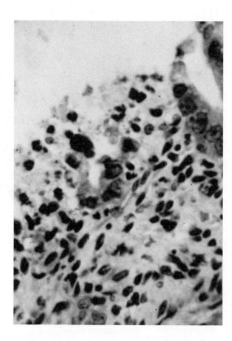

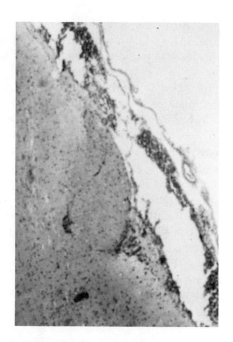

FIGURE 40. A photomicrograph through the wall of the cecum of an albino rat, fed from weaning on a low protein diet, that died following oral administration of cottonseed oil in a dose of 60 ml/kg at eight weeks from weaning, showing necrosis of Lieberkühn's glands. Hematoxylin-phloxine-saffron, x 450. (A previously unpublished figure from the studies of Boyd and Krijnen.[13])

FIGURE 42. A photomicrograph of the meninges and adjacent brain of a rat, fed from weaning on a low protein diet, that died following oral administration of cottonseed oil in a dose of 60 ml/kg at eight weeks from weaning, showing capillary-venous congestion of the meninges. Hematoxylin-phloxine-saffron, x 40. (From Boyd and Krijnen[13] with the permission of *Food and Cosmetics Toxicology,* copyright © 1971, Pergamon Press, England.)

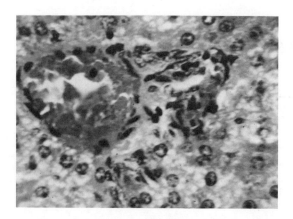

FIGURE 41. A photomicrograph of the periphery of a hepatic lobule in an albino rat, fed from weaning on a protein-deficient diet, that died following oral administration of cottonseed oil in a dose of 80 ml/kg at eight weeks from weaning. Note the deposition of oil droplets in the hepatic cells adjacent to the portal vein, hepatic artery, and bile ducts. Hematoxylin-phloxine-saffron, x 450. (A previously unpublished photograph from the studies of Boyd and Krijnen.[13])

Figure 43, and for the region of the ascending limb of Henle's loop in Figure 44. Congestion of the lungs was frequently accompanied by hemorrhage into the respiratory airway where cilia in the bronchioles could be seen propelling the red blood cells in respiratory tract fluid[14] toward the trachea, as illustrated in Figure 45.

The Oral $LD_{50\ (100\ days)}$ of Cottonseed Oil

Boyd and Krijnen[15] reported studies of the multiposal toxicity of cottonseed oil given to albino rats in doses at the range of the oral $LD_{50\ (100\ days)}$. The techniques of measuring toxicity at the $LD_{50\ (100\ days)}$ have been reviewed by Boyd.[16] The animals were fed from weaning on a low protein diet containing 3% protein as casein prepared after Hegsted and Chang.[17] The diet contained 3% casein, 82% cornstarch, 8% hydrogenated cottonseed oil, 4% salt mix, and 3% multivitamin mixture. Cottonseed oil was given by gavage once daily in doses ranging from 1.8 to 20 ml/kg/24 hr.

The oral $LD_{50\ (100\ days)}$ ± S.E. or estimated

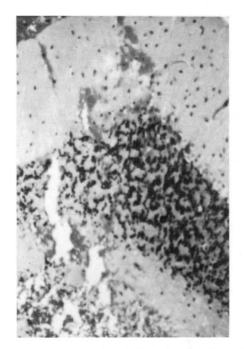

FIGURE 43. A photomicrograph of the cerebellum of a rat, fed from weaning on a low protein diet, that died from oral administration of a lethal dose of cottonseed oil at eight weeks from weaning, showing congestion and hemorrhage in the outer molecular layer (top), in the region of Purkinje's cells, in the granular layer and in the inner layer of white matter (bottom). Hematoxylin-phloxine-saffron, x 100. (A previously unpublished figure from the studies of Boyd and Krijnen.[13])

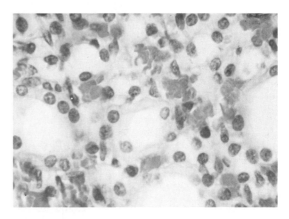

FIGURE 44. A section through the region of the ascending limb of Henle's loop in the kidney of a rat, fed from weaning on a low protein diet, that died from oral administration of cottonseed oil in a dose of 80 ml/kg at eight weeks from weaning, showing marked capillary congestion of the supporting connective tissue. Hematoxylin-phloxine-saffron, x 450. (A previously unpublished figure from the studies of Boyd and Krijnen.[13])

daily dose that killed 50% of the animals over a period of 100 days was found to be 8.1 ± 1.4 ml/kg/day or 6.6 ± 1.1 g/kg/day. The acute oral $LD_{50 \, (1 \, dose)}$ in rats fed the same diet for 16 weeks was previously estimated at 53 ± 13 ml/kg, as noted in Table 43. The 100-Day LD_{50} Index, or $LD_{50 \, (100 \, days)}$ expressed as a percentage of the $LD_{50 \, (1 \, dose)}$,[16] was therefore 15.3 ± 2.6. The estimated $LD_{1 \, (100 \, days)}$ was 1 ml/kg/day and the $LD_{99 \, (100 \, days)}$ 18 ml/kg/day in animals fed the protein deficient diet. Protein deficient diets ordinarily augment the susceptibility of weanling rats to the toxic effects of chemical agents.[11]

The clinical signs of toxicity at the oral $LD_{50 \, (100 \, days)}$ included loss of body weight, anorexia, oligodipsia, oliguria, aciduria, a slight fever from smaller daily doses, and listlessness. After the first month of administration, there appeared increasing alopecia, a dry scaly dermatitis, penile erection, piloerection, tail-biting, and hypertrophy of the lower incisor teeth. The latter sign also appeared to a lesser degree in

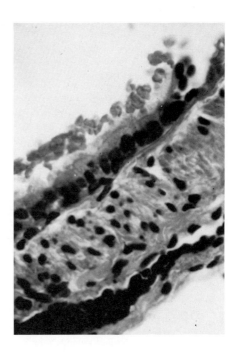

FIGURE 45. A section through a small bronchiole of the lung of a rat, fed from weaning on a low protein diet, that died from oral administration of cottonseed oil in a dose of 60 ml/kg at eight weeks from weaning, showing congestion of the bronchiole (bottom) and hemorrhaged red blood cells in the lumen of the bronchiole being propelled upward by cilia (top). Hematoxylin-phloxine-saffron, x 450. (A previously unpublished figure from the studies of Boyd and Krijnen.[13])

animals fed the low protein diet without cotton-seed oil; a photograph of the condition in controls has been presented by Boyd.[11] Incisor hypertrophy was augmented by daily doses of cottonseed oil. Most of the clinical signs were dose dependent. The common premortem sign was hypothermic coma.

Histopathological observations recorded at death are summarized in Table 44. It will be noted that the gastrointestinal tract had become tolerant to the irritant effect of large daily doses of cottonseed oil, the mucosa was intact, and microscopic oil droplets were not absorbed through it. Pathology was confined to a stress reaction, mild

tissue inflammation, and degenerative changes in many organs.

The zona glomerulosa of the adrenal gland was relatively hypertrophied and hyperemic, as illustrated in Figure 46. The meninges were edematous and infiltrated with round cells, as exemplified in Figure 47. There was hyperemia or mild congestion about the descending limb of Henle's loop of the kidneys. The latter is illustrated in Figure 48. Degenerative changes were present in many organs as listed in Table 44; an example of partial atrophy of skeletal muscle is presented in Figure 50. There was a marked inhibition of spermatogenesis in the testes which was due to the protein deficient diet. Cottonseed oil produced

TABLE 44

Histopathologic Observations at Autopsy on Albino Rats Fed from Weaning on a Diet Containing 3% Protein as Casein and Given Cottonseed Oil Daily at Doses in the Range of the LD_{50} (100 days)[a]

Organ	Histopathology
Adrenal glands	Zona glomerulosa hyperemic; zona fasciculata occasionally hydropic
Brain	Meningeal congestion with hemorrhage, edema, and infiltration of inflammatory round cells
Gastrointestinal tract	
Cardiac stomach	Hyperemic with an occasional healed ulcer
Pyloric stomach	Hyperemic
Small bowel	Hyperemic: Peyer's patches prominent
Cecum	Peyer's patches prominent
Colon	Normal
Heart	Myofibrils occasionally granulated
Kidneys	Glomeruli ischemic and compressed by swollen (cloud) tubules; fine fatty degeneration of tubules; capillary congestion with hemorrhage in the region of Henle's loop, especially about the descending limb
Liver	Areas of sinusoidal congestion; areas of cloudy swelling or hydropic degeneration with loss of basophilic staining in the hepatic cells
Lungs	Mild congestion; areas of lymphocytic infiltration; occasionally venous stasis and thrombosis
Muscle (ventral abdominal wall)	Excess connective tissue between myofibrils
Salivary (submaxillary) glands	Areas of necrosis of the serous glands; excretory ducts empty of secretion
Skin	Normal appearance
Spleen	Normal appearance
Testes	Inhibition of spermatogenesis plus pyknosis and degeneration of spermatocytes and spermatogonial cells
Thymus gland	Marked loss of thymocytes

[a]The effects of the low protein diet alone, described by Boyd,[11] are not included.

congestion of the testes and extensive toxic necrosis of spermatogenic tissue, as illustrated in Figure 49.

The weight and water content of body organs were measured on animals that survived to 100 days. Changes in organ weights are summarized in Table 45. There was a dose dependent loss of body weight, and of the weights of residual carcass, skeletal muscle, spleen, testes, and thymus gland. Loss of weight was less than that of the total body in most parts of the gastrointestinal tract, heart, kidneys, and liver. The weights of the adrenal glands, brain, and lungs were unaffected by repeated oral administration of cottonseed oil.

Shifts in the water levels of body organs are summarized in Table 46. The smaller daily doses tended to produce hydration of certain organs, while dehydration was the common effect of large daily doses. Shifts in individual organs are indicated in Table 46.

Conclusions Regarding Cottonseed Oil

The acute oral $LD_{50 \text{ (4 days)}}$ ± S.E. of cottonseed oil in young male albino rats fed a standard laboratory chow was 252 ± 20 g/kg. Reducing dietary protein intake to approximately 10% of optimal amounts augmented the acute toxicity of cottonseed oil approximately tenfold. The main clinical sign was depression of the central nervous system with death in hypothermic coma. At autopsy, cottonseed oil was found to have produced a violent local inflammation of the

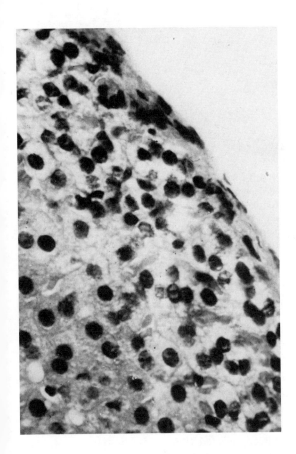

FIGURE 46. A photomicrograph of the cortex of the adrenal gland of a rat, fed from weaning on a protein-deficient diet, that died after 13 days of daily oral administration by gavage of cottonseed oil in a dose of 7.1 ml/kg/day, showing hypertrophy of the zona glomerulosa with mild congestion, and some hydropic degeneration of the adjacent zona fasciculata. Hematoxylin-phloxine-saffron, x 450. (A previously unpublished figure from the studies of Boyd and Krijnen.[15])

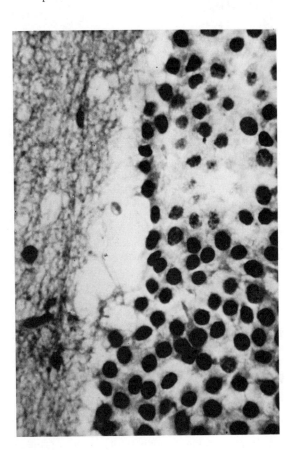

FIGURE 47. A photomicrograph of the brain of a rat, fed from weaning on a low protein diet, that died on the 43rd day of daily oral administration by gavage of cottonseed oil in a dose of 14.2 ml/kg/day, showing round cell infiltration of the meninges (right half of figure). Hematoxylin-phloxine-saffron, x 450. (A previously unpublished figure from the studies of Boyd and Krijnen.[15])

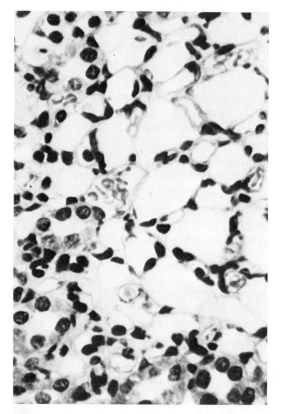

FIGURE 48. A photomicrograph of the kidney of a rat, fed from weaning on a low protein diet, that died on the 24th day of daily administration of cottonseed oil by gavage in a dose of 14.2 ml/kg/day. The section shows the mildly congested descending limbs of Henle's loop (lined by squamous epithelium, to the right and upper half of center) with relatively normal ascending limbs (lined by cuboidal epithelium, to the left and at the bottom). Hematoxylin-phloxine-saffron, x 450. (A previously unpublished photograph from the studies of Boyd and Krijnen.[15])

FIGURE 49. A photomicrograph of the testes of a rat, fed from weaning on a low protein diet, that died on the 86th day of daily administration by gavage of cottonseed oil in a dose of 7.1 ml/kg/day. Inhibition of spermatogenesis, shown to the left at center, is due to protein deficiency. Congestion and necrosis, seen especially at the right side of the figure, were due to cottonseed oil. Hematoxylin-phloxine-saffron, x 40. (A previously unpublished photograph from the studies of Boyd and Krijnen.[15])

gastrointestinal tract through which microscopic oil droplets were absorbed. The oil droplets were deposited in tissues where they produced a local vascular congestion, degenerative changes, dehydration, and loss of organ weights.

Repeated daily doses of 20 ml/kg produced a toxic inhibition of growth with no deaths in rats fed from weaning on one third of the optimal dietary intake of protein. When dietary protein was reduced to 10% of optimal, weanling albino rats did not grow and were highly susceptible to daily cottonseed oil given by gavage. The $LD_{50 \ (100 \ days)} \pm S.E.$ was 6.6 ± 1.1 g/kg/day with a 100-day LD_{50} index of 15.3 ± 2.6 in animals fed 10% of optimal protein intake. Clinical signs at the $LD_{50 \ (100 \ days)}$ were those of

depression of the central nervous system plus an extensive dermatitis. At autopsy, the intestinal tract had adapted to daily gavage of cottonseed oil and was relatively normal in appearance. Degenerative changes were present in many body organs most of which had lost weight with some tendency to dehydration at large daily doses of cottonseed oil in animals fed 10% optimal amounts of protein.

Extrapolated to man, it would appear that cottonseed oil is not likely to be consumed in amounts that would produce toxicity and death in persons eating optimal amounts of dietary protein. If a person were eating 10% or less of optimal amounts of dietary protein, cottonseed oil could produce toxicity in amounts of the probable order of 1 ml/kg/day and death in larger daily doses.

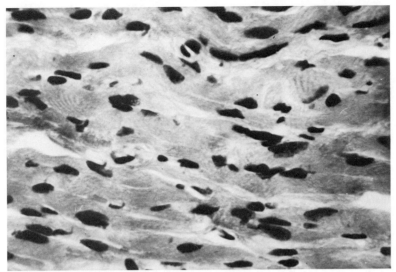

FIGURE 50. A photomicrograph of skeletal muscle in a rat, fed from weaning on a low protein diet, that died on the 86th day of daily administration of cottonseed oil by gavage in a dose of 7.1 ml/kg/day, showing an excess of connective tissue between myofibrils. Hematoxylin-phloxine-saffron, x 450. (A previously unpublished photograph from the studies of Boyd and Krijnen.[15])

TABLE 45

Changes in the Wet Weight of Organs of Surviving Albino Rats Fed from Weaning on a 3% Protein Diet and Given Cottonseed Oil Daily for 100 Days[a]

Organ	Daily dose of cottonseed oil (ml/kg)		
	1.8 (N = 5 plus 18 controls)	3.6 (N = 5 plus 18 controls)	7.1 (N = 5 plus 18 controls)
Adrenal glands	+ 2.0	– 5.8	– 0.3
Brain	– 3.2	– 0.6	– 3.2
Gastrointestinal tract			
Cardiac stomach	–16.9**	–23.1**	–10.0*
Pyloric stomach	– 5.8	– 0.8	–25.7**
Small bowel	+ 1.2	+ 7.8	–11.6*
Cecum	– 7.8*	– 3.0	–23.5**
Colon	– 7.9*	0.0	–19.4**
Heart	+ 8.8	– 2.0	–10.3*
Kidneys	+ 2.8	– 1.7	–12.5**
Liver	+ 0.7	– 2.3	– 5.4*
Lungs	+ 0.2	– 6.0	– 6.2
Muscle (ventral abdominal wall)	–15.2**	–20.7**	–33.4**
Salivary (submaxillary) glands	+14.9*	+13.0*	–14.1*
Skin	–15.5**	– 9.9*	–34.7**
Spleen	+ 2.1	–19.3*	–29.2**
Testes	– 1.1	–20.1**	–62.6**
Thymus	–40.0**	–50.2**	–33.6**
Residual carcass	–12.0**	–11.2**	–21.3**
Autopsy body weight	– 6.6*	– 9.3**	–22.0**

[a]Wet weight was measured in grams. The results are expressed as a mean percent change from controls fed the 3% protein diet but given no other agent, specifically as $[(X_O - \overline{X}_c)/\overline{X}_c] \times 100$, where $\overline{X}_O$ is the mean in cottonseed oil-treated rats and $\overline{X}_c$ in the controls. One asterisk indicates that $\overline{X}_O - \overline{X}_c$ was significant at P = 0.05 to 0.02 and two asterisks at P = 0.01 or less.

TABLE 46

Changes in the Water Content of Body Organs of Surviving Albino Rats Fed from Weaning on a 3% Protein Diet and Given Cottonseed Oil Daily for 100 Days[a]

Organ	Daily dose of cottonseed oil (ml/kg)		
	1.8 (N = 5 plus 18 controls)	3.6 (N = 5 plus 18 controls)	7.1 (N = 5 plus 18 controls)
Adrenal glands	+ 0.7	+14.9	−16.3*
Brain	+ 0.5	+ 0.7	− 0.4
Gastrointestinal tract			
Cardiac stomach	+ 2.1	+ 5.8	+ 5.3
Pyloric stomach	+ 6.7*	+ 7.0*	+ 5.4
Small bowel	− 3.1	− 0.6	− 3.2
Cecum	+ 9.0*	+13.3**	+ 8.2*
Colon	+ 5.2	+ 6.8	− 5.4
Heart	0.0	+ 1.3	− 0.7
Kidneys	+ 3.2	+ 4.1	− 0.4
Liver	+ 7.8**	+ 5.8	− 2.2
Lungs	+ 5.3*	− 3.5	− 4.1
Muscle (ventral abdominal wall)	+ 4.2*	+ 7.2*	− 8.9*
Salivary (submaxillary) glands	− 7.6*	+ 1.8	−14.8**
Skin	+18.9**	+12.8*	−11.1**
Spleen	− 3.3	− 1.2	− 4.0
Testes	− 1.8	− 4.5*	− 9.8**
Thymus gland	0.0	− 7.8	−47.1**
Residual carcass	+ 3.2	+ 0.2	− 0.7

[a]Water content was measured as grams water per 100 g dry weight of tissue. The results are expressed as a mean percent change from controls fed the 3% protein diet but given no other agent, specifically as $[(\overline{X}_O - \overline{X}_C)/\overline{X}_C] \times 100$, where $\overline{X}_O$ is the mean in cottonseed oil-treated rats and $\overline{X}_C$ in controls. One asterisk indicates that $\overline{X}_O - \overline{X}_C$ was significant at $P = 0.05$ to 0.02 and two asterisks at $P = 0.01$ or less.

REFERENCES

1. Stecher, P. G., Windholz, M., Leahy, D. S., Bolton, D. M., and Eaton, L. G., *The Merck Index. An Encyclopedia of Chemicals and Drugs,* 8th ed., Merck and Company, Inc., Rahway, N.J., 1968.
2. Kaunitz, H., Slanetz, C. A., and Johnson, R. E., Antagonism of fresh fat to the toxicity of heated and aerated cottonseed oil, *J. Nutr.,* 55, 577, 1955.
3. Edgren, B., Tolerance of the dog to intravenous fat emulsions, *Acta Pharmacol. Toxicol.,* 16, 260, 1960.
4. Orö, L. and Wretlind, A., Pharmacological effects of fatty acids, triolein and cottonseed oil, *Acta Pharmacol. Toxicol.,* 18, 141, 1961.
5. Munro, I. C., Salem, F. A., Goodman, T., and Hasnain, S. H., Biochemical and pathological changes in the heart and liver of rats given brominated cottonseed oil, *Toxicol. Appl. Pharmacol.,* 19, 62, 1971.
6. Boyd, E. M. and Boulanger, M. A., Acute oral toxicity of cottonseed oil, *Toxicol. Appl. Pharmacol.,* 14, 432, 1969.
7. Boyd, E. M. and Knight, L. M., Postmortem shifts in the weight and water levels of body organs, *Toxicol. Appl. Pharmacol.,* 5, 119, 1963.
8. Boyd, E. M., Toxicological studies, in *Clinical Testing of New Drugs,* Herrick, A. D. and Cattell, M., Eds., Revere Publishing Co., New York, 1965, 13.
9. Croxton, F. E., *Elementary Statistics with Applications in Medicine and the Biological Sciences,* Dover, New York, 1959.

10. **Boyd, E. M. and Horne, C. J.,** The toxicity of daily administration of cottonseed oil in albino rats fed from weaning on a diet containing one third the optimal intake of protein, unpublished data, 1972.

11. **Boyd, E. M.,** *Protein Deficiency and Pesticide Toxicity,* Charles C Thomas, Springfield, Ill., 1972.

12. **Krijnen, C. J. and Boyd, E. M.,** Susceptibility to captan pesticide of albino rats fed from weaning on diets containing various levels of protein, *Food Cosmet. Toxicol.,* 8, 35, 1970.

13. **Boyd, E. M. and Krijnen, C. J.,** Intolerance to cottonseed oil in rats fed a low protein diet, *Food Cosmet. Toxicol.,* 9, 389, 1971.

14. **Boyd, E. M.,** *Respiratory Tract Fluid,* Charles C Thomas, Springfield, Ill., 1972.

15. **Boyd, E. M. and Krijnen, C. J.,** The toxicity of dicophane and cottonseed oil at the $LD_{50 \, (100 \, days)}$ in albino rats fed from weaning on a diet containing 3% protein as casein, Paper presented at The Second International Congress of Pesticide Chemistry, Tel Aviv, February 21–27, 1971.

16. **Boyd, E. M.,** *Predictive Toxicometrics,* Scientechnica (Publishers) Ltd., Bristol, England, 1972.

17. **Hegsted, D. M. and Chang, Y.-O.,** Protein utilization in growing rats. I. Relative growth index as a bioassay procedure, *J. Nutr.,* 85, 159, 1965.

Chapter 9

MINERAL OIL

The similarity of results obtained with cotton-seed oil, described in Chapter 8, to those with corn oil, described in Chapter 7, suggested the possibility that the physical property of oiliness may have been a common denominator in these toxicity tests. To investigate this possibility, the acute toxicity of mineral oil given by gavage was studied.[1] The acute oral toxicity of mineral oil differed in many respects from that of corn oil and cottonseed oil. The toxicity of all three oils did not appear to depend, therefore, on their physical consistency.

Mineral oil is a mixture of liquid hydrocarbons obtained from petroleum. It is known under various other names such as paraffin oil, liquid paraffin, liquid petrolatum, Adepsine oil, Nujol[®], Kaydol[®], Alboline, Paroleine, Saxol[®], and Glymol. It is a colorless, odorless, and almost tasteless oil of specific gravity 0.83 to 0.91, used as a laxative in medicine and gastrointestinal impaction in veterinary medicine, and as a solvent for certain drugs.[2]

Used as a laxative, mineral oil may retain water in emulsified form and increase the bulk of the stool in addition to its main action of lubrication.[3] Long continued use as a laxative may interfere with the absorption of certain essential food elements, such as carotene, the precursor of vitamin A.[4] Mineral oil may be absorbed as fine droplets through the mucosa of the gastro-intestinal tract. It is treated as a foreign body which may be eliminated, for example in the macrophages of sputum,[5] or collect in granulomas or fibrous tissue.[6] Mineral oil taken by mouth may coat the pharynx and small amounts may make their way into the lungs. Intrapulmonary deposits may also follow the use of nose drops or inhalation of drugs dissolved in mineral oil. The result is mineral oil granulomas of the lungs or mineral oil pneumonia with an x-ray picture which resembles bronchogenic carcinoma.

Prigal[7] notes that mineral oil has been classed as a carcinogen based upon production of plasmacytomas from the intraperitoneal injection of mineral oil into an highly inbred, cancer-susceptible strain of mice. He finds that similar plasmacytomas are produced by other inert substances and reviews a wide body of evidence that mineral oil is not carcinogenic. Shubik et al.[8] also concluded that hard paraffin or petroleum waxes are not carcinogenic.

Chaudhuri and Chakravarty[9] reported that a cheap variety of mineral oil called white oil given in the diet to monkeys produced widespread tissue congestion and death in one to two weeks following administration of a total of from 36 to 96 ml of the oil. In view of the fact that Boyd and Horne[1] obtained no deaths in albino rats given mineral oil daily by gavage in total doses up to 2 l/kg over a period of 15 days, it would appear possible that deaths in monkeys may have been due to toxic impurities in the cheap variety of mineral oil used in the study on monkeys.[9] Shubik et al.[8] reported that hard paraffin fed to rats at 10% of the diet did not shorten their life span and produced no deaths or other signs of toxicity such as inhibition of growth.

Acute Oral Toxicity in Rats

Boyd and Horne[1] gave mineral oil by gavage daily to unstarved young male albino rats in a series of doses up to 150 ml/kg/day for 15 days. When the amount given by intragastric cannula exceeded 50 ml/kg, appreciable volumes of the oil were evacuated through the anus within 1 or 2 min of oral administration. Representative data upon the percentages immediately evacuated through the anus are collected in Table 47.

Measurements of clinical signs of toxicity are summarized in Table 48. There were no deaths over the period of 15 days of daily oral adminis-tration of mineral oil in total doses up to twice body weight. There was an inhibition of growth with no anorexia or even a slight increase in food (chow) intake. There was a consistent slight average hypothermia which was not great enough to be statistically significant in any one dosage group. The volume of urine and intake of water were augmented. No hematuria or glycosuria appeared but there was a proteinuria which was dose dependent.

The rats given huge oral doses of mineral oil

TABLE 47

The Percentage of Daily Oral Doses of Mineral Oil that Was Immediately Evacuated Through the Anus of Young Male Albino Rats

Daily dose administered (ml/kg)	Percent immediately evacuated		
	On the 5th day	On the 10th day	Average/day (± standard deviation)
80	45.1	39.3	40.8 ± 15.2
100	51.5	44.2	51.6 ± 13.2
150	53.4	62.4	55.2 ± 8.6

TABLE 48

Clinical Signs of Toxicity in Young Male Albino Rats at the end of 15 Days of Daily Administration of Mineral Oil by Gavage

Sign	Daily dose of mineral oil (ml/kg)		
	80	100	150
Body weight: g	−24.4*	−40.0*	−19.0*
Food intake: g/kg/24 hr	+22.2*	+37.1*	+ 3.8
Water intake: ml/kg/24 hr	+98.5*	+96.4*	+21.8
Colonic temperature: °F	− 0.63	− 0.51	− 0.38
Urinary volume: ml/kg/24 hr	+271*	+252*	+180*
Urinary blood: units/kg/24 hr	0.0	0.0	0.0
Urinary glucose: mg/kg/24 hr	0.0	0.0	0.0
Urinary protein: mg/kg/24 hr	+242*	+513*	+534*
Urinary pH: 24-hr sample	+21.5*	+18.6*	+10.0
Listlessness: units	0.6	1.1*	0.0
Maniacal excitement: % incidence	30.0*	28.0*	32.0*
Fur soiling: units	3.9*	4.0*	4.0*
Dermatitis: % incidence	20.0*	56.0*	100.0*
Alopecia: % incidence	40.0*	100.0*	100.0*
Diarrhea: units	0.5	1.0*	3.0*

The results are expressed as mean percentage changes from values in controls not given mineral oil except for the last six signs which are entered as mean differences from controls.
*Significant at $P = 0.05$ or less

were either listless or exhibited maniacal excitement, consisting of jumping about the cage, screaming, and biting themselves or objects in their cage. Their fur became soiled with mineral oil and areas of the skin were first bruised and then became inflamed. Areas affected included the nose, mouth, legs, and abdomen. These areas appeared to be itchy to the animal, as scratch marks were common. The incidence of skin lesions was dose dependent, as was alopecia. Diarrhea

appeared with increasing intensity as the daily dose was increased.

Histopathology

Since there were no deaths, gross and microscopic pathology were recorded on representative rats of each dosage group at the end of 15 days of daily administration of mineral oil by gavage. The results of histopathological studies are summarized in Table 49. Mineral oil produced a mild to

TABLE 49

Microscopic Findings in Young Male Albino Rats Given Large Daily Doses of Mineral Oil by Gavage for 15 Days

Organ	Histopathology
Adrenal glands	Lipoid droplets prominent in zona glomerulosa and fasciculata; sinusoids congested
Brain	Areas of congestion of the meninges and brain
Gastrointestinal tract	
Cardiac stomach	Capillary-venous congestion of the submucosa
Pyloric stomach	Congestion of the lamina propria in the tips of the gastric glands
Small bowel	Mild congestion in the lamina propria of the villi
Cecum	Mild capillary-venous congestion of the lamina propria
Colon	Mild congestion of the lamina propria and submucosa
Heart	Mild capillary congestion of the myocardium
Kidneys	Mild congestion of the glomeruli and tubules
Liver	Mild sinusoidal congestion
Lungs	Areas of edema and congestion
Muscle (ventral abdominal wall)	Normal appearance
Salivary (submaxillary) glands	Normal appearance
Skin	Skin lesions show necrosis of the stratum corneum and infiltration of leukocytes, and occasionally similar lesions of the stratum malpighi
Spleen	Normal appearance
Testes	Minor deficiency of spermatocytes
Thymus gland	Capillary-venous congestion and loss of thymocytes

moderate irritant local inflammatory reaction in the gastrointestinal tract. Several body organs were mildly inflamed, including the brain and meninges, heart, kidneys, liver, lungs, and thymus gland. There was a mild stress reaction in the adrenal and thymus glands.

The earliest effect of mineral oil on the skin was an augmentation of granulation in the stratum corneum. This early lesion is illustrated in Figure 51. The second stage was characterized by the appearance of areas of necrosis in the stratum corneum and stratum dysjunctum, as may be seen in Figure 52. This stage was followed by infiltration of the stratum corneum by white blood cells, as shown in Figure 53. The fourth stage consisted of infiltration of the stratum malpighi by leukocytes and complete destruction of the epidermis, as shown in Figure 54. The reaction finally spread to the dermis where there occurred edema of cells lining the hair follicles, the disappearance of hair, and general inflammation of the area affected, as illustrated in Figure 55.

Organ Weights

Data on the weight of body organs of albino rats at the end of 15 days of daily administration by gavage of representative doses of mineral oil are collected in Table 50. Compared with corresponding data in controls given no mineral oil, there was a loss of weight of about one quarter of that in controls in autopsy body weight and weight of residual carcass. The percentage loss of weight was greater than that of body weight in the instances of skeletal muscle, skin, spleen, and thymus gland. There was no significant change in the weight of adrenal glands, brain, cardiac stomach, colon, and salivary glands from most daily doses. Changes in weight of the other organs listed in Table 50 were losses intermediary between these two extremes.

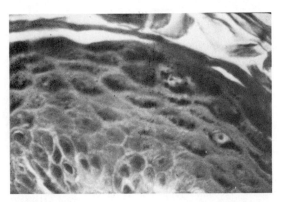

FIGURE 51. A photomicrograph through the epidermis of a rat that had received mineral oil by gavage in a dose of 100 ml/kg/24 hr for 15 days, showing early proliferation of granulations in the stratum corneum.[1] Hematoxylin-phloxine-saffron, x 450.

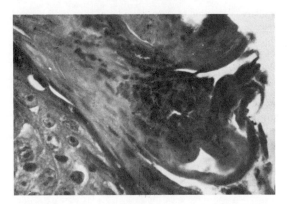

FIGURE 52. The second stage in the development of skin lesions from large doses of mineral oil given by gavage daily for 15 days to albino rats, showing an area of necrosis of the stratum corneum.[1] Hematoxylin-phloxine-saffron, x 450.

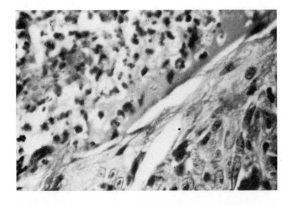

FIGURE 53. The third stage in the development of skin lesions from large doses of mineral oil given by gavage to albino rats daily for 15 days, showing infiltration of the stratum corneum by white blood cells.[1] Hematoxylin-phloxine-saffron, x 450.

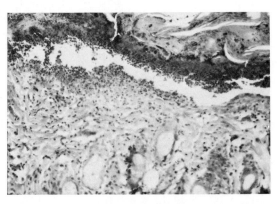

FIGURE 54. A photomicrograph through the epidermis and adjacent dermis of a rat that had been given mineral oil by gavage once daily in a dose of 100 ml/kg/24 hr for 15 days, showing infiltration of the stratum malpighi by leukocytes and complete breakdown of the epidermis. There is some leukocytic infiltration of the adjacent dermis.[1] Hematoxylin-phloxine-saffron, x 100.

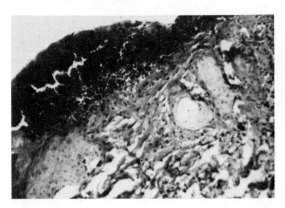

FIGURE 55. A late stage in the development of skin lesions to mineral oil given by gavage once daily for 15 days to albino rats in a dose of 100 ml/kg/24 hr, showing necrosis of the epidermis, edema of the hair follicles, and absence of hair in the follicles.[1] Hematoxylin-phloxine-saffron, x 100.

Organ Water Levels

Data on water levels of the organs listed in Table 50 are assembled in Table 51 as mean percentage changes from corresponding values in controls given no mineral oil. It will be noted that shifts in water content of body organs were minor and somewhat inconsistent. The larger daily doses of mineral oil produced a hydration of pyloric stomach, small bowel, cecum, and colon; a daily dose of 80 ml/kg caused an increase in the water level of cecum and then only at $P = 0.05$ to 0.02. The hydration of cecum and colon was dose dependent. There were no consistent changes in

TABLE 50

Changes in the Wet Weight of Body Organs in Albino Rats at the End of 15 Days of Daily Administration of Mineral Oil by Gavage[a]

Organ	Daily dose of mineral oil: ml/kg		
	80	100	150
Adrenal glands	− 6.1	− 4.1	+15.2*
Brain	− 4.0	− 8.8*	− 1.8
Gastrointestinal tract			
Cardiac stomach	− 4.2	− 8.9*	− 1.3
Pyloric stomach	−19.8**	−24.7**	−10.3*
Small bowel	+ 0.4	+ 3.3	+11.8**
Cecum	+ 2.2	+ 6.2	+16.3**
Colon	− 4.8	− 1.7	+ 4.1**
Heart	−17.1**	−25.4**	−12.1**
Kidneys	−10.0*	−12.6**	−10.0**
Liver	−21.3**	−22.8**	−16.4**
Lungs	−22.2**	−27.8**	+ 1.1
Muscle (ventral abdominal wall)	−35.5**	−51.2**	−36.6**
Salivary (submaxillary) glands	+ 0.2	− 2.3	+ 0.7
Skin	−31.3**	−35.5**	−29.8**
Spleen	−36.8**	−41.2**	−28.3**
Testes	−12.3*	−25.5**	− 1.8
Thymus gland	−48.3**	−71.2**	−40.2**
Residual carcass	−26.0**	−38.9**	−23.4**
Autopsy body weight	−21.7**	−31.5**	−18.4**

[a]Wet weight was measured in grams. The results are expressed as mean percent changes from corresponding values in controls given no mineral oil, specifically as $[(\bar{X}_O - \bar{X}_C)/\bar{X}_C] \times 100$, where $\bar{X}_O$ is the mean in rats which received mineral oil and $\bar{X}_C$ in the controls. One asterisk indicates that $\bar{X}_O - \bar{X}_C$ was significant at $P = 0.05$ to 0.02 and two asterisks at $P = 0.01$ or less.

TABLE 51

Changes in the Water Content of Body Organs in Albino Rats at the End of 15 Days of Daily Administration of Mineral Oil by Gavage[a]

Organ	Daily dose of mineral oil: ml/kg		
	80	100	150
Adrenal glands	− 8.1	+ 8.1	+ 1.6
Brain	+ 5.1	+ 6.2*	− 1.9
Gastrointestinal tract			
Cardiac stomach	− 3.1	+ 1.8	− 2.7
Pyloric stomach	− 0.3	+ 9.1*	+ 8.6**
Small bowel	+ 1.3	+10.8***	+ 8.1**
Cecum	+ 5.7*	+ 9.2***	+13.9***
Colon	− 0.2	+ 9.3**	+10.5**
Heart	− 2.0	+ 1.2	− 4.6*
Kidneys	− 2.2	+ 5.9	+ 2.4
Liver	+ 1.8	+ 4.2	− 2.8
Lungs	− 4.8	+ 1.2	− 9.7
Muscle (ventral abdominal wall)	− 0.7	+ 3.4	+ 1.2
Salivary (submaxillary) glands	− 7.1*	− 3.2	− 1.1
Skin	+11.6**	+ 8.2*	− 2.2
Spleen	− 2.0	+ 1.4	− 0.3
Testes	− 5.2*	− 3.2	− 3.1*
Thymus gland	− 5.3	− 3.6	+ 2.8
Residual carcass	− 6.9*	− 2.1	+ 1.3

[a]Water content was measured as g water per 100 g dry weight of tissue. The results are expressed as a mean percentage change from corresponding values in controls given no mineral oil, specifically as $[(\bar{X}_O - \bar{X}_C)/\bar{X}_C] \times 100$, where $\bar{X}_O$ is the mean in rats given mineral oil and $\bar{X}_C$ in controls. One asterisk indicates that $\bar{X}_O - \bar{X}_C$ was significant at $P = 0.05$ to 0.02 and two asterisks at $P = 0.01$ or less.

the water content of other organs listed in Table 51.

Conclusions Regarding Mineral Oil

Mineral oil given by gavage once daily for 15 days to young male albino rats produced no deaths in daily doses up to 150 ml/kg. Since approximately half of the daily dose was evacuated through the anus within a couple of minutes of intragastric administration, the total amount retained beyond this period was up to approximately 1 kg/kg body weight. These results indicate that deaths from smaller amounts of corn oil and cottonseed oil were due to properties of these fatty oils other than their physical consistency.

While mineral oil produced no deaths under these circumstances, it did produce toxic effects. Growth was reduced by about 25% in spite of no change or an increase in food (chow) intake. Inhibition of growth was accompanied by a diuresis, polydipsia, a slight hypothermia, proteinuria, and alkalinuria. There was either listlessness or maniacal excitement, diarrhea, soiling of the fur, lesions of the skin, and alopecia. At 15 days there were found at autopsy a mild inflammatory reaction in the gastrointestinal tract and many body organs, a stress reaction, loss of weight with minor changes in water content of most body organs, and little or no evidence of degenerative change in these survivors.

While deaths might have occurred had the dosing been continued beyond 15 days, this was not done because of the probability of producing vitamin deficiencies through inhibition of absorption of fat-soluble vitamins.

REFERENCES

1.   Boyd, E. M. and Horne, C. J., The acute oral toxicity of mineral oil, unpublished data, 1972.
2.   Stecher, P. G., Windholtz, M., Leahy, D. S., Bolton, D. M., and Eaton, L. G., *The Merck Index. An Encyclopedia of Chemicals and Drugs,* 8th ed., Merck and Company, Inc., Rahway, N.J., 1968.
3.   Krantz, J. C., Carr, C. J., and LaDu, B. N., Jr., *The Pharmacologic Principles of Medical Practice,* 7th ed., Williams and Wilkins, Baltimore, 1969.
4.   AMA, *New Drugs Evaluated by the A.M.A. Council on Drugs,* American Medical Association, Chicago, 1967.
5.   Meyler, L., Dalderup, C., Van Dijl, W., and Bouma, H. G. D., *Side Effects of Drugs,* Vol. 5, Excerpta Medica Foundation, Amsterdam, 1966.
6.   Campbell, J. S., Nigam, S., Hurtig, A., Sahasrabudhe, M. R., and Marino, J., Mineral oil granulomas of the uterus and parametrium and granulomatous salpingitis with Schaumann bodies and oxalate deposits, *Fert. Steril.,* 15, 278, 1964.
7.   Prigal, S. J., Mineral oil as a human carcinogen, fact and fiction, *Ann. Allergy,* 25, 449, 1967.
8.   Shubik, P., Saffiotti, U., Lijinsky, W., Pietra, G., Rappaport, H., Toth, B., Raha, C. R., Tomatis, L., Feldman, R., and Ramaki, H., Studies on the toxicity of petroleum waxes, *Toxicol. Appl. Pharmacol.,* 4, Supplement, November, 1962.
9.   Chaudhuri, R. N. and Chakravarty, N. K., Observations on the toxicity of white oil, *Indian J. Med. Sci.,* 6, 137, 1952.

Chapter 10

RANCID FATS

Rancidity is due to the slow and spontaneous oxidation of unsaturated fatty acids.[1] Double bonds in fatty acids are reacted upon by peroxide radicals to form a variety of products. Rancidity is frequently quantitated in terms of the peroxide value of fats, but this value is not a measure of the toxicity of the rancid fat.[2] Mild oxidation yields glycols at the site of double bonds:

$$- CH_2 - CH = CH - CH_2 - \xrightarrow{\text{O}}$$
$$- CH_2 - CH(OH) - CH(OH) - CH_2 -$$

Peroxide radicals first produce unstable hydroperoxides:

$$- CH_2 - CH = CH - CH_2 - \xrightarrow{\text{O}}$$

As oxidation continues, the glycols split to form carboxy acids:

$$- CH_2 - CH(OH) - CH(OH) - CH_2 - \xrightarrow{\text{O}}$$

and the hydroperoxides or ozonides split to form aldehydes:

The nature of compounds producing rancidity, therefore, depends upon the degree of oxidation involved.[3]

It has been known for some time that rancidity may interfere with nutritional studies.[4,5] The seriousness of the interference has been viewed as of minor and major significance. Burr and Barnes,[6] for example, concluded that rancidity may render fats "unpalatable, destructive to other food and possibly slightly toxic in themselves." As noted in Chapter 8, Kaunitz, Slanetz, and Johnson[7] found that aerated cottonseed oil, heated to 95°C for 200 to 300 hr, produced hepatomegaly, enlarged kidneys and adrenal glands, diarrhea, and death within three weeks when added to the diet of rats in amounts up to 15 to 20%. Fresh cottonseed oil was nontoxic. Peters[8] reported that caffeine given by gavage to albino rats produced a fulminating lethal reaction when the animals were fed a high egg white biotin deficient diet. Peters and Boyd[9] found the toxic reaction to be much more severe during the winter months of the year. It was noted later[10] that augmented toxicity was due to the formation of rancidity in the diet fed to the animals.

The significance of rancidity was accidentally discovered in the author's laboratory. A supply of high egg white biotin deficient diet had been purchased to find its effect on drug toxicity. The diet was stored at room temperature. Boyd and Sargeant[11] used the diet initially and found that young adult rats grew and acted normally when fed the biotin deficient diet. The supply of diet remained stored at room temperature and was subsequently used by Peters,[8] who found that it now produced toxicity when fed to young adult rats. The diet was prepared after the formula of Rubin, Drekter, and Moyer;[12] its composition is listed in Table 52. The formula given in Table 52 is an adaptation of that of Boas[13] who was the first to describe biotin deficiency. The diet of Boas[13] was originally used in 1922 by Bond[14] in a study

TABLE 52

The Composition of the Biotin Deficient Diet of Rubin, Drekter, and Moyer[12]

Ingredient	Concentration in diet (%)
Raw egg white powder, spray-dried	30.0
Cornstarch	48.0
Cottonseed oil	14.0
Cod liver oil	3.0
Salt mix, Phillips-Hart IV	5.0
Choline chloride	0.1
Vitamin supplements	Adequate

of calcium metabolism. Bond[14] used 14% cottonseed oil; Boas[13] changed this to olive oil, György in 1939[15] to arachis oil, and in 1944 Dittmer et al.[16] changed it back to cottonseed oil. Cod liver oil was originally given separately in drops,[13] but was subsequently incorporated in the diet.[15]

Earlier investigators apparently prepared this diet at short intervals because they did not report that it turned rancid and became toxic on standing. Peters and Boyd[10] found that rancidity developed when the diet was stored at room temperature for six months or longer. In studies to be reviewed in this chapter, they found that the rancid diet produced a biphasic toxic reaction, an initial reaction during the first week of feeding from which the animals partially recovered, followed by a delayed reaction which appeared at about three weeks. The initial toxic reaction was shown to be due to the rancid fats and the delayed

reaction to raw egg white augmented by the presence of rancid fats.

The Biphasic Reaction to Rancid Fats

The initial toxic reaction in young albino rats fed a rancid biotin deficient diet consisted of listlessness, hypothermia, a marked loss of body weight, anorexia, oligodipsia, diuresis, diarrhea, proteinuria, and loss of absolute weight in all body organs except the adrenal glands, brain, and gastrointestinal tract. There was a slight dehydration of body tissues which was not due to rancidity since it appeared in controls fed fresh biotin deficient diet. Loss of body weight during the initial toxic reaction of the first week of feeding the rancid diet is illustrated as regression line "(e)" of Figure 56 and the anorexia and diuresis as regression line "(c)" in Figure 57. These toxic signs, except diuresis, did not appear in the

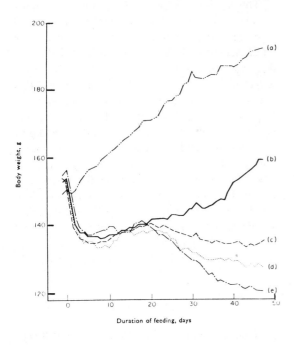

FIGURE 56. Mean changes in the body weight of young female albino rats fed either laboratory chow [regression line (a)], a denatured rancid biotin deficient diet plus vitamin supplements [regression line (b)], a rancid biotin deficient diet plus supplemental oral vitamins [regression line (c)], a rancid biotin deficient diet plus supplemental vitamins given subcutaneously [regression line (d)], or a rancid biotin deficient diet [regression line (e)]. (From Peters and Boyd[10] with the permission of the authors and of *Food and Cosmetics Toxicology,* copyright © 1969, Pergamon Press, England.)

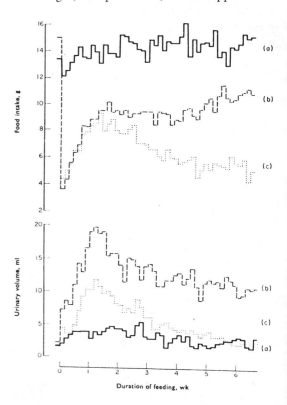

FIGURE 57. Mean changes in food intake and urinary volume of young female albino rats fed either laboratory chow [regression line (a)], a denatured rancid biotin deficient diet [regression line (b)], or a rancid biotin deficient diet [regression line (c)]. (From Peters and Boyd[10] with the permission of the authors and of *Food and Cosmetics Toxicology,* copyright © 1969, Pergamon Press, England.)

studies of Boyd and Sargeant[11] who fed a fresh (nonrancid) biotin deficient diet to albino rats. All of the signs of toxicity of the initial toxic reaction except diuresis appeared to be due to the rancidity of dietary fats.

A period of recovery from the initial toxic reaction appeared during the second and third weeks of feeding the rancid biotin deficient diet. Food and water intake increased (Figure 57), diuresis persisted (Figure 57), and there was no further loss of, or even a slight gain in, body weight (Figure 56).

The delayed toxic reaction began to appear after about 21 days of feeding the rancid biotin deficient diet. Food and water intake, urinary volume, and body weight started to decline slowly (Figures 56 and 57). The animals slowly became cachectic and deaths began to appear at the sixth week. Autopsy at seven weeks disclosed a further loss in weight of body organs, particularly in skeletal muscle, skin, and thymus gland. At seven weeks, most of the organs were hydrated.

Burr and Barnes[6] concluded that starvation due to anorexia from the unpalatable nature of rancid diets was responsible for their toxic effects. The toxic reaction to starvation alone is somewhat different from that produced by the rancid diet, however. Peters[17] reported that starvation produced oliguria, rather than diuresis, in rats. The significance of dehydration during the initial toxic reaction and of hydration during the delayed toxic reaction is somewhat obscure. Peters and Boyd[18] found that starvation alone produced a hydration of body organs in albino rats. Peters and Krijnen[19] noted that dehydration of body organs appeared in rats fed fresh biotin deficient diet. It would appear, therefore, that the diet alone (excluding rancidity) may produce dehydration, while starvation alone produces hydration.

The most interesting histopathological finding at autopsy in rats previously fed a rancid biotin deficient diet for seven weeks was degeneration of the proximal renal tubular epithelium with reflux of the necrotic epithelium into the subcapsular space of the glomerulus. This finding is illustrated in Figure 58. The histopathological picture shown in Figure 58 is identical to that reported in vitamin E deficient rats[20] in which the lesion appears to be due to rapid postmortem autolysis of the proximal tubular epithelium with reflux of debris into the subcapsular space of the glomerulus. Peters and Boyd[10] noted that the renal lesion was

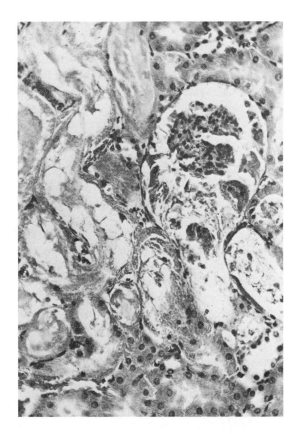

FIGURE 58. A photomicrograph of the kidney of a rat previously fed a rancid biotin deficient diet for 47 days, showing degeneration of the proximal convoluted tubules and reflux of debris into the subcapsular space of the glomerulus. Hematoxylin-phloxine-saffron, x 450. (From Peters and Boyd[10] with the permission of the authors and of *Food and Cosmetics Toxicology,* copyright © 1969, Pergamon Press, England.)

encountered more frequently in thick than in thin blocks of tissue removed for preparation of slides for microscopic observation. This evidence supports the view that the lesion found in rats fed rancid diets was also due to rapid postmortem autolysis. Since the lesion in vitamin E deficient rats is prevented by giving the animals 0.25 mg of a-tocopherol weekly, Peters and Boyd[10] gave up to 1 mg of a-tocopherol daily to rats fed the rancid diet, but this treatment did not prevent the appearance of the glomerular reflux. While the lesion appeared to be due to rapid postmortem hydrolysis, it did not seem to be due to a deficiency of vitamin E in rats fed a rancid diet.

The Initial Toxic Reaction

Studies were made by Peters and Boyd[10] to define the significance of factors concerned with development of the initial toxic reaction to rancid diets. The interval of exposure to room temperature required for development of the reaction was investigated in five groups of rats each fed a biotin deficient diet which had been exposed for a certain length of time, from 0 to 16 weeks. It was found that a maximal initial toxic reaction was produced by a diet which had been exposed to room temperature in a thin layer 6 cm in thickness for four weeks.

In a second series of studies, it was found that the initial toxic reaction in male rats was the same as that in females.

Third, a series of rats of different ages were fed rancid biotin deficient diet. The toxic reaction was most marked in weanling rats weighing 44 ± 4 g (mean ± standard deviation). The initial toxic reaction decreased in intensity in older rats. The age effect may be due to the fact that young rats eat relatively more food, expressed as g food/kg body weight/24 hr, than older rats. The younger rats receive relatively more rancid fats per kg body weight, therefore, than do the older rats.

In a fourth study, season was found to affect the initial toxic reaction. During the winter months of February and March, rats fed the rancid diet at Kingston, Ontario, Canada developed a more severe reaction than did rats fed during other seasons of the year. Death began to appear at one week, and by three weeks half the animals in the winter study were dead. Clinical signs of winter toxicity included sunken eyes, erect and greenishly discolored fur, ataxia, arched back, abducted legs, abdominal bloating, automutilation of the tail, severe diarrhea, greenish stools containing mucous pledgets, anorexia, loss of body weight, oligodipsia, and hemoconcentration. The animals died of respiratory failure following mild asphyxial convulsions and a period of hypothermic coma. At autopsy, most organs were congested, there were ulcers in the pyloric stomach, a stress reaction, organ weights were reduced, and the renal glomerular reflux reaction was found in many animals. Maignon and Chahine[21] reported seasonal variations in the response of weanling rats to vitamin deficient diets.

The effect of aggregation and segregation on the initial toxic reaction was investigated in a fifth study which was performed during the winter months. Aggregated rats were assembled with six to nine animals per cage. Segregated rats were isolated one to a cage. The rancid diet was fed to both groups. Toxicity was much more severe in the aggregated animals, as exemplified in Figure 59.

The sixth study investigated the influence of a cortisone preparation on the initial toxic reaction. In 1953, Greenberg and Frazer[22] reported that cortisone did not influence the toxic reaction of rats to rancid diets. Peters and Boyd[10] gave decamethasone in daily oral doses of from 60 to 120 μg and fed them a rancid biotin deficient diet. The toxic reaction was the same as that in controls not given decamethasone.

Finally, recovery from the initial toxic reaction was studied in 33 female rats placed on the rancid diet for 30 days and then transferred to a standard laboratory chow. Recovery began during the first 24 hr. By the 11th day on laboratory chow, the clinical signs and autopsy findings were within or

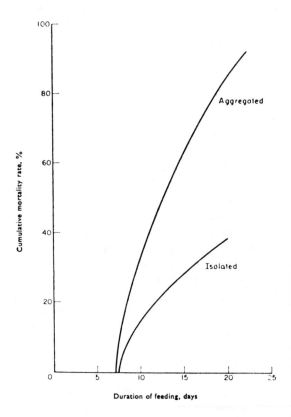

FIGURE 59. Mortality rates at one week in aggregated rats housed six to nine per cage and in segregated rats isolated one to a cage and fed a rancid biotin deficient diet during the winter months of the year at Kingston, Ontario, Canada. (From Peters and Boyd[10] with permission of the authors and of *Food and Cosmetics Toxicology,* copyright © 1969, Pergamon Press, England.)

approaching the range of values in controls fed laboratory chow for the full 41 days.

Factors Responsible for the Initial Toxic Reaction

In one series of studies,[10] it was found that development of the toxic rancid factor required a certain percentage of fatty oils in the biotin deficient diet. For example, when the concentration of cottonseed oil was lowered from 14% (Table 52) to 4%, cod liver oil omitted (vitamins A and D being added), and the diet exposed to laboratory temperature for six weeks, it produced no toxic effects.

In a second series of investigations, the presence of raw egg white powder was found necessary for the development of toxicity in the rancid oil fraction. For example, toxicity did not develop in an exposed diet containing 14% cottonseed oil and 3% cod liver oil added to laboratory chow. The initial toxic reaction did not occur from feeding an exposed diet containing 18% casein, 60% sucrose, 12% fatty oils, 6% fiber, 4% salt mix, and adequate vitamin supplements. In a control test, the initial toxic reaction continued to appear in albino rats fed an exposed biotin deficient diet, as listed in Table 52.

Finally, it was demonstrated that while raw egg white powder was necessary for the production of rancidity in the oil fraction, the rancid oils alone were responsible for the initial toxic reaction. Biotin deficient diet was exposed for six months, the oils were extracted with ether, and the extract was evaporated to dryness, yielding an oil which was thick, discolored, and had a rancid smell. In experiment one, the rancid oil was used to prepare a diet similar to that listed in Table 52, but with 17% of rancid oil in place of the fresh oils; feeding this diet produced an initial toxic reaction in rats. In experiment two, a diet was prepared which was identical to that of experiment one, but with 30% raw egg white powder replaced by denatured egg white powder. An initial toxic reaction was produced in albino rats fed the diet of experiment two, indicating that raw egg white powder was not necessary for the production of this toxic reaction. This conclusion was confirmed in experiment three in which an initial toxic reaction appeared in rats fed a diet similar to that used in experiment one, but in which 30% casein replaced the egg white protein. The conclusion from these studies was that the initial toxic reaction was due entirely to rancid fats. On the basis of evidence then

available, Narayan and Kummerow[23] proposed in 1963 that the toxicity of rancid fats was due to formation of a complex between proteins and the oils. To the extent that the toxic factor was completely extractable with ether, no evidence was obtained by Peters and Boyd[10] that the rancid fats had to combine with protein to produce the initial toxic reaction.

Peters and Boyd[10] realized that there was a possibility that the residue left after extracting the rancid oils from the exposed biotin deficient diet, noted in the previous paragraph, might produce the initial toxic reaction. To investigate this possibility, they added 14% fresh cottonseed oil and 3% fresh cod liver oil to the ether-extracted residue and fed this to albino rats. No toxic reaction occurred. Control groups in this study added confirmation to the previously demonstrated facts that no toxicity developed in rats fed a fresh biotin deficient diet, or a fresh biotin deficient diet with casein replacing raw egg white powder, or laboratory chow containing the same concentrations of fresh cottonseed and cod liver oils. The evidence obtained by Peters and Boyd,[10] therefore, indicated that the initial toxic reaction was due entirely to rancidity of the fatty oil fraction of the diet.

The Delayed Toxic Reaction

The features of the delayed toxic reaction were established in a series of studies reported by Peters and Boyd.[10] The delayed toxic reaction appeared in both male and female albino rats. It was more marked in young than in older rats. Segregation of the animals one to a cage did not lessen the severity of the delayed toxic reaction as it did of the initial toxic reaction, as shown in Figure 59. During the winter months of the year, delayed deaths occurred in rats fed a rancid biotin deficient diet, but there was no obvious period of recovery from the initial toxic reaction. Delayed deaths in the winter appeared to be due to an extension of the initial toxic reaction. In other words, no proof was obtained that season had a marked influence on the delayed toxic reaction, as it did on the initial toxic reaction. In place of the hemoconcentration recorded in the initial toxic reaction, there was a fall in blood hemoglobin in the delayed toxic reaction. At 75 days, for example, blood hemoglobin in rats fed a rancid biotin deficient diet was 10.3 ± 2.4 g/100 ml (mean ± standard deviation), compared with 14 to

16 g/100 ml in controls fed laboratory chow or a fresh biotin deficient diet.

Finally, several experiments were designed to establish the factor or factors in the rancid diet which was or were responsible for the development of the delayed toxic reaction. In a first series of such studies, evidence was obtained that the rancid diet augmented slightly the need for vitamins such as biotin. When biotin supplementation was given daily to such rats, as 200 μg either orally or subcutaneously, loss of body weight in the delayed toxic reaction was slightly less than that in animals given no biotin supplementation, as shown in Figure 56 as regressions (c) and (d) compared with (e). Autopsy, however, revealed no significant differences in the degree of loss of weights in most body organs from biotin supplementation. As noted in Table 52, rats fed rancid diets were receiving amounts of all vitamins which were deemed adequate. It was possible, however, that feeding rancid diets augmented the need for vitamins, as suggested by Holman.[3] To study this possibility, rats were fed the rancid diet and given orally each day 200 mg of a complete vitamin supplement. The delayed toxicity syndrome was found to be insignificantly affected by the vitamin supplementation. The conclusion from these investigations was that while the delayed toxic reaction was not due to vitamin deficiencies, it could possibly be increased slightly by an augmented need for some vitamins such as biotin.

In a second series of experiments, it was shown that the delayed toxic reaction was due to the sublethal toxicity of raw egg white augmented by the presence of dietary rancid oils and possibly, as noted above, to a minor degree by increased need for certain vitamins. Peters and Boyd[10] fed albino rats a rancid biotin deficient diet which was autoclaved just before feeding for 3 min at 125°C to denature the egg white. During denaturation the color of the diet changed from pale yellow to ocher. It was then fed to albino rats together with vitamin supplementation in the form of 200 mg daily of an all-vitamin mixture. As controls, other rats were fed rancid diet which had not been denatured and they developed a typical delayed toxic reaction. A typical initial toxic reaction was produced in rats fed the denatured rancid diet, but there was no delayed toxic reaction whatsoever. Growth rate was similar to that in controls fed laboratory chow, as shown in Figure 56. Food

intake calculated as calories was also the same as in chow-fed controls, but calculated as grams was somewhat lower in rats fed the denatured rancid diet because this diet contains about 25% more calories per gram than laboratory chow (see Figure 57). The diuresis that began during the initial toxic reaction persisted in rats fed the denatured rancid diet, as shown in Figure 57. Markley[24] has quoted evidence indicating that heat can alter the chemical nature of rancid oils so it is possible that nontoxic products were formed during denaturation.

These results suggested that the main dietary factor responsible for the delayed toxic reaction was raw egg white. Peters[25] fed albino rats diets containing increasing percentages of raw egg white powder and found that anorexia and inhibition of growth appeared when the amount of egg white reached 80% of the diet. When the egg white was previously denatured, a level of 80% in the diet produced no toxicity. Boyd, Peters, and Krijnen[26] demonstrated that raw egg white powder produced death in albino rats when given by gavage in doses about equal to one tenth of the animals' body weight. These results and corresponding studies on the toxicity of other proteins will be discussed in Part 4. The effects of rancid oils have been discussed in considerably more detail in the reviews of Peters.[27-29]

Relative Hepatomegaly in Rats Fed a Rancid Diet

Peters[8] demonstrated that the cachexia in albino rats induced by feeding a rancid biotin deficient diet made the animals highly susceptible to caffeine toxicity. Peters and Boyd[30] investigated the possibility that anorexia had been responsible for the augmented toxicity of caffeine in rats fed a rancid biotin deficient diet. They found that partial starvation did augment the susceptibility of rats to caffeine toxicity. Dixon, Shultice, and Fouts[31] reported that other drugs such as hexobarbital were more toxic in starved animals. Peters and Boyd[32] considered that a useful principle to demonstrate to medical students would be that cachexia augments susceptibility to drug action. They decided to show that sleeping time to pentobarbital was lengthened in albino rats fed a cachexigenic rancid biotin deficient diet. During the afternoon of the demonstration, sleeping time of the cachectic rats proved to be significantly shorter — not longer — than that in healthy controls fed laboratory chow!

Further studies suggested that a relative hypertrophy of the liver in rats fed the rancid diet had been responsible for a rapid breakdown of pentobarbital and hence a reduction in sleeping time.

Changes in body weight and in the duration of sleeping time to pentobarbital sodium given intraperitoneally in a dose of 25 mg/kg are shown in Figure 60. At autopsy it was found that while there was a decrease in the absolute weight of all organs, the weight of liver and of certain other organs, such as adrenal glands, was increased relative to body weight. Pentobarbital dosage had been calculated on a mg/kg body weight basis.

In a second experiment, pentobarbital was given in a range of doses indicated in Figure 61. The maximal sleeping time was about 5 hr. This duration was produced from doses of pentobarbital of about 50 mg/kg in rats fed laboratory (fox) chow and of about 75 mg/kg in rats fed the rancid diet. Doses in excess of these amounts produced deaths. As in the first experiment, sleeping time to pentobarbital in doses calculated

as mg/kg body weight was longer in rats fed a standard chow than in rats fed the rancid diet. The weight of the liver in the former group was 8.87 ± 0.38 g (mean ± standard deviation) and in the latter group 8.18 ± 0.56 g. The chow-fed rats, therefore, received about 60% more pentobarbital per g of liver weight than the rats fed a rancid diet. Had rats fed the rancid diet been given 60% more pentobarbital, they would have slept about the same length of time as chow-fed rats.

The results suggest, therefore, that the relative hepatomegaly of rats fed a rancid diet was responsible for their resistance to the hypnotic action of pentobarbital. This did not occur in a control group of rats fed a fresh biotin deficient diet, as shown by data summarized in Table 53. It should be noted, however, that there were other factors in the rats fed a rancid diet which might have affected their reaction to pentobarbital. For example, they exhibited a stress reaction and stress has been reported to both augment[33] or di-

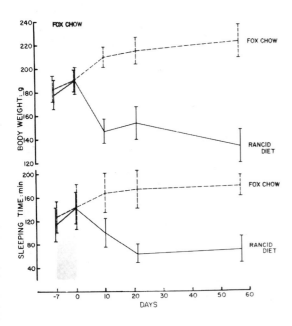

FIGURE 60. The effect of feeding a rancid biotin deficient diet for the number of days indicated on the abscissa upon body weight and pentobarbital sleeping time in albino rats. The results are shown as means plus and minus their standard deviations. Results in a pretreatment control week when all rats were fed laboratory (fox) chow are shown to the left of the figure. (From Peters and Boyd[32] with the permission of the authors and of *Toxicology and Applied Pharmacology,* copyright © 1966, Academic Press, New York.)

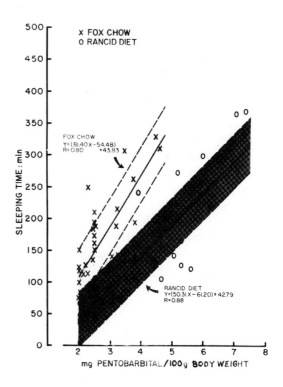

FIGURE 61. The regression of sleeping time on dosage of pentobarbital sodium given intraperitoneally to albino rats fed for up to 75 days on a rancid biotin deficient diet or on laboratory (fox) chow. (From Peters and Boyd[32] with the permission of the authors and of *Toxicology and Applied Pharmacology,* copyright © 1966, Academic Press, New York.)

TABLE 53

The Effect of Feeding a Fresh Biotin Deficient Diet to Albino Rats on Pentobarbital Sleeping Time, Body Weight, Liver Weight, and Liver Water Content[a]

Diet	Sleeping time (min)	Body weight (g)	Liver weight (g)[b]	Liver water (%)
Control (fox chow)	100 ± 50	210 ± 20	8.21 ± 0.42	71.9 ± 0.8
Biotin deficient	88 ± 38	192 ± 19	6.66 ± 0.50	72.8 ± 0.7
Probability (P)[c]	0.4	0.01	<0.001	0.02

[a]Results are expressed as the mean ± S.D.
[b]Wet weight
[c]Probability that the mean of the biotin deficient animals equals that of the controls.
(From Peters and Boyd[32] with the permission of the authors and of *Toxicology and Applied Pharmacology*, copyright © 1966, Academic Press, New York.)

minish[34] responses to drugs. They also had relative hypertrophies of the kidneys, gastrointestinal tract, adrenal glands, and salivary glands, and a relative atrophy of the thymus gland, skeletal muscle, and skin.

Conclusions Regarding Rancid Fats

Feeding a biotin deficient diet containing rancid fatty oils produces a biphasic toxic reaction in albino rats, an initial toxic reaction during the first week, and a delayed toxic reaction beginning at about three weeks.

The initial toxic reaction is due to rancid oils produced in the diet on standing at room temperature with the aid of certain other dietary items such as raw egg white powder. The initial toxic reaction consists of a fulminating anorectic cachexia, which is particularly marked in weanling rats and in the winter months of the year. During the second and third weeks, the animals recover from the initial toxic reaction even though they continue to be fed a rancid diet.

The delayed toxic reaction sets in slowly at about 21 days in rats fed a rancid diet. It consists of a gradual loss of body weight, with death appearing at six weeks and longer. Most body organs become edematous and there is degeneration of the proximal renal tubular epithelium with reflux of debris into the glomerulus. Many clinical features are different from those of the initial toxic reaction; for example, the delayed reaction is accompanied by anemia rather than hemoconcentration, as in the initial toxic reaction. The delayed reaction is due to the large amount of raw egg white powder, assisted by rancid oils, and aided to a minor degree by relative vitamin deficiencies.

Feeding rancid oils produces a relative hepatomegaly in the cachectic rats which may enable the animals to metabolize more rapidly certain agents such as pentobarbital. Sleeping time to pentobarbital, given in doses calculated as mg/kg body weight, is shorter in cachectic rats fed a rancid diet than in healthy controls fed a standard chow.

REFERENCES

1. White, A., Handler, P., and Smith, E. L., *Principles of Biochemistry,* 4th ed., McGraw-Hill, New York, 1968.
2. Poling, C. E., Warner, W. D., Mone, P. E., and Rice, E. E., The influence of temperature, heating time, and aeration upon the nutritive value of fats, *J. Am. Oil Chem. Soc.,* 39, 315, 1962.
3. Holman, R. T., Autoxidation of fats and related substances, in *Progress in the Chemistry of Fats and Other Lipids,* Vol. 2, Holman, R. T., Lundberg, W. O., and Malkin, T., Eds., Pergamon Press, Oxford, England.
4. Fitzhugh, O. G., Nelson, A. A., and Calvery, H. O., Rancid fat in experimental diets, *Proc. Soc. Exp. Biol. Med.,* 56, 129, 1944.
5. Fox, M. R. S. and Mickelsen, O., Salt mixtures for purified-type diets. I. Effect of salts in accelerating oxidative rancidity, *J. Nutr.,* 67, 123, 1959.
6. Burr, G. O. and Barnes, R. H., Non-caloric functions of dietary fats, *Physiol. Rev.,* 23, 256, 1943.
7. Kaunitz, H., Slanetz, C. A., and Johnson, R. E., Antagonism of fresh fat to the toxicity of heated and aerated cottonseed oil, *J. Nutr.,* 55, 577, 1955.
8. Peters, J. M., A fulminating toxic reaction to daily administration of caffeine in albino rats on a biotin deficient diet, Am. Ind. Hyg. Conf. Abstr., 1963, 18.
9. Peters, J. M. and Boyd, E. M., Clinical and pathological signs of winter toxicity from biotin deficient raw egg white diet in albino rats, *Pharmacologist,* 5, 232, 1963.
10. Peters, J. M. and Boyd, E. M., Toxic effects from a rancid diet containing large amounts of raw egg white powder, *Food Cosmet. Toxicol.,* 7, 197, 1969.
11. Boyd, E. M. and Sargeant, E. J., The production of skin reactions to benzylpenicillin in animals on a biotin-deficient diet, *J. New Drugs,* 2, 283, 1962.
12. Rubin, S. H., Drekter, L., and Moyer, E. H., Biological activity of synthetic d,1-desthiobiotin, *Proc. Soc. Exp. Biol. Med.,* 58, 352, 1945.
13. Boas, M. A., The effect of desiccation upon the nutritive properties of egg-white, *Biochem. J.,* 21, 712, 1927.
14. Bond, M., A modification of basal diet for rat feeding experiments, *Biochem. J.,* 16, 479, 1922.
15. György, P., The curative factor (vitamin H) for egg white injury, with particular reference to its presence in different foodstuffs and in yeast, *J. Biol. Chem.,* 131, 733, 1939.
16. Dittmer, K., du Vigneaud, V., György, P., and Rose, C. S., A study of biotin sulfone, *Arch. Biochem.,* 4, 299, 1944.
17. Peters, J. M., Caffeine toxicity in starved rats, *Toxicol. Appl. Pharmacol.,* 9, 390, 1966.
18. Peters, J. M. and Boyd, E. M., Organ weights and water levels of the rat following reduced food intake, *J. Nutr.,* 90, 354, 1966.
19. Peters, J. M. and Krijnen, C. J., Organ weights and water contents of rats fed purified diets, *Growth,* 30, 99, 1966.
20. Moore, T., Sharman, I. M., and Symonds, K. R., Kidney changes in vitamin E-deficient rats, *J. Nutr.,* 65, 183, 1958.
21. Maignon, F. and Chahine, M. A., Les variations saisonnières de la sensibilité de l'organisme'a l'intoxication proteique s'observent encore en presence de vitamines, *C. R. Séances Soc. Biol. Fil.,* 108, 868, 1931.
22. Greenberg, S. M. and Frazer, A. C., Some factors affecting the growth and development of rats fed rancid fat, *J. Nutr.,* 50, 421, 1953.
23. Narayan, K. A. and Kummerow, F. A., Factors influencing the formation of complexes between oxidized lipids and proteins, *J. Am. Oil Chem. Soc.,* 49, 339, 1963.
24. Markley, K. S., *Fatty Acids. Their Chemistry and Physical Properties,* Interscience, New York, 1947.
25. Peters, J. M., A separation of the direct toxic effect of dietary raw egg white powder from its action in producing biotin deficiency, *Br. J. Nutr.,* 21, 801, 1967.
26. Boyd, E. M., Peters, J. M., and Krijnen, C. J., The acute oral toxicity of reconstituted spray-dried egg white, *Ind. Med. Surg.,* 35, 782, 1966.
27. Peters, J. M., Caffeine Toxicity in Rats on A Biotin Deficient Diet, M.Sc. Thesis, Douglas Library, Queen's University, Kingston, Ontario, Canada, 1964.
28. Peters, J. M., Factors in Caffeine Toxicity, Ph.D. Thesis, Douglas Library, Queen's University, Kingston, Ontario, Canada, 1966.
29. Peters, J. M., Factors affecting caffeine toxicity, *J. Clin. Pharmacol.,* 7, 131, 1967.
30. Peters, J. M. and Boyd, E. M., Secondary factors in caffeine toxicity, *Proc. Can. Fed. Biol. Soc.,* 7, 37, 1964.
31. Dixon, R. L., Shultice, R. W., and Fouts, J. R., Factors affecting drug metabolism by liver microsomes. IV. Starvation, *Proc. Soc. Exp. Biol. Med.,* 103, 333, 1960.
32. Peters, J. M. and Boyd, E. M., Resistance to pentobarbital in rats fed a cachexigenic diet, *Toxicol. Appl. Pharmacol.,* 8, 464, 1966.
33. Prioreschi, P., Stress e anestesia da bromuro di sodio, *Atti. Soc. Lombarda Sci. Med. Biol.,* 14, 215, 1959.
34. Selye, H., *The Pluricausal Cardiopathies,* Charles C Thomas, Springfield, Ill., 1961.

PART IV. THE ORAL TOXICITY OF PROTEINS

Chapter 11

RAW EGG WHITE POWDER

An indication that raw egg white powder might produce toxicity and death in high doses appeared during studies on the effect of feeding a biotin deficient diet described by Peters,[1] Boyd and Peters,[2] Peters and Krijnen,[3] and discussed in Chapter 10. The biotin deficient diet used in these studies was that of Rubin, Drekter, and Moyer[4] which contains 30% raw egg white powder. This amount of dietary raw egg white produces biotin deficiency in weanling rats but has little effect on adult animals. Peters[5] traced the origin of the content of raw egg white powder. The diet was first reported in 1916 by Bateman,[6] who fed adult white rats a diet containing from 20 to 80% raw egg white mixed with unspecified amounts of milk powder, bread meal, and lard. Diets containing the larger amounts of raw egg white produced anorexia, diarrhea, and loss of body weight. Parsons[7] distinguished between what she called an "early nutritive disaster" and a later vitamin deficiency syndrome in weanling rats fed a diet containing 66% raw egg white. Tscherkes[8] and Maignon and Chahine[9] reported that a diet containing 100% raw egg white produced death within three to five days. From these earlier data, Boyd, Peters, and Krijnen[10] estimated that the single killing oral dose of raw egg white would probably be of the order of 100 to 200 g/kg.

The Acute Oral LD$_{50}$

Boyd et al.[10] determined the acute oral toxicity of raw egg white in male albino rats weighing 150 to 200 g. The preparation used was egg white solids (spray dried) obtained from General Biochemicals of Chagrin Falls, Ohio. It was dissolved in distilled water to a concentration of 40% (w/v) and given by mouth slowly through an intragastric cannula in a volume of 100 ml/kg, repeated at hourly intervals for 0 to 4 times, to animals which had been starved overnight to empty the stomach. Controls were given the same volumes of distilled water. Clinical observations were recorded daily for one week and, in survivors,

at a fortnight and at one month. Autopsies were performed not later than 30 min after death in animals which died, upon representative groups of survivors at two weeks and at one month, and upon controls at the same intervals.

As illustrated in Figure 62, the regression of doses of raw egg white between 80 and 120 g/kg was linear and fitted by the equation $Y = (84.1 + 0.332X) \pm 6.4$. By substituting 50 for X, the LD$_{50}$ $\pm$ S.E. may be calculated to be 100.7 ± 6.4 g/kg. The maximal LD$_0$ may be estimated from figure 62 to be 84 g/kg and the minimal LD$_{100}$ to be 117 g/kg. Actually, a dose of 80 g/kg produced 7% mortality and 120 g/kg produced 90% mortality. Doses greater than 120 g/kg produced 100% mortality.

The mean $\pm$ standard error interval to death was 4.4 ± 0.7 hr. The interval was somewhat shorter

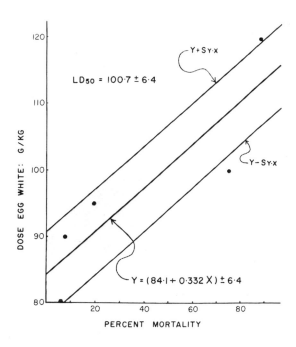

FIGURE 62. The regression of dose of raw egg white powder given by stomach tube to young adult male rats on percent mortality. (From Boyd et al.[10] with the permission of *Industrial Medicine and Surgery*, copyright © 1966, Industrial Medicine Publishing Co., Miami, Fla.)

than the mean in rats receiving the higher doses of raw egg white and somewhat longer in animals given the smaller doses.

Clinical Signs of Toxicity

At the acute oral LD_{50}, the albino rats had received 250 ml/kg of distilled water over a period of 2 hr. Clinical signs in controls given this dose of distilled water are exemplified in Figure 63. Clinical signs began to appear at 1 hr when piloerection was quite marked. They reached a peak of intensity at 3 hr or 1 hr after giving the last dose of distilled water (50 ml/kg). The signs were predominantly those of depression of the central nervous system such as listlessness and hyporeflexia. Piloerection appeared to be due to a fall in body temperature. There was no frank diarrhea but the stools were soft and the fur soiled. All except the last two signs had decreased in intensity at 4 hr.

Premortem clinical signs in animals given raw egg white are shown in Figure 64. To indicate the effect of lethal oral doses of raw egg white, the degree of each sign seen in water-treated controls and illustrated in Figure 63 has been subtracted from that recorded in rats given egg white plus distilled water and the difference is entered in Figure 64. Diarrhea was marked in rats given egg white. It consisted of repeated evacuations of what appeared to be mostly suspensions of egg white. Diarrhea was accompanied by abdominal bloating and soiling of the fur. Otherwise, the dominant effect of raw egg white was depression of the central nervous system which took the form of hyporeflexia, prostration, dyspnea, listlessness, and cyanosis. In contrast to the fall in body temperature of controls given distilled water, rats receiving raw egg white developed a fever which reached a peak at 3 hr. Death was due to respiratory or cardiac failure following tonoclonic convulsions.

Autopsy Observations

Gross pathology at death due to oral administration of raw egg white consisted of lesions in the brain, lungs, liver, spleen, and residual carcass. The brain and lungs were congested and the residual carcass was of a dark red color. The spleen was pale and the liver was dark.

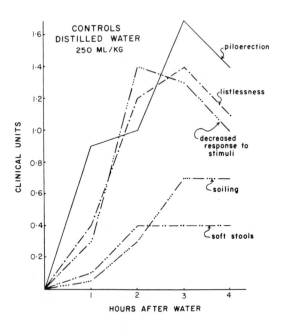

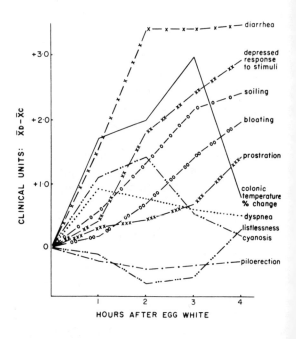

FIGURE 63.   The clinical signs of toxicity of distilled water given by stomach tube to young male albino rats in a dose of 250 ml/kg over a period of 2 hr. (From Boyd et al.[10] with the permission of *Industrial Medicine and Surgery*, copyright © 1966, Industrial Medicine Publishing Co., Miami, Fla.)

FIGURE 64.   Clinical signs of toxicity to raw egg white given by mouth to young adult male albino rats. The results are entered as minus the degree of each sign in controls given distilled water to indicate the net effect of raw egg white. (From Boyd et al.[10] with the permission of *Industrial Medicine and Surgery,* copyright © 1966, Industrial Medicine Publishing Co., Miami, Fla.)

TABLE 54

Histopathological Findings in Young Adult Male Albino Rats Following Oral Administration of Lethal Doses of Raw Egg White

Organ	At death	Survivors at 1 to 3 days
Adrenal glands	Vacuolation of zona glomerulosa	Alternating hyperemia and ischemia
Brain	Meningeal congestion and minute brain hemorrhages	Mild meningeal congestion
Gastrointestinal tract		
Cardiac stomach	Normal or excess mucus	Normal or hypertrophied epithelium
Pyloric stomach	Minor venous congestion of submucosa	Normal
Small bowel	Egg white adherent to villi	Normal or hypertrophied glands
Cecum	Minor congestion of lamina propria and submucosa	Egg white adherent and parasites seen in egg white
Colon	Normal	Parasites in egg white residue
Heart	Normal	Minor venous thrombosis
Kidneys	Congestion and tubular edema	Minor capillary-venous congestion
Liver	Diffuse peripheral lobular vacuolation and edema of von Kupffer's cells	Diffuse fine fatty degeneration of periphery of lobule and minor venous thrombosis
Lungs	Areas of capillary congestion and hemorrhage	Minor congestion, edema and venous thrombosis
Muscle (ventral abdominal wall)	Normal	Normal
Pancreas islets	Ischemic	Ischemic
Salivary (submaxillary) glands	Normal	Normal
Skin	Hypovascular	Normal
Spleen	Contracted red pulp	Normal
Testes	Pyknosis of spermatocytes	Sperm shrunken and irregular
Thymus gland	Mild capillary-venous congestion	Minor loss of thymocytes

(From Boyd et al.[10] with the permission of *Industrial Medicine and Surgery,* copyright © 1966, Industrial Medicine Publishing Co., Miami, Fla.)

The microscopic findings at death are summarized in Table 54. Egg white produced a very minor irritant inflammatory reaction in the gastrointestinal tract. There was a hemorrhagic inflammation of the meninges, brain, and lungs and congestion of the kidneys and thymus gland. The renal tubules and hepatic cells were edematous. The pancreas and skin were ischemic.

There was a stress reaction in the adrenal glands, spleen, and thymus gland.

Shifts in the wet weight of body organs at death following lethal oral doses of raw egg white are indicated in Table 55. In the 4 hr to death, the albino rats had lost a mean of 10% body weight. Loss of weight was particularly marked in the tissues of the gastrointestinal tract, skeletal

TABLE 55

Changes in the Wet Weight of Body Organs at Autopsy on Albino Rats Following Oral Administration of Lethal Doses of Raw Egg White[a]

Organ	At death (N = 28 plus 13 controls)	Fortnight survivors (N = 16 plus 14 controls)	Month survivors (N = 21 plus 16 controls)
Adrenal glands	– 9.5	– 9.7	+10.3*
Brain	– 1.2	– 3.1	+ 2.8
Gastrointestinal tract			
Cardiac stomach	–21.5*	– 4.7*	– 3.1
Pyloric stomach	–24.9**	– 5.9	– 3.1
Small bowel	–27.1**	+ 1.1	+ 4.2
Cecum	–34.8**	– 8.3*	– 0.5
Colon	–23.9**	– 0.8	+ 9.3*
Heart	– 7.3**	– 4.4	+ 0.1
Kidneys	–15.2**	– 2.0	– 1.8
Liver	–17.8**	– 3.7	+ 4.8
Lungs	+17.1*	– 9.8*	0.0
Muscle (abdominal wall)	–25.9**	+ 0.7	+ 2.4
Salivary (submaxillary) glands	– 1.5	– 6.0	– 4.7
Skin	– 5.8	+ 7.4	+ 1.6
Spleen	–23.6*	+36.9*	–35.3*.
Testes	–22.5**	+ 3.2	– 3.1
Thymus gland	–23.1**	–17.5*	+19.4*
Residual carcass	–10.1**	0.0	+ 4.3
Autopsy body weight	– 9.5**	0.0	+ 3.3

[a]Wet weight was measured in grams. The results are expressed as mean percent change from controls, specifically as $[(\bar{X}_d – \bar{X}_c)/\bar{X}_c] \times 100$, where $\bar{X}_d$ is the mean in the drug-treated rats and $\bar{X}_c$ in the controls. Mean differences significant at $P = 0.05$ to 0.02 are indicated by one asterisk and at $P = 0.01$ or less by two asterisks. (From Boyd et al.[10] with the permission of *Industrial Medicine and Surgery*, copyright © 1966, Industrial Medicine Publishing Co., Miami, Fla.)

muscle, spleen, testes, and thymus gland. The lungs had gained weight due to congestion and there was no significant change in the weight of some organs such as adrenal glands, brain, and salivary glands.

Mean changes in the water levels of body organs at death due to oral administration of raw egg white are summarized in Table 56. It may be seen that intragastric administration of concentrated aqueous solutions of raw egg white powder produced a dehydration of all body organs. Water was drawn particularly from the tissues of the gastrointestinal tract, muscle, testes, and thymus gland and dehydration accounted for part or most of the loss of wet weight in these organs.

The cause of death, therefore, was cardio-respiratory failure following convulsions. This was associated with a marked dehydration of body organs, congestion of several organs such as the brain and meninges, mild degenerative changes in the liver and kidneys, and a mild stress reaction.

Survivors of Raw Egg White

Clinical measurements in survivors were calculated as mean percentage changes from similar measurements made before administration of raw egg white and of distilled water. Results in animals given a total of 250 ml/kg of distilled water are summarized in Table 57. During the first 24 hr after giving distilled water, there was an average loss of body weight of 2.2% which was uniform and therefore significant at $P = 0.05$ or less. Loss of weight was associated with anorexia, a diuresis, alkalinuria, piloerection, and listlessness. During

TABLE 56

Mean Changes in the Water Content of Body Organs in Albino Rats Following Oral Administration of Lethal Doses of Raw Egg White[a]

Organ	At death (N = 28 plus 13 controls)	Fortnight survivors (N = 16 plus 14 controls)	Month survivors (N = 21 plus 16 controls)
Adrenal glands	−12.3**	− 8.6*	−3.4
Brain	−13.4**	− 0.6	+0.3
Gastrointestinal tract			
Cardiac stomach	−30.5**	− 1.2	−1.6
Pyloric stomach	−21.9**	− 7.0*	+2.5
Small bowel	−14.0**	− 4.4*	+1.2
Cecum	−26.7**	−16.4**	+0.8
Colon	−20.8**	− 4.5	+2.3
Heart	−14.2**	− 1.7	+0.9
Kidneys	−14.5**	− 0.3	−0.7
Liver	−12.8**	− 1.6	−2.9
Lungs	−18.3**	− 1.3	−0.6
Muscle (abdominal wall)	−22.3**	− 3.4	+0.4
Salivary glands (submaxillary)	−13.7**	− 3.6	−1.3
Skin	−17.0**	+ 5.4	−1.1
Spleen	− 9.9**	− 2.9	+2.8
Testes	−23.8	− 1.4	+0.9
Thymus gland	−21.1**	− 4.5*	+2.3
Residual carcass	−12.8**	− 4.0*	−1.9

[a]Water levels were measured as g water per 100 g dry weight of tissue. The results are expressed as percent change from controls, specifically as $[(\bar{X}_d - \bar{X}_c)/\bar{X}_c] \times 100$, where $\bar{X}_d$ is the mean in the drug-treated animals and $\bar{X}_c$ in the controls. Mean differences significant at $P = 0.05$ to 0.02 are indicated by one asterisk and at $P = 0.01$ or less by two asterisks. (From Boyd et al.[10] with the permission of *Industrial Medicine and Surgery*, copyright © 1966, Industrial Medicine Publishing Co., Miami, Fla.)

the second and subsequent days, growth resumed and signs of toxicity to distilled water disappeared.

Data on clinical signs in survivors of oral administration of lethal doses of raw egg white are summarized in Table 58. Inhibition of growth was somewhat more evident in rats surviving administration of raw egg white than in water-treated controls. Recovery of growth did not appear as early in rats receiving egg white in spite of an increase in food and water intake during the second and subsequent days. There was a slight initial fever at 24 hr followed by a rebound hypothermia and return to normal body temperature at the end of the first week in survivors. At 24 hr there was a marked diuresis with a residual less marked diuresis persisting through the remainder of the first week in survivors. Marked proteinuria during the first few days may have

been due, at least in part, to contamination of urine with diarrheal egg white. Alkalinuria alternated with aciduria, as indicated in Table 58. Many of the clinical signs seen at 4 hr in nonsurvivors and illustrated in Figure 64 were present in survivors at 24 hr. These clinical signs gradually disappeared during the second and subsequent days, as indicated by values for the last seven entries in Table 58.

Residual histopathology in survivors at one to three days after oral administration of lethal doses of raw egg white is indicated in Table 54. Most of the mild local inflammatory reaction in the gastrointestinal tract had disappeared. Egg white remaining in the lumen of the cecum and colon could be seen to be infected with various parasites. There was some residual congestion in the meninges, kidneys, and lungs with minor venous

TABLE 57

Clinical Signs in Control Albino Rats Given Distilled Water Orally in a Dose of 250 ml/kg over a Period of 2 hr

Sign	Units	Pre-water control day $\bar{X} \pm$ S.D.	Days after distilled water (Mean % change from pre-water control day)[1] 1	2	3	4	5	14
Body weight	g	174 ± 11	− 2.2*	+ 1.6	+ 4.9*	+ 7.6*	+ 12.4*	+45.3*
Food intake	g/kg/day	127 ± 18	− 12.3*	+ 1.6	+ 3.3	+ 1.6	+ 4.9	−20.5*
Water intake	ml/kg/day	120 ± 30	− 4.2	+ 14.2*	+ 14.2	+13.3	+ 9.2	−16.8*
Colonic temperature	°C	37.4 ± 0.4	− 0.6	− 0.1	+ 0.1	+ 0.3	− 0.9	− 0.1
Urinary volume	ml/kg/day	5.7 ± 5.7	+1686*	+ 43	+ 64	+21	− 22	+69
Urinary protein output	mg/kg/day	5.1 ± 4.0	− 4.2	+100	+167	−17	+100	0
Urinary pH	24-hr sample	6.3 ± 0.4	+ 17.2*	+ 14.0*	0.0	− 1.6	+ 9.4	+ 6.2
Urinary glucose output[2]	mg/kg/day	0.0 ± 0.0	0.0	0.0	0.0	0.0	0.0	0.0
Piloerection[2]	1+ to 4+	0.0 ± 0.0	+ 0.9*	0.0	0.0	0.0	0.0	0.0
Listlessness[2]	1+ to 4+	0.0 ± 0.0	+ 0.4*	0.0	0.0	0.0	0.0	0.0
Diarrhea[2]	1+ to 4+	0.0 ± 0.0	0.0	0.0	0.0	0.0	0.0	0.0
Hyporeflexia[2]	1+ to 4+	0.0 ± 0.0	0.0	0.0	0.0	0.0	0.0	0.0
Prostration[2]	1+ to 4+	0.0 ± 0.0	0.0	0.0	0.0	0.0	0.0	0.0
Soiling[2]	1+ to 4+	0.0 ± 0.0	0.0	0.0	0.0	0.0	0.0	0.0
Abdominal bloating[2]	1+ to 4+	0.0 ± 0.0	0.0	0.0	0.0	0.0	0.0	0.0

[1] Mean changes which differed at P = 0.05 or less from the mean in the pre-water control day are indicated by an asterisk.
[2] Results of this measurement for days after distilled water are expressed as $\bar{X}_a - \bar{X}_b$, where $\bar{X}_a$ is the mean on the respective day after distilled water and $\bar{X}_b$ the mean on the pre-water control day. In each instance $\bar{X}_b$ is zero. (From Boyd et al.[10] with the permission of *Industrial Medicine and Surgery*, copyright © 1966, Industrial Medicine Publishing Co., Miami, Fla.)

TABLE 58

Clinical Signs in Albino Rats that Survived Oral Administration of Lethal Doses of Raw Egg White[a]

Sign	Expressed as	Days after egg white 1	2	3	4	5	14
Body weight	% Change	− 2.0*	− 2.1*	− 0.9	− 0.7	− 2.3	+ 5.0
Food intake	% Change	− 46.5**	+ 8.7*	+ 11.6*	+ 11.5*	+ 13.4*	+ 9.3
Water intake	% Change	+ 62.5**	+ 8.6*	+ 8.0	+ 0.2	+ 0.1	+ 3.3
Colonic temperature	% Change	+ 1.1*	− 0.5	− 1.4*	− 1.4*	+ 0.1	− 0.3
Urinary volume[b]	% Change	+3800.0**	+265.4*	+286.8*	+186.1	+298.5*	+150.6
Urinary protein output[b]	% Change	+9728.1**	+304.3*	+152.2*	+ 19.0	− 36.1	+ 45.2
Urinary pH	% Change	+ 3.4*	− 7.8**	+10.2*	+ 12.1*	+ 12.0**	+ 4.7
Urinary glucose output	Difference	+ 2.1	+ 36.0**	+ 9.2	+ 2.1	+ 2.0	0.0
Piloerection	Difference	+ 0.1	0.0	0.0	0.0	0.0	0.0
Listlessness	Difference	+ 0.3*	+ 0.2	0.0	0.0	0.0	0.0
Diarrhea	Difference	+ 0.4*	0.0	0.0	0.0	0.0	0.0
Hyporeflexia	Difference	+ 0.4	0.0	0.0	0.0	0.0	0.0
Prostration	Difference	0.0	0.0	0.0	0.0	0.0	0.0
Soiling	Difference	+ 1.3**	+ 0.05	0.0	0.0	0.0	0.0
Abdominal bloating	Difference	0.0	0.0	0.0	0.0	0.0	0.0

[a] The results are expressed either as percent change from controls, specifically as $[(\bar{X}_d - \bar{X}_c)/\bar{X}_c] \times 100$, or as differences from the control specifically as $(\bar{X}_d - \bar{X}_c)$, where $\bar{X}_d$ is the mean of the observations in drug (egg white) treated rats and $\bar{X}_c$ in the controls. One asterisk indicates that $\bar{X}_d - \bar{X}_c$ is significant at P = 0.05 to 0.02 and two asterisks at P = 0.01 or less.
[b] Urine at 24 hr was contaminated with diarrheal egg white.
(From Boyd et al.[10] with the permission of *Industrial Medicine and Surgery*, Copyright © 1966, Industrial Medicine Publishing Co., Miami, Fla.)

thrombosis in the heart and liver. In the liver, a fine peripheral fatty degeneration was evident. Residual inhibition of spermatogenesis persisted in the testes.

Shifts in the weight of body organs in survivors at two weeks and at one month are summarized in Table 55. In animals autopsied at a fortnight after giving raw egg white, there was minor loss of weight in cardiac stomach, cecum, lungs, and thymus gland. In general, however, organ weights at two weeks were similar to those in water-treated controls. At one month, organ weights in rats surviving oral administration of raw egg white were essentially the same as those in water-treated controls.

Changes in the levels of organ water in rats surviving raw egg white are indicated in Table 56. At two weeks there was some residual dehydration of adrenal glands, pyloric stomach, small bowel, cecum, thymus gland, and residual carcass. Organ water levels had returned to values in the controls at one month after raw egg white in surviving albino rats.

The results on survivors indicate, therefore, that albino rats recover quickly from the toxic effects of lethal oral doses of raw egg white. Some signs of toxicity persist for a few days, at two weeks there is a minor dehydration of body organs, but at one month the survivors are essentially normal.

Discussion

The acute oral LD_{50} of raw egg white powder dissolved in distilled water and given as repeated doses of a 40% (w/v) solution to young male albino rats was approximately one tenth of body weight. It is obvious that this amount of raw egg white is not likely to be consumed by man over a period of 2 or 3 hr. Even in small children, the dose required to kill is not likely to be taken orally. A child weighing 20 lb would have to ingest some 2 lb of raw egg white powder to get the equivalent of a lethal dose in rats.

In most studies on acute oral toxicity, the volume of the vehicle is kept constant and the amount of agent dissolved in this volume varied. This rule was not followed in the present study of acute oral toxicity of raw egg white powder because of the limits of solubility of the egg white in distilled water. The maximal amount of the preparation of egg white powder used which could be dissolved in distilled water was 40 g/100 ml of final solution. The maximal volume of this solution which could be given without producing marked immediate evacuation through the anus was 100 ml/kg. It was necessary to repeat this maximal volume and an interval of 1 hr between administrations was selected from preliminary studies as being the shortest interval not followed by massive immediate evacuation through the anus. The studies of Ferguson[11] and of Constantopoulos and Boyd[12] have shown that death rates from toxic doses of raw egg white powder increase in proportion to the volume of vehicle used to dissolve the powder. Presumably this phenomenon is related to rates of absorption of the agent dissolved in a vehicle, such as distilled water, and given intragastrically. Had it been possible to give the largest volume of solution of raw egg white powder, namely 400 ml/kg, at one time and dissolved other doses in this volume, the LD_{50} would presumably have been somewhat lower than that found. Had it been possible to dissolve more raw egg white powder in a given volume of distilled water and had smaller volumes of the solution been given, the LD_{50} would presumably have been higher than that found by the technique used herein.

Expressed as g/kg, the LD_{50} of raw egg white is obviously quite high. Expressed as millimoles per kg (mM/kg) body weight it is much lower. From data on the molecular weight of proteins[13] it may be estimated that the LD_{50} of raw egg white is of the order of from less than 1 to 10 mM/kg body weight. It is probable that some of the raw egg white was digested during the 4 hr before death. If it had all been converted to amino acids, the LD_{50} of these would be roughly 1000 mM/kg. Assuming that 10% of the raw egg white was converted to amino acids and peptides during the 4 hr before death, the LD_{50} of the mixture would be approximately 100 mM/kg. The type of death was similar to that from sucrose, glucose, sodium chloride, and potassium chloride. The oral LD_{50} of these three agents, calculated as mM/kg body weight is, respectively, 103,[14] 138,[15] 64,[16] and 41.[16] Expressed as mM/kg, the acute oral LD_{50} of raw egg white may not be too much different from that of water-soluble agents producing a similar type of death. These relationships have been discussed further in Chapter 3.

Conclusions Regarding Raw Egg White

The acute oral LD_{50} ± S.E. of aqueous solutions of raw egg white powder in young adult male albino rats is 100.7 ± 6.4 g/kg. Expressed as mM/kg body weight, the oral LD_{50} of partially digested raw egg white may be estimated as approximately the same as that of sucrose, glucose, sodium chloride, and potassium chloride.

Death occurred at 4.4 ± 0.7 hr (mean $\pm$ standard error) and was immediately due to cardiorespiratory failure following tonoclonic convulsions. The initial signs of toxicity were due mainly to depression of the central nervous system and to the presence of bulk in the gastrointestinal tract. Autopsy revealed a mild irritant gastro-enteritis, tissue inflammation, degeneration and dehydration, and a mild stress reaction.

Recovery in survivors began to appear at 24 hr, was evident at five days, and complete by two to four weeks.

REFERENCES

1. **Peters, J. M.,** Toxicity due to other than biotin deficiency in adult albino rats on a biotin-deficient, dried egg white diet, *Fed. Proc.,* 22, 311, 1963.
2. **Boyd, E. M. and Peters, J. M.,** Clinical and pathological signs of winter toxicity from biotin-deficient raw egg white diet in albino rats, *Pharmacologist,* 5, 232, 1963.
3. **Peters, J. M. and Krijnen, C. J.,** Organ weights and water contents of rats fed purified diets, *Growth,* 30, 99, 1966.
4. **Rubin, S. H., Drekter, L., and Moyer, E. H.,** Biological activity of synthetic d, l-desthiobiotin, *Proc. Soc. Exp. Biol. Med.,* 58, 352, 1945.
5. **Peters, J. M.,** A separation of the direct toxic effects of dietary raw egg white powder from its action in producing biotin deficiency, *Br. J. Nutr.,* 21, 801, 1967.
6. **Bateman, W. G.,** The digestibility and utilization of egg proteins, *J. Biol. Chem.,* 26, 263, 1916.
7. **Parsons, H. T.,** Physiological effects of diets rich in egg white, *J. Biol. Chem.,* 90, 351, 1931.
8. **Tscherkes, L. A.,** Proteinogene Toxikosen, *Biochem. Ztschr.,* 182, 35, 1927.
9. **Maignon, F. and Chahine, M. A.,** Les variations saisonnières de la sensibilité de l'organisme a l'intoxication protéique s'observent encore in presence de vitamines, *C.R. Soc. Biol.,* 108, 868, 1931.
10. **Boyd, E. M., Peters, J. M., and Krijnen, C. J.,** The acute oral toxicity of reconstituted spray-dried egg white, *Ind. Med. Surg.,* 35, 782, 1966.
11. **Ferguson, H. C.,** Dilution of dose and acute oral toxicity, *Toxicol. Appl. Pharmacol.,* 4, 759, 1962.
12. **Constantopoulos, G. and Boyd, E. M.,** Factors affecting sucrose toxicity, *Int. J. Clin. Pharmacol. Ther. Toxicol.,* 1, 539, 1968.
13. **White, A., Handler, P., and Smith, E. L.,** *Principles of Biochemistry,* 4th ed., McGraw-Hill, New York, 1968.
14. **Boyd, E. M., Godi, I., and Abel, M.,** Acute oral toxicity of sucrose, *Toxicol. Appl. Pharmacol.,* 7, 609, 1965.
15. **Boyd, E. M. and Carsky, E.,** Maximal tolerated amounts of dextrose given intragastrically to albino rats, *Acta Diabetol. Lat.,* 4, 538, 1967.
16. **Boyd, E. M. and Shanas, M. N.,** The acute oral toxicity of sodium chloride, *Arch. Int. Pharmacodyn. Ther.,* 144, 86, 1963.

Chapter 12

CASEIN PREPARATIONS

Boyd, Krijnen, and Peters[1] reported an investigation of the acute oral toxicity of seven preparations of casein. The preparations studied were

a. Certified casein, purchased from the Fisher Scientific Company, Ltd. of Don Mills, Ontario, Canada, was given by intragastric cannula to overnight-starved young, male albino rats weighing 150 to 200 g. From the observations of Davies,[2] it was suspended in 0.12% aqueous solution of ammonium hydroxide. At this pH, casein is present as an anion and electrostatic repulsive forces between molecules are at a maximum, making the casein more soluble.[3] Following preliminary studies, casein was given as 100 ml/kg of a 30% (w/v) suspension, warmed to body temperature, and repeated at intervals of 1 hr to yield total doses of from 30 to 150 g/kg. Controls received 100 ml/kg of the 0.12% solution of ammonium hydroxide at the same intervals.

b. High protein casein, purchased from General Biochemicals, Inc. of Chagrin Falls, Ohio, was prepared by the lactic acid fermentation of skim milk. It contains 85% protein, 11% water, 1.9% ash, and 1.5% milk fat, with adequate vitamin and mineral supplements. It was given in a dose of 50 ml/kg of a 15% (w/v) suspension at five successive hourly intervals for three days and then the amount was gradually increased to nine administrations per day until death occurred, or for three weeks, whichever occurred first.

c. Vitamin-free test casein, purchased from General Biochemicals of Chagrin Falls, Ohio, was prepared by multiple extractions with hot alcohol and vacuum drying. It contains 89% protein, 8% water, 2% ash, and 0.5% fat. Alcohol extraction removes most, but not all, of the vitamins. It was administered to albino rats in the same doses and amounts as was done with high protein casein.

d. Sodium caseinate, obtained from General Biochemicals of Chagrin Falls, Ohio, contains 93.5% protein, 4% ash (1.3% sodium), and 1.5% fat. It was found to be soluble in water to 20% (w/v) at room temperature and was given to rats as 50 ml of a 15% (w/v) solution in distilled water

per kg body weight at intervals of 0.5 hr for ten successive administrations per day. The total daily dose of 75 g/kg was repeated daily for one week to a total weekly dose of 525 g/kg.

e. Casein sodium, purchased from the Nutritional Biochemicals Corp. of Cleveland, Ohio, was given in the same doses and at the same intervals as sodium caseinate.

f. Casein calcium, obtained from the Nutritional Biochemicals Corp. of Cleveland, Ohio, was also given in the same doses and at the same intervals as sodium caseinate.

g. Enzymatic casein hydrolysate, made by General Biochemicals of Chagrin Falls, Ohio, is prepared by treating casein with pancreatin.[4] It contains amino acids and peptides. It is edible and is present in certain infant food formulas[5] for the treatment of babies with feeding problems[6] such as those associated with allergenic sensitivity to intact proteins, pancreatic deficiencies, and it is used in the tube feeding of infants. The recommended dose for babies is up to 5 g/kg/day[6] which, as will be noted below, is one fifth of the acute oral LD_{50} per kg body weight in albino rats. Enzymatic casein hydrolysate was found to be soluble in distilled water to 60% (w/v). It was given to albino rats by stomach tube in doses of from 10 to 50 g/kg, each dose dissolved in water to a volume of 100 ml final aqueous solution per kg body weight.

Casein

The suspensions of certified casein gradually coagulated on standing in vitro and in vivo in the stomach of the albino rats.[1] The latter coagulation caused casein to remain in the stomach and the introduction of further suspensions produced death in 6 to 14 hr by nonspecific gastric rupture. The fresh suspension was light enough to be regurgitated and some deaths were due to nonspecific inhalation of the suspension into the lungs where blockage of the air passages caused death within 30 min from asphyxia. The larger doses of the casein suspension produced deaths following convulsions at 0.5 to 4 hr after the last administration. Convulsive deaths were found to be due to the 0.12% ammonium hydroxide solution. The

LD_{50} of NH_3OH was estimated to be 0.45 g/kg and at autopsy a violent gastritis was found. This value for the acute oral LD_{50} of NH_3OH is similar to that reported in cats.[7] No deaths could be attributed to casein in animals given certified casein.

The reaction of rats to oral administration of high protein casein was similar to that of vitamin-free test casein. Fifty percent of the animals died of stomach rupture, mostly during the first day, and 30% from aspiration asphyxia. Of the survivors, 37.5% died from what appeared to be casein intoxication following oral administration of total doses of casein of from 140 to 830 g/kg. By extrapolation, the acute oral LD_{50} of casein was estimated to be of the order of 1,200 g/kg given over a period of two to three weeks. This dose corresponds to administration of some 5 to 20 mM/kg. Had all of the casein been hydrolyzed to amino acids, the LD_{50} would have been about 25 g/kg or about 100 to 150 mM/kg. It would appear, therefore, that a very small fraction of the dose of these two preparations of casein was digested and absorbed as amino acids. It is obvious that ingestion of such amounts of casein by man is extremely unlikely, confirming the conclusions of Biochoff in 1932[8] and of Hegsted in 1964[9] that man and animals can tolerate huge amounts of proteins without signs of direct toxicity. On the other hand, it may be noted that the LD_1 of these two forms of casein was of the order of 50 g/kg in albino rats, which corresponds to a child of 20 to 25 lb eating and retaining, over a short period of time, about 1 lb of casein.

Ability of the albino rats to withstand stomach rupture appeared to be due to ability of the stomach to expand and accommodate the large volumes of administered casein suspension. The clinical signs, presumably of casein intoxication, in these latter rats included inhibition of growth, anorexia (for laboratory chow), diuresis (due to the large volume of administered water), proteinuria, aciduria, and listlessness. At autopsy, there was a mild, local, irritant, inflammatory reaction in the gastrointestinal tract, congestion and areas of necrosis in the liver, an inflammation of certain organs such as the brain, heart, kidneys, and lungs, and some atrophy of muscle and of the thymus gland.

Casein Salts

Thirty percent of the rats given either sodium caseinate or casein sodium died within five days from the toxic effects of the preparations. This corresponds to a total dose of 375 g/kg and suggested an LD_{50} of the order of 400 to 500 g/kg. The clinical signs of toxicity were a marked loss of body weight, marked anorexia, marked diuresis and proteinuria, alkalinuria, diarrhea, listlessness, and premortem hypothermia. At autopsy, the cecum was inflamed. An inflammatory reaction was present in many body organs such as the adrenals, brain, heart, kidneys, liver, lungs, spleen, testes, and thymus gland. There occurred fatty degeneration in the renal tubules. Survivors had a marked diuresis and augmented water intake. The signs of intoxication were a combination of those due to large volumes of water[10] and, in particular, large daily doses of sodium chloride.[11,12] The amount of sodium given with the casein per day was approximately the amount of sodium chloride which will kill 50% of rats when given by daily oral administration through a stomach tube.[12] Death from sodium caseinate and casein sodium appeared to be due, therefore, largely to the salt component of the preparations.

There were no deaths due to casein calcium apart from nonspecific death from stomach rupture. Survivors had clinical signs similar to those recorded in rats given the sodium salts of casein. Lack of deaths due to casein calcium was probably due to the fact that the LD_{50} of most salts of calcium is higher than that of sodium chloride.[7]

Enzymatic Casein Hydrolysate

Results with this preparation of casein were quite different from those noted above. The LD_{50} ± S.E. was found to be 26.0 ± 1.6 g/kg, the LD_1 was estimated at 24, and the LD_{99} at 29 g/kg. The range of lethal doses was, therefore, quite narrow and suggested that doses of the order of 70 g and over given orally to a baby weighing 6 lb could produce death. Since the recommended dose of hydrolyzed casein is up to 15 g for a baby weighing 6 lb,[6] it is obvious that this amount might produce signs of toxicity due to hydrolyzed casein. Such babies are usually already in a cachetic state from feeding problems, and it is even possible that this dose could produce death. As will be noted below, the signs of intoxication to hydrolyzed casein are similar to those recorded in such cachetic babies. The higher the dose of hydrolyzed casein, the shorter the interval to death, and the LD_{50} was 3.6 ± 1.4 hr (mean ± standard deviation) with an occasional death delayed to 24 hr or longer.

The clinical signs of toxicity appeared during the first hour and included listlessness, cyanosis, and diarrhea. Hemoconcentration developed within a few minutes, as shown in Figure 65. Blood hemoglobin levels became concentrated by about one third in 1 hr and remained at that level until death. The degree of hemoconcentration increased with increasing dose of orally administered hydrolyzed casein, as shown by data charted in Figure 66. The regression of values for blood hemoglobin on dose of casein hydrolysate was linear within the range of doses given, and was fitted by the equation $Y = (13.9 + 0.19X) \pm 1.2$. As might be expected, the spread of values for hemoglobin was greater at the higher doses of casein hydrolysate. Death was due to respiratory failure in a deep cyanotic coma.

Gross pathology at death consisted of intense congestion of the brain, hemorrhagic inflammation of the gastrointestinal tract, and a dark liver.

Histopathological findings are summarized in Table 59. There was an intense irritant inflammatory reaction with areas of lysis of the lining mucosa in the gastrointestinal tract. Tissue inflammation appeared in organs such as the adrenal glands, brain, meninges, heart, kidneys, and liver. The congestion had produced capillary hemorrhages in some organs such as the brain, meninges, and lungs. Blood coagulation and clotting were seen in organs such as the adrenal glands, heart, liver, spleen, testes, and thymus gland. Most deaths occurred within a few hours, which was too early for the development of histologically evident degenerative changes, but some evidence of such was present in the adrenal glands, kidneys, testes, and thymus gland.

Data on organ weights are summarized in Table 60. Since the lumen of the gastrointestinal tract was distended with the aqueous solution of enzymatic casein hydrolysate in these early deaths, there was no significant loss of body weight, but the weight of residual carcass (which did not include weight of intestinal contents) was reduced by some 14%. Marked losses of wet weight were recorded in most parts of the gastrointestinal tract, muscle, spleen, skin, testes, and thymus gland.

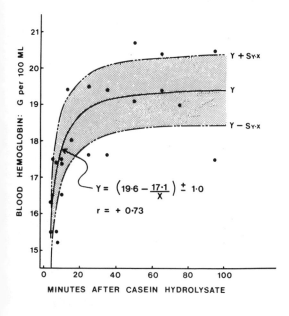

FIGURE 65. The regression, on time in minutes, of values for hemoglobin concentration in the blood of albino rats given enzymatic casein hydrolysate orally in a dose of 26 g/kg. (From Boyd et al.[1] with the permission of *The Journal of Nutrition,* copyright © 1967, The Wistar Institute.)

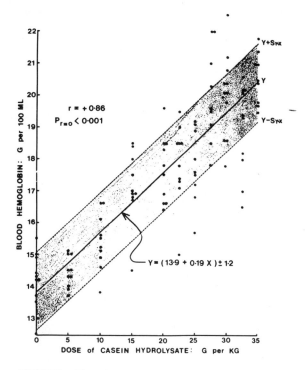

FIGURE 66. The regression, on dose of casein hydrolysate administered to albino rats by stomach tube, of changes in the concentration of hemoglobin in blood measured 30 min after giving the casein preparation. (From Boyd et al.[1] with the permission of *The Journal of Nutrition,* copyright © 1967, The Wistar Institute.)

TABLE 59

Histopathological Observations in Albino Rats at Death due to Oral Administration of Lethal
Doses of Enzymatic Casein Hydrolysate

Organ	Histopathology
Adrenal glands	Sinusoidal erythrocytes packed and distorted; clotting; minute areas of early necrosis
Brain	Marked capillary-venous congestion and hemorrhages in the meninges and brain
Gastrointestinal tract	
Cardiac stomach	Capillary-venous congestion of the submucosa with areas of lysis of the stratified squamous epithelium
Pyloric stomach	Capillary-venous congestion of the lamina propria and submucosa
Small bowel	Capillary-venous congestion of the lamina propria and submucosa and shrunken villi
Cecum	Capillary-venous congestion and hemorrhage of the lamina propria and submucosa and lysis of glands
Colon	Capillary-venous congestion of the lamina propria and submucosa
Heart	Coronary capillaries and veins congested and occasionally blood clots present
Kidneys	Vascular congestion especially in the loop region and tubular fatty degeneration in late deaths
Liver	Sinusoids packed with distorted erythrocytes and areas of venous clotting
Lungs	Venous clots in early deaths and areas of edema and hemorrhage in late deaths
Muscle	Fibers shrunken but otherwise normal in appearance
Salivary (submaxillary) glands	Normal appearance
Skin	Ischemic
Spleen	Red pulp shrunken, packed erythrocytes, venous clots
Testes	Tubules shrunken, extravascular clots, some tubular lysis
Thymus gland	Venous clots and some loss of thymocytes

(From Boyd et al.[1] with the permission of *The Journal of Nutrition,* copyright © 1967, The
Wistar Institute.)

Water contents of body organs were reduced, as shown by data summarized in Table 61. All changes were significant at $P = 0.01$ or less. It is obvious that many of the losses of organ weight, noted in Table 60, were due to organ dehydration as might have been anticipated due to the short interval to death. Dehydration was particularly marked in the organ first exposed to the concentrated aqueous solution of enzymatic casein hydrolysate, namely, the stomach. Dehydration was due to the osmotic attraction of water from the tissues into the blood and into the lumen of the gastrointestinal tract to counteract hypertonicity.

Survivors at 24 hr had lost body weight and exhibited anorexia, hyperdipsia, a mild fever, diuresis, aciduria, and proteinuria. The listlessness, cyanosis, and diarrhea seen during the early hours of intoxication had disappeared at 24 hr and the rats looked normal. Data on survivors are summarized in Table 62. There was some residual loss of body weight at 48 hr but by day three the animals had started to recover some of the lost body weight. Most other signs of toxicity had dis-

TABLE 60

Changes in the Fresh Weight of Body Organs at Autopsy in Albino Rats Given Doses of Casein Enzymatic Hydrolysate in the Range of the Oral LD$_{50}$ [a]

Organ	At death (N = 17 + 19 controls)	2-week survivors (N = 15 + 14 controls)	1-month survivors (N = 18 + 16 controls)
Adrenal glands	− 4.3	− 3.8	−12.5**
Brain	− 3.2*	− 0.3	+ 0.1
Gastrointestinal tract			
Cardiac stomach	−24.1**	−17.7*	+ 2.0
Pyloric stomach	−21.2**	− 8.8	− 0.7
Small bowel	− 5.2	− 9.2	+ 9.5**
Cecum	−19.7**	+ 4.9	− 0.1
Colon	−18.9**	−10.8*	+ 3.6
Heart	− 2.4	+ 2.9	− 3.4
Kidneys	− 5.2*	− 5.9*	+ 4.0
Liver	− 6.6	− 5.0	+ 8.4*
Lungs	+13.6	− 7.6*	+ 1.5
Muscle (ventral abdominal wall)	−30.8**	− 3.6	−17.5**
Salivary (submaxillary) glands	− 2.3	+ 1.5	− 0.6
Skin	−11.2**	− 0.5	− 2.9
Spleen	−28.4**	− 8.5	− 7.8
Testes	−17.1**	− 2.3	− 3.0
Thymus gland	−17.4*	−11.4*	− 7.9
Residual carcass	−13.7**	− 3.7*	− 0.2
Autopsy body weight	− 2.4	− 3.2*	− 0.7

[a]The organs were weighed in grams and the results are expressed as mean percent change from controls, specifically as $[(\bar{X}_d - \bar{X}_c)/\bar{X}_c] \times 100$, where $\bar{X}_d$ is the mean in the drug (casein) treated rats and $\bar{X}_c$ in the respective controls.

* A mean difference significantly different from zero at P = 0.05 to 0.02.

** A mean difference significantly different from zero at P = 0.01 or less.

(From Boyd et al.[1] with the permission of The Journal of Nutrition, copyright © 1967, The Wistar Institute.)

TABLE 61

Changes in the Water Content of Body Organs at Autopsy on Albino Rats Given Doses of Casein Enzymatic Hydrolysate in the Range of the Oral LD$_{50}$ [a]

Organ	At death (N = 17 + 19 controls)	2-week survivors (N = 15 + 14 controls)	1-month survivors (N = 18 + 16 controls)
Adrenal glands	−24.6**	+8.3*	+7.6
Brain	−15.2**	−0.3	+0.2
Gastrointestinal tract			
Cardiac stomach	−41.0**	−5.3	−0.2
Pyloric stomach	−41.9**	−2.6	+3.2
Small bowel	−30.3**	−0.6	+0.8
Cecum	−24.6**	+0.9	+2.5
Colon	−33.2**	+1.0	+3.9*
Heart	−17.3**	−0.6	−0.2
Kidneys	−17.8**	−0.7	−0.4
Liver	−17.0**	+0.5	−6.0*
Lungs	−16.0**	−2.2	+1.2
Muscle (ventral abdominal wall)	−24.0**	+0.9	−1.0
Salivary (submaxillary) glands	−16.2**	+0.6	+2.5
Skin	−23.6**	−2.2	−2.7
Spleen	−11.3**	−0.7	+0.7
Testes	−17.6**	+1.6*	+0.6
Thymus gland	−19.5**	−2.2	+2.3
Residual carcass	−21.3**	−4.8*	+3.0

[a]Water content was measured as grams water/100 g dry weight of tissue and the results are expressed as mean percent change from controls, specifically as $[(\bar{X}_d - \bar{X}_c)/\bar{X}_c] \times 100$, where $\bar{X}_d$ is the mean in the drug (casein) treated rats and $\bar{X}_c$ in the respective controls.

* A mean difference significantly different from zero at P = 0.05 to 0.02.

** A mean difference significantly different from zero at P = 0.01.

(From Boyd et al.[1] with the permission of The Journal of Nutrition, copyright © 1967, The Wistar Institute.)

TABLE 62

Clinical Measurements on Survivors of Death due to Oral Administration of Casein Enzymatic Hydrolysate to Albino Rats[a]

	Days after casein		
Measurement	1	2	3
	% change		
Body weight, g	− 3.3**DD	− 4.1**DD	− 1.8*
Food intake, g/kg/24 hr	− 44.5**	− 4.9	+ 0.2
Water intake, ml/kg/24 hr	+ 80.8**DD	+ 21.2**	+ 3.6*
Colonic temperature, °C	+ 0.7**DD	+ 0.4	+ 0.1
Urinary volume, ml/kg/24 hr	+ 82.3**DD	+ 35.8	+16.8
Urinary pH, 24-hr sample	− 4.4**	− 0.2	−10.1
Urinary glucose output, mg/kg/24 hr	−100.0**	+109.0	+36.1
Urinary protein output, mg/kg/24 hr	+494.0**DD[b]	− 6.0	−53.2*
Listlessness, cyanosis, diarrhea; clinical units	0.0	0.0	0.0

[a]The results are expressed as mean percentage change from controls specifically as $[(\bar{X}_d - \bar{X}_c)/\bar{X}_c] \times 100$, where $\bar{X}_d$ is the mean in the drug (casein) treated survivor and $\bar{X}_c$ in the controls. Dose dependence of the mean percentage change is indicated by "DD."

[b]Urine during the first 24 hr was contaminated with diarrheal casein hydrolysate which may have contributed to the markedly increased output of urinary protein.

*$\bar{X}_d - \bar{X}_c$ significantly different from zero at $P = 0.05$ to 0.02.

**$\bar{X}_d - \bar{X}_c$ significantly different from zero at $P = 0.01$ or less. (From Boyd et al.[1] with the permission of *The Journal of Nutrition,* copyright © 1967, The Wistar Institute.)

(From Boyd et al.[1] with the permission of *The Journal of Nutrition,* copyright © 1967, The Wistar Institute.)

appeared at 48 and at 72 hr. Autopsy at two weeks disclosed some residual loss of weight in certain organs such as cardiac stomach, colon, kidneys, lungs, thymus gland, and residual carcass, as indicated in Table 60. Loss of weight at a fortnight was not due to dehydration which, as indicated in Table 61, had disappeared at this interval. By one month, organ weights and water levels of surviving albino rats were essentially within the range of those in controls.

Conclusions Regarding Casein

The acute oral LD_{50} of casein protein in albino rats is probably of the order of 1,200 g/kg given over a period of several days. The signs of intoxication include listlessness, anorexia, inhibition of growth, diuresis, proteinuria, and an inflammatory reaction in many body organs. It is unlikely that death would occur from this type of intoxication in man due to the high dose necessary to produce it. The toxicity of casein sodium and calcium is due to their salt content.

Predigested casein, a mixture of amino acids and peptides used in infant feeding problems, has an acute oral LD_{50} of 26 g/kg. Doses approaching this level could be expected to produce signs of intoxication in human infants. Death occurred in about 4 hr following a period of listlessness, cyanosis, hemoconcentration, coma, and respiratory failure. At autopsy, the concentrated solutions of predigested casein were found to have drawn water out of the tissues and produced a general inflammatory reaction with capillary hemorrhages and extensive blood clotting. Recovery began to appear in survivors within a few days and was essentially complete at one month.

REFERENCES

1.   **Boyd, E. M., Krijnen, C. J., and Peters, J. M.,** Lethal amounts of casein, casein salts and hydrolysed casein given orally to albino rats, *J. Nutr.,* 93, 429, 1967.
2.   **Davies, W. L.,** *The Chemistry of Milk,* Chapman and Hall, London, 1936.
3.   **White, A., Handler, P., and Smith, E. L.,** *Principles of Biochemistry,* 4th ed., McGraw-Hill, New York, 1968.
4.   *British Pharmaceutical Codex,* The Pharmaceutical Press, London, 1963.
5.   *Vademecum International V-I Canada,* 14th ed., J. Morgan Jones Publications, Montreal, 1967.
6.   **Ebbs, J. H.,** The nutrition and feeding of infants, in *Nutrition, A Comprehensive Treatise,* Vol. 3, Beaton, G. H. and McHenry, E. W., Eds., Academic Press, New York, 1966.
7.   **Spector, W. S.** Ed., *Handbook of Toxicology,* Vol. 1, Acute Toxicities of Solids, Liquids and Gases to Laboratory Animals, W. B. Saunders, Philadelphia, 1956.
8.   **Bischoff, F.,** The influence of diet on renal and blood vessel changes, *J. Nutr.,* 5, 431, 1932.
9.   **Hegsted, D. M.,** Proteins, in *Nutrition, A Comprehensive Treatise,* Vol. 1, Beaton, G. H. and McHenry, E. W., Eds., Academic Press, New York, 1964.
10. **Boyd, E. M. and Godi, I.,** Acute oral toxicity of distilled water in albino rats, *Ind. Med. Surg.,* 36, 609, 1967.
11. **Boyd, E. M. and Shanas, M. N.,** The acute oral toxicity of sodium chloride, *Arch. Int. Pharmacodyn. Ther.,* 144, 86, 1963.
12. **Boyd, E. M., Abel, M. M., and Knight, L. M.,** The chronic oral toxicity of sodium chloride at the range of the $LD_{50}(0.1L)$, *Can. J. Physiol. Pharmacol.,* 44, 157, 1966.

Chapter 13

HIGH PROTEIN DIETS

Optimal Protein Intake

There are various methods employed to estimate the optimal amount of dietary protein. These methods have been reviewed by nutritionists such as Hegsted[1] under the headings of (a) biological methods and (b) chemical constituents of diet. Most methods are based upon estimates of the efficiency of the body to utilize the amount of protein in the diet and 1,500 publications have been reviewed by Kuppnswamy et al.[2] A widely used method is estimating the biological value or percent of absorbed nitrogen which is retained, originally proposed in 1909 by Thomas.[3] In 1919, Osborne, Mendel, and Ferry[4] introduced estimates of the protein efficiency ratio or gain in weight of young rats per gram of protein eaten. Hegsted and Chang[5] proposed plotting gain in body weight against nitrogen intake in grams and were able to calculate the relative potencies of proteins by comparing the slopes of the linear portions of the regressions. An analysis of their charts indicates that the regression lines flattened at higher nitrogen intakes. Miller and Payne[6] state that dietary protein has three actions: for growth, for maintenance of body proteins, and for oxidation to yield energy. They conclude that large intakes are increasingly oxidized but do not mention possible toxicity. It has been known for many years that excessive ingestion of amino acids, such as tyrosine,[7] may produce toxicity.

The nitrogen requirements of growing animals vary with the rate of growth and, therefore, with protein building. Ebbs[8] notes that while the relatively slower growing human infants require 2.5 to 4 g/kg/day, the relatively faster growing weanling rat needs at least 20 g/kg/day. The Canadian standard for humans varies from about 4 g/kg/day at age one to about 1 g/kg/day for an adult.[1]

Excessive intake of proteins in the form of highly concentrated baby formulas has been reported to place a marked demand upon the kidneys, dehydration, and an increase in water requirements.[9] On the other hand, McClellan and Dubois[10] found that men could live on meat (plus fat) alone for at least one year with little or no evidence of toxicity. Hegsted[1] notes that Eskimos apparently thrive on high protein (plus fat) diets. He also states that high protein diets cause hypertrophy of the kidneys. Boyd and Semple[11] found that weanling albino rats fed for 100 days on a diet containing 81% casein exhibited inhibition of growth and a relative hypertrophy of the kidneys.

Early studies on protein requirements disclosed that there were differences due to the nature of protein and led to the discovery of the essential amino acids.[1,12] This progressed to estimates of the effect of proteins as per gram or per gram of nitrogen rather than to studies based upon estimates of maximal growth vs. optimal percentage or amount of protein in the diet. Other parameters of efficacy vs. amount of dietary protein were also largely overlooked. One study providing such information was that of Boyd, Boulanger, and DeCastro on phenacetin toxicity.[13]

Phenacetin was given by stomach tube to male albino rats in a dose of 4.0 g/kg, which Boyd and Hottenroth[14] had reported as an approximate acute oral LD_{50} in rats. The animals had been previously fed for four weeks from weaning on diets of varying protein content. They were then given water but no food for 16 hr (overnight) to empty the stomach and phenacetin was administered as 20 ml/kg of a 20% suspension in distilled water. The clinical signs of toxicity in animals previously fed diets containing from 9 to 81% casein are listed in Table 63. It will be noted that the death rate was significantly higher in rats previously fed a diet high in casein. The pathological signs recorded at autopsy were a combination of those due to phenacetin[15] and to high casein diets.[16]

In rats previously fed a diet containing 26% protein as lactalbumin,[13] phenacetin killed 42% of the animals in 42 ± 21 hr (mean ± standard deviation). In the previous feeding of a diet containing 26% protein as soy assay protein, the death rate from phenacetin was significantly increased to values comparable to those in rats fed a diet of 81% casein. The results of these studies indicated that on diets containing from 9 to 27%

TABLE 63

The Clinical Signs of Toxicity to Phenacetin Given Orally in a Dose of 4 g/kg to Male Albino Rats Previously Fed for 28 Days from Weaning on Diets Containing Increasing Amounts of Casein[a]

Clinical Sign	Percentage of casein in diet		
	9	27	81
Hypothermia	61	59	8*
Pallor	75	74	85
Prostration	76	59	61
Drowsiness	91	82	97
Corneal reflex depressed	75	74	81
Respiratory rate slowed	76	73	61
Sialorrhea	82	82	85
Dacryorrhea	84	84	81
Exophthalmos	81	86	85
Ataxia	85	84	85
Righting reflex depressed	61	59	75
Hair soiling	6	18	14
Diarrhea	0	18	37
Hours to death	26 ± 17	28 ± 12	31 ± 17
Percent mortality	50	46	87*

[a]The results are expressed as percentage incidence during the period of 24 hr after giving phenacetin except that hours to death are expressed as mean ± standard deviation and death rates as percent mortality. Results which differed at $P = 0.05$ or less from those in rats fed 27% casein are indicated by an asterisk. (From Boyd et al.[13] with the permission of *Pharmacological Research Communications*.)

protein as casein albino rats were more resistant to phenacetin toxicity than on diets containing larger amounts of casein.

Hegsted and Chang[5] fed albino rats for three weeks from weaning on diets of varying protein content and recorded an increase in body weight and itrogen intake. They studied four proteins, namely, lactalbumin, casein, soy protein, and wheat gluten. Maximal increases in body weight occurred in each case at the maximal amount of protein in the diet. The maximal dietary amounts were 15% lactalbumin (mean weight gain 112 g), 26% casein (gain 137 g), 43% soy protein (gain 116 g), and 41% wheat gluten (gain 64 g). In each instance, the protein efficiency ratio was highest at a percentage of dietary protein less than the amount which produced maximal growth.

Optimal Casein Intake in Weanling Rats

The data noted above suggested that a diet containing 20 to 30% protein as casein would permit optimal growth of weanling albino rats and make them most resistant to noxious influences such as the toxic effects of chemical agents. DeCastro and Boyd[17] measured growth rate in albino rats fed for four weeks from weaning on a diet containing 27% protein as casein and compared their results with those in similar animals fed a standard laboratory chow (Purina Laboratory Chow Checkers) which contained not less than 20% mixed proteins. The results are summarized in Table 64. The data demonstrated that rats fed the purified optimal casein diet grew as well as rats fed a standard chow. At 28 days, rats fed the purified optimal casein diet weighed a significant 6.3% less than animals fed laboratory chow, mainly due to a decrease in the bulk of the contents of the gastrointestinal tract and to some inhibition of muscle growth.

Since Purina Laboratory Chow Checkers is bulky and contains fewer calories per gram than the purified optimal casein diet, food intake was calculated as kcal/kg/day. As shown in Table 64, food intake was practically identical in the two

TABLE 64

Weekly Clinical Measurements in Albino Rats Fed from Weaning on Different Diets Apparently Adequate in Protein[a]

Diet	Week 1 (N = 45/group)	Week 2 (N = 30/group)	Week 3 (N = 20/group)	Week 4 (N = 10/group)
Daily gain in body weight (g)				
Laboratory chow	5.0 ± 1.0	6.6 ± 0.6	6.5 ± 1.2	6.7 ± 2.4
27% casein	5.1 ± 1.4	6.0 ± 0.7	6.0 ± 2.2	6.5 ± 0.9
Daily food intake (kcal/kg body weight)				
Laboratory chow	432 ± 33	418 ± 14	367 ± 18	336 ± 25
27% casein	422 ± 66	390 ± 29	368 ± 18	355 ± 22
Daily water intake (ml/kg body weight)				
Laboratory chow	162 ± 20	147 ± 14	130 ± 10	115 ± 12
27% casein	116 ± 15	104 ± 3	96 ± 4	84 ± 3

[a]Expressed as mean ± standard deviation of daily measurements. (From DeCastro and Boyd[17] with the permission of the authors and of the *Bulletin of the World Health Organization.*)

groups. Water intake was higher in rats fed laboratory chow probably because the salt intake was somewhat higher in these animals than in those fed the casein diet. Laboratory chow also contains more cellulose bulk which could retain more water in the gastrointestinal tract and account for the augmented water intake and bulkier stools.

DeCastro and Boyd[17] measured the weight and water content of body organs at weekly intervals during their study. The organs of rats fed the purified optimal casein diet were slightly dehydrated compared with those in controls fed laboratory chow. Loss of body water could also have contributed to loss of body weight. Changes in the weights of body organs at 28 days are assembled in Table 65 as percentage differences from initial weights which, in turn, were calculated as a percent of body weight. Expressed in this manner, it is possible to see what organs comprised a greater and what organs comprised a lesser percentage of body weight over the growth period of four weeks.

It may be noted from data in Table 65 that at the end of 28 days, muscle, skin, and testes formed a greater percentage of body weight than they did at weaning. Loss of relative organ weight was most marked in the brain and adrenal glands

of rats fed laboratory chow. In rats fed the purified optimal casein diet, the weight of most parts of the gastrointestinal tract was a much smaller percentage of body weight at 28 days than at zero days from weaning. Skeletal muscle and salivary glands grew relatively less in the casein-fed rats than in the chow-fed animals.

In general, the growth of weanlings fed the purified optimal casein diet was similar to that of rats fed laboratory chow. In other studies, the body weight of albino rats fed from weaning on the purified optimal casein diet has been reported both slightly lower[18-23] and slightly higher[24-26] than that of controls fed a standard laboratory chow. There were also minor and insignificant differences in body weight between rats fed one type of standard laboratory chow and those fed another type.

Another indication that rats fed from weaning on a purified optimal casein diet acted like those of controls fed a standard laboratory chow was obtained in studies on the acute oral toxicity of a series of agents listed in Table 66. Of 16 agents, the acute oral LD_{50} in casein-fed rats was higher in 8, lower in 4, and insignificantly different in another 4 instances than in chow-fed controls. In 14 of the 16 studies, the interval to death at the acute oral LD_{50} was statistically the same in each

TABLE 65

Changes in the Weights of Body Organs of Male Albino Rats at the End of 28 Days from Weaning[a]

Organ	Fed laboratory chow	Fed a purified optimal casein diet
Adrenal glands	−50.0	−54.2
Brain	−66.7	−64.7
Gastrointestinal tract		
Cardiac stomach	−25.6	−31.3
Pyloric stomach	−38.5	−46.1
Small bowel	−35.5	−43.8
Cecum	−32.3	−58.9
Colon	−21.5	−60.0
Heart	−22.7	−20.5
Kidneys	−21.7	−15.9
Liver	− 4.6	− 5.0
Lungs	−31.3	−26.1
Muscle (ventral abdominal wall)	+53.0	+38.0
Skin	+28.9	+35.4
Spleen	−25.1	−25.0
Submaxillary salivary glands	− 9.5	−23.0
Testes	+22.5	+27.1
Thymus gland	−25.8	−22.7
Residual carcass	− 9.8	− 5.3
Body weight after 28 days (g)	229 ± 14	214 ± 23

[a]Weights of organs were calculated as percentages of body weight. The results are expressed as mean percentage changes from controls at zero days, specifically as $[(\bar{X}_{28} - \bar{X}_0)/\bar{X}_0] \times 100$, where $\bar{X}_{28}$ is the mean weight, as percentage of body weight, after the 28-day feeding period and $\bar{X}_0$ is the corresponding mean before feeding. (From DeCastro and Boyd[17] with the permission of the authors and of the *Bulletin of the World Health Organization*.)

group. The incidences of clinical and pathological signs of toxicity at the LD_{50} in casein-fed rats were essentially the same as in chow-fed controls. When a few differences were recorded, there was no consistent trend from agent to agent. For example, diarrhea was more marked in casein-fed rats given captan[18] and less marked in similar animals given dicophane[30] than in chow-fed controls.

These various studies indicate that albino rats fed from weaning on purified diets containing 26 or 27% casein, starch, fats, salts, and vitamins behave like controls fed a standard laboratory chow insofar as parameters of comparison have been made. The main differences were that casein-fed rats exhibited a minor degree of tissue de-hydration and the bulk of the intestinal contents was lower than in chow-fed controls.

Optimal Casein Intake of Adult Rats

As noted above, the protein needs of the adult are about one quarter of those in the weanling per kg body weight per day. The needs of the adult are mainly to replace tissues destroyed by wear and tear, to meet certain situations of augmented need such as pregnancy, lactation, and certain disease states associated with augmented catabolism such as fever and infection, and to replace nitrogen lost in the excreta. Data on excretion of nitrogen have been reviewed by Brody[34] and indicate that it varies with the basal metabolic rate and surface area. The average minimal nitrogen excretion is

TABLE 66

A Comparison of Some Parameters of Acute Oral Toxicity in Albino Rats Previously Fed for 28 Days from Weaning on a Purified Optimal Casein Diet with Those in Controls Fed a Standard Laboratory Chow

| | Result in casein-fed rats vs. that in chow-fed controls | | |
Agent studied	LD_{50}	Interval to death	Reference
Captan	No difference	No difference	18
Carbaryl	Higher	No difference	27
Chlordane	No difference	Longer	28
Chlorpropham	Higher	No difference	21
Demeton	Lower	No difference	23
Diazinon	No difference	No difference	29
Dicophane	Higher	No difference	30
Dimethoate	Lower	No difference	24
Diuron	Higher	No difference	25
Endosulfan	Lower	No difference	19
Endrin	Lower	No difference	31
Lindane	No difference	No difference	32
Malathion	Higher	No difference	20
Monuron	Higher	Longer	33
Parathion	Higher	No difference	22
Toxaphene	Higher	No difference	26

about 2 mg nitrogen per basal kcal. This is a useful figure for estimating protein needs of the adult. For example, an adult man with a basal metabolic rate of 1,600 kcal per day requires a minimum of 1,600 x 2 mg nitrogen or some 200 g of readily available protein per day. Under normal circumstances, mixed diets of man contain much more protein than this minimum and protein deficiency in adults is uncommon in persons who obtain sufficient food to prevent starvation. Most such diets of human adults also contain a good supply of the essential amino acids.

Since casein is frequently used as a source of dietary protein to measure the effects of protein toxicity in studies on adult animals as well as on weanlings, it became necessary to find out if animals fed optimal amounts of protein as casein differed from animals fed optimal amounts of protein as the mixed natural proteins in laboratory chow. Casein (vitamin-free) is frequently used by nutritionists to prepare diets deficient in one or other of the B vitamins for feeding to animals. Carbohydrate is usually provided as sucrose or glucose to a total of 80 to 90% of the diet. The remainder is made up of fats, salts, and vitamins. Initial studies

in the author's laboratory suggested that young adult albino rats fed such purified diets grew and acted as well as controls fed laboratory chow but became highly susceptible to certain toxic influences, such as large doses of benzyl-penicillin[35,36] or caffeine.[37,38] Augmented susceptibility to drug toxicity in these circumstances was later found to be due to the large amounts of dietary sucrose.[39,40] The toxicity of sucrose was discussed in Chapter 3.

Peters and Krijnen[41] reported a study of organ weights and water contents of young adult female rats fed two types of purified diets over a period of two to four weeks followed by laboratory chow for two weeks. Their Purified Diet I was obtained from the Nutritional Biochemicals Corp. of Cleveland, Ohio, and contained 18% vitamin-free casein, 68% sucrose, 10% vegetable oil, 4% salt mix, and supplements of all vitamins. Purified Diet II was obtained from General Biochemicals of Chagrin Falls, Ohio, and contained 30% dried egg white, 48% cornstarch, 14% cottonseed oil, 3% cod liver oil, 5% salt mix, and vitamin supplements. Results were compared with those in controls fed Purina Laboratory Chow Checkers

133

and the comparisons were correlated in a computer with days on the diet.

Body weight in rats fed the purified diets was the same at two weeks as in controls fed laboratory chow. The bulk of the intestinal contents was some 50% higher in rats fed laboratory chow than in rats fed the purified diets. Changes in the weight and water content of individual body organs at 14 days are summarized in Table 67. In rats fed the purified diets, there was a relative loss of weight in the intestinal tissues and a relative minor gain in weight of the heart, skin, and residual carcass. The most consistent change in organ water levels was some degree of dehydration. Somewhat similar data on gastrointestinal weight were obtained by Moinuddin and Lee[42],[43] and McCall et al.[44] Loss of intestinal weight appears to be due to decreased stimulus to intestinal movements from a smaller bulk of intestinal contents in rats fed the purified diets. When placed upon a diet of laboratory chow after two weeks on the purified diets, there was a

rapid recovery of gastrointestinal weight (Figure 67) and water content (Figure 68).

The results of these various studies suggest that a diet containing 20 to 30% protein as casein is optimal for growth and nitrogen balance in weanling and in adult albino rats. A purified casein-containing diet is less bulky than laboratory chow, reduces bulk in the lumen of the intestines, and lessens the weight and water content of intestinal tissues. Otherwise, an optimal casein diet appears to have effects no different from those of standard laboratory chows.

High Protein Diets in Weanling Rats

As noted above, excessive intake of concentrated protein formulas by babies produces dehydration, polydipsia, and an excessive load on the kidneys.[9] In a study of obesity in mice, Fenton and Dowling[45] found that diets high in protein prevented the development of nutritional obesity in this species. Boyd and Semple[11] studied the

TABLE 67

Organ Weights and Water Contents in Young, Adult Albino Rats Fed Laboratory Chow or Purified Diets for 14 Days

Organ	Weight			Water content		
	Laboratory chow[1]	Diet 1[2]	Diet 2[2]	Laboratory chow[3]	Diet 1[2]	Diet 2[2]
Adrenal glands	0.0312 ± 0.0009	+ 4.3	+ 7.4	72.2 ± 1.8	−1.92	−2.14
Brain	0.961 ± 0.081	+10.1	+ 4.0	78.2 ± 0.2	−0.04	+0.17
Gastrointestinal tract						
Cardiac stomach	0.123 ± 0.013	+ 5.2	+ 7.8	76.3 ± 1.4	−1.03	+0.87
Pyloric stomach	0.365 ± 0.036	− 6.8	−10.4*	76.8 ± 0.6	−1.87**	−0.37
Small bowel	1.181 ± 0.088	−15.6**	−24.6**	79.7 ± 0.6	−0.43	+1.33*
Cecum	0.329 ± 0.056	−30.0**	−28.7**	79.6 ± 1.0	−2.35**	−2.46
Colon	0.640 ± 0.060	−37.2**	−47.0**	79.7 ± 0.5	−3.39**	−1.28*
Heart	0.345 ± 0.016	+12.9**	+ 7.0*	77.6 ± 0.7	−0.53	−0.28
Kidneys	0.854 ± 0.035	+ 3.6	− 0.2	78.4 ± 1.0	−0.25	−0.47
Liver	4.855 ± 0.209	− 0.8	− 4.2	71.6 ± 0.7	−0.23	−0.14
Lungs	0.625 ± 0.129	+ 9.8	−11.0	79.4 ± 0.5	−0.27	+0.15
Muscle (ventral abdominal wall)	1.368 ± 0.126	+ 4.9	− 5.4	75.4 ± 0.3	−0.91**	−0.98*
Ovaries	0.0349 ± 0.0039	+ 2.8	−10.8	78.8 ± 1.1	−1.49*	−0.17
Skin	18.96 ± 1.46	+ 8.8**	+14.3**	64.1 ± 2.7	−2.81	+0.86
Spleen	0.378 ± 0.073	− 4.7	+ 4.0	76.7 ± 2.8	−0.26	−0.43
Submaxillary salivary glands	0.170 ± 0.016	− 7.9	+ 5.5	76.1 ± 1.1	−1.59*	−0.70
Thymus	0.0969 ± 0.0260	+ 5.0	+22.0	79.1 ± 0.9	−0.56	−0.39
Residual carcass	51.65 ± 1.37	+ 4.4**	+ 6.2*	68.8 ± 1.0	−1.77*	−2.49

[1] Expressed as mean ± S.D. % of autopsy body weight.
[2] Changes in organ weight and water content are expressed as mean % change from controls fed laboratory chow. Means that differed at P = 0.05 to 0.02 from corresponding means for controls are indicated by one asterisk, at P = 0.01 or less by two asterisks.
[3] Measured as mean ± S.D. % wet weight.
(From Peters and Krijnen[41] with the permission of the authors and of *Growth*.)

clinicopathological syndrome of toxicity to a high casein diet fed for 100 days from weaning to male albino rats. The diet was prepared after the formulas of Hegsted and Chang[5] and contained 81% casein, 4% starch, 8% hydrogenated cotton-seed oil, 4% salt mix USP XIV, 2% cod liver oil, and 1% of an all-vitamin mixture. This study will be described to exemplify the effects of a high protein diet fed to weanling albino rats.

Clinicopathological Syndrome

The most common clinical sign of toxicity in weanlings to a diet of 81% casein was diarrhea with fur soiling.[11] Evidence of disturbance of the autonomic nervous system consisted of rhinorrhea and sialorrhea. Most of the clinical signs, however, were referrable to the central nervous system. They included ataxia, aggressiveness, automatism, catalepsy, dyspnea, dysphonia, hyperkinesia, hyperreflexia, hyporeflexia, listlessness, nystagmus, phonation, and piloerection. None of these signs appeared in all animals; they occurred in a few and at varying intervals while eating the high protein diet.

Deaths occurred in the early days of feeding. At the end of 3 weeks, 5% of the animals had died and there were no further deaths during the remainder of the 100 days of the experiment, as shown in Table 68. Loss of weight was most marked during the initial weeks when body weight dropped to one third of that in controls fed optimal amounts of casein. Loss of appetite was also most evident in the early feeding period, as shown by data listed in Table 68.

While these results could suggest an adaptation to the high casein diet, other signs of toxicity became progressively more marked with continuance of the feeding. These included hypothermia, diuresis, and proteinuria. Aciduria persisted throughout the dieting period.

An autopsy was performed on survivors at 100 days.[11] Histopathological signs are summarized in Table 69. The high protein diet produced areas of hyperemia and capillary-venous congestion in the pyloric stomach and small bowel and, after absorption, in a few body organs such as the kidneys,

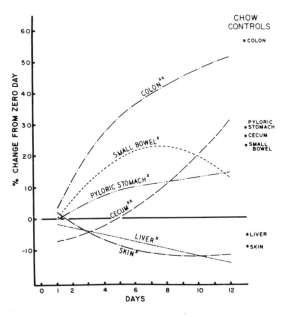

FIGURE 67. Percentage changes, from values in rats previously fed purified diet II, in the dry weight (calculated as percent of autopsy body weight), of the gastrointestinal organs, liver, and skin, when the animals were again fed laboratory chow. One "x" indicates that the correlation coefficient was significant at P = 0.05 to 0.02 and "xx" at P = 0.01 or less. (From Peters and Krijnen[41] with the permission of the authors and of *Growth.*)

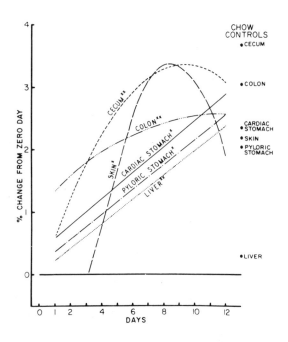

FIGURE 68. Percentage changes in the water content, calculated as percent wet weight, of the gastrointestinal organs, skin, and liver in young adult albino rats following change to a diet of laboratory chow after the previous feeding of purified diet II for 14 days. One "x" indicates that the correlation coefficient differed at P = 0.05 to 0.02 from zero and "xx" at P = 0.01 or less. (From Peters and Krijnen[41] with the permission of the authors and of *Growth.*)

TABLE 68

The Clinical Signs of Toxicity to a Diet Containing 81% Casein Fed for 100 Days from Weaning to Male Albino Rats[a][1]

	Days of feeding			
Sign	21	53	76	100
Mortality: percent	5	5	5	5
Body weight: g	− 49**	− 66**	− 67**	− 66**
Food intake: g/kg/day	− 52**	− 37**	− 38**	− 31*
Water intake: ml/kg/day	− 24*	− 10	− 11	+ 33*
Colonic temperature: °F	− 0.6	− 1.8*	2.4**	− 2.5**
Urinary volume: ml/kg/day	+ 63	+ 75*	+ 261**	+ 264**
Urinary glucose: mg/kg/day	0	0	0	0
Urinary protein: mg/kg/day	+2560**	+4080**	+6370**	+8560**
Urinary pH: 24-hr sample	− 30.1**	− 33.4**	− 29.7*	− 32.0**

[a]The results, except for mortality, are expressed as a mean percentage change from controls fed a diet containing 27% casein, specifically as $[(\bar{X}_p - \bar{X}_c)/\bar{X}_c] \times 100$, where $\bar{X}_p$ is the mean in rats fed the high protein diet and $\bar{X}_c$ the corresponding mean in the controls. One asterisk indicates that $\bar{X}_p - \bar{X}_c$ was significant at $P = 0.05$ to 0.02 and two asterisks at $P = 0.01$ or less.

TABLE 69

Histopathological Findings in Albino Rats Fed for 100 Days from Weaning on a Diet Containing 81% Casein[1]

Organ	Histological appearance
Adrenal glands	Lipoid globules prominent in the zona fasciculata and zona reticularis
Brain	Normal appearance
Gastrointestinal tract	
Cardiac stomach	Normal appearance
Pyloric stomach	Areas of congestion at one month; areas of fatty degeneration and necrosis at the base of the gastric glands at two to three months
Small bowel	Areas of congestion of the tips of the villi at two to three months
Cecum	Normal appearance
Colon	Normal appearance
Heart	Normal appearance
Kidneys	Areas of congestion and cloudy swelling of the renal tubules
Liver	Hypertrophy of the Purkinje's cells at one month; areas of fatty degeneration and necrosis at two to three months
Lungs	Areas of mild congestion; proliferation of the pulmonary lymph nodes at two to three months
Muscle, skeletal	Normal appearance
Salivary (submaxillary) glands	Areas of fatty degeneration and necrosis of the serous glands at two to three months
Skin	Normal appearance
Spleen	White pulp prominent
Testes	Few normal sperm at one month; areas of degeneration of spermatogenic tissue at two to three months
Thymus gland	Hyperemic at one month; lymphocytic hyperplasia at two to three months

lungs, and thymus gland. With continued feeding, there developed an increasing stressor reaction in the adrenal glands, spleen, and thymus gland and evidence of degenerative changes in organs such as the pyloric stomach, kidneys, liver, salivary glands, and testes. Excessive proliferation of lymphocytes was seen in some organs, such as the lungs and thymus gland. It should be emphasized that these microscopic findings were obtained at autopsy on animals that survived. Histopathology is usually less marked in a survivor than in an animal that dies from the effects of a toxic agent.

Changes in the weight and water content of body organs in survivors at 100 days are summarized in Table 70. There was a significant inhibition of the growth of all organs except the adrenal glands. At 100 days, loss of body weight was 66.7% of that in the controls. Loss of weight was particularly marked in muscle, skin, and thymus gland. Relatively resistant to inhibition of growth were the brain, gastrointestinal tract, kidneys, lungs, salivary glands, and testes. Dehydration was the common change in organ water levels. Dehydration was particularly marked in the adrenal glands, cecum, skeletal muscle, spleen, and thymus gland. There was no significant change in the water content of stomach, small bowel, heart, kidneys, liver, and testes, as shown in Table 70.

In short, the main toxic effects of feeding weanling rats a diet high in casein were inhibition of growth, diarrhea, hypothermia, dysfunction of the central nervous system, dehydration, and inflammatory and degenerative changes in body organs. Loss of weight was due mainly to inhibition of growth of skeletal muscle and skin.

Susceptibility to Starvation

Boyd, Chen, and Muis[46] reported that male

TABLE 70

The Wet Weight and Water Content of Body Organs in Albino Rats at the End of 100 Days of Feeding from Weaning of a Diet Containing 81% Casein[a] [1]

Organ	Wet weight[b]	Water content[c]
Adrenal glands	− 4.8	−21.5**
Brain	−16.9**	− 6.1*
Gastrointestinal tract		
Cardiac stomach	−28.3**	+ 6.3
Pyloric stomach	−38.9**	− 9.2
Small bowel	−16.8**	+ 5.9
Cecum	−49.9**	−23.3**
Colon	−50.9**	− 9.0*
Heart	−63.1**	− 1.8
Kidneys	−26.7**	− 1.1
Liver	−53.8**	− 0.4
Lungs	−49.8**	− 2.7
Muscle (ventral abdominal wall)	−70.1**	−21.5**
Salivary (submaxillary) glands	−48.2**	−16.0**
Skin	−71.2**	− 6.6*
Spleen	−57.0**	−17.7**
Testes	−14.4**	− 1.8
Thymus gland	−80.0**	−43.1**
Residual carcass	−68.7**	−12.2**
Autopsy body weight	−66.7**	

[a]The results are expressed as mean percent changes from corresponding data in controls fed an optimal protein diet containing 27% casein, specifically as $[(\overline{X}_p - \overline{X}_c)/\overline{X}_c] \times 100$, where $\overline{X}_p$ is the mean in rats fed a high protein diet and $\overline{X}_c$ the corresponding mean in controls. One asterisk indicates that $\overline{X}_p - \overline{X}_c$ was significant at $P = 0.05$ to 0.02 and two asterisks at $P = 0.01$ or less.
[b]Measured in grams.
[c]Measured as g water per 100 g dry weight of tissue.

albino rats fed for 28 days from weaning on a diet containing 81% casein and of the same composition as that used by Boyd and Semple,[11] noted above, became more susceptible to the effects of absolute starvation (water but no food). Starvation produced an augmented loss of body weight, hypothermia, and aciduria with a decrease in water intake, urinary volume, and proteinuria. As indicated by data shown in Table 71, starvation killed two thirds of rats fed the high casein diet in 7 days compared with 13 to 14 days in animals previously fed 9 to 27% casein. Starvation-induced necrotic ulcers in pyloric stomach were more marked in rats fed the high protein diet, while infiltrative ulcers of the cardiac stomach were less marked than in rats fed diets containing 9 to 27% protein as casein. Starvation produced a congestion of the brain, gastrointestinal tract, kidneys, liver, and pancreas, a stress reaction, and degenerative changes in the kidneys (cloudy swelling), liver (hepatic cells atrophied), pancreas (deficiency of zymogenic granules in the acinar glands), and testes (inhibition of spermatogenesis).

Shifts in the wet weight and water content of body organs following starvation for 14 days in animals previously fed an optimal (27%) casein diet and for 7 days in rats given excessive amounts of dietary casein (81%) are summarized in Table 72. The day of autopsy, as noted above, was the day on which two thirds of the animals had died from the effects of absolute starvation. The common effect of starvation was a loss of weight and hydration of body organs. Animals previously fed excessive amounts of dietary casein were unable to tolerate as marked a loss of organ weight and as marked a degree of hydration of body organs as were animals previously fed an optimal casein diet. In other words, animals fed high casein diets died at less loss of organ weight and less gain in organ water content than did controls fed an optimal percentage of dietary casein. There were a few exceptions to this rule, as may be noted in Table 72. Gain in weight of cardiac stomach in the optimal casein group, for example, was due to the presence of ulcers infiltrated with white blood cells in these animals. With death prolonged to 14 days, such proliferative ("starvation") ulcers had a longer time to grow than in the high casein group where death occurred earlier.

In brief, therefore, albino rats fed from weaning on diets containing an excess of protein as casein do not grow as well as rats fed optimal amounts of casein and are much more susceptible to the effects of starvation. They tolerate the loss of weight and hydration of body organs produced by starvation for a much shorter period of time.

Susceptibility to Toxic Doses of Chemical Agents

In addition to being highly susceptible to the effects of starvation, albino rats fed from weaning on toxic amounts of dietary casein are more susceptible to toxic doses of various chemical agents. As noted by data in Table 63, they are more susceptible to death from oral administration of phenacetin in a dose of 4 g/kg. Krijnen and Boyd[47] summarized data on the values of the acute oral LD_{50} of a series of chemical agents in albino rats previously fed for 28 days from weaning on diets containing from 0 to 81% casein. The diets contained casein and starch to a total of 85%. The other constituents were 8% hydrogenated cottonseed oil, 4% salt mix, and 3% multivitamin mixture, as used by Boyd and Semple.[11]

To compare acute toxicities, Krijnen and Boyd[47] used an index obtained by dividing the oral LD_{50} in rats fed from weaning on an optimal protein diet containing 26 or 27% casein by the LD_{50} in rats fed diets containing other levels of dietary casein. The results are assembled in Table 73. It will be noted that there is some variation from agent to agent. Carbaryl and endosulfan were equally toxic in both groups of animals. Captan, diazinon, dicophane, lindane, and malathion were two times (or greater) more toxic in rats pre-

TABLE 71

Death Rates and the Percentage Incidence of Pathological Lesions Seen at Death due to Starvation in Albino Rats Previously Fed for 28 days from Weaning on a Diet Containing 81% Protein as Casein

Lesion	Percent casein in diet		
	9	27	81
Days to 67% mortality	13	14	7
Congestion of the brain	75	100	100
Infiltrative ulcers in cardiac stomach	100	100	0
Necrotic ulcers in pyloric stomach	25	67	100
Small bowel contained dark fluid	25	77	100
Congested lungs	75	100	85
Minced carcass dark red	100	100	0

(From Boyd et al.[46] with the permission of *Growth*.)

TABLE 72

Changes in the Wet Weight and Water Content of Body Organs in Albino Rats Following Starvation for a Period Sufficient to Produce a 67% Mortality Rate in Animals Previously Fed for 28 days from Weaning on Diets Containing Optimal (27%) or Excessive (81%) Amounts of Dietary Protein as Casein[a]

| | Percent casein diet | | | |
| | Wet weight[b] | | Water content[c] | |
Organ	27.0 (N = 9 plus 10 controls)	81.0 (N = 7 plus 10 controls)	27.0 (N = 9 plus 10 controls)	81.0 (N = 7 plus 10 controls)
Adrenal glands	0.0	+14.2*	+16.7*	+29.5**
Brain	+ 0.1	− 2.8	− 0.2	+ 0.4
Gastrointestinal tract				
Cardiac stomach	+50.2**	− 8.3	+29.3**	+27.1**
Pyloric stomach	−23.7**	−35.0**	+20.2**	+26.7**
Small bowel	−39.3**	−30.5**	+25.5**	+47.1**
Cecum	−32.0**	−40.0**	+ 3.1	+15.4**
Colon	−32.2**	−12.8*	+ 7.1*	+13.8*
Heart	−50.0**	−30.4**	− 3.2	+ 2.1
Kidneys	−42.2**	−33.5**	+ 7.0*	+13.7**
Liver	−74.9**	−66.6**	+20.9**	+16.6**
Lungs	−31.1**	−27.5**	− 6.3**	− 5.9*
Muscle (ventral abdominal wall)	−68.3**	−46.0**	+44.3**	+17.2*
Salivary (submaxillary) glands	−67.2**	−48.2**	+ 2.8	+ 3.3
Skin	−55.8**	−34.0**	+ 0.2	− 0.7
Spleen	−69.2**	−63.2**	−10.2*	− 2.8
Testes	−30.5**	−17.6**	−10.8**	− 9.5**
Thymus gland	−88.1**	−76.2**	+ 1.2	+ 6.8*
Residual carcass	−51.8**	−30.5**	+25.7**	+17.2**
Autopsy body weight	−55.0**	−36.3**		

[a]Changes are expressed as mean percent change from corresponding values in controls fed the same diet but not starved, specifically as $[(\bar{X}_s - \bar{X}_c)/\bar{X}_c] \times 100$, where $\bar{X}_s$ is the mean in starved animals and $\bar{X}_c$ in controls. One asterisk indicates that $\bar{X}_s - \bar{X}_c$ was significant at P = 0.05 to 0.02 and two asterisks at P = 0.01 or less.
[b]Wet weight was measured in grams.
[c]Water content was measured as g water per 100 g dry weight of tissue.
(From Boyd et al.[46] with the permission of *Growth*.)

viously fed a diet containing toxic amounts of dietary casein. As indicated by data in Table 73, however, the toxicity of these agents was augmented much more by lowering than by raising the level of dietary casein. This conclusion applied to the degree of the raising dietary protein employed — no data are available, for example, on the effects of diets containing more than 81% casein on the toxicity of these agents.

In brief, therefore, albino rats fed from weaning on diets containing toxic amounts of protein as casein are not only hypersusceptible to the toxic effects of starvation but also to the toxic effects of certain chemical agents.

High Protein Diets in Adults

One of the earliest nutritionists to suggest that high levels of dietary proteins could be toxic to adults was Chittenden in 1907.[55] He questioned the figure of Voit who postulated that an adult man should consume some 100 to 125 g of protein per day. Voit's figure was calculated from the average human intake and was based on the premise that the average man would instinctively select the amount of dietary protein which he needed. Chittenden gave evidence that man was actually healthier on a diet containing only about one quarter to one third of this amount of dietary protein and claimed that excessive protein intake

TABLE 73

The Indices of Comparative Toxicity Obtained by Dividing the Value of the Acute Oral LD_{50} of a Series of Chemical Agents in Albino Rats Previously Fed for 28 Days from Weaning on a Diet Containing Optimal Amounts of Dietary Casein (26 or 27%), by the LD_{50} in Rats Fed Diets Containing Other Amounts of Dietary Casein

Chemical agent	Percentage casein in diet				Reference
	0	3.5	9.0	81	
Captan	2100.0	26.3	1.2	2.4	48
Carbaryl	8.6	6.5	1.1	1.0	49
Chlorpropham	8.7	4.0	1.7	—	21
Diazinon	7.4	1.9	1.8	2.0	50
Dicophane (DDT)	4.0	2.9	1.5	3.7	51
Endosulfan	20.0	4.3	1.8	1.0	52
Lindane	12.3	1.9	1.0	1.8	53
Malathion	2.6	2.3	1.8	2.2	54
Monuron	11.5	3.0	1.8	—	33

(From Krijnen and Boyd[47] with the permission of the authors and of *Comparative and General Pharmacology,* copyright © 1971, Scientechnica Publishers Ltd., Bristol, England.)

yielded large amounts of nitrogenous waste products which placed a burden on the body, particularly on the kidneys. Gamble reached similar conclusions in 1946[56] and in 1959, Ross[57] presented evidence that high protein diets lower the length of life and augment the incidence of cancer in man. Most reviews of human protein requirements, however, stress protein deficiency rather than protein excess.[1,12] This is probably because protein excess is less likely to occur than is protein deficiency due to the high cost of most protein-containing foods such as meat.

In studies on animals, Gullino et al.[58] reported the acute LD_{50} values of ten essential amino acids. They found that the toxicity of the l-isomers was in general similar to that of the d-isomers; leucine was the least toxic and arginine and tryptophane the most toxic. The toxicity of a mixture of nine amino acids (without l-arginine) was additive but was reduced by including l-arginine in the mixture. Adrian and Terroine[59] found that a high protein diet reduced the urinary loss of riboflavin and nicotinic acid but not of pyridoxine in male rats. Van Dam-Bakker et al.[60] noted that feeding a high protein diet to albino rats every other day followed by a low protein diet on alternate days inhibited growth rate, lactation, and hemoglobin formation.

Kato et al.[61] reported that albino rats fed a diet containing 50% protein were able to detoxify strychnine, pentobarbital, and zoxazolamine more rapidly than were rats fed diets low in protein. Wergedal and Harper[62] found that glycine, in a dose of 66 mM/kg, was 100% lethal in fasted rats fed a diet containing 80% of casein because the diet induced enzymes concerned with the deamination of glycine to ammonia. Ammonia reached toxic levels in blood because fasting had depleted the liver of intermediates required for conversion of ammonia to urea. When the intermediates were fed to such rats, the animals survived. McLean and McLean[63] cite this study as "the most perfect example of interaction between diet and toxicity." There is evidence that high protein diets may augment the development of cancer in animals.[64] Cohn et al.[65] reported that force-feeding adult male albino rats diets containing 67% protein increased their fat content.

There are indications that dietary soy protein is particularly liable to produce toxic effects. Schultze[66] fed pregnant female rats a diet containing 24% protein as purified soybean proteins and recorded a failure of lactation with up to 80% mortality rates in the pre-weaning suckling animals. In a subsequent study, Schultze[67] concluded that lactation failure was not due to vitamin deficiencies but found it could be prevented by substituting vitamin-free casein for soybean protein. Boyd et al.[13] found that rats previously fed a diet containing 26% protein as soy protein were more susceptible to phenacetin toxicity than were animals fed 26% protein as casein. Peters[68] also noted a difference in toxicity between different dietary proteins, raw egg white powder being more toxic than casein.

The studies of Peters[68] will be cited in exemplification of the toxic and nontoxic effects of high protein diets in young adult albino rats. Peters fed adult albino rats for two to four weeks on diets containing from 20 to 80% protein as raw egg white powder with the balance to 90% composed of maize starch and with 5% cottonseed oil, 5% salt mix, and a general vitamin supplement. Other groups received 80% of heat-denatured egg white powder, 80% casein, or 100% raw egg white; results were compared with those in controls fed Purina laboratory chow.

The clinical signs of toxicity increased in intensity with increasing amount of raw egg white powder in the diet. Diuresis was the most sensitive sign, urinary volume increasing by 50% following 20% egg white in the diet and rising to 600% at 80% egg white. Diuresis was accompanied by proteinuria, alkalinuria, and polydipsia; the latter is illustrated in Figure 69. Soft stools appeared in rats receiving 60% and over raw egg white and at 100% there was a marked diarrhea. The latter group of animals exhibited glycosuria, a loss of body weight and a mortality rate of 8% over two weeks of feeding. Changes in body weight are summarized in Table 74. Loss of body weight was accompanied by loss of wet weight in all body organs except brain, cardiac stomach, kidneys, and salivary glands. Loss of organ weight was associated with loss of organ water content which was not dose-dependent, as indicated by data exemplified in Table 75 for female rats.

While large amounts of raw egg white protein produced toxic effects in young adult albino rats, similar large amounts (80%) of heat-denatured egg white protein or of casein had no or minor toxic effects. Clinical measurements in albino rats fed such diets are summarized in Table 76. It should be noted that one group of rats was fed raw egg white and received in addition 100 μg biotin subcutaneously every second day to eliminate the possibility that the toxic effect of raw egg white was due to a relative deficiency of biotin. Diets of

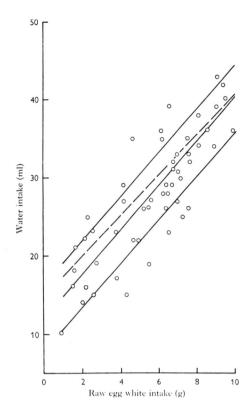

FIGURE 69.   The regression of water intake on amount of raw egg white powder eaten on the fifth day of feeding shown as a solid regression line ± its standard error calculated from the equation $Y = (12.0 + 2.8X) \pm 4.2$. The interrupted line is the regression on the 11th day of feeding. (From Peters[68] with the permission of the author and of the *British Journal of Nutrition.*)

80% casein or denatured egg white produced some loss of weight in the tissues and luminal contents of cecum and colon and a slight gain in the absolute weight of kidneys and liver plus dehydration of many organs of young adult albino rats. Diets containing 80% raw egg white protein, with or without biotin supplementation, produced loss of weight without dehydration in all organs except brain.

In brief, therefore, young adult albino rats are relatively resistant to the toxic effects of large amounts of dietary casein but not of dietary raw egg white protein. The results with casein are in contrast to the considerable toxicity of large amounts of this protein in weanling rats.

Conclusions Regarding High Protein Diets
Optimal Protein Diets

High protein diets are those that contain amounts of proteins in excess of the optimal

TABLE 74

The Growth of Albino Rats Fed Diets Containing Increasing Amounts of Raw Egg White Powder

Percent raw egg white powder	2 weeks feeding Body weight gain[a]	4 weeks feeding Body weight gain[a]
20	61 ± 9	111 ± 17*
40	65 ± 12*	108 ± 14
60	65 ± 23	108 ± 33
80	36 ± 12*	83 ± 32
100	−5 ± 6*	
0 (chow)	51 ± 13	96 ± 7

[a]Expressed as percentage gain (mean ± S.D.) from initial body weight. Means that differed at P = 0.05 to 0.02 from corresponding means for controls fed on laboratory chow are indicated by an asterisk. (From Peters[68] with the permission of the author and of the *British Journal of Nutrition*.)

amount. There are various criteria for estimating optimal amounts which vary from one protein to another. More evidence is available on casein than on any other protein. This evidence indicates that a diet containing some 20 to 30% casein is optimal for the growth of weanling rats and for maintenance of adult rats. Compared with standard laboratory chows, diets containing optimal amounts of casein are less bulky and therefore reduce the weight of intestinal contents and the stimulus to growth of intestinal muscle. Optimal casein diets may also produce a slight dehydration of body organs.

High Protein Diets

Diets containing three times the optimal amount of dietary casein are toxic to weanling but not to adult albino rats. High casein diets inhibit the growth of weanlings and produce hypothermia, aciduria, diarrhea, dehydration, CNS signs, and death. The weanling animals become

TABLE 75

Shifts in the Water Content, Calculated as Percent Wet Weight, of Body Organs of Female Albino Rats at the End of Two Weeks of Feeding Diets Containing Increasing Percentages of Raw Egg White Powder

Organ	Percent raw egg white[a] 20	40	60	80	100
Adrenal glands	−1.38	−3.45*	−2.26*	−2.67*	−2.19
Brain	+0.07	+0.04	−0.01	+0.14	−0.42*
Gastrointestinal tract					
Cardiac stomach	+1.04	−0.41	−0.83	+0.01	+0.38
Pyloric stomach	−0.05	−1.37*	−1.02	−0.45	+0.18
Small bowel	−1.26**	−0.93*	−0.76	−1.14*	+0.41
Cecum	−1.55	−1.63*	−1.13	−0.55	+0.17
Colon	−2.47**	−2.78**	−2.29**	−2.53**	−1.28**
Heart	−0.27	−0.60	−0.61	−0.73*	−0.47
Kidneys	+0.86	+0.49	+2.60	+0.19	+0.12
Liver	+0.53	−0.65	−1.16**	−1.16	−0.57
Lungs	−0.69*	−0.66*	−0.61*	−0.79	−0.89**
Muscle (ventral abdominal wall)	−0.71	−1.14*	−0.91**	−0.56	+0.12
Ovaries	−1.07	−2.07*	−1.52	−2.56**	−2.44*
Skin	−3.38	−3.93	−3.64	−3.36	+0.38
Spleen	−0.30	−0.84**	−0.77**	−0.77**	−1.25**
Submaxillary salivary glands	−1.57	−0.91	−0.61	−1.53*	−2.04*
Thymus	−0.27	−1.34	−0.89	−0.67	−0.03
Residual carcass	−1.73*	−1.55	−2.58*	−1.48	−0.98

[a]Changes in rats fed on raw egg white powder are expressed as mean percentage change from the animals fed on chow. Means that differed at P = 0.05 to 0.02 from corresponding means for rats fed on chow are indicated by one asterisk and at P ≤ 0.01 by two asterisks. (From Peters[68] with the permission of the author and of the *British Journal of Nutrition*.)

TABLE 76

Clinical Measurements in Albino Rats During 14 Days of Administration of Large Amounts of Dietary Protein[a]

Diet	Daily gain in body weight (mean ± S.D.) (g)	Daily food intake (mean ± S.D.) (g)	Daily water intake (mean ± S.D.) (ml)	Daily urinary volume (mean ± S.D.) (ml)
80% raw egg white powder	3.9 ± 0.8	12 ± 1	37 ± 7	26 ± 4
80% raw egg white powder plus biotin supplement	4.2 ± 1.2	13 ± 1	39 ± 6	26 ± 4
80% denatured egg white powder	5.7 ± 1.0	—	44 ± 5	—
80% casein	6.0 ± 1.4	14 ± 1	39 ± 5	25 ± 3
Laboratory chow	5.8 ± 0.7	14 ± 1	23 ± 1	3 ± 1

[a]Clinical measurements are expressed as the mean ± S.D. of daily values during the 14 days of the experiment. The food intake of animals fed on laboratory chow was calculated as calorie-equivalent to that of animals given the high protein diet (i.e., the g intake of laboratory chow was 1.3 times the figures listed above). Animals fed denatured egg white spilled their food and this made accurate readings of food intake and urinary volume impossible. (From Peters[68] with the permission of the author and of the *British Journal of Nutrition*.)

hypersusceptible to the toxic effects of starvation and of some chemical agents. Adult rats are relatively immune to the toxic effects of diets high in casein but become susceptible to large amounts of other dietary proteins such as raw egg white powder.

REFERENCES

1. **Hegsted, D. M.,** Proteins, in *Nutrition. A Comprehensive Treatise,* Vol. 1, Beaton, G. H. and McHenry, E. W., Eds., Academic Press, New York, 1964, Chap. 3, 115.

2. **Kuppnswamy, S., Srinivasan, M., and Subrahmaxyan, V.,** Proteins in Foods, Special Report Series No. 33, Indian Council of Medical Research, New Delhi, India, 1958.

3. **Thomas, K.,** Ueber die biologische Westigkeit der Stickstoff-substanzen in verschiedenen Nahrungsmitteln, *Arch. Physiol.,* 219, 1909.

4. **Osborne, T. B., Mendel, L. B., and Ferry, E. L.,** A method of expressing numerically the growth-promoting value of proteins, *J. Biol. Chem.,* 37, 223, 1919.

5. **Hegsted, D. M. and Chang, Y.-O.,** Protein utilization in growing rats. I. Relative growth index as a bioassay procedure, *J. Nutr.,* 85, 159, 1965.

6. **Miller, D. S. and Payne, P. R.,** Problems in the prediction of protein values of diets. The use of food composition tables, *J. Nutr.,* 74, 413, 1961.

7. **Schweizer, W.,** Studies on effect of 1-tyrosine on white rat, *J. Physiol.,* 106, 167, 1947.

8. **Ebbs, J. H.,** Nutritional status: assessment and application, *in Nutrition. A Comprehensive Treatise,* Vol. 3, Beaton, G. H. and McHenry, E. W., Eds., Academic Press, New York, 1966, Chap. 1.

9. **Hoag, L. A., Riykin, H., Levine, S. Z., Wilson, J. R., Berliner, F., Weigele, C., and Anderson, A. F.,** A study of alimentary "protein fever," *Am. J. Dis. Child.,* 34, 150, 1927.

10. McClellan, W. S. and Dubois, E. F., Clinical calorimetry; prolonged meat diets with study of kidney function and ketosis, *J. Biol. Chem.,* 87, 651, 1930.

11. Boyd, E. M. and Semple, M. A., Inhibition of growth in weanling albino rats fed a diet containing 81% of casein, unpublished data, 1972.

12. White, A., Handler, P., and Smith, E. L., *Principles of Biochemistry,* 4th ed., McGraw-Hill, New York, 1968.

13. Boyd, E. M., Boulanger, M. A., and DeCastro, E. S., Phenacetin toxicity and dietary protein, *Pharmacol. Res. Commun.,* 1, 15, 1969.

14. Boyd, E. M. and Hottenroth, S. M. H., The toxicity of phenacetin at the range of the oral LD_{50} (100 days) in albino rats, *Toxicol. Appl. Pharmacol.,* 12, 80, 1968.

15. Boyd, E. M., The acute oral toxicity of phenacetin, *Toxicol. Appl. Pharmacol.,* 1, 240, 1959.

16. Boyd, E. M., Food and drug toxicity: a summary of recent studies, *J. Clin. Pharmacol.,* 8, 281, 1968.

17. DeCastro, E. S. and Boyd, E. M., Organ weights and water content of rats fed protein-deficient diets, *Bull. W.H.O.,* 38, 971, 1968.

18. Boyd, E. M. and Krijnen, C. J., Toxicity of captan and protein-deficient diet, *J. Clin. Pharmacol.,* 8, 225, 1968.

19. Boyd, E. M. and Dobos, I., Protein deficiency and tolerated oral doses of endosulfan, *Arch. Int. Pharmacodyn. Ther.,* 178, 152, 1969.

20. Boyd, E. M. and Tanikella, T. K., The acute oral toxicity of malathion in relation to dietary proteins, *Arch. Toxikol.,* 24, 292, 1969.

21. Boyd, E. M. and Carsky, E., The acute oral toxicity of the herbicide chlorpropham in albino rats, *Arch. Environ. Health,* 19, 621, 1969.

22. Boyd, E. M., Chen, C. P., and Liu, S. J., The acute oral toxicity of parathion in relation to dietary protein, *Arch. Toxikol.,* 25, 238, 1969.

23. Boyd, E. M. and Krupa, V., The acute oral toxicity of demeton in albino rats fed from weaning on diets of varying protein content, *Can. J. Pharm. Sci.,* 4, 35, 1969.

24. Boyd, E. M. and Muis, L. F., Acute oral toxicity of dimethoate in albino rats fed a protein-deficient diet, *J. Pharm. Sci.,* 59, 1098, 1970.

25. Boyd, E. M. and Krupa, V., Protein-deficient diet and diuron toxicity, *J. Agric. Food Chem.,* 18, 1104, 1970.

26. Boyd, E. M. and Taylor, F. I., Toxaphene toxicity in protein-deficient rats, *Toxicol. Appl. Pharmacol.,* 18, 158, 1971.

27. Boyd, E. M. and Boulanger, M. A., Insecticide toxicity. Augmented susceptibility to carbaryl toxicity in albino rats fed purified casein diets, *J. Agric. Food Chem.,* 16, 834, 1968.

28. Boyd, E. M. and Taylor, F. I., The acute oral toxicity of chlordane in albino rats fed 28 days from weaning on a protein-deficient diet, *Ir.J. Med. Surg.,* 38, 434, 1969.

29. Boyd, E. M. and Carsky, E., Kwashiorkorigenic diet and diazinon toxicity, *Acta Pharmacol. Toxicol.,* 27, 284, 1969.

30. Boyd, E. M. and DeCastro, E. S., Protein-deficient diet and DDT toxicity, *Bull. W.H.O.,* 38, 141, 1968.

31. Boyd, E. M. and Stefec, J., Dietary protein and pesticide toxicity: with particular reference to endrin, *Can. Med. Assoc. J.,* 101, 335, 1969.

32. Boyd, E. M. and Chen, C. P., Lindane toxicity and protein-deficient diet, *Arch. Environ. Health,* 17, 156, 1968.

33. Boyd, E. M. and Dobos, I., Acute oral toxicity of monuron in albino rats fed from weaning on different diets, *J. Agric. Food Chem.,* 17, 1213, 1969.

34. Brody, S., *Bioenergetics and Growth,* Reinhold Publishing Co., New York, 1945.

35. Boyd, E. M., Mulrooney, D. A., Pitman, C. A., and Abel, M., Benzylpenicillin toxicity in animals on a synthetic, high sucrose diet, *Can. J. Physiol. Pharmacol.,* 43, 47, 1965.

36. Boyd, E. M., Covert, E. L., and Pitman, C. A., Benzylpenicillin toxicity in albino rats fed synthetic high sugar diets, *Chemotherapia,* 11, 320, 1966.

37. Peters, J. M., Factors affecting caffeine toxicity, *J. Clin. Pharmacol.,* 7, 131, 1967.

38. Peters, J. M. and Boyd, E. M., Diet and caffeine toxicity in rats, *Toxicol. Appl. Pharmacol.,* 8, 350, 1966.

39. Boyd, E. M., Dobos, I., and Taylor, F., Benzylpenicillin toxicity in albino rats fed synthetic high starch versus high sugar diets, *Chemotherapia,* 15, 1, 1970.

40. Boyd, E. M., Diet and drug toxicity, *Clin. Toxicol.,* 2, 423, 1969.

41. Peters, J. M. and Krijnen, C. J., Organ weights and water contents of rats fed purified diets, *Growth,* 30, 99, 1966.

42. Moinuddin, J. F. and Lee, H. W., Effects of feeding diets containing sucrose, cellobiose or glucose on the dry weights of cleaned gastrointestinal organs in the rat, *Am. J. Physiol.,* 192, 417, 1958.

43. Moinuddin, J. F. and Lee, H. W., Possible associations of dietary residues with growth of the large gut, *Am. J. Physiol.,* 197, 903, 1959.

44. McCall, M. G., Newman, G. E., and Valberg, L. S., Enlargement of the cecum in the rat in iron deficiency, *Br. J. Nutr.,* 16, 333, 1962.

45. Fenton, P. F. and Dowling, M. T., Studies on obesity. 1. Nutritional obesity in mice, *J. Nutr.,* 49, 319, 1953.

46. Boyd, E. M., Chen, C. P., and Muis, L. F., Resistance to starvation in albino rats fed from weaning on diets containing from 0 to 81% of protein as casein, *Growth,* 34, 99, 1970.

47. **Krijnen, C. J. and Boyd, E. M.,** The influence of diets containing from 0 to 81% of protein on tolerated doses of pesticides, *Comp. Gen. Pharmacol.,* 2, 373, 1971.

48. **Krijnen, C. J. and Boyd, E. M.,** Susceptibility to captan pesticide of albino rats fed from weaning on diets containing various levels of protein, *Food Cosmet. Toxicol.,* 8, 35, 1970.

49. **Boyd, E. M. and Krijnen, C. J.,** The influence of protein intake on the acute oral toxicity of carbaryl, *J. Clin. Pharmacol.,* 9, 292, 1969.

50. **Boyd, E. M., Carsky, E., and Krijnen, C. J.,** The effects of diets containing from 0 to 81% of casein on the acute oral toxicity of diazinon, *Clin. Toxicol.,* 2, 295, 1969.

51. **Boyd, E. M. and Krijnen, C. J.,** Dietary protein and DDT toxicity, *Bull. Environ. Contam. Toxicol.,* 4, 256, 1969.

52. **Boyd, E. M., Dobos, I., and Krijnen, C. J.,** Endosulfan toxicity and dietary protein, *Arch. Environ. Health,* 21, 15, 1970.

53. **Boyd, E. M., Chen, C. P., and Krijnee, C. J.,** Lindane and dietary protein, *Pharmacol. Res. Commun.,* 1, 403, 1969.

54. **Boyd, E. M., Krijnen, C. J., and Tanikella, T. K.,** The influence of a wide range of dietary protein concentration on the acute oral toxicity of malathion, *Arch. Toxikol.,* 26, 125, 1970.

55. **Chittenden, R.,** Physiological Economy in Nutrition, with Special Reference to the "Minimal Protein Requirements of the Healthy Man: An Experimental Study," F.A. Stokes Company, New York, 1907.

56. **Gamble, J. L.,** Harvey Lectures, Vol. 42, 1946–1947.

57. **Ross, M. H.,** Protein, calories and life expectancy, *Fed. Proc.,* 18, 1190, 1959.

58. **Gullino, P., Winitz, M., Birnbaum, S. M., Cornfield, J., Otey, M. C., and Greenstein, J. P.,** Studies on the metabolism of amino acids and related compounds in vivo. I. Toxicity of essential amino acids, individually and in mixtures, and the protective effect of l-arginine, *Arch. Biochem. Biophys.,* 64, 319, 1956.

59. **Adrian, J. and Terroine, T.,** Influence du taux protidique de la ration et de la qualité des protéines alimentaires sur l'excrétion urinaire de riboflavine, pyridoxine et niacine, *C. R. Acad. Sci.,* 250, 1120, 1960.

60. **Van Dam-Bakker, A. W. I., De Groot, A. P., and Luyken, R.,** The influence of alternate high-protein and low-protein feeding on growth and reproduction and on regeneration of haemoglobin in rats, *Br. J. Nutr.,* 12, 259, 1958.

61. **Kato, R., Oshima, T., and Tomizawa, S.,** Toxicity and metabolism of drugs in relation to dietary protein, *Jap. J. Pharmacol.,* 18, 356, 1968.

62. **Wergedal, J. E. and Harper, A. E.,** Metabolic adaptations in higher animals. IX. Effect of high protein intake on amino nitrogen catabolism in vivo, *J. Biol. Chem.,* 239, 1156, 1964.

63. **McLean, A. E. M. and McLean, E. K.,** Diet and toxicity, *Br. Med. Bull.,* 25, 278, 1969.

64. **Homburger, F., Ed.,** *The Physiology of Cancer,* 2nd ed., Cassell and Company, London, 1958.

65. **Cohn, C., Joseph, D., Bell, L., and Oler, A.,** Feeding frequency and protein metabolism, *Am. J. Physiol.,* 205, 71, 1963.

66. **Schultze, M. O.,** Nutritional value of plant materials. VIII. Lactation failure of rats fed diets containing purified soybean proteins, *J. Nutr.,* 49, 231, 1953.

67. **Schultze, M. O.,** Nutritional value of plant materials. IX. The effect of various supplements on lactation failure of rats fed diets containing purified soybean proteins, *J. Nutr.,* 49, 245, 1953.

68. **Peters, J. M.,** A separation of the direct toxic effects of dietary raw egg white powder from its action in producing biotin deficiency, *Br. J. Nutr.,* 21, 801, 1967.

PART V. THE ORAL TOXICITY OF WATER AND SALTS

Chapter 14

DISTILLED WATER

Under normal circumstances, water intoxication in man is of rare occurrence. Habener, Dashe, and Solomon[1] gave fluids to healthy male subjects in doses increasing to some 100 ml/kg/day over a period of four weeks and found no change in serum osmolality. Body water balance was maintained through diuresis and oligodipsia. Le Magnen[2] reported similar adjustments in albino rats. Boyd and Godi[3] found that the largest single dose of distilled water which could be given intragastrically to young male albino rats without ill effects was 70 ml/kg warmed to body temperature and administered slowly over a period of 2 min. Larger single doses were either aspirated into the lungs or, if 200 ml/kg or over, produced gastric rupture. A dose of 70 ml/kg repeated at intervals of less than 20 min was in part evacuated through the anus. If the interval between administrations was lengthened much beyond 20 min, a major part of the water given was absorbed and eliminated through the kidneys.

Water intoxication may be produced in man by the antidiuretic activity of hormones of the posterior pituitary gland present in oxytocin and vasopressin. A single dose of oxytocin injected rapidly has little or no antidiuretic activity[4-6] but infused over a period of several minutes, oxytocin reduces the renal clearance of free water.[7-9] Similar antidiuretic activity is obtained by giving vasopressin either as a single dose or by infusion.[10] The site of action is the area of the distal convoluted and collecting tubules of the kidneys which is excited to augment reabsorption of water.[6] Signs of water intoxication have occurred in obstetric patients given oxytocin at the rate of from 43 to 1367 mU/min for 4 to 42 hr.[10]

The syndrome of water intoxication was first described by Rowntree in 1923[11] during studies designed to investigate the toxic effects of excessive activity of pituitary antidiuretic hormone in animals. In a series of studies by authors such as Rowntree,[12] Underhill and Sallick,[13] and Gaunt et al.,[14,15] it was shown that distilled water given orally to animals in divided doses totaling some 200 to 900 ml/kg produced lethargy, vomiting, confusion, convulsions, coma, and death. Wasterlain and Torak[16] found that the neurological signs were due to edema of the interstitial space of the brain and swelling of the astrocytes during vasopressin-induced water intoxication in rats. Astrocytes contain large amounts of sodium chloride[17] which could account for their peculiar susceptibility to water intoxication.

The studies of Boyd and Godi[3] will be described in exemplification of the acute toxicity of distilled water. These authors gave distilled water warmed to 99°F to male albino rats starved overnight to empty the stomach. Distilled water was administered intragastrically through a stomach tube in amounts of 70 ml/kg repeated at intervals of 20 min (for reasons noted above) to the total doses listed in Table 77. Of the 29 controls given no distilled water, noted in Table 77, 15 received a stomach tube insertion at the same intervals distilled water was given and 14 received no treatment apart from being placed in a

TABLE 77

Total Amounts of Distilled Water Given by Stomach Tube to Adult Male Albino Rats

ml/kg	Number of rats
0	29 (controls)
280	14
350	8
385	14
420	22
455	14
490	15
525	19
560	12
595	20

(From Boyd and Godi[3] with the permission of *Industrial Medicine and Surgery*, copyright © 1967, Industrial Medicine Publishing Co., Miami, Fla.)

metabolism cage for observation. Clinical observations were made, as indicated, until death, and for a period of one month in survivors. Autopsies were performed immediately after death to avoid postmortem changes described by Boyd and Knight,[18] and on survivors at two weeks and one month.

Clinical Signs of Acute Water Intoxication

The acute oral LD_{50} ± S.E. of distilled water given to albino rats as described by Boyd and Godi[3] was calculated to the 469 ± 51 ml/kg. It should be emphasized that this was an estimate of the minimal LD_{50}; if water is given in single doses in excess of 70 ml/kg or at intervals greater or less than 20 min, the LD_{50} is higher for reasons discussed above. Furthermore, and as also noted above, amounts of distilled water greatly in excess of 70 ml/kg given as one single intragastric administration can cause death by mechanical means, such as aspiration asphyxia and gastric rupture. Approximately 15% of the administered dose of water was eliminated in the urine before death occurred. The 50% killing dose of retained water was, therefore, of the order of 400 ml/kg. The estimated maximal nonlethal dose of distilled water was 352 ml/kg (= 300 ml/kg of retained water) and the minimal LD_{100} was 586 ml/kg (500 ml/kg of retained water).

Ninety-five percent of the rats died at 154 ± 36 min (mean ± standard deviation) from the start of water administration. The LD_{50} required 140 min for administration and most of the animals died during and shortly after the last or seventh administration of distilled water. Five percent of the animals had delayed deaths at from 1.5 to 16 days.

The clinical signs of water intoxication in albino rats appeared during progressive oral administrations and included weakness, ataxia, and finally prostration. There occurred frequency of urination, polyuria, dacryorrhea, abdominal bloating, pallor, cyanosis, and diarrhea. As death approached, there developed tremors, first in the limbs and then of the whole body. The latter was associated with a Straub reaction (extension of the tail), exophthalmos, and tachypnea. The various clinical signs were dose dependent, as exemplified for four signs in Figure 70.

Autopsy Signs of Acute Intoxication

Histopathological observations on albino rats

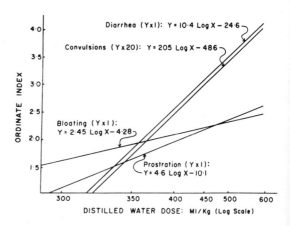

FIGURE 70. The regression, on log total dose of distilled water given by stomach tube to adult male albino rats, of severity of diarrhea (graded 1+ to 4+), percentage of animals exhibiting convulsions (multiply ordinate index by 20), degree of abdominal bloating (1+ to 4+), and extent of prostration (1+ to 4+) measured at the end of the period of water administration. (From Boyd and Godi[3] with the permission of *Industrial Medicine and Surgery,* copyright © 1967, Industrial Medicine Publishing Co., Miami, Fla.)

that died of water intoxication are summarized in Table 78. It is apparent from information listed in Table 78 that the volume of distilled water required to produce death overwhelmed the mechanisms of the body for maintenance of water and salt balance. Exposure of the gastrointestinal tissue to huge amounts of water in the lumen of the gut produced edema and hydration of the lining mucosa and of supporting connective tissue particularly of the lamina propria, which supports the lining mucosa and lies between it and the muscularis mucosae. Water entering the blood vessels produced a swelling and distortion of appearance of the red blood cells which tended to clump together and form thromboses.

When the large volume of distilled water was carried by blood to body tissues, it entered the cells of organs in huge amounts and produced hydration and swelling. This was evident in such cells as the Purkinje's cells of the cerebellum, the brush border of the proximal renal tubules, erythrocytes in the hepatic sinusoids, the mucous salivary gland cells, the lymphocytes of white pulp in the spleen, the subcutaneous cells of skin, and in the spermatogenic tissue of the testes. Distorted erythrocytes tended to cling to the endothelium lining the capillaries, veins, and arteries, for example, in the adrenal sinusoids. This led to clotting

TABLE 78

Histopathological Observations on Albino Rats that Died from Oral Administration of Distilled Water in Doses at the Range of the Acute LD_{50}

Organ	Histopathology
Adrenal glands	Erythrocytes in the cortical sinusoids swollen and adherent to sinusoid wall, medulla ischemic
Brain	Swelling noticeable in some cells such as Purkinje's cells of the cerebellum
Gastrointestinal tract	
Cardiac stomach	Stratified squamous epithelium edematous, thrombosis of small veins in the submucosa
Pyloric stomach	Parietal cells edematous and small veins thrombosed, ulcers in delayed deaths
Small bowel	Pale-staining of Lieberkuhn's glands, edema of the lamina propria and of erythrocytes in capillaries, veins and arteries shrunken in delayed deaths
Cecum	Same as small bowel
Colon	Same as small bowel
Heart	Venous thrombosis
Kidneys	Brush border of proximal renal tubules edematous, casts, venous thrombosis, congestion in delayed deaths with pyknosis and necrosis of the tubules
Liver	Thrombosis in the portal veins, erythrocytes in the sinusoids distorted in appearance and adherent to sinusoidal wall, central veins ischemic, atrophy of hepatic tissue in delayed deaths
Lungs	Venous thrombosis, congestion and pulmonary edema in delayed deaths
Muscle (skeletal)	Normal appearance
Salivary (submaxillary) glands	Venous thrombosis, mucous glands edematous
Skin	Edema of subcutaneous tissue
Spleen	White pulp edematous, red pulp full of particulate matter, ischemia and splenic contraction and edema in delayed deaths
Testes	Edema and venous thrombosis
Thymus gland	Venous thrombosis, thymocytes edematous

(From Boyd and Godi[3] with the permission of *Industrial Medicine and Surgery*, copyright © 1967, Industrial Medicine Publishing Co., Miami, Fla.)

of blood seen particularly in veins of the heart, kidneys, portal veins of the liver, pulmonary veins, and veins of the salivary glands, testes, and thymus gland. In the early stages of tissue hydration, the large amount of water in blood vessels first exposed seemed to produced ischemia of distal adjacent tissue, such as ischemia of the adrenal medulla, which is supplied mostly with blood that has previously passed through the sinusoids of the adrenal cortex.

In animals that survived early death from water intoxication, the body was freed of water by diuresis. Of necessity, this resulted in some loss of body electrolytes and inability of cells to hold the normal amount of water. Many cells of survivors, therefore, appeared shrunken, for example, the cells of the small bowel, cecum, colon, kidneys, and hepatic tissue. This led to degenerative changes which could produce a delayed death. Degenerative changes took the form of necrotic ulcers in pyloric stomach, pyknosis, and necrosis of the renal tubular cells, atrophy of parietal cells in the liver, and loss of red pulp in the spleen. Degeneration was occasionally associated with a local capillary-venous congestion, such as that seen in the kidneys and lungs.

As might be expected, hydration of body tissue resulted in a substantial increase in their wet weight (see Table 79) due to a marked increase in their water content (see Table 80) at the time of death due to water intoxication. Increase in wet weight was particularly marked in the adrenal glands, stomach, cecum, heart, kidneys, lungs, skin, thymus gland, and residual carcass. Hydration was marked in the same organs (except adrenal glands and thymus gland) and also in the brain, small bowel, colon, skeletal muscle, and salivary glands.

Signs in Survivors

In survivors at 24 hr, there was a loss of body weight which was dose dependent, as shown in Figure 71. Loss of weight was due to a decrease in food and water intake, as indicated in Figure 71, and a considerable diuresis, as shown in Figure 72. Loss of body water and salt in urine contributed to the loss of body weight. There was also a dose dependent increase in urinary pH accompanied by

a glycosuria and proteinuria. For comparison, values for these various measurements in control rats not given distilled water are summarized in Table 81.

In survivors at two weeks, the weight and water content of most body organs had returned to the range of values in controls not given distilled water. These data are summarized in Tables 79 and 80. At one month there was a rebound hydration of most body organs, as noted in Table 80. Most body organs had lost wet weight at one month (Table 79) so that loss of dry weight was even more marked. The studies of Boyd and Godi[3] were terminated by autopsy of survivors at one month so that no information was available on the ultimate fate of such animals.

Acute Toxicity in Rabbits

Boyd and Boyd[19] reported a study of the effect of oral administration of warmed distilled water on the output and composition of respiratory tract fluid in urethanized rabbits. Distilled water was given through a gastric cannula in single

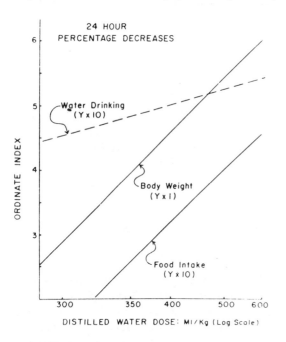

FIGURE 71. The regression, on log total dose of distilled water given by stomach tube to adult male albino rats, of percentage decreases, from values in controls given no distilled water, in water intake (as ml/kg/24 hr), body weight (g/day), and food intake (g/kg/24 hr) of survivors at 24 hr. The ordinate index is multiplied by the respective factors (Y x factor) to yield mean percentage decreases. (From Boyd and Godi[3] with the permission of *Industrial Medicine and Surgery,* copyright © 1967, Industrial Medicine Publishing Co., Miami, Fla.)

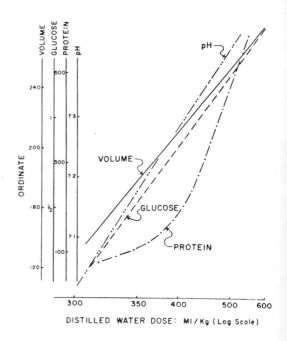

FIGURE 72. The regression, on log total dose of distilled water given by stomach tube to male albino rats, of changes in the volume of urine calculated as ml/kg/24 hr, pH of 24-hr samples, and urinary concentration of glucose and protein calculated as mg/kg/24 hr, during the first day after water administration. (From Boyd and Godi[3] with the permission of *Industrial Medicine and Surgery,* copyright © 1967, Industrial Medicine Publishing Co., Miami, Fla.)

TABLE 79

Shifts in the Wet Weight of Body Organs of Albino Rats Given Distilled Water in Amounts at the Range of the Acute Oral LD$_{50}$ [a]

Organ	At death	Fortnight survivors	Month survivors
Adrenal glands	+ 27.7*	+ 2.1	+ 7.1
Brain	– 1.8	– 1.8	– 0.1
Gastrointestinal tract			
Cardiac stomach	+ 34.1**	– 2.4	– 9.4*
Pyloric stomach	+ 30.3**	– 7.6	– 4.1
Small bowel	+ 2.6	+ 2.8	–24.9**
Cecum	+ 29.4**	+11.3*	–12.7*
Colon	+ 2.3	+17.4*	–15.6**
Heart	+ 32.0*	– 4.2	–10.4*
Kidneys	+ 24.7**	– 2.0	– 5.0*
Liver	+ 5.0	+ 5.3	–10.8*
Lungs	+130.2*	+ 7.3	–14.7**
Muscle (abdominal wall)	+ 16.2*	– 7.9	– 5.3
Salivary glands (submaxillary)	0.0	+ 5.3	+ 5.8
Skin	+ 26.3**	0.0	– 7.3*
Spleen	– 31.3**	–24.7*	+ 4.2
Testes	+ 14.5**	+ 0.3	– 4.6*
Thymus gland	+ 27.0**	– 4.0	+ 7.5
Residual carcass	+ 39.4**	– 0.9	+ 3.1
Autopsy body weight	+ 30.0**	0.0	– 4.8

[a]Wet weight was measured in grams. Results are expressed as percent change from controls, specifically as $[(\bar{X}_W - \bar{X}_c)/\bar{X}_c] \times 100$, where $\bar{X}_W$ is the mean in animals given distilled water and $\bar{X}_c$ is the mean in controls. Differences significant at $P = 0.05$ to 0.02 are indicated by one asterisk and at $P < 0.01$ by two asterisks. (From Boyd and Godi[3] with the permission of *Industrial Medicine and Surgery*, copyright © 1967, Industrial Medicine Publishing Co., Miami, Fla.)

TABLE 80

Shifts in the Water Levels of Body Organs of Albino Rats Given Distilled Water in Doses at the Range of the Acute Oral LD$_{50}$ [a]

Organ	At death	Fortnight survivors	Month survivors
Adrenal glands	+ 4.5	– 4.8	– 6.4
Brain	+10.2**	+ 0.3	+ 5.8*
Gastrointestinal tract			
Cardiac stomach	+34.0**	– 9.7*	+ 8.8
Pyloric stomach	+45.3**	– 4.3	+15.6*
Small bowel	+29.6**	– 2.5	+ 3.4
Cecum	+36.4**	–13.1*	+ 6.1
Colon	+25.9**	+ 2.7	+10.4*
Heart	+25.3**	– 0.9	+ 3.9
Kidneys	+26.9**	+ 1.8	+10.4*
Liver	+ 8.9**	– 5.7*	+ 4.8
Lungs	+23.2*	+ 2.1	+ 5.7
Muscle (abdominal wall)	+20.1**	– 2.3	+ 6.8*
Salivary glands (submaxillary)	+16.1*	+ 3.2	+11.3
Skin	+59.0**	+ 8.0	+ 6.8
Spleen	+ 2.2	– 0.9	+16.8**
Testes	+ 9.8*	+ 4.2	+ 2.3
Thymus gland	+ 4.4	+ 7.5	+ 6.8*
Residual carcass	+18.4**	+ 3.2	+21.2*

[a]Water levels measured as g H$_2$O/100 g dry weight of organ. Results are expressed as percent change from controls, specifically as $[(\bar{X}_W - \bar{X}_c)/\bar{X}_c] \times 100$, where $\bar{X}_W$ is the mean in animals given distilled water and $\bar{X}_c$ is the mean in the controls. Differences significant at $P = 0.05$ to 0.02 are indicated by one asterisk and at $P < 0.01$ by two asterisks. (From Boyd and Godi[3] with the permission of *Industrial Medicine and Surgery*, copyright © 1967, Industrial Medicine Publishing Co., Miami, Fla.)

TABLE 81

A Summary of Clinical Measurements Expressed as Mean ± Standard Deviation in Control Albino Rats not Given Distilled Water

Measurement	Day 1	Day 4
Increase in body weight: g/24 hr	5.2 ± 0.54	6.6 ± 0.82
Food intake: g chow/kg/24 hr	158 ± 33	158 ± 53
Water intake: ml/kg/24 hr	211 ± 63	186 ± 42
Colonic temperature: °F	99.4 ± 0.9	98.9 ± 0.8
Urinary volume: ml/kg/24 hr	9.2 ± 15.2	0.8 ± 1.5
Urinary glucose output: g/kg/24 hr	0.0 ± 0.0	0.0 ± 0.0
Urinary protein output: mg/kg/24 hr	24.8 ± 17.0	1.15 ± 0.65
Urinary pH: 24-hr sample	6.1 ± 0.4	6.5 ± 0.6

(From Boyd and Godi[3] with the permission of *Industrial Medicine and Surgery,* copyright © 1967, Industrial Medicine Publishing Co., Miami, Fla.)

doses of from 10 to 100 ml/kg and in higher total doses of 180, 270, 360, and 450 ml/kg given as 90 ml/kg every 20 min as required to yield the total doses indicated. Deaths followed administration of doses of 180 ml/kg and over. Death was preceded by hypothermia, abdominal bloating, diuresis, diarrhea, and occasionally nosebleed. The acute oral LD_{50} ± S.E. was calculated to be 342 ± 14 ml/kg in these urethanized animals. The anesthetic agent prevented the appearance of signs of stimulation of the central nervous system such as tremors and a Straub reaction seen in unanesthetized albino rats. On the other hand, urethane may have accentuated signs of depression of the central nervous system, such as weakness, ataxia, and prostration recorded in unanesthetized albino rats.[3] The acute oral LD_{50}, therefore, could be higher or lower in unanesthetized rabbits. It could be unchanged from the value found in urethanized rabbits which was of the same general high order of 469 ± 51 ml/kg reported in unanesthetized albino rats.[3]

The Acute Toxicity of Nonlethal Doses

As noted by Boyd,[20] distilled water is frequently used as the solvent or vehicle for administration of drugs by mouth. In some reports of such studies, the effects of the distilled water alone have been described. A representative group of such reports will be reviewed here. Boyd and Liu[21] noted that the psychic trauma associated with the insertion of an intragastric cannula produced minor effects in albino rats such as a slight temporary inhibition of growth rate, a decrease in water intake and urinary volume, and a slight aciduria. Boyd and Liu[21] obtained these results by comparing clinical signs in rats given stomach tube insertions with those in controls given no stomach tube insertion. They inserted the stomach tube at intervals of 2.5 hr four times per day. Presumably one stomach tube insertion would have even less effect upon the animals.

20 ml/kg

Boyd and Shanas[22] studied the acute oral toxicity of potassium chloride dissolved in distilled water and given by gastric cannula to overnight-starved adult female albino rats in a volume of 20 ml/kg. The distilled water produced no change in food intake, colonic temperature, and the amounts of sugar, albumin, occult blood, acetone, or bilirubin in urine. There was a slight increase in water intake and a decrease in urinary volume during but not after the first 24 hr of water administration.

60 ml/kg

Boyd, Godi, and Abel[23] reported on the acute toxicity of sucrose given orally as a solution in distilled water at a volume of 60 ml/kg. They found that this volume of distilled water produced hypokinesia, prostration, abdominal bloating, and diarrhea. Constantopoulos and Boyd[24] gave sucrose orally to albino rats in increasing volumes of distilled water of from 35 to 60 ml/kg. In volumes of 45 to 60 ml/kg, the death rate from sucrose in a dose of 36 g/kg was 7 to 12 times higher than in volumes of 35 or 40 ml/kg. This

TABLE 82

Clinical Measurements in Young Adult Male Albino Rats Following Oral Administration of Distilled Water in Single Doses of 75 to 100 ml/kg[a]

Measurement	Days 1 to 3	Days 4 to 6	Days 7 to 9	Days 10 to 12
Food intake: g/kg/day	95 ± 29	98 ± 25	103 ± 20	98 ± 13
Water intake: ml/kg/day	138 ± 50	127 ± 45	132 ± 29	123 ± 18
Urine volume: ml/kg/day	12 ± 10	8 ± 9	6 ± 9	5 ± 5
Urine protein: mg/100 ml	49 ± 29	78 ± 40	84 ± 41	74 ± 23
Urine glucose: g/100 ml	0.1 ± 0.2	0.1 ± 0.2	0.2 ± 0.3	0.1 ± 0.1
Urine pH	7.3 ± 0.7	6.9 ± 1.1	6.9 ± 1.0	6.4 ± 0.4

[a]The results are expressed as mean ± standard deviation. (From Boyd and Shanas[25] with the permission of the *Canadian Medical Association Journal*.)

could have been due to (a) a combination of the toxicity of distilled water and that of sucrose or (b) to impairment of digestion and absorption of sucrose by highly concentrated aqueous solution of the sugar. Constantopoulos and Boyd[24] found that levels of blood glucose were not appreciably affected by this volume of distilled water used to dissolve sucrose. This suggested that explanation (b) was probably not correct and favored explanation (a).

75 to 100 ml/kg

Boyd and Shanas[25] measured the acute toxicity of medicinal iron powder given by stomach tube to albino rats as suspension in volumes of distilled water ranging from 75 to 100 ml/kg. As indicated by data summarized in Table 82, these doses of distilled water produced a possible temporary decrease in food intake and urinary protein output, and a possible slight temporary increase in water intake, urinary volume, and urinary pH.

185 ml/kg

Boyd and Abel[26] studied the acute oral toxicity of barium sulfate given by stomach tube as suspensions containing 150 g in distilled water to a final volume of 100 ml. The acute oral LD_{50} ± S.E. of barium sulfate was calculated to be 364 ± 41 g/kg with death due to bowel obstruction. The LD_{50} dose of barium sulfate was suspended in 185 ml/kg of distilled water and clinical measurements following oral administration of this dose of distilled water over a period of 6 hr are summarized in Table 83. The results were similar to those reported by Boyd and Shanas[25] and are shown in

Table 82. Distilled water, at this dose, produced a slight inhibition of growth and reduction in food intake and a slight increase in water intake, urinary volume and urinary pH.

250 ml/kg

Boyd, Peters, and Krijnen[27] investigated the acute toxicity of dried egg white powder dissolved in distilled water as a 40% (w/v) solution given by stomach tube to young adult male albino rats. One hundred milliliters of this solution were administered at first and repeated at hourly intervals to a maximal dose of 160 g of egg white per kg body weight (= 400 ml/kg of the aqueous solution). The acute oral LD_{50} ± S.E. of spray-dried egg white was found to be 100.7 ± 6.4 g/kg. As controls, 46 rats received 250 ml/kg of distilled water given by stomach tube, 100 ml/kg initially followed by a further 100 ml/kg in 1 hr and the remaining 50 ml/kg after 2 hr. This dose of distilled water produced piloerection, listlessness, hyporeflexia, soft stools, and fur soiling. These signs reached a peak of intensity at 2 to 3 hr after water administration.

As indicated by data summarized in Table 84, at 24 hr after water administration there was some loss of body weight due to a reduction in food intake. Urinary volume was markedly elevated during the first 24 hr and the urine tended to be alkaline. There were some residual piloerection and listlessness at 24 hr but not thereafter, and other signs noted at 2 to 3 hr had disappeared even at 24 hr. During the second and subsequent days, growth resumed and there was no evidence of consistent changes in the other parameter, as may be seen from data in Table 84.

TABLE 83

Clinical Measurements in Young Adult Male Albino Rats Following Oral Administration of Distilled Water in a Dose of 185 ml/kg over a Period of 6 hr[a]

Measurement	Units	Control day	Days after water		
			1	2	3
Body weight	g	143.0 ± 9.0	141.0 ± 11.0	147.0 ± 12.0	152.0 ± 12.0
Food intake	g/kg/24 hr	130.0 ± 26.0	124.0 ± 29.0	129.0 ± 24.0	121.0 ± 24.0
Water intake	ml/kg/24 hr	182.0 ± 46.0	191.0 ± 47.0	192.0 ± 31.0	172.0 ± 33.0
Colonic temperature	°F	98.8 ± 1.1	98.9 ± 1.0	98.9 ± 0.9	99.3 ± 1.0
Urinary volume	ml/kg/24 hr	2.7 ± 4.2	20.6 ± 20.4	4.3 ± 6.6	2.3 ± 5.1
Urinary glucose	mg/kg/24 hr	0.0 ± 0.0	0.0 ± 0.0	0.0 ± 0.0	0.0 ± 0.0
Urinary protein	mg/kg/24 hr	1.6 ± 0.3	4.0 ± 4.2	2.0 ± 2.8	2.1 ± 1.9
Urinary pH	24-hr sample	6.4 ± 0.6	8.2 ± 1.2	6.2 ± 0.3	6.3 ± 0.3

[a]The results are expressed as mean ± standard deviation. (From Boyd and Abel[26] with the permission of the *Canadian Medical Association Journal*.)

TABLE 84

Clinical Signs of Toxicity to Distilled Water Administered Orally to Young Male Albino Rats in a Total of 250 ml/kg

Sign	Units	Pre-water control day $\bar{X}$ ± S.D.	Days after distilled water (Mean % change from pre-water control day)[a]					
			1	2	3	4	5	14
Body weight	g	174 ± 11	− 2.2*	+ 1.6	+ 4.9*	+ 7.6*	+ 12.4*	+45.3*
Food intake	g/kg/day	127 ± 18	− 12.3*	+ 1.6	+ 3.3	+ 1.6	+ 4.9	−20.5*
Water intake	ml/kg/day	120 ± 30	− 4.2	+ 14.2*	+ 14.2	+13.3	+ 9.2	−16.8*
Colonic temperature	°C	37.4 ± 0.4	− 0.6	− 0.1	+ 0.1	+ 0.3	− 0.9	− 0.1
Urinary volume	ml/kg/day	5.7 ± 5.7	+1686*	+ 43	+ 64	+21	− 22	+69
Urinary protein output	ml/kg/day	5.1 ± 4.0	− 42	+100	+167	−17	+100	0
Urinary pH	24-hr sample	6.3 ± 0.4	+ 17.2*	+ 14.0*	0.0	− 1.6	+ 9.4	+ 6.2
Urinary glucose output[b]	mg/kg/day	0.0 ± 0.0	0.0	0.0	0.0	0.0	0.0	0.0
Piloerection[b]	1+ to 4+	0.0 ± 0.0	+ 0.9*	0.0	0.0	0.0	0.0	0.0
Listlessness[b]	1+ to 4+	0.0 ± 0.0	+ 0.4*	0.0	0.0	0.0	0.0	0.0
Diarrhea[b]	1+ to 4+	0.0 ± 0.0	0.0	0.0	0.0	0.0	0.0	0.0
Hyporeflexia[b]	1+ to 4+	0.0 ± 0.0	0.0	0.0	0.0	0.0	0.0	0.0
Prostration[b]	1+ to 4+	0.0 ± 0.0	0.0	0.0	0.0	0.0	0.0	0.0
Soiling[b]	1+ to 4+	0.0 ± 0.0	0.0	0.0	0.0	0.0	0.0	0.0
Abdominal bloating[b]	1+ to 4+	0.0 ± 0.0	0.0	0.0	0.0	0.0	0.0	0.0

[a]Mean changes which differed at P = 0.05 or less from the mean in the pre-water control day are indicated by an asterisk.
[b]Results of this measurement for days after distilled water are expressed as $\bar{X}_a - \bar{X}_b$, where $\bar{X}_a$ is the mean on the respective day after distilled water and $\bar{X}_b$ the mean on the pre-water control day. In each instance $\bar{X}_b$ is zero.
(From Boyd et al.[27] with the permission of *Industrial Medicine and Surgery*, copyright © 1966, Industrial Medicine Publishing Co., Miami, Fla.)

The Chronic Toxicity of Nonlethal Doses
20 ml/kg/day

Information on clinical measurements in young adult male albino rats given distilled water in a dose of 20 ml/kg was provided by Boyd, Abel, and Knight[28] in a study of the toxicity of sodium chloride at the range of the oral LD_{50} (100 days), a daily dose that killed 50% of animals over 100 days of administration. Sodium chloride was dissolved in 20 ml/kg of distilled water and the LD_{50} (100 days) ± S.E. was found to be 2.69 ± 0.12 g/kg/day, which was 72% of the acute oral LD_{50} in overnight-starved rats. Controls were given 20 ml/kg of distilled water daily for the same period of time. Animals given water appeared normal and healthy. Clinical measurements were made weekly and the results were compared with those in other albino rats given no distilled water. Data on the comparisons are summarized at representative intervals of water administration in Table 85.

Daily oral administration of this dose of distilled water caused some inhibition of growth during the first half of the period of dosing. A small part of the loss of body weight was due to the effects of daily insertion of the stomach tube. The animals gradually became tolerant to distilled water and lost little or no body weight during the second 50 days of daily administration. At the end of the 100 days, body weight of the water-treated rats was 7.3% less than in controls given no distilled water.

The initial inhibition of growth was due to a slight decrease in food and water intake and a slight increase in body temperature. When the animals gained weight in the second half of the study, it was due to a slight increase in food and water intake. There were minor and inconsistent shifts in urinary volume and in urinary glucose and protein output. The pH of urine was consistently more alkaline than that of controls given no distilled water. Alkalinization of the urine appeared to be one of the most sensitive indicators of the effect of oral administration of distilled water.

At the end of the 100 days of water administration, the animals were chloroformed and autopsied. Changes in the weight and water content of body organs at this time are summarized in Table 86. There were no significant changes in the gross or microscopic appearances of body tissues at 100 days. It may be seen from data in Table 86 that loss of body weight was due mainly to loss of weight in skin. There was also loss of weight in brain, heart, kidneys, liver, and residual carcass. Organs that gained a significant amount of wet weight included cecum, lungs, muscle, spleen, and thymus gland.

There were few consistent changes in the water

TABLE 85

Clinical Measurements in Young Adult Male Albino Rats Given Distilled Water in a Dose of 20 ml/kg/day Compared with Data in Controls Given no Distilled Water[a]

Measurement	Days given distilled water			
	0	28	56	100
Body weight: g	− 0.1	−11.4**	− 6.5*	+ 1.2
Food intake: g/kg/day	− 3.3	− 3.8	+17.2*	+ 3.8
Water intake: ml/kg/day	0.0	− 1.1	− 5.2	+12.2*
Colonic temperature: °F	+ 1.0	+ 2.6*	+ 1.8	+ 1.7
Urine volume: ml/kg/day	+ 1.0	−30.2*	+ 2.6	+30.3*
Urine glucose: mg/kg/day	0.0	0.0	+10.0	+10.0
Urine protein: mg/kg/day	−13.2	+24.2*	−15.0	−18.2*
Urine pH: 24-hr sample	+ 0.3	+ 4.2*	+ 5.8*	+ 9.8*

[a]The results are expressed as mean percent change from controls, specifically as $[(\bar{X}_w - \bar{X}_c)/\bar{X}_c] \times 100$, where $\bar{X}_w$ is the mean in rats given distilled water and $\bar{X}_c$ in controls. One asterisk indicates that $\bar{X}_w - \bar{X}_c$ is significant at $P = 0.05$ to 0.02 and two asterisks at $P = 0.01$ or less. (The data are calculated in part from information in the report of Boyd et al.[28])

TABLE 86

The Wet Weight and Water Content of Body Organs of Albino Rats at the End of 100 Days of Daily Oral Administration of Distilled Water in a Dose of 20 ml/kg/day[a]

Organ	Wet weight	Water content
Adrenal glands	− 7.5	+11.5**
Brain	−13.0**	−10.4*
Gastrointestinal tract		
Cardiac stomach	4.6	− 0.3
Pyloric stomach	+ 2.0	+ 3.0
Small bowel	+ 2.4	− 2.1
Cecum	+31.1**	− 0.7
Colon	+ 0.8	− 0.6
Heart	− 7.9*	− 4.0
Kidneys	−10.7*	− 4.2
Liver	− 9.4*	−14.2**
Lungs	+10.1*	− 0.2
Muscle (ventral abdominal wall)	+ 8.6*	+ 5.2*
Skin	−12.4**	− 1.8
Spleen	+18.6**	− 2.8
Testes	− 1.7	− 3.0
Thymus gland	+13.2*	− 8.9*
Residual carcass	− 6.6**	+ 5.7*
Autopsy body weight	− 7.3**	

[a]Wet weight was measured in grams and water content in g water per 100 g dry weight of tissue. The results are expressed as a mean percentage change from values in controls not given distilled water, specifically as $[(\bar{X}_w - \bar{X}_c)/\bar{X}_c] \times 100$, where $\bar{X}_w$ is the mean in water-treated rats and $\bar{X}_c$ the corresponding mean in the controls. One asterisk indicates that $\bar{X}_w - \bar{X}_c$ was significant at P = 0.05 to 0.02 and two asterisks at P = 0.01 or less. (The data are calculated in part from information provided by Boyd et al.[28])

content of body organs at the end of 100 days of administration of distilled water in a dose of 20 ml/kg/day. As shown in Table 86, there was a significant gain in the water content of adrenal glands, skeletal muscle, and residual carcass. Significantly dehydrated were brain, liver, and thymus gland. Loss of wet weight in brain and liver, therefore, was due in part to loss of organ water. Loss of wet weight in adrenal glands and residual carcass was due to loss of dry weight. Gain in wet weight of muscle was due in part to hydration, while gain in weight of thymus gland was due to a gain in dry weight. Gain in weight of cecum, lungs, and spleen occurred without a significant change in their water content, and so did loss of weight in heart, kidneys, and skin.

Boyd and Hottenroth[29] reported on the "withdrawal syndrome" to distilled water in albino rats. Distilled water was given by stomach tube daily in a dose of 20 ml/kg for 100 days and then water administration was abruptly terminated. The animals were controls in a study of the oral LD_{50} (100 days) of phenacetin which was found to be 1.12 ± 0.02 g/kg/day, or 27.1% of the acute oral LD_{50} in overnight-starved rats. Exemplary measurements following 14 days of withdrawal of distilled water are collected in Table 87. Statistically significant changes included an increase in food intake, water intake, and in the weight of stomach, lungs, and residual carcass and a decrease in urinary volume, urinary pH, and weight of thymus gland. By comparing these changes with those cited in Tables 85 and 86, it may been seen that they represented, for the most part, a return to normal in measurements made during daily administration of distilled water. There was no consistent or significant change in locomotor activity, which ordinarily indicates that

TABLE 87

The Effect of Abrupt Withdrawal of Oral Administration of Distilled Water at the End of 100 Days of Administration in a Dose of 20 ml/kg/day[a]

Measurement	Mean percent change
Body weight gain	+ 3.8
Food intake	+33.3*
Water intake	+63.3**
Urinary volume	−34.3*
Urinary glucose output	+ 1.5
Urinary pH	−13.7**
Locomotor activity, 1st week	− 9.0
Locomotor activity, 2nd week	+ 5.0
Weight of cardiac stomach	+10.6*
Weight of pyloric stomach	+10.7*
Weight of lungs	+13.3*
Weight of skeletal muscle	+ 3.3
Weight of salivary glands	+ 4.7
Weight of skin	− 2.3
Weight of spleen	− 2.9
Weight of testicles	− 1.7
Weight of thymus gland	−20.4*
Weight of residual carcass	+ 8.0*
Water content of spleen	− 0.2
Water content of residual carcass	− 0.2

[a]The results are expressed as mean percent change at 14 days from measurements made during the last week of daily distilled water administration. Mean changes that differed at P = 0.05 to 0.02 are indicated by one asterisk and at P = 0.01 or less by two asterisks. (From Boyd and Hottenroth[29] with the permission of *Toxicology and Applied Pharmacology*, copyright © 1968, Academic Press, New York.)

there was no physical dependence upon the agent given.

In brief, therefore, repeated daily oral administration of distilled water in a dose of 20 ml/kg/day produced minor and, for the most part, statistically insignificant changes in young adult male albino rats. There were some inhibition of growth and an increase in urinary pH which disappeared upon cessation of daily water administration at 100 days. This daily dose of distilled water corresponds, on a body weight basis, to the drinking of about 3 pt of water per day by an adult man weighing 80 kg over and above the normal intake of water. It is apparent that while this amount of distilled water produced certain measurable effects they are of a minor nature.

Larger Daily Doses

Boyd and Liu[21] reported on the effects of daily oral administration of distilled water in amounts from 60 to 480 ml/kg/day for 14 days to albino rats and in increasing daily doses up to 760 ml/kg/day for 49 days. These animals were used as controls in a study of the oral toxicity of starch described in Chapter 6 in which it is noted that the water was given in amounts of 15 to 190 ml/kg every 2.5 hr, the amounts being gradually increased as tolerance developed.

The clinical signs of chronic toxicity to distilled water are summarized in Table 31 of Chapter 6. They included loss of body weight associated with inhibition of food and water intake, increasing with increasing daily dose of distilled water. Diuresis also increased with increase in the volume of administered water, which was anticipated. The pH value of urine, on the other hand, was maximally augmented by the lower daily doses of water and was increased less by very large daily doses which, however, produced a hematuria. There were no deaths.

Autopsy at the end of the period of administration of distilled water disclosed hypertrophy of the stratified squamous epithelium, muscularis mucosae, and muscularis externa of cardiac stomach. Hypertrophy of smooth muscle was also noted in the small bowel, to a lesser extent in pyloric stomach, and not at all in cecum and colon. In addition, occasionally there were found early degenerative changes in the liver, venous stasis and thrombosis in the kidneys, and hyperemia in several organs such as the adrenal glands, most parts of the gastrointestinal tract, heart, lungs, salivary glands, testes, and thymus gland.

60 ml/kg/day

Changes in the wet weight of body organs at the end of 14 days of daily administration of distilled water are summarized in Table 88 and in organ water content in Table 89. A daily dose of 60 ml/kg, corresponding to about 5 l./day for a man weighing 80 kg, produced a significant decrease in the weight of pyloric stomach and colon. As noted by data summarized in Table 89, no significant changes in organ water levels occurred at this daily dose of distilled water. Relatively minor effects were produced, therefore, by a daily dose of 60 ml/kg. It is quite possible that tolerance

TABLE 88

Changes in the Wet Weight of Body Organs of Albino Rats Following Oral Administration of Distilled Water Daily for 14 Days[a]

Organ	Daily dose of distilled water (ml per kg)			
	60	120–200	280–340	400–480
Adrenal glands	+ 3.1	+ 6.0	– 1.5	+ 19.2**
Brain	+ 1.0	– 0.9	– 2.6	– 3.4**
Gastrointestinal tract				
Cardiac stomach	+ 4.0	+22.5**	+95.1**	+135.1**
Pyloric stomach	–16.8**	– 7.2*	+ 4.7	+ 12.2**
Small bowel	+ 0.8	+12.9**	+19.2**	+ 21.4**
Cecum	– 7.9	+ 3.4	– 5.2	– 1.7
Colon	–20.0**	– 2.0	–11.5*	– 7.0
Heart	–	3.4	– 5.5*	– 7.3**
Kidneys	– 5.8	– 7.9*	–13.3**	– 15.1**
Liver	– 5.9	+ 1.9	– 6.2*	– 12.4**
Lungs	+ 5.8	– 1.8	– 3.4	3.8
Muscle (ventral abdominal wall)	–	–12.3**	–14.2**	– 17.4**
Skin	– 2.2	– 2.7	–11.5**	– 18.3**
Spleen	– 1.7	– 6.4	–13.3**	– 20.6**
Submaxillary salivary glands	–	+ 5.4	+ 2.5	1.5
Testicles	+ 0.2	– 2.2	– 3.8	7.5**
Thymus gland	+ 0.8	+ 1.2	–16.9**	– 16.9**
Residual carcass	– 3.3	– 4.5*	– 7.8**	– 14.3**

[a]Weight of organs was fresh weight measured in grams. The results are expressed as mean percent change from controls given only gastric tube insertions, specifically as [($\bar{X}_d - \bar{X}_c)/\bar{X}_c$] x 100, where $\bar{X}_d$ is the mean in rats given distilled water and $\bar{X}_c$ the mean in tube insertion controls. One asterisk indicates that $\bar{X}_d - \bar{X}_c$ was significant at P = 0.05 to 0.02 and two asterisks at P = 0.01 or less. (From Boyd and Liu[21] with the permission of the Canadian Medical Association Journal.)

TABLE 89

Changes in the Water Content of Body Organs of Albino Rats Following Oral Administration of Distilled Water Daily for 14 Days[a]

Organ	Daily dose of distilled water (ml per kg)			
	60	120–200	280–340	400–480
Adrenal glands	+0.9	–7.9	–5.5	+ 0.4
Brain	+0.8	–0.8	–2.2*	– 1.0
Gastrointestinal tract				
Cardiac stomach	+2.4	+0.4	+7.2**	+3.1**
Pyloric stomach	+1.2	–4.5*	–0.2	+ 8.5**
Small bowel	+2.5	–4.1*	–5.3*	+ 1.1
Cecum	+4.3	–1.7	+1.6	+10.3**
Colon	+4.0	–7.0*	–6.2*	– 4.4
Heart	–0.1	–2.5*	–3.2*	– 2.9*
Kidneys	–0.4	–4.9**	–5.0**	– 4.6*
Liver	+4.5	–2.3	+0.9	– 1.4
Lungs	+0.8	0.0	–2.4	– 1.9
Muscle (ventral abdominal wall)	+4.9	–5.2**	–4.8*	– 4.2
Skin	–1.4	–2.2	–4.3*	+ 1.5
Spleen	+0.9	+0.2	–2.2*	– 0.9
Submaxillary salivary glands	–4.7	–7.0**	–8.5**	– 7.3**
Testicles	+0.8	–2.0**	–1.3	– 1.2
Thymus gland	+1.3	–2.0	–4.9*	– 3.2
Residual carcass	+1.3	–2.3	–3.0	+ 0.1

[a]Water content was measured as grams per 100 g dry weight. The results are expressed as mean percent change from controls given only gastric tube insertions, specifically as [($\bar{X}_d - \bar{X}_c)/\bar{X}_c$] x 100, where $\bar{X}_d$ is the mean in rats given distilled water and $\bar{X}_c$ the mean in tube insertion controls. One asterisk indicates that $\bar{X}_d - \bar{X}_c$ was significant at P = 0.05 to 0.02 and two asterisks at P = 0.01 or less. (From Boyd and Liu[21] with the permission of the Canadian Medical Association Journal.)

to the minor changes would have been produced by continued dosing with 60 ml/kg.

120 to 200 ml/kg/day

A daily dose of 120 to 200 ml/kg would correspond, on a body weight basis, to amounts between about 10 and 15 l./day by a man weighing 80 kg. Doses of this order produced a statistically significant loss of wet weight in kidneys, skeletal muscle, pyloric stomach, and residual carcass and a significant gain (due to hypertrophy of the mucosa and smooth muscle) in wet weight of cardiac stomach and small bowel. The same daily doses resulted in dehydration of several body organs, including pyloric stomach, small bowel, colon, heart, kidneys, skeletal muscle, salivary glands, and testes. Dehydration was presumably due to the fact that these doses produced a marked diuresis along with loss of body weight and a decrease in food and water intake, as shown in Table 31 of Chapter 6. These effects plus the histological changes noted above indicate a moderate degree of toxicity from distilled water in a dose of 120 to 200 ml/kg/day. The animals looked healthy, however, and probably had no change in serum osmotic pressure since Habener et al.[1] reported no change in healthy men taking daily amounts of water up to 100 ml/kg/day.

280 to 340 ml/kg/day

Distilled water in daily doses of from 280 to 340 ml/kg produced loss of wet weight in colon, heart, kidneys, liver, skeletal muscle, skin, spleen, thymus gland, residual carcass, and autopsy body weight. The cardiac stomach and small bowel had hypertrophied to accommodate these large volumes of distilled water. Part of the increase in wet weight of cardiac stomach was due to an increase in its water content, as indicated in Table 89. Otherwise, most body organs were dehydrated by daily doses of 280 to 340 ml/kg for the same reason that dehydration was produced by daily doses of 120 to 200 ml/kg. Organs dehydrated included brain, small bowel, colon, heart, kidneys, muscle, skin, spleen, salivary glands, and thymus gland with lesser and statistically insignificant losses of water in other body organs. These doses correspond, on a body weight basis, to some 22 to 25 l. of distilled water per day by a man weighing 80 kg. The effects of such daily doses may be labeled as definitely toxic but not lethal at the intervals used between administration (2.5 hr).

400 to 480 ml/kg/day

The relatively long interval of 2.5 hr between daily water administration appears to have been responsible for the lack of deaths from daily doses of from 400 to 480 ml/kg. From studies on acute toxicity, when distilled water was given as 70 ml/kg at intervals of 20 min, one would have expected deaths from 400 to 480 ml/kg. The LD_{50} from distilled water given as 70 ml/kg every 20 min was 469 ± 51 ml/kg. It would appear from these results that the $LD_{50\ (100\ days)}$ of distilled water given as 70 ml/kg every 20 min to albino rats on a full stomach is rather close to the acute LD_{50} given on an empty stomach. This would yield a 100-day LD_{50} index which is near the bottom of those listed in Table 18 in Chapter 3. Daily doses of 400 to 480 ml/kg divided and given at intervals of 2.5 hr produced a reactive hypertrophy of the pyloric stomach as well as of the cardiac stomach and small bowel, as may be noted from data listed in Table 88. The gastrointestinal accommodation hypertrophy was associated with an increase in the water content of most parts of the gastrointestinal tract (Table 89). There was a stress reaction in the adrenal glands, spleen, and thymus gland. Most organs had lost considerably more wet weight than was lost following the next lower daily doses of distilled water, but were less dehydrated. Daily doses of 400 to 480 ml/kg correspond on a body weight basis to some 32 to 38 l. water per 80 kg man. Depending upon the rate of administration, such doses may produce death from water intoxication.

Conclusions Regarding Distilled Water
Acute Toxicity

Distilled water, given by stomach tube to young adult albino rats at the rate of 70 ml/kg every 20 min, had an oral LD_{50} ± S.E. of 469 ± 51 ml/kg. The corresponding value in urethanized rabbits was 342 ± 14 ml/kg. Most of the animals died within 2½ hr of the start of dosing following a period of weakness, ataxia, polyuria, dacryorrhea, diarrhea, pallor, cyanosis, and muscular tremors. The huge volume of distilled water had overcome body mechanisms for control of salt and water, producing widespread hydration of body organs and distortion and clotting of the red blood cells.

Diuresis freed the body of excess water but also eliminated considerable amounts of body salt resulting in a delayed loss of organ weights and some degenerated changes in tissues of the kidney, liver, and other organs. There were a few (5%) delayed deaths from such changes.

In survivors, there occurred a temporary loss of body weight with a decrease in food and water intake, a diuresis, proteinuria, glycosuria, and alkalinuria. By two weeks, the weight and water content of body organs had returned to normal values but at one month there occurred a rebound hydration and loss of organ weight.

Acute Toxicity of Nonlethal Doses

A dose of 20 ml/kg produced practically no signs of toxicity. Raising the single dose to 60 ml/kg produced diarrhea and signs of depression of the central nervous system. Raising the dose to 75 to 100 ml/kg added alkalinuria to the observed toxic signs. A dose of 185 ml/kg produced a similar toxic reaction. At 250 ml/kg, given as 100 ml followed by a further 100 ml/kg in 1 hr and 50 ml/kg in 2 hr, distilled water produced some loss of body weight and other signs of toxicity lasting up to 24 hr.

Chronic Toxicity of Nonlethal Doses

A daily dose of 20 ml/kg given by stomach tube once daily for 100 days produced minor evidence of toxicity. Similar results followed a daily dose of 60 ml/kg. Daily doses of 120 and 200 ml/kg produced inhibition of growth and dehydration of many body organs. Daily doses of 280 to 340 ml/kg, divided into four equal parts each given at intervals of 2.5 hr, produced definite signs of toxicity which were more marked when the daily dose was raised to 400 to 480 ml/kg. Deaths appeared when the interval between daily administration was shortened to 20 min. At intervals less than 20 min the lethal effect was less marked because excess orally administered water was eliminated through the anus.

REFERENCES

1. Habener, J. F., Dashe, A. M., and Solomon, D. H., Response of normal subjects to prolonged high fluid intake, *J. Appl. Physiol.,* 19, 134, 1964.
2. Le Magnen, J., Nouvelles données sur le processus de régulation des consommations hydrique et saline chez le rat blanc, *C. R. Soc. Biol.,* 147, 21, 1953.
3. Boyd, E. M. and Godi, I., Acute oral toxicity of distilled water in albino rats, *Ind. Med. Surg.,* 36, 609, 1967.
4. Chalmers, T. M., Lewis, A. A. G., and Pawan, G. L. S., The effect of posterior pituitary extracts on the renal excretion of sodium and chloride in man, *J. Physiol.,* 112, 238, 1951.
5. Abdul-Karim, R. and Assali, N. S., Renal function in human pregnancy, *J. Lab. Clin. Med.,* 57, 522, 1961.
6. Saunders, W. G. and Munsick, R. A., Antidiuretic potency of oxytocin in women post partum, *Am. J. Obstet. Gynecol.,* 95, 5, 1966.
7. Thomson, W. B., The effect of oxytocin and vasopressin and of phenylalanyl[3]-oxytocin on the urinary excretion of water and electrolytes in man, *J. Physiol.,* 150, 284, 1960.
8. Liggins, G. C., The treatment of missed abortion by high dosage syntocinon intravenous infusion, *J. Obstet. Gynaecol. Br. Commonw.,* 69, 277, 1962.
9. Whalley, P. J. and Pritchard, J. A., Oxytocin and water intoxication, *J.A.M.A.,* 186, 601, 1963.
10. Bilek, W. and Dorr, P., Water intoxication and grand mal seizure due to oxytocin, *Can. Med. Assoc. J.,* 103, 379, 1970.
11. Rowntree, L. G., Water intoxication, *Arch. Intern. Med.,* 32, 157, 1923.
12. Rowntree, L. G., The effects on mammals of the administration of excessive quantities of water, *J. Pharmacol. Exp. Ther.,* 29, 135, 1926.
13. Underhill, F. P. and Sallick, M. A., On the mechanism of water intoxication, *J. Biol. Chem.,* 63, 61, 1925.
14. Gaunt, R., Remington, J. W., and Schweizer, M., Some effects of intraperitoneal glucose injections and excess water in normal, adrenalectomized and hypophysectomized rats, *Am. J. Physiol.,* 120, 532, 1937.

15. Gaunt, R., Nelson, W. O., and Loomis, E., Cortical hormone-like action of progesterone and non-effect of sex hormones on "water intoxication," *Proc. Soc. Exp. Biol. Med.*, 39, 319, 1939.
16. Wasterlain, C. G. and Torack, R. M., Cerebral edema in water intoxication, *Arch. Neurol.*, 19, 79, 1968.
17. Ruch, T. C. and Patton, H. D., Eds., *Physiology and Biophysics*, 19th ed., W. B. Saunders, Philadelphia, 1965.
18. Boyd, E. M. and Knight, L. M., Postmortem shifts in the weight and water levels of body organs, *Toxicol. Appl. Pharmacol.*, 5, 119, 1963.
19. Boyd, E. M. and Boyd, C. E., Expectorant activity of water in acute asthma attacks, *Am. J. Dis. Child.*, 116, 397, 1968.
20. Boyd, E. M., Food and drug toxicity. A summary of recent studies, *J. Clin. Pharmacol.*, 8, 281, 1963.
21. Boyd, E. M. and Liu, S. J., Toxicity of starch administered by mouth, *Can. Med. Assoc. J.*, 98, 492, 1968.
22. Boyd, E. M. and Shanas, M. N., The acute oral toxicity of potassium chloride, *Arch. Int. Pharmacodyn. Ther.*, 133, 275, 1961.
23. Boyd, E. M., Godi, I., and Abel, M., Acute oral toxicity of sucrose, *Toxicol. Appl. Pharmacol.*, 7, 609, 1965.
24. Constantopoulos, G. and Boyd, E. M., Factors affecting sucrose toxicity, *Int. J. Clin. Pharmacol. Ther. Toxicol.*, 1, 539, 1968.
25. Boyd, E. M. and Shanas, M. N., The acute oral toxicity of reduced iron, *Can. Med. Assoc. J.*, 89, 171, 1963.
26. Boyd, E. M. and Abel, M., The acute toxicity of barium sulfate administered intragastrically, *Can. Med. Assoc. J.*, 94, 849, 1966.
27. Boyd, E. M., Peters, J. M., and Krijnen, C. J., The acute oral toxicity of reconstituted spray-dried egg white, *Ind. Med. Surg.*, 35, 782, 1966.
28. Boyd, E. M., Abel, M., and Knight, L. M., The chronic oral toxicity of sodium chloride at the range of the LD_{50} (0.1 L), *Can. J. Physiol. Pharmacol.*, 44, 157, 1966.
29. Boyd, E. M. and Hottenroth, S. M. H., The toxicity of phenacetin at the range of the oral $LD_{50(100 \text{ days})}$ in albino rats, *Toxicol. Appl. Pharmacol.*, 12, 80, 1968.

Chapter 15

SODIUM CHLORIDE

Acute Toxicity of Sodium Chloride

Sodium chloride occurs in nature as the mineral halite from which rock salt is made. It is also produced by the evaporation of seawater and is called sea salt. Other names are common salt and table salt. Its general properties have been comprehensively reviewed by many authors such as Kaufmann.[1] Meneely[2] notes that sodium chloride is present in almost all living material and has been a natural constituent of food from time immemorial. He records that chlorine was discovered in 1774 and that sodium and chloride were recognized as elements by Davy in the early 19th century. Sodium is one of the most abundant elements in the earth's crust and may gain access to the body in one or more of five ways: (a) in drinking water, (b) in natural food, (c) in additions to food during processing, (d) in additions to food during cooking, and (e) in additions to food at the table. Meneely discusses each of these sources of sodium and notes that the daily human requirement of sodium chloride has been estimated at from 15 g to less than 1 g. The toxic effects of sodium chloride in congestive heart failure and hypertension were recognized as early as 1904 by Ambard and Beaujard.[3]

Sodium chloride is a white, crystalline, granular or powdery substance. Contamination with small amounts of calcium and magnesium chlorides enables it to absorb water and to cake. It is soluble in water to about 40% and is the natural chemical source of most compounds containing sodium or chlorine. Sodium chloride has a wide variety of uses in the food, chemical, pottery, and metallurgical industries. It is used in medicine in salt depletion, orally as an emetic agent, rectally as an enema in constipation, and topically in infections of the skin and mucous membranes.

Acute toxicity in man has been caused mainly by the mistaken substitution of salt for sugar in feeding formulas for babies. Kvalvik[4] reported fever, intense thirst, and cerebral and pulmonary edema in a human infant given approximately 4 g

of sodium chloride per kg body weight per day for five days in dietary form. Markley et al.[5] found that a dose of about 0.8 g/kg was tolerated by man when given by intragastric drip over a period of 21 hr. Götze[6] reported epileptiform convulsions, somnolence, and stupor in an adult man following intravenous infusion by mistake of a 20% solution of sodium chloride at a dose of about 1 g of NaCl per kg body weight.

Spector[7] reviewed data on published figures for lethal doses of sodium chloride given parenterally. He found that the lethal range of parenteral doses is from 2.5 to 5.0 g/kg in mice, rats, and guinea pigs. Ussing et al.[8] reviewed evidence[9] indicating that a dose of about 3 g/kg is lethal to mice when given intravenously as physiological saline solution, the death rate increasing with increase in the rate of infusion. Sollman[10] reported that toxic oral doses of the order of 1 to 15 g/kg produced a severe and fatal gastroenteritis accompanied by restlessness, thirst, polyuria, fever, convulsions, coma, and death within 8 hr. Boyd and Shanas[11] and Shanas and Boyd[12] reported the acute oral LD_{50} ± S.E. of sodium chloride to be 3.89 ± 0.30 g/kg in young adult male albino rats and 3.62 ± 0.30 g/kg in young adult females. The studies of Boyd and Shanas[11] will be described in exemplification of the acute oral toxicity of sodium chloride. Sodium chloride was given in doses of from 0.8 to 16.0 g/kg, each dose dissolved in distilled water to a final volume of 20 ml/kg, orally by stomach tube to overnight-fasted young adult albino rats of a Wistar strain. Clinical signs were recorded until death and for two weeks in survivors. Autopsies were performed at death and at two weeks in survivors. Statistical methods were those of Croxton[13] and Waugh.[14]

Clinical Signs of Acute Oral Toxicity

At doses of from 3.0 to 5.0 g/kg, the regression of dose (Y axis) on percent mortality (X axis) was linear.[11] The estimating equations ± their standard errors were calculated to be Y = (3.05 + 0.0168 X) ± 0.30 for males and Y = (2.69 + 0.0185 X) ± 0.30 for females. Estimated values for the acute oral

LD$_{50}$ ± S.E. were, therefore, 3.89 ± 0.30 g/kg for males and 3.62 ± 0.30 g/kg for females. The difference between these two estimates of the LD$_{50}$ is not statistically significant (P > 0.05) and the value for animals of both sexes was 3.75 ± 0.43 g/kg. The median lethal dose was approximately equivalent to the total amount of sodium chloride reported normally present in the body of albino rats.[8]

All animals given doses of 10.0 and 16.0 g/kg died within 0.5 to 4.25 hr and no rats given 0.8 g/kg died. The mean intervals to death at other doses are illustrated in Figure 73. The regression of dose on mean interval to death was best fitted by an equation involving the reciprocal of Y (dose) on X (interval), as indicated in Figure 73. The correlation coefficient of the regression for males was insignificantly different from that for females, i.e., P = 0.07. In rats receiving 3 to 5 g/kg, the time to death was 9.8 ± 4.1 hr for males and 6.9 ± 3.7 hr for females. Values are expressed as mean ± S.E. The difference between the two means is not statistically significant (P > 0.05). The interval for

males plus females was 8.6 ± 5.3 hr. One animal was given 5 g/kg, died at five days, and was excluded in calculating the mean interval to death.

The clinical signs of toxicity to sodium chloride in doses at the range of the acute oral LD$_{50}$ in male rats were the same as those in females. There was also no significant difference in the incidence of toxic signs between the two sexes over a period of 7 hr following administration of the salt. During this period, 56% of the animals had convulsive movements. As shown in Figure 74, the percentage incidence increased logarithmically from about 10% following a dose of 3.0 g/kg to 80% after 4.0 g/kg. The average incidence of animals that ran to the drinking water immediately after being given sodium chloride was 25%. This action was considered to be the result of thirst and its incidence is plotted against dose of sodium chloride in Figure 74 as Y$_t$. The regression on dose was logarithmically negative, probably because the

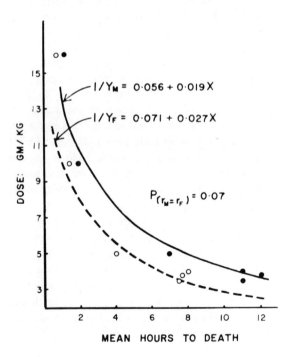

FIGURE 73. The regression of dose of sodium chloride, given by stomach tube to young adult albino rats, on mean hours to death in males (Ym, solid circles and solid line) and females (Yf, open circles and interrupted line). (From Boyd and Shanas[11] with the permission of the *Archives Internationales de Pharmacodynamie et de Therapie.*)

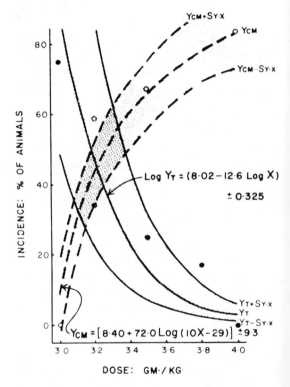

FIGURE 74. The regression, on dose of sodium chloride given orally to young adult albino rats, of the percentage incidence of convulsive movements (Ym, open circles and interrupted lines) and immediate drinking of water or thirst (Yt, solid circles and solid lines) during the first seven hours following salt administration. (From Boyd and Shanas[11] with the permission of the *Archives Internationales de Pharmacodynamie et de Therapie.*)

convulsive movements produced by higher doses prevented the animals from running to the source of drinking water. The mean incidence of mucous diarrhea was 35% and of flexor rigidity 15%, both of which were dose dependent. The immediate cause of death was respiratory failure in deep prostration.

Pathological Signs at Autopsy

When it is recalled that doses in the range of the acute oral LD_{50} were given dissolved in distilled water as 20 ml of solution containing 15 to 20% sodium chloride per kg body weight, it is not surprising that these highly concentrated solutions produced a violent local inflammatory reaction in the gastrointestinal tract. The common histopathological findings at death were capillary and venous congestion of the lamina propria and submocosa of the pyloric stomach, small bowel, cecum, and colon. Absorption of these hypertonic solutions of sodium chloride produced a widespread tissue inflammatory reaction, as indicated by congestion of the cerebrum, cerebellum, meninges, and of most other organs except skeletal muscle and skin.

Shifts in the wet weight and water content of body organs at death are summarized in Table 90 as mean percentage changes from corresponding values in controls given no sodium chloride. The dehydrating action of oral administration of hypertonic aqueous solutions of sodium chloride was manifested in all tissues, usually to a statistically significant degree. There was a mean loss of water in each of small bowel, cecum, lungs, and skin but the individual mean changes were not quite statistically significant. Dehydration was marked in other body organs, especially in the adrenal glands, brain, pyloric stomach, liver, ovaries, and spleen. Ussing et al.[8] note that there is an increase in blood volume in acute sodium chloride poisoning. Increase in blood volume may have been produced by the entry into the blood of tissue water, presumably in an attempt to maintain the isotonicity of blood. Augmentation of blood volume may have accounted for some of the vascular congestion of body organs noted in the previous paragraph.

Loss of wet weight of body organs was in general not as marked as loss of water. Since 70 to 80% of the wet weight of most organs is due to water, one would have anticipated losses of wet weight equal to 70 to 80% of the losses of water if there was no change in the dry weight of body organs. Losses of wet weight were less than anticipated on this basis in adrenal glands, brain, cardiac stomach, pyloric stomach, heart, lungs, skeletal muscle, ovaries, skin, spleen, thymus gland, and residual carcass. Loss of wet weight was equivalent to loss of water in colon, kidneys, and testicles and more than equivalent in the liver, small bowel, and cecum. While some of these differences may have been due to experimental variation, the large incidence of organs with less loss of wet weight than of water content suggests acquisition of dry weight which probably came from thick, stagnant blood.

Boyd and Krijnen[15] have shown that the weight of certain organs of the body is more constant than body weight. These organs include brain, kidney, and liver. If so, the same dose of sodium chloride calculated as g/kg body weight would represent a larger amount per 100 g weight of these organs in large rats than in small rats. To test this possibility, the water content of these organs was plotted against g of sodium chloride per rat in a group of animals given the same dose per kg body weight, namely 10 g/kg body weight. The dose of 10 g/kg was selected because all of the animals given this dose died at the same interval of 2 to 4 hr after administration of sodium chloride. The results in brain are plotted in Figure 75 as an example. It may be seen that the water content of brain decreased in proportion to the increase in administered grams of sodium chloride and increase in body weight in spite of the fact that all animals received the same dose per kg body weight, i.e., 10 g/kg. Water levels of kidney and of liver were also negatively correlated with grams sodium chloride per rat in this group of animals. The results exemplify certain fallacies inherent in expressing dosage as g/kg body weight especially where there is a large variation in body weight in an experimental group. Boyd and Krijnen[15] found that effects of chemical agents were more constant when expressed as g/kg weight of certain body organs than as g/kg body weight. Since weight of body organs is usually not known when a drug is given, it is probable that the standard method of calculating dose as g/kg body weight is the most suitable general method available. As discussed in Chapter 3, there may be advantages in calculating doses as millimoles per kg body weight.

TABLE 90

Shifts in the Wet Weight and Water Levels of Body Organs of Albino Rats Given Doses of Sodium Chloride in the Range of the Oral Median Lethal Dose[a]

	Nonsurvivors		Survivors at 2 weeks	
Organ	Weight	Water	Weight	Water
Adrenal glands	− 3.2	−20.4*	+ 1.3	− 1.9
Brain	− 5.8*	−31.1*	+ 4.9	− 0.8
Gastrointestinal tract				
Cardiac stomach	+ 6.8	−14.4*	+ 5.0	− 8.8*
Pyloric stomach	− 6.5	−22.3*	+ 5.7	− 3.7
Small bowel	−14.8	− 5.0	− 9.9	−16.9*
Cecum	−13.9	− 2.9	+ 8.9	− 4.7
Colon	−16.6*	−17.5*	+ 3.9	− 3.7
Heart	− 3.6	−17.2*	− 0.9	+ 1.1
Kidneys	−12.9*	−14.6*	+ 3.0	+ 1.6
Liver	−38.4*	−23.2*	+11.1*	− 1.1
Lungs	− 1.5	− 7.4	+14.4	+ 1.1
Muscle (ventral abdominal wall)	− 5.7	−14.8*	+ 3.5	+ 6.4
Ovaries	−11.3	−24.3*	−11.3	+10.1
Skin	+ 8.7	−10.7	+ 3.7	+ 3.5
Spleen	− 7.9	−22.8*	− 3.1	+ 0.5
Testicles	−13.9*	−14.5*	− 5.2	− 0.5
Thymus gland	− 9.0	−15.3*	−12.4	− 1.5
Residual carcass	− 0.4	−15.0*	+ 4.0	− 1.3

[a]Wet weight was measured in grams and water levels in g per 100 g dry weight of tissue. Shifts are expressed as a mean percentage change from corresponding values in controls given no sodium chloride, specifically as $[(\bar{X}_d - \bar{X}_c)/\bar{X}_c] \times 100$, where $\bar{X}_d$ refers to the mean in the drug-treated and $\bar{X}_c$ in the control animals. Shifts significantly different from control values at $P \leqslant 0.05$ are indicated by an asterisk.

(From Boyd and Shanas[11] with the permission of the *Archives Internationales de Pharmacodynamie et de Therapie*.)

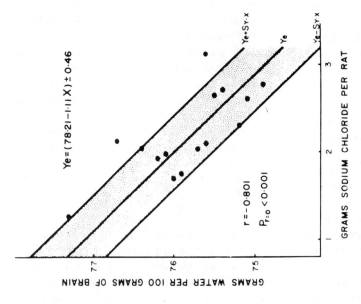

$Ye = (78\cdot21 - 1\cdot11\ X) \pm 0\cdot46$

$r = -0\cdot801$

$P_{r=0} < 0\cdot001$

GRAMS WATER PER 100 GRAMS OF BRAIN

GRAMS SODIUM CHLORIDE PER RAT

FIGURE 75. The regression of brain water levels, expressed as grams per 100 g wet weight, on grams of sodium chloride given orally to albino rats at a dose of 10 g/kg body weight. Note that body weights of individual rats may be obtained by multiplying the figures on the abscissa by 100. (From Boyd and Shanas[11] with the permission of the *Archives Internationales de Pharmacodynamie et de Therapie*.)

Signs of Recovery in Survivors of Acute Oral Toxicity

Measurements of clinical signs in albino rats that survived oral administration of sodium chloride in doses at the range of the acute LD_{50} are shown in Tables 91 and 92. The animals were starved for 16 hr (overnight) to empty the stomach prior to intragastric administration of sodium chloride. The marked gain in body weight during the first 24 hr, seen in controls and in rats given the lower doses of salt, was due to recovery of weight lost during the fasting period. Gain in body weight (Table 91) during the first 24 hr was less the higher the dose of sodium chloride. During the second and third days there were no consistent or significant differences between body weight of salt-treated animals and that of controls given no sodium chloride. Food intake varied inversely with the dose of sodium chloride the animal had received; this relationship held during the first three days in survivors. On the other hand, there were no significant differences among survivors of various doses of sodium chloride in their water intake which was uniformly high throughout these days. Selye[16] reported that large doses of sodium chloride stimulate the zona glomerulosa of the adrenal cortex. Body temperature tended to be somewhat elevated in survivors during the first 24 hr; this elevation persisted into the second and third days, especially in survivors of the higher doses.

Urinary volume was elevated during the first 24 hr, more or less in direct proportion to dose of sodium chloride as shown in Table 92. The diuresis gradually disappeared during the second and third days. There were no significant changes in the urinary output of glucose, and output of protein tended to decrease in survivors of oral administration of sodium chloride in doses at the range of the acute LD_{50}. During the first 24 hr there was an acidosis in rats surviving salt administration. The pH of urine became normal during the second and third days.

The wet weight and water content of body organs were measured in survivors of administration of sodium chloride at two weeks after giving the salt. The results are summarized in Table 90. It may be seen that these two parameters had values which were essentially in the range of normal controls at this period following sodium chloride administration.

In brief, therefore, oral administration of sodium chloride in doses at the range of the LD_{50} produced death in young adult albino rats due to respiratory failure associated with an acute encephalopathy and accompanied by a fulminating gastroenteritis, dehydration, and congestion of most body organs. Recovery of survivors was evident during the first 24 hr and was complete by two weeks.

Chronic Toxicity of Sodium Chloride

The rapid recovery of albino rats that survived oral administration of toxic doses of sodium chloride suggested that the animals could survive relatively high fractions or percentages of the acute oral LD_{50} given daily by gavage. This was found to be so by Boyd et al.[17] who reported the oral $LD_{50\ (100\ days)}$ of sodium chloride was 72% of the acute oral LD_{50}. This again is not surprising in view of wide variations in the consumption of sodium chloride by man and other animal species. The animal body possesses mechanisms for dealing with deficiencies and excesses of salt intake so as to maintain the normal osmotic pressure of intracellular and extracellular fluid. The common controlling mechanisms are the posterior hypophysial antidiuretic hormone; aldosterone from the adrenal cortex; thirst, which is stimulated by osmoreceptors in the hypothalamus; and body pH.[18]

Blood volume is a variable figure[18] and alterations may be divided into six main categories. Welt[19] has termed these categories as (a) hypotonic expansion or accumulation of excess water without salt, (b) isotonic expansion or accumulation of water and salt as an isotonic solution, (c) hypertonic expansion or retention of more salt than water, (d) hypotonic contraction or loss of body salt without loss of water, (e) isotonic contraction, and (f) hypertonic contraction. These changes in extracellular fluid are followed by changes in intracellular fluid leading to various pathological conditions. An example of hypotonic expansion is water intoxication with hypotonicity of intracellular fluid, discussed in Chapter 14. Isotonic expansion may lead to hypoproteinemia and nephrotic edema. Excessive ingestion of seawater produces hypertonic expansion and death from encephalopathy. Hypotonic contraction occurs in adrenal cortical insufficiency due to loss of sodium chloride. Isotonic contraction is encountered in severe diarrhea in which appreciable volumes of digestive fluids are lost — the total

TABLE 91

Shifts in the Body Weight, Food Intake, Water Intake, and Colonic Temperature of Albino Rats Surviving Oral Doses of Sodium Chloride in the Range of the LD_{50} [a]

Dose: g/kg	N	Days after sodium chloride		
		1	2	3

Body weight gain per 24 hr: grams (+ or −)

Dose: g/kg	N	1	2	3
0.0	44	+17.6 ± 8.5	+3.7 ± 5.6	+2.0 ± 4.8
0.8	12	+16.1 ± 4.2	−0.3 ± 5.5	+8.3 ± 5.0
3.0	12	+15.0 ± 7.7	+1.4 ± 5.4	+2.4 ± 3.1
3.2	9	+ 7.0 ± 9.0	+8.6 ± 7.5	+1.2 ± 4.0
3.5	7	+11.7 ± 9.8	−1.4 ± 7.9	+0.7 ± 3.5
3.8	5	+ 4.6 ± 8.8	+7.1 ± 6.3	+4.2 ± 3.3
4.0	2	+ 4.7 ± 9.1	+3.7 ± 3.3	−0.3 ± 5.5

Food intake: g/kg/24 hr

Dose: g/kg	N	1	2	3
0.0	44	110 ± 17	101 ± 17	102 ± 13
0.8	12	122 ± 6	101 ± 15	114 ± 14
3.0	12	84 ± 19	106 ± 11	104 ± 14
3.2	9	75 ± 18	90 ± 8	83 ± 22
3.5	7	53 ± 29	98 ± 36	71 ± 23
3.8	5	63 ± 12	91 ± 13	97 ± 10
4.0	2	49 ± 31	81 ± 14	88 ± 6

Water intake: ml/kg/24 hr

Dose: g/kg	N	1	2	3
0.0	44	216 ± 39	165 ± 45	167 ± 29
0.8	12	228 ± 20	142 ± 29	175 ± 48
3.0	12	216 ± 89	177 ± 43	173 ± 35
3.2	9	229 ± 59	193 ± 52	160 ± 45
3.5	7	219 ± 88	150 ± 68	130 ± 67
3.8	5	224 ± 40	163 ± 50	180 ± 8
4.0	2	253 ± 64	196 ± 53	129 ± 28

Colonic temperature: °F

Dose: g/kg	N	1	2	3
0.0	44	99.3 ± 0.5	99.4 ± 0.9	99.2 ± 0.8
0.8	12	99.0 ± 0.8	99.3 ± 0.6	98.8 ± 0.5
3.0	12	100.2 ± 0.7	99.6 ± 0.6	99.8 ± 0.6
3.2	9	99.5 ± 0.9	99.4 ± 0.9	98.5 ± 1.4
3.5	7	99.7 ± 0.7	100.5 ± 0.5	99.6 ± 0.9
3.8	5	100.5 ± 0.4	100.0 ± 0.7	99.4 ± 0.4
4.0	2	101.5 ± 1.1	100.5 ± 1.1	100.0 ± 1.0

[a]The results are expressed as mean ± standard deviation

TABLE 92

Urinary Volume and Composition in Albino Rats Surviving Oral Doses of Sodium Chloride in the Range of the LD_{50} [a]

Dose g/kg	N	Days after sodium chloride		
		1	2	3

Volume: ml/kg/24 hr

Dose g/kg	N	1	2	3
0.0	44	40 ± 19	36 ± 22	38 ± 24
0.8	12	46 ± 9	41 ± 17	37 ± 16
3.0	12	141 ± 57	48 ± 32	10 ± 9
3.2	9	108 ± 25	54 ± 22	56 ± 32
3.5	7	83 ± 34	29 ± 27	35 ± 30
3.8	5	150 ± 12	35 ± 8	58 ± 17
4.0	2	173 ± 38	53 ± 10	34 ± 12

Glucose: g/100 ml

Dose g/kg	N	1	2	3
0.0	44	0.02 ± 0.07	0.08 ± 0.11	0.06 ± 0.10
0.8	12	0.12 ± 0.12	0.17 ± 0.12	0.19 ± 0.17
3.0	12	0.00 ± 0.00	0.00 ± 0.00	0.00 ± 0.00
3.2	9	0.00 ± 0.00	0.02 ± 0.04	0.00 ± 0.00
3.5	7	0.05 ± 0.05	0.10 ± 0.11	0.04 ± 0.06
3.8	5	0.00 ± 0.00	0.07 ± 0.07	0.00 ± 0.00
4.0	2	0.00 ± 0.00	0.00 ± 0.00	0.10 ± 0.10

Protein: mg/100 ml

Dose g/kg	N	1	2	3
0.0	44	80 ± 51	58 ± 36	65 ± 35
0.8	12	19 ± 11	54 ± 17	65 ± 26
3.0	12	14 ± 11	51 ± 36	77 ± 24
3.2	9	13 ± 13	42 ± 17	90 ± 61
3.5	7	14 ± 12	53 ± 36	39 ± 22
3.8	5	5 ± 2	41 ± 24	75 ± 64
4.0	2	3 ± 2	53 ± 25	22 ± 11

pH: 24-hr sample

Dose g/kg	N	1	2	3
0.0	44	8.1 ± 0.8	7.7 ± 0.9	7.2 ± 0.9
0.8	12	7.4 ± 0.9	7.6 ± 0.8	7.0 ± 0.9
3.0	12	7.7 ± 0.4	7.9 ± 0.6	7.3 ± 0.5
3.2	9	8.1 ± 0.5	8.2 ± 0.5	7.9 ± 0.2
3.5	7	7.6 ± 0.6	7.6 ± 0.4	7.3 ± 0.7
3.8	5	6.9 ± 0.5	8.6 ± 0.4	8.0 ± 0.3
4.0	2	6.8 ± 0.5	7.5 ± 0.4	7.2 ± 0.5

[a]The results are expressed as mean ± standard deviation

daily volume of the digestive fluids is about two thirds of the volume of extracellular fluid. Hypertonic contraction occurs in any situation in which large volumes of water are lost without a concomitant loss of salt as in persons lost in a hot desert with no drinking water.

Most studies on chronic sodium chloride intoxication have been concerned with high dietary levels of the salt. Meneely[20] reported that albino rats fed diets containing 0.15 to 2.0% sodium chloride (equivalent to 0.75 to 10 g per day by an adult man) had minor and insignificant changes in growth rate and no obvious pathology. When dietary sodium chloride was increased to 2.8 to 5.6% (14 to 28 g per day by man), the life span of albino rats was shortened and mild hypertension developed. A dietary level of 7.0 to 9.8% (35 to 49 g per day by man) was markedly hypertensigenic and life-shortening. Okano et al.[21] reported that albino rats given drinking water containing 3% of sodium chloride ate little food and eventually died from the hypertonic saline.

Meneely, Tucker and Darby[22] found that as levels of dietary sodium chloride were increased above those of the control group, growth rate was progressively inhibited. Inhibition of growth was associated with augmentation of water intake and urinary volume.[22] In a later communication, Meneely et al.[23] reported a gradual increase in mean group blood pressure after one half to one year of the feeding of diets containing large amounts of sodium chloride. Hypertension was associated with increases in serum cholesterol and electrocardiographic evidence of impaired cardiac action. These changes were more marked in male than in female albino rats. Dahl[24] noted an increase in plasma cholesterol in dogs fed diets high in sodium chloride but the change was not related directly to hypertension, renal disease, loss of body weight, or decrease in food intake. He concluded that atherogenesis is not related directly to hypercholesterolemia.

Dahl and Schackow[25] inbred Sprague-Dawley rats and developed strains which were resistant (R) and others which were sensitive (S) to hypertension following ingestion of high levels of dietary sodium chloride. Other studies by Dahl and co-workers established that the R and S genetic strain differences applied to hypertension induced by renal artery compression,[26] administration of cortisone,[27] and vasoactive drugs.[28] These findings suggest that genetic differences influence susceptibility to hypertension in general, a suggestion confirmed by Jaffé et al.[29] who reported histopathological lesions of hypertension in genetically susceptible (S) strains of rats given diets both low and high in sodium chloride.

Jaffé et al.[29] regard growth of arterial branch pads as the primary lesion in these types of hypertension. Branch pads are musculoelastic thickenings of the arterial wall adjacent to formation of a branch of the vessel. These branch pads may proliferate in any artery. In the kidney, proliferation yields a decreased blood supply to the glomeruli, which become enlarged and hypovascular, to the tubules, which develop hyperplastic epithelium, and both effects lead to degenerative fatty change[30] and granulation of the juxtaglomerular cells.[31] Diethylstilbestrol-induced rupture of the aorta in turkeys, but not hyperlipemia, hypercholesterolemia, or hypercalcemia, is augmented by feeding the birds a diet high in sodium chloride.[32]

Several investigators have reported on the influence of diets high in sodium chloride on organ weights. Kaunitz[33] found that increased dietary salt ingestion produced increase in the weight of kidneys but not of adrenal glands in rats. Morrison and Sarett[34] reported that a relative increase in the weight of kidneys, adrenal glands, and heart, induced by feeding rats diets high in sodium chloride, was augmented by feeding a diet deficient in B vitamins. They noted that organ water levels were not affected by feeding the high salt diet. Meneely[2] explained that increase in weight of the adrenal gland is variable and significant only at very high levels of intake of sodium chloride in rats.

The relationship of intake of sodium chloride to hypertension in man is clear when comparisons are made between different populations but not within the same population.[35-37] This is probably due to the fact that levels of salt intake are more or less uniform in any one population, but may vary significantly between populations and to genetic differences between human populations.[2] There may also be differences in the dietary intake of potassium which tend to offset many of the toxic effects of excess ingestion of sodium.[2]

The Oral LD$_{50}$ (100 days) of Sodium Chloride

From studies reviewed above,[2] it is apparent that albino rats can tolerate up to 5 to 10 g of sodium chloride per kg body weight per day, given in dietary form, for six months to one year before deaths begin to appear. From the work of Boyd et al.[17] it is equally apparent that much smaller daily amounts of sodium chloride are toxic and lethal to albino rats when given by a single daily intragastric administration. The lesser toxicity of sodium chloride taken in the diet as opposed to its toxicity by gavage is seen also for other common dietary articles such as sugar,[38] casein,[39] starch,[40] and caffeine.[41] This relationship is due to the fact that such substances can be rapidly detoxified, which permits the ingestion without death of relatively toxic doses spread over the day in the diet. To compare chronic toxicity from dietary administration with acute toxicity from intragastric cannula administration poses the anomaly that doses of these foods larger than the acute oral LD_{50} can be taken daily in the diet. Boyd[42] has proposed, therefore, that the method of administration employed in studying chronic toxicity should be similar to that used in measuring acute toxicity. In the case of oral administration, this involves comparing daily oral administration by gavage in chronic studies with single intragastric cannula administration in acute studies. The number of days of chronic daily gavage is indicated in the subscript, i.e., the oral $LD_{50\ (100\ days)}$ is the dose given once daily by gavage which kills 50% of animals over a period of 100 days of administration. In no study to date has the $LD_{50\ (100\ days)}$ so determined been greater than the acute oral LD_{50}.[42] This may also be seen from data assembled in Table 18 of Chapter 3.

The oral $LD_{50\ (100\ days)}$ of sodium chloride was determined in young male albino rats by Boyd et al.[17] Since the salt was given by gavage once daily to unstarved animals, the acute oral LD_{50} was first determined in such animals, giving the sodium chloride, each dose dissolved in distilled water to a final volume of 20 ml/kg, in the morning following overnight eating of a standard laboratory (Purina) chow. The acute oral $LD_{50} \pm$ S.E. was found to be 6.14 ± 0.31 g/kg in overnight-unstarved rats compared with 3.75 ± 0.43 g/kg in overnight-starved animals. The presence of food in the stomach had reduced the acute oral toxicity of sodium chloride to almost half that in overnight-starved animals with an empty stomach.

Sodium chloride was then given once daily by stomach tube for five days a week in decreasing fractions of the acute oral LD_{50} in unstarved

animals. Each dose was given to 14 to 40 rats for 100 days or until an appreciable number of rats had died, whichever occurred first. When the daily dose was given for one week or more, it was multiplied by 5/7 to obtain the daily dose, each dose given seven days a week. The relation of 5-vs. 7-day dosing has been discussed by Boyd.[42] Daily doses so given were 6.14, 5.32, 4.73, 4.22, 3.69, 3.25, 3.07, 2.95, 2.84, 2.70, and 2.57 g/kg/24 hr with controls given only 20 ml/kg/24 hr of distilled water. Clinical observations were recorded at weekly or shorter intervals, an autopsy was performed upon each rat that died, and survivors were necropsied at 100 days.

The daily dose that produced 50% mortality at the end of each week of administration was calculated and plotted against weeks of administration. The results are shown in Figure 76. From the regression equation the $LD_{50\ (100\ days)} \pm$ S.E. or $LD_{50\ (0.1L)}$ was calculated to be 2.69 ± 0.12 g/kg/24 hr. The term "$LD_{50\ (0.1L)}$" indicates that this is the dose which kills 50% of animals when given once daily by gavage for 100 days or approximately for one tenth of their expected normal life span (i.e., 0.1L). As indicated in Table 18 of Chapter 3, the oral $LD_{50\ (100\ days)}$ of 2.69

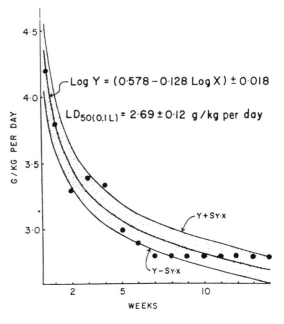

FIGURE 76. The regression, on weeks of administration, of the daily oral dose of sodium chloride which killed 50% of the animals. (From Boyd et al.[17] with the permission of the National Research Council of Canada, publishers of the *Canadian Journal of Physiology and Pharmacology.*)

± 0.12 g/kg/24 hr is 71.7 ± 3.2% of the acute oral LD_{50} of 3.75 g/kg determined in overnight-starved albino rats. The figure of 71.7 ± 3.2 is termed the "100-day LD_{50} index," which is an estimate of chronic toxicity in relation to acute toxicity.

Boyd et al.[17] found that the range of chronic lethal doses from the $LD_{1\ (100\ days)}$ to $LD_{99\ (100\ days)}$ was extremely narrow. They proposed a value of 2.06 g/kg/24 hr for the $LD_{1\ (100\ days)}$ or maximal $LD_{0\ (100\ days)}$ and 3.23 g/kg/24 hr for the $LD_{99\ (100\ days)}$ or minimal $LD_{100\ (100\ days)}$. They also calculated that the total cumulative amount of sodium chloride required to kill 50% of albino rats over a period of 100 days of daily oral administration by gavage was 269 g/kg. This is about 100 times the total amount of sodium chloride, expressed as g/kg, in the body of a rat[8] and indicates that the animals eliminated practically all of the daily administered dose of salt. Boyd et al.[17] reviewed evidence presented by Sapirstein, Brandt, and Drury,[43] Koletsky,[44,45] Kleiner and Dotti,[46] Richter and Mosier,[47] and others indicating that when sodium chloride is added to the diet or drinking water the amount required to kill 50% of animals in a period of 100 days would be of the order of 10 to 15 g/kg/24 hr. This indicates that sodium chloride can be eliminated from the body in even greater daily amounts when added to the diet or drinking water than when given once daily by gavage.

Clinical Signs of Chronic Oral Toxicity

Clinical signs in rats given sodium chloride daily were compared with corresponding measurements in control rats given only distilled water at a volume of 20 ml/kg. Representative measurements in controls are summarized in Table 93. When animals that died were assigned a value of -100% growth rate and included in estimates of daily doses which inhibited growth rate by 50% the value for *50% growth inhibition* was 2.61 ± 0.11 g/kg/day or practically the same as the value of the $LD_{50\ (100\ days)}$. The regression of daily dose producing 50% inhibition of growth on weeks of administration was practically identical to that shown in Figure 76 for 50% lethal doses, again when data on dead animals were included in the estimation. When inhibition of growth, calculated as a percentage of that in controls, was measured only on survivors, the daily doses producing 10, 25, and 50% inhibition of growth were somewhat higher than when dead animals were included. The regressions of daily doses producing these percentage inhibitions of growth, on weeks of administration, are shown in Figure 77. The estimating equation for 50% inhibitions was Y = (3.19 − 0.021X) ± 0.063, for 25% inhibition Y = (2.93 −

TABLE 93

Representative Clinical Measurements on Control Male Albino Rats Given Distilled Water in a Dose of 20 ml/kg/24 hr Five Days a Week for 100 Days

Measurement	Days[a]							
	0	7	14	28	42	56	70	100
Body weight (g)	158 ± 15[b]	189[c]	218[c]	277[c]	318[c]	349[c]	366[c]	413[c]
Food intake (g/kg/day)	104 ± 12	89	79	76	64	66	58	55
Water intake (ml/kg/day)	130 ± 19	109	98	89	76	72	79	68
Colonic temperature (°F)	98.7 ± 1.0	98.5	98.9	99.1	99.6	99.8	99.0	99.4
Urine volume (ml/kg/day)	5.1 ± 4.1	5.7	12.8	9.9	9.7	9.5	12.6	13.1
Urine protein (mg/100 ml)	74 ± 11	89	68	82	114	85	69	87
Urine glucose (g/100 ml)	0 ± 0	0	0	0	0.02	0.05	0	0.02
Urine pH (24-hr sample)	6.4 ± 0.4	7.2	7.1	6.6	6.8	6.8	7.1	7.1

[a]The average standard deviation at days 7 to 100 was the same percentage of the mean as at zero day.
[b]Each value for day zero is expressed as mean ± S.D.
[c]Each value for days 7 to 100 is expressed as $\bar{X}$.

(From Boyd et al.[17] with the permission of the National Research Council of Canada, publishers of the *Canadian Journal of Physiology and Pharmacology*.)

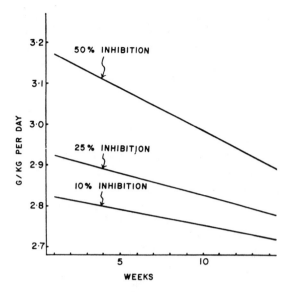

FIGURE 77. The regression, on weeks of administration, of the daily oral dose of sodium chloride which produced 10, 25, and 50% inhibition of growth in albino rats which survived death. (From Boyd et al.[17] with the permission of the National Research Council of Canada, publishers of the *Canadian Journal of Physiology and Pharmacology.*)

0.011X) ± 0.035, and for 10% inhibition Y = (2.83 – 0.0084X) ± 0.092. From these equations the daily dose that inhibited growth of survivors by 50% of that in controls given no salt may be calculated to be 2.89 ± 0.063 g/kg/24 hr at the end of 100 days of administration. The corresponding value for 10% inhibition of growth is 2.71 ± 0.092 g/kg/day.

Inhibition of growth was not due to inhibition of *food intake*. Food intake was decreased only premortally in animals that died. Food intake of survivors was otherwise insignificantly different from that of controls with no relation between food intake and daily dose of sodium chloride. For this reason, pair-fed animals were not introduced as controls for animals given daily oral sodium chloride administration.

Practically all albino rats had a marked decrease in *water intake* during the few days before death. On the other hand, survival appeared to be associated with ability to drink more water. When daily doses of sodium chloride required to augment water intake to four times the volume in controls were plotted against duration of administration of the salt, a logarithmic regression was obtained which was almost identical to that shown in Figure 76. Corresponding regressions of daily

doses which augmented water intake to three and two times the volume in controls were similar to that shown in Figure 76, but with ordinate values at progressively lower levels. All three regressions approached each other at 100 days when the daily dosage of all three calculations approached the oral LD_{50} (100 days).

These calculations on water intake in relation to daily dose of sodium chloride suggested that water intake per gram of salt administered was higher at the end than at the beginning of the 100 days of oral administration of sodium chloride. To investigate this possibility, an estimate of water intake per gram of salt intake was obtained by subtracting water intake of the controls from that of animals given sodium chloride. Water intake of the controls was primarily related to food intake. The differences indicated the water intake per gram of sodium chloride intake and such figures were calculated for all survivors at each daily dose for intervals up to 100 days. Water intake calculated per gram of sodium chloride bore no relationship to dose of sodium chloride administered, but did increase linearly with duration of daily administration of the salt, as illustrated in Figure 78. It will be noted that the intake of water

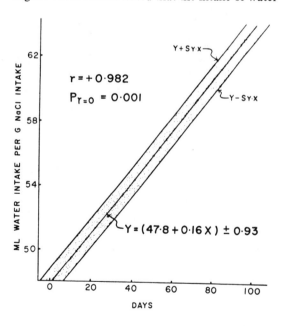

FIGURE 78. The regression, on days of daily oral administration of sodium chloride to male albino rats, of milliliters of water intake per gram of sodium chloride administered to surviving animals. (From Boyd et al.[17] with the permission of the National Research Council of Canada, publishers of the *Canadian Journal of Physiology and Pharmacology.*)

per gram of sodium chloride increased significantly from about 48 ml/g at 0 days to about 62 ml/g at 100 days. Richter and Mosier[47] calculated that rats drink 50 to 60 ml of water for each gram of sodium chloride added to their diet.

The volume of urine per gram of sodium chloride administered was calculated in a manner similar to that of water intake, i.e., by subtracting urinary volume in the controls from that in rats given sodium chloride. The volume of urine per gram of sodium chloride also increased with increase in the number of days of administration of sodium chloride and the regression was similar to that of water intake shown in Figure 78. The volume of urine was found to be equal to 0.69 ± 0.4 (mean ± standard deviation) times the volume of water intake per gram of sodium chloride administered. Since most of the salt administered was eliminated in urine, the concentration of sodium chloride in urine may be estimated from the figures noted. The concentration of sodium chloride in urine at zero days, for example, was 3.01 g/100 ml, at 10 days 2.91, at 60 days 2.57, and at 100 days 2.36 g/100 ml. These results suggest that the kidneys may have experienced increasing inability to concentrate urine with increase in the duration of oral administration of toxic doses of sodium chloride. An alternative explanation is that the kidneys adapted to continued administration of sodium chloride by diluting the salt in increasing volumes of urine, thus lowering its toxicity. The alternative explanation is favored by the fact that most deaths occurred in the first few weeks of daily administration of toxic doses of sodium chloride. Survivors became increasingly resistant to the lethal effect of sodium chloride as time went on. Boyd et al.[17] discuss other explanations.

Urinalysis revealed changes which varied with duration of sodium chloride administration but not with dosage of the salt within the range of doses employed by Boyd et al.[17] The output of protein in urine, calculated as mg/kg/24 hr, increased by about 50% during the first two weeks of administration of toxic doses of sodium chloride. There was no significant augmentation of urinary glucose at any interval following any used daily dose of sodium chloride. There were no premortem changes in urinary protein, glucose, or pH. In survivors, urinary pH became somewhat more alkaline during the first 5 weeks of daily oral administration of sodium chloride and then fell significantly below the pH of controls during the second half of the 100 days of administration. As illustrated in Figure 79, the regression of urinary pH on days of administration of sodium chloride was quadratic[14] and best fitted by the equation

$$Y = (0.113 + 0.0044 \, X - 0.000122 \, X^2) \pm 0.072$$

Colonic temperature of the albino rats also followed a bimodal variation with duration of oral administration of toxic doses of sodium chloride.[17] During the first month, oral administration of the salt produced a slight fever which was not dose dependent within the range of doses of sodium chloride administered. During the second month, the body temperature of salt treated rats returned to the range of values in controls given no salt and listed in Table 93. During the last month of oral administration of toxic doses of sodium chloride, a slight but

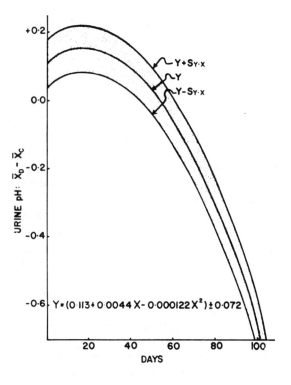

FIGURE 79. The regression, on days of oral administration of toxic doses of sodium chloride to male albino rats, of changes in the pH of 24-hr samples of urine expressed as the mean in salt-treated rats (X_d) minus the mean in controls given no sodium chloride (X_c). (From Boyd et al.[17] with the permission of the National Research Council of Canada, publishers of the *Canadian Journal of Physiology and Pharmacology*.)

statistically significant degree of hypothermia occurred and again was not dose dependent within the range of doses of salt given. These various changes are summarized by data presented in Figure 80.

Premortem signs were recorded by Boyd et al.[17] during the week before death. The larger daily doses of sodium chloride produced death in less than one week and death was preceded by a marked diarrhea and convulsive movements, i.e., signs similar to those noted in the acute, single dose toxicity studies. Death after the first week of daily oral administration of toxic doses of sodium chloride was preceded by hypothermic coma and respiratory failure. This was accompanied by a rapid loss of body weight, anorexia, oligodipsia, and oliguria.

Histopathological Effects of Chronic Sodium Chloride Toxicity

The microscopic findings in albino rats that died from daily oral administration of sodium chloride are summarized in Table 94 as changes (a) in animals that died during the first two weeks of

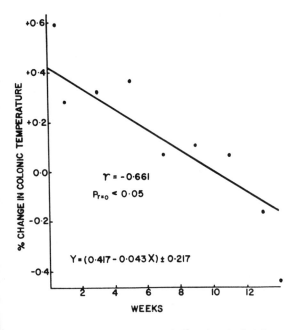

FIGURE 80. The regression, on days of oral administration of toxic doses of sodium chloride to male albino rats, of mean percent changes in colonic temperature calculated as $[(\bar{X}_s - \bar{X}_c)/\bar{X}_c]$, x 100, where $\bar{X}_s$ is the mean in salt-treated rats and $\bar{X}_c$ in controls given no sodium chloride. (From Boyd et al.[17] with the permission of the National Research Council of Canada, publishers of the *Canadian Journal of Physiology and Pharmacology*.)

daily salt administration and (b) in animals that died after the first two weeks. Early deaths were associated with a violent inflammatory reaction in the gastrointestinal tract which has also been reported by Scott and Rotondo.[48] Absorption of toxic amounts of sodium chloride into the blood and tissues produced an initial inflammation of many organs including the adrenal glands, brain, heart, kidneys, liver, lungs, meninges, thymus gland, and ureter. Encephalitis has been reported by Kvalvick[4] and by Sautter, Sorenson, and Clark,[49] and generalized inflammation of tissues in acute salt intoxication by Boyd and Shanas.[11]

In early deaths there also occurred degenerative changes in the kidneys, liver, salivary glands, spleen, testes and thymus gland. These changes are summarized in Table 94. There have been other reports of hepatitis[46,48] and nephritis.[22,23,43-46,49,50] Bronchopneumonia was a contributing cause of early deaths, as noted by several authors.[4,44,45,48,49]

The histopathological appearance of body organs in animals that died after the first two weeks of daily oral administration of toxic doses of sodium chloride was quite different. The gastrointestinal tract had adapted to the presence of large daily amounts of hypertonic saline and had hypertrophied. There was but a mild inflammatory reaction in a few organs such as the stomach, heart, and meninges. A stress reaction was noted in the adrenal glands, spleen, and thymus gland. Infection occurred in some organs such as the brain and lungs. Degenerative changes appeared in the kidneys, liver, testes, the arteriolar media, and in some veins such as the portal vein. The arteriolitis of late deaths has been extensively described by many authors.[23,25,44,45,50-52]

Observations on Survivors of Chronic Sodium Chloride Toxicity

Ability to survive daily oral administration of toxic doses of sodium chloride was associated with ability to inhibit development of pneumonia and tubular nephritis. The arteriolitis was present in survivors and the heart had a mild capillary congestion with small areas of infiltration of mononuclear cells and fibroblasts. Areas of perivascular edema were occasionally seen in the lungs. The cardiac stomach and cecum were hypertrophied and other organs were essentially normal in microscopic appearance.

The weight of body organs was measured either

TABLE 94

Histopathological Observations in the Organs of Male Albino Rats which Died from Daily Oral Administration of Sodium Chloride

Organ	At death within the first 2 weeks	At death after the first 2 weeks
Adrenal glands	Capillary-venous congestion	Diffuse vacuolation
Brain	Capillary-venous congestion	Occasional abscess
Gastrointestinal tract		
Cardiac stomach	Capillary-venous congestion Capillary hemorrhage	Mild capillary-venous congestion
Pyloric stomach	Capillary-venous congestion Capillary hemorrhage Small ulcers	Mucosal hypertrophy Mild capillary-venous congestion
Small bowel	Capillary-venous congestion Shrunken villi Edema	Mucosal hypertrophy
Cecum	Capillary-venous congestion Small ulcers	Mucosal hypertrophy
Colon	Capillary-venous congestion Capillary hemorrhage Small ulcers	Normal
Heart	Capillary congestion	Mild capillary-venous congestion
Kidneys	Capillary-venous congestion Edema of glomeruli and tubules Areas of tubular necrosis Tubular debris in glomerular space	Tubular edema
Liver	Capillary-venous congestion Mild central lobular vacuolation Pyknosis of Kupffer's cells	Diffuse vacuolation
Lungs	Capillary-venous congestion Areas of edema Bronchopneumonic areas	Bronchopneumonia
Meninges	Capillary-venous congestion Capillary hemorrhage	Mild capillary-venous congestion
Muscle (abdominal wall)	Hypovascular	Normal
Salivary glands (submaxillary)	Areas of edema	Normal
Skin	Hypovascular	Normal
Spleen	Edema Billroth cords	Contracted
Testes	Areas of edema of spermatogenic cells Inhibition of spermatogenesis Sertoli's and Leydig's cells normal	Inhibition of spermatogenesis
Thymus gland	Moderate atrophy Capillary-venous congestion	Moderate atrophy
Ureter	Capillary-venous congestion	Normal
Blood vessels	Normal arterioles	Vacuolation of arteriolar media and portal vein media and intima

(From Boyd et al.[17] with the permission of the National Research Council of Canada, publishers of the *Canadian Journal of Physiology and Pharmacology*.)

(a) at the interval when 50% of animals had died from daily oral administration of toxic doses of sodium chloride or (b) on other survivors at 100 days. When autopsy was performed on group (a) at less than 100 days, the weight of certain organs was related to the total cumulative dose of sodium chloride which had been previously given. This relationship is illustrated in Figure 81 for the adrenal glands and the gastrointestinal organs. The correlation coefficients for the quadratic regression of changes in fresh weight of the adrenal glands, pyloric stomach, and small bowel and the linear regressions of cardiac stomach and cecum were statistically significant at $P < 0.02$. The fresh weight of other organs declined with increasing cumulative dose of sodium chloride.

Animals that survived to 100 days were divided into two groups: (a) those in which less than half the animals had previously died from daily oral administration of toxic doses of sodium chloride and (b) those in which there had been no deaths during the 100 days. Animals of group (a) had received larger daily doses of sodium chloride than had animals of group (b). Changes in organ fresh

weights in groups (a) and (b) at 100 days are summarized in Table 95. Confirming the hypertrophy noted microscopically, the weight of the gastrointestinal organs, particularly cardiac stomach and cecum, was increased in both groups (a) and (b). The weight of the adrenal glands was insignificantly changed (and hence increased relative to body weight) in both groups. The weight of all other organs in group (a) and of most other organs in group (b) was decreased at 100 days. In general, loss of organ weight was less in animals of group (b), that had received the smaller daily doses of sodium chloride, than in animals of group (a). As noted in Table 95, the loss of weight in four organs of group (b) was significantly less than corresponding losses in group (a).

Changes in the water content of body organs of albino rats that survived daily oral administration of toxic doses of sodium chloride for 100 days are summarized in Table 96. The changes were not dose dependent and data on all survivors are grouped together in Table 96. There was a significant increase in the water levels of small bowel, cecum, and colon. Significant dehydration was present in pyloric stomach, heart, lungs, spleen, testes, and thymus gland. Changes in other organs were statistically insignificant. Essentially similar changes in water levels were found in survivors autopsied before 100 days.

Conclusions Regarding Sodium Chloride
Acute Oral Toxicity

The $LD_{50} \pm S.E.$ of sodium chloride, dissolved in distilled water and given by stomach tube to young adult male and female albino rats previously starved for 16 hr (overnight) to empty the stomach, was found to be 3.75 ± 0.43 g/kg. The mean $\pm$ standard deviation interval to death was 8.6 ± 5.3 hr. The clinical toxic syndrome in males was duplicated in females and consisted of diarrhea, convulsive movements, muscular rigidity, prostration, respiratory failure, and death.

At autopsy on animals that died there was found a fulminating irritant gastroenteritis which permitted absorption of hypertonic volumes of the saline solution. This in turn produced inflamed and dehydrated body organs.

Survivors exhibited some signs of toxicity at 24 hr, such as inhibition of growth, anorexia, a slight fever, diuresis, and aciduria. Most clinical measurements in survivors were within the normal range in the second and subsequent days after administra-

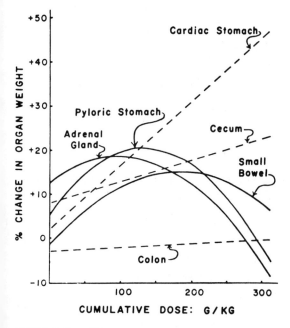

FIGURE 81. The regression, on cumulative total dose of sodium chloride that had been administered orally to male albino rats over a period to 50% mortality, of percentage changes from controls in the wet weight of the adrenal glands and gastrointestinal organs of survivors. (From Boyd et al.[17] with the permission of the National Research Council of Canada, publishers of the *Canadian Journal of Physiology and Pharmacology.*)

TABLE 95

The Effect of Daily Oral Administration for 100 Days of Toxic Doses of Sodium Chloride on the Fresh Weight of Body Organs of Male Albino Rats

Organ	Controls, g wet weight mean ± S.D. (N = 38)	Group A: survivors in groups with 50% or less earlier deaths (N = 39)		Group B: Survivors in groups with no previous deaths (N = 30)[a]	
		% change from controls	P	% change from controls	P
Adrenal glands	0.049 ± 0.008	− 0.1	1.00	+ 0.7	0.5
Brain	1.803 ± 0.118	− 5.7	<0.001	− 4.9	0.005
Gastrointestinal tract					
Cardiac stomach	0.406 ± 0.043	+43.2	<0.001	+36.8	<0.001
Pyloric stomach	1.026 ± 0.125	+ 2.5	0.3	+ 3.6	0.01
Small bowel	8.60 ± 0.863	+11.9	0.02	+ 9.3	0.05
Cecum	1.053 ± 0.143	+20.4	<0.001	+47.0	0.05
Colon	2.241 ± 0.241	+ 0.1	1.00	+10.9	0.10
Heart	1.164 ± 0.104	−12.4	<0.001	−10.9	0.02
Kidneys	3.018 ± 0.355	− 7.7	0.001	+ 0.1	0.8*
Liver	16.26 ± 1.992	−16.7	<0.001	−13.8	0.001*
Lungs	1.627 ± 0.249	−23.9	<0.001	+ 1.5	0.7*
Muscle (abdominal wall)	14.63 ± 2.067	−13.8	<0.001	−10.9	0.01
Skin	92.39 ± 11.04	−23.3	<0.001	−16.8	0.02
Spleen	0.825 ± 0.122	−22.4	0.001	−11.1	0.5
Testicles	3.465 ± 0.261	− 8.0	0.001	− 8.8	<0.001
Thymus gland	0.169 ± 0.044	−21.8	<0.001	−18.9	0.1
Residual carcass	225.0 ± 24.1	−15.3	<0.001	−13.7	0.005
Autopsy body weight	413.9 ± 43.1	−11.1	<0.001	− 9.4	<0.001*

[a]Mean changes significantly different (P ≤ 0.02) from those in group A are indicated by an asterisk.

(From Boyd et al.[17] with the permission of the National Research Council of Canada, publishers of the *Canadian Journal of Physiology and Pharmacology*.)

tion of sodium chloride. Autopsy in survivors at two weeks disclosed that the appearance, weight, and water contents were essentially normal.

Chronic Oral Toxicity

The oral $LD_{50 (100 days)}$ ± S.E. of sodium chloride given once daily by gavage to male albino rats was found to be 2.69 ± 0.12 g/kg/24 hr. Sodium chloride given by stomach tube as a hypertonic aqueous solution once daily is about two to seven times more lethal than when the salt is added to the diet or drinking water of albino rats. The presence of food in the stomach delays absorption of sodium chloride and when taken with drinking water or in the diet, the intake is spread over 24 hr. Since the salt is quickly

detoxified, an appreciable amount of sodium chloride in the diet or drinking water is eliminated before it can produce serious toxic effects. The oral $LD_{50 (100 days)}$ corresponds on a body weight basis to a man of 80 kg swallowing and retaining ½ lb salt dissolved in 1½ qt water each day for 100 days. This is obviously unlikely to happen under ordinary circumstances. Sodium chloride deaths in the human population have been reported mainly in babies given formulas in which salt was added by mistake in place of sugar. Hypertension in certain populations appears to be related to a high intake of dietary sodium chloride.

The oral $LD_{50 (100 days)}$ of sodium chloride in albino rats was more than 70% of the acute oral LD_{50}. This indicates that a rather large percentage

TABLE 96

The Effect of Daily Oral Administration of Toxic Doses of Sodium Chloride on the Water Content of Body Organs of Male Albino Rats which Survived to 100 Days

Organ	Controls, mean ± S.D. g/100 g dry weight (N = 38)	Rats treated with sodium chloride (N = 69)	
		% change from controls	P
Adrenal glands	211 + 28	+ 0.1	1.0
Brain	344 ± 6	− 0.5	0.5
Gastrointestinal tract			
Cardiac stomach	317 ± 17	+ 3.6	0.2
Pyloric stomach	309 ± 12	−10.0	0.001
Small bowel	371 ± 26	+ 6.8	0.02
Cecum	349 ± 19	+12.8	0.001
Colon	409 ± 20	+ 4.4	0.02
Heart	339 ± 11	− 3.9	<0.001
Kidneys	332 ± 10	+ 3.8	0.1
Liver	245 ± 15	− 1.2	0.6
Lungs	359 ± 12	− 4.4	0.01
Muscle (abdominal wall)	261 ± 15	− 0.8	0.7
Skin	135 ± 23	+13.4	0.1
Spleen	319 ± 6	− 3.2	0.01
Testicles	648 ± 11	− 4.1	<0.001
Thymus gland	327 ± 46	− 7.4	0.05
Residual carcass	185 ± 21	− 3.4	0.3

(From Boyd et al.[17] with the permission of the National Research Council of Canada, publishers of the *Canadian Journal of Physiology and Pharmacology*.)

of the acutely lethal dose can be given daily without producing death. The estimated maximal LD_0 (100 days) is of the order of 2 g/kg/24 hr in albino rats somewhat more than 50% of the acute oral LD_{50}. This percentage is much higher than that seen for phenacetin, acetylsalicylic acid, atropine, pilocarpine, and certain pesticides.

Albino rats appeared to adapt to daily administrations of sodium chloride. In the early weeks they had a slight fever, proteinuria, alkalinuria, polydipsia, polyuria, and inhibition of growth without anorexia. Toward the end of 100 days of daily administration, survivors developed a slight hypothermia and aciduria. Early deaths were of a type similar to those seen in acute oral toxicity. Late deaths followed a few days of hypothermic cachexia and were due to pneumonia, hepatitis, nephritis, and arteriolitis.

Survivors developed the ability to dilute sodium chloride in urine and were able to eliminate huge amounts of the salt daily. They had some inhibition of growth associated with arteriolitis and occasionally minor toxic effects on body organs.

REFERENCES

1. Kaufmann, D. W., *Sodium Chloride,* American Chemical Society, Monograph Number 145, Reinhold Publishing Co., New York, 1960.
2. Meneely, G. R., Toxic effects of dietary sodium chloride and the protective effect of potassium, in *Toxicants Occurring Naturally in Foods,* Publication 1354, National Academy of Sciences, National Research Council, Washington, D.C., 1966.
3. Ambard, L. and Beaujard, E., Causes de l'hypertension arterielle, *Arch. Gen. Med.,* 1, 520, 1904.
4. Kvalvik, K., Koksaltintoksikas jon. Et tilfelle, *Tidsskr. Nor. Laegeforen,* 77, 839, 1957.
5. Markley, K., Bocanegra, M., Morales, G., and Chiappari, M., Oral sodium loading in normal individuals, *J. Clin. Invest.,* 36, 303, 1957.
6. Götze, H., Kocksalzuergiftung infolge übergrosser parenteraler Zufuhr, *Arch. Toxikol.,* 19, 284, 1962.
7. Spector, W. S., Ed., *Handbook of Toxicology,* Vol. 1, W. B. Saunders, Philadelphia, 1956, 272.
8. Ussing, H. H., Kruhoffer, P., Thaysen, J. H., and Thorn, N. A., *The Alkali Metal Ions in Biology,* Springer-Verlag, Berlin, 1960.
9. Winbury, M. M. and Crittenden, P. J., Intravenous saline tolerances in mice, *Proc. Soc. Exp. Biol. Med.,* 69, 220, 1948.
10. Sollmann, T., *A Manual of Pharmacology,* 8th ed., W. B. Saunders, Philadelphia, 1957.
11. Boyd, E. M. and Shanas, M. N., The acute oral toxicity of sodium chloride, *Arch. Int. Pharmacodyn. Ther.,* 144, 86, 1963.
12. Shanas, M. N. and Boyd, E. M., The acute oral toxicity of sodium chloride, *Am. Ind. Hyg. Conf. Abstr.,* 1963, 129.
13. Croxton, F. E., *Elementary Statistics with Applications in Medicine,* Prentice-Hall, New York, 1953.
14. Waugh, A. E., *Elements of Statistical Method,* 3rd ed., McGraw-Hill, New York, 1952.
15. Boyd, E. M. and Krijnen, C. J., Tolerated doses of phenacetin in relation to body weight and organ weights, *Jap. J. Pharmacol.,* 19, 386, 1969.
16. Selye, H., Adrenal changes produced by parenteral administration of highly hypertonic solutions, *Acta Neuroveg.,* 6, 212, 1953.
17. Boyd, E. M., Abel, M. M., and Knight, L. M., The chronic oral toxicity of sodium chloride at the range of the $LD_{50 (0.1L)}$, *Can. J. Physiol. Pharmacol.,* 44, 157, 1966.
18. White, A., Handler, P., and Smith, E. L., *Principles of Biochemistry,* 4th ed., McGraw-Hill, New York, 1968.
19. Welt, L. G., *Clinical Disorders of Hydration and Acid-Base Equilibrium,* Little, Brown and Company, Boston, 1955.
20. Meneely, G. R., Salt, *Am. J. Med.,* 16, 1, 1954.
21. Okano, T., Esaki, H., Miyazaki, Y., Fujita, T., and Ogishima, H., Experimental studies of excessive intake of NaCl. 1. The effect of salt water intake on the growth of rats, *Kurume Med. J.,* 9, 40, 1962.
22. Meneely, G. R., Tucker, R. G., and Darby, W. J., Chronic sodium chloride toxicity in albino rats. I. Growth on a purified diet containing various levels of sodium chloride, *J. Nutr.,* 48, 489, 1952.
23. Meneely, G. R., Tucker, R. G., Darby, W. J., and Auerbach, S. H., Chronic sodium chloride toxicity in albino rats. II. Occurrence of hypertension and syndrome of edema and renal failure, *J. Exp. Med.,* 98, 71, 1953.
24. Dahl, L. K., Effect of chronic salt feeding. Elevation of plasma cholesterol in rats and dogs, *J. Exp. Med.,* 112, 635, 1960.
25. Dahl, L. K. and Schackow, E., Effects of chronic excess salt ingestion: experimental hypertension in the rat, *Can. Med. Assoc. J.,* 90, 155, 1964.
26. Dahl, L. K., Heine, M., and Tassinari, L., Effects of chronic excess salt ingestion: role of genetic factors in both DOCA-salt and renal hypertension, *J. Exp. Med.,* 118, 605, 1963.
27. Dahl, L. K., Heine, M., and Tassinari, L., Effects of chronic excess salt ingestion: further demonstration that genetic factors influence the development of hypertension: evidence from experimental hypertension due to cortisone and to adrenal regeneration, *J. Exp. Med.,* 122, 533, 1965.
28. Dahl, L. K., Heine, M., and Tassinari, L., Effects of chronic excess salt ingestion: vascular reactivity in two strains of rats with opposite genetic susceptibility to experimental hypertension, *Circulation,* 30, 11, 1964.
29. Jaffé, D., Sutherland, L. E., Barker, D. M., and Dahl, L. K., Effects of chronic excess salt ingestion. Morphologic findings in kidneys of rats with differing genetic susceptibilities to hypertension, *Arch. Pathol.,* 90, 1, 1970.
30. Meneely, G. R., Tucker, R. G., Darby, W. J., and Auerbach, S. H., Chronic sodium chloride toxicity. Renal and vascular lesions, *Ann. Intern. Med.,* 39, 991, 1953.
31. Tobian, L., Janecek, J., and Tombaulian, A., The effect of high sodium intake on the development of nephrosclerotic hypertension. Effect of nephrosclerotic hypertension on the granularity of the juxtaglomerular cells, *J. Lab. Clin. Med.,* 53, 842, 1959.
32. Simpson, C. F., Harms, R. H., and Kling, J. M., Relationship of dietary sodium chloride to aortic ruptures in turkeys induced by diethylstilbestrol, *Proc. Soc. Exp. Biol. Med.,* 121, 633, 1966.
33. Kaunitz, H., Relation of chloride, sodium and potassium intake to renal and adrenal size, *Lab. Invest.,* 5, 132, 1956.
34. Morrison, A. B. and Sarett, H. P., The effects of deficiency of B vitamins on salt toxicity in the rat, *J. Nutr.,* 68, 231, 1959.

35. **Dahl, L. K.,** Medical progress. Salt intake and salt need, *N. Engl. J. Med.,* 258, 1152, 1958.
36. **Dahl, L. K.,** Possible role of salt intake in development of essential hypertension, in *Essential Hypertension, An International Symposium,* Springer-Verlag, Heidelberg, 1960.
37. **Dahl, L. K.,** Studies on the role of salt and genetics in hypertension, *Acad. Med. N.J. Bull.,* 10, 269, 1964.
38. **Constantopoulos, G. and Boyd, E. M.,** Maximal tolerated amounts of sucrose given by daily intragastric administration to albino rats, *Food Cosmet. Toxicol.,* 6, 717, 1968.
39. **Boyd, E. M. and Semple, A.,** The chronic toxicity of casein in the diet of albino rats, Unpublished data, 1972.
40. **Boyd, H. M. and Liu, S.-J.,** Toxicity of starch administered by mouth, *Can. Med. Assoc. J.,* 98, 492, 1968.
41. **Peters, J. M.,** Factors affecting caffeine toxicity, *J. Clin. Pharmacol.,* 7, 131, 1967.
42. **Boyd, E. M.,** *Predictive Toxicometrics,* Scientechnica (Publishers) Ltd., Bristol, England, 1971.
43. **Sapirstein, L. A., Brandt, W. L., and Drury, D. R.,** Production of hypertension in rats by substituting hypertonic sodium chloride solutions for drinking water, *Proc. Soc. Exp. Biol. Med.,* 73, 82, 1950.
44. **Koletsky, S.,** Role of salt renal mass in experimental hypertension, *Arch. Pathol.,* 68, 11, 1959.
45. **Koletsky, S.,** Hypertensive vascular disease produced by salt, *Lab. Invest.,* 7, 377, 1958.
46. **Kleiner, I. S. and Dotti, L. B.,** Effects of repeated administration of chlorates and chlorides of potassium and sodium in massive doses, *N. Y. Med. Coll. Flower Hosp. Bull.,* 3, 309, 1940.
47. **Richter, C. P. and Mosier, H. D., Jr.,** Maximum sodium chloride intake and thirst in domesticated and wild Norway rats, *Am. J. Physiol.,* 176, 213, 1954.
48. **Scott, E. P. and Rotondo, C. C.,** Salt intoxication; accidental ingestion of large amounts of sodium chloride; report of case with autopsy of 2 year old patient, *Kent. Med. J.,* 45, 107, 1947.
49. **Sautter, J. H., Sorenson, D. K., and Clark, J. J.,** Salt poisoning in swine, *J. Am. Vet. Med. Assoc.,* 130, 12, 1957.
50. **Meneely, G. R. and Dahl, L. K.,** Electrolytes in hypertension: the effects of sodium chloride. The evidence from animal and human studies, *Med. Clin. North Am.,* 45, 271, 1961.
51. **Tobian, L.,** Interrelationship of electrolytes, juxtaglomerular cells and hypertension, *Physiol. Rev.,* 40, 280, 1960.
52. **Gross, F.,** Sodium metabolism and hypertension, *Schweiz. Med. Wochenschr.,* 93, 1065, 1963.

Chapter 16

POTASSIUM CHLORIDE

Potassium is the main cation of intracellular fluid where its concentration is about 20 times that in extracellular fluid. Potassium is present in all natural foods from plant and animal sources and occurs in the mineral sylvite. Potassium chloride is a white crystalline powder, soluble in water, forming a solution of neutral pH. It is used to combat hypokalemic states and large doses may produce gastrointestinal irritation and ulceration, diarrhea, weakness, and circulatory disturbances in man.[1] Many potassium salts have a disagreeable taste — salt of wormwood, for example, is potassium carbonate. Hypokalemia and hyperkalemia are extremely uncommon in normal man[2] and occur mainly from use of certain diuretic agents (hypokalemia) or during certain types of renal inability to excrete potassium (hyperkalemia).

The human diet ordinarily contains 2 to 4 g of potassium per day which is more than sufficient to meet the needs of the body.[3] The total potassium of a man weighing 70 kg is about 4,000 mEq, 115 mEq/l. in cell water, and 3.8 to 5.4 mEq/l. in serum. Hyperkalemia is uncommon and is seen in conditions such as premortem states, Addison's disease, uremia, certain shock conditions associated with hemoconcentration, or following intravenous infusion of fluids rich in potassium.

Potassium deficiency may occur in cachexia, in excessive vomiting and diarrhea, during the parenteral administration of fluids deficient in potassium, in excessive use of salt-excreting diuretics, and in conditions associated with negative nitrogen balance.[4] There is usually deficiency of potassium in both the intracellular and extracellular fluids. The syndrome includes lethargy, muscular weakness, anorexia, paralysis, and cardiac irregularities. The body attempts to retain potassium by excreting an acidic urine containing large amounts of ammonium ion. Aldosterone and deoxycorticosterone cause retention of sodium with a decrease in blood potassium. Potassium is filtered into urine in the proximal renal tubules and actively secreted into urine in the distal convoluted tubules.[5] Potassium

is involved in many body functions including acid-base balance,[6] the transport of glucose[7] and amino acids,[8] the permeability of cells,[9] and many enzyme reactions.[10] Potassium depletion is a common feature of kwashiorkor.[11]

The maximal nontoxic amount of potassium in man has been estimated at from 0.2[12,13] to 1 g/kg/day.[14] Drescher et al.[15] recorded that potassium chloride added to the diet in amounts equal to 20 to 30 g/kg/day killed 50% of albino rats in three days. Meneely, Ball, and Youmans[16] found that addition of potassium chloride to the diet of rats protected the animals from the toxic effects of high levels of dietary sodium chloride. Meneely[2] noted that the results of addition of sodium and potassium chlorides to the diet of rats could be divided into five categories, namely (a) optimal amounts of each salt, (b) moderately toxic amounts of sodium chloride plus optimal amounts of potassium chloride, (c) moderately toxic amounts of sodium chloride plus extra amounts of potassium chloride, (d) markedly toxic amounts of sodium chloride plus optimal amounts of potassium chloride, and (e) markedly toxic amounts of sodium chloride plus extra amounts of potassium chloride. Animals of category (a) were considered as controls and lived out their normal lifespan without developing hypertension. Animals of category (b) had a shortened lifespan and moderate hypertension; extra potassium chloride given to animals of category (c) prolonged their lifespan but did not influence their moderate hypertension. Animals of category (d) developed a marked hypertension and their lifespan was markedly shortened; addition of extra potassium chloride in animals of category (e) reduced the hypertension to moderate levels and lengthened the lifespan. Meneely[2] notes that these differences could explain variation in the response of hypertensive patients to administration of potassium chloride. Morrison and Sarett[17] have reported on the ability of potassium chloride to counteract the toxic effects of high levels of dietary sodium chloride.

Boyd and Shanas[18] reviewed data on the acute toxicity of potassium chloride given by stomach tube to albino rats previously starved overnight to empty the stomach. They noted that the acute oral LD_{50} had been reported to lie between 2 g/kg[19] and 4 g/kg.[20] Boyd and Shanas[18] found the acute oral LD_{50} ± S.E. of potassium chloride to be 3.02 ± 0.14 g/kg in young adult female albino rats. The LD_{50} of potassium chloride given parenterally is lower than that when given by mouth.[21] The studies of Boyd and Shanas[18] will be cited in exemplification of the acute oral toxicity of potassium chloride.

Boyd and Shanas[18] used albino rats of a Wistar strain which has been bred in the animal quarters of the Department of Pharmacology at Queen's University. The animals were females weighing 200 to 300 g and were fed Purina fox chow checkers. They were placed in metabolism cages and given water but no food for 16 hr (overnight) prior to administration of potassium chloride. Potassium

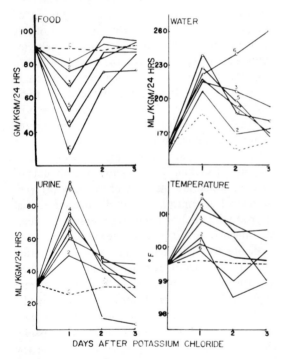

FIGURE 82. The regression, on days after oral administration of toxic doses of potassium chloride to albino rats, of changes in food intake, water intake, urinary volume, and colonic temperature. C = controls given no potassium chloride; 1 = 2.1 g potassium chloride per kg body weight; 2 = 2.4 g/kg; 3 = 2.7 g/kg; 4 = 3.3 g/kg; 5 = 3.6 g/kg; and 6 = 3.9 g/kg. Open circles indicate that the difference from controls was significant at P < 0.025. (From Boyd and Shanas[18] with the permission of the *Archives Internationales de Pharmacodynamie et de Therapie*.)

chloride was given in doses of from 2.1 to 3.9 g/kg, each dose dissolved in distilled water to a final volume of 20 ml/kg body weight. Clinical signs were recorded at hourly or other intervals as indicated and autopsies were performed on animals that died. Clinical and pathological parameters were also recorded on survivors over a period of two weeks following administration of potassium chloride.

Clinical Signs of Acute Potassium Chloride Toxicity

Death from oral administration of lethal doses of potassium chloride occurred at from 1 to 12 hr following administration, the mean ± standard deviation interval to death being 3.3 ± 3.2 hr. The LD_{50} ± S.E. was 3.02 ± 0.14 g/kg. The clinical signs of intoxication in animals that died included tonoclonic convulsions followed by prostration and respiratory failure. Animals that did not die had convulsive movements, diarrhea or constipation, and periods of dyspnea. They had anorexia, polydipsia, diuresis, and a fever, all of which signs were more or less dose dependent at 24 hr, as illustrated in Figure 82. Recovery was rapid in survivors and by the second or third day, measurements noted in Figure 82 had returned to or toward normal. Potassium chloride had no significant effect upon the amount of urinary acetone, albumin, occult blood, bilirubin, or glucose.

Signs at Autopsy

Potassium chloride was found on autopsy to have produced an irritant gastroenteritis in animals that died. The parietal cells, mucous neck cells, and surface epithelium of pyloric stomach were shrunken and occasionally necrotic or hemorrhagic; there was capillary-venous congestion of the lamina propria and submucosa. The columnar epithelium of the intestinal villi was shrunken and the goblet cells were dilated.

Absorption of hypertonic amounts of potassium chloride produced toxic signs in body organs which were particularly evident in animals with a delayed death. Necrosis appeared in the renal tubular epithelium as an early, somewhat restricted change which probably would have been more evident had death been postponed to 24 hr or longer. The heart was dilated with blood at death. The alveoli of the lungs were frequently collapsed.

TABLE 97

Changes in the Mean Wet Weight of Body Organs of Albino Rats Following Oral Administration of Toxic Doses of Potassium Chloride

Organ	Controls Mean ± S.D. (g)	Nonsurvivors % change from controls	P	Survivors at 2 weeks Compared with nonsurvivors % change	P	Compared with controls % change	P
Spleen	0.721 ± 0.091	−23.6	<0.001	+34.6	0.001	+ 2.9	0.7
Abdominal muscle	5.13 ± 0.81	−20.1	0.005	+19.3	0.02	− 4.7	0.5
Pyloric stomach	1.00 ± 0.19	−19.0	0.05	+17.3	0.05	− 5.0	0.5
Kidneys	2.02 ± 0.26	−16.8	0.005	+ 7.7	0.2	−10.4	0.05
Lungs	1.29 ± 0.23	−14.7	0.05	+29.1	0.05	+10.1	0.4
Jejunum	3.21 ± 0.55	−14.0	0.1	+11.2	0.2	− 4.4	0.6
Ileum	3.48 ± 0.73	− 9.8	0.2	+ 4.5	0.5	− 5.7	0.5
Colon	1.89 ± 0.30	− 9.5	0.2	+ 4.6	0.4	− 5.3	0.4
Skin	38.6 ± 5.4	− 9.1	0.2	+ 5.4	0.3	− 4.1	0.4
Adrenal glands	0.067 ± 0.006	− 9.0	0.1	+ 8.2	0.3	− 1.5	0.8
Liver	10.3 ± 1.2	− 7.8	0.2	+ 8.4	0.2	0.0	1.0
Ovaries	0.111 ± 0.024	− 6.3	0.4	+ 9.6	0.2	+ 2.7	0.8
Brain	1.31 ± 0.08	− 6.1	0.1	+ 3.3	0.4	− 4.6	0.1
Cecum	0.85 ± 0.20	− 4.7	0.6	+ 4.9	0.6	0.0	1.0
Residual carcass	131 ± 20	− 3.8	0.6	+ 1.6	0.8	− 2.3	0.7
Cardiac stomach	0.344 ± 0.058	+ 1.7	0.8	+ 1.2	0.9	+ 2.9	0.7
Heart	0.796 ± 0.072	+11.3	0.025	−12.0	0.02	− 2.0	0.6

(From Boyd and Shanas[18] with the permission of the *Archives Internationales de Pharmacodynamie et de Therapie.*)

Changes in the wet weight of body organs are summarized in Table 97. At death, most organs were found to have lost weight. This was particularly so in the spleen, the muscular layer of the ventral abdominal wall, pyloric stomach, kidneys, and lungs. The heart had gained weight due to the large volume of blood in its dilated chambers. In survivors, organ wet weight was within the range of that in controls at two weeks.

Corresponding shifts in the water content of body organs are indicated in Table 98. The early deaths in these animals were associated with loss of water in most body organs. Dehydration was particularly evident in pyloric stomach, skin, cardiac stomach, lungs, kidneys, colon, liver, and heart. In survivors, organ water content was found to be within the limits of that of the controls at two weeks after giving potassium chloride.

Conclusions Regarding Potassium Chloride

The acute oral LD_{50} ± S.E. of potassium chloride in young adult female albino rats was found to be 3.02 ± 0.14 g/kg. Animals tolerated larger daily doses if potassium chloride was incorporated into their diet.

Death occurs at 3.3 ± 3.2 hr (mean ± standard deviation). Death is due to respiratory failure in marked prostration following tonoclonic convulsions. Animals that do not die have convulsive twitchings, diarrhea, anorexia, polydipsia, diuresis, and fever. Recovery of survivors is rapid and by the second or third day measurements of clinical signs are essentially within the normal range.

Hypertonic doses of potassium chloride produced a local irritant inflammatory reaction in the gastrointestinal tract. Absorption of large toxic amounts of potassium chloride into the bloodstream produced dehydration, loss of wet weight, and toxic effects in many body organs. Organ weights and water levels returned to normal limits in survivors at two weeks after administration of potassium chloride.

TABLE 98

Changes in the Mean Water Content, Measured as gram Water per 100 g Dry Weight of Tissue, of Body Organs of Albino Rats Following Oral Administration of Toxic Doses of Potassium Chloride

Organ	Controls Mean ± S.D. (g/100 g dry wt)	Nonsurvivors		Survivors at 2 weeks			
				Compared with nonsurvivors		Compared with controls	
		% change from controls	P	% change	P	% change	P
Pyloric stomach	349 ± 37	−22.9	<0.001	+30.9	<0.001	+ 0.9	0.9
Skin	146 ± 13	−14.3	<0.001	+12.8	<0.001	− 3.4	0.3
Cardiac stomach	355 ± 26	−13.5	0.01	+15.6	<0.001	+ 0.3	0.9
Lungs	241 ± 15	−11.7	<0.001	+18.0	<0.001	+ 4.1	0.1
Kidneys	332 ± 22	−10.5	<0.001	+12.1	<0.001	+ 0.3	0.9
Colon	449 ± 67	−10.2	0.05	+13.6	0.025	+ 2.0	0.7
Liver	283 ± 13	− 8.8	<0.001	+ 9.7	0.005	0.0	1.0
Heart	351 ± 8	− 8.3	<0.001	+ 9.6	<0.001	+ 0.6	0.6
Cecum	344 ± 44	− 7.6	0.2	+12.9	0.025	+ 4.4	0.3
Abdominal muscle	224 ± 24	− 5.3	0.3	+ 5.2	0.5	− 0.4	0.9
Ovaries	265 ± 39	− 4.2	0.6	+ 0.1	0.3	+ 4.5	0.7
Residual carcass	201 ± 20	− 4.0	0.4	+ 8.3	0.1	+ 4.0	0.3
Brain	365 ± 11	− 3.8	0.02	+ 4.8	0.005	+ 0.8	0.5
Spleen	316 ± 9	− 1.6	0.4	+ 2.6	0.2	+ 0.9	0.6
Jejunum	415 ± 67	+ 1.0	0.9	+10.0	0.2	+11.3	0.2
Adrenal glands	240 ± 31	+ 1.6	0.7	+ 5.7	0.1	+ 7.5	0.1
Ileum	338 ± 65	+ 8.9	0.4	+ 7.4	0.4	+16.9	0.05

(From Boyd and Shanas[18] with the permission of the *Archives Internationales de Pharmacodynamie et de Therapie.*)

REFERENCES

1. Stecker, P. G., Windholtz, M., Leahy, D. S., Bolton, D. M., and Eaton, L. G., *The Merck Index. An Encyclopedia of Chemicals and Drugs,* 8th ed., Merck and Company, Rahway, N.J., 1968.
2. Meneely, G. R., Toxic effects of dietary sodium chloride and the protective effect of potassium, in *Toxicants Occurring Naturally in Foods,* Publication 1354, National Academy of Sciences, National Research Council, Washington, D.C., 1966, 267.
3. White, A., Handler, P., and Smith, E. L., *Principles of Biochemistry,* 4th ed., McGraw-Hill, New York, 1968.
4. Bland, J. H., Ed., *Clinical Metabolism of Body Water and Electrolytes,* W.B. Saunders, Philadelphia, 1963.
5. Pitts, R. F., *Physiology of the Kidney and Body Fluids,* Year Book Medical Publishers, Chicago, 1963.
6. Forster, R. P., Kidney, water and electrolytes, *Ann. Rev. Physiol.,* 27, 183, 1965.
7. Balazs, E. A. and Jeanloz, K. W., Eds., *The Amino Sugar,* Vols. II A, 1965, and II B, 1966, Academic Press, New York.
8. Greenberg, D. W., Ed., *Metabolic Pathways,* Vol. 2, Academic Press, New York, 1961.
9. Harris, E. J., *Transport and Accumulation in Biological Systems,* Butterworths, London, 1956.
10. Boyes, P. D., Lardy, H., and Myrbäch, K., Eds., *The Enzymes,* Academic Press, New York, 1960.
11. Hepsted, D. W., Proteins, in *Nutrition. A Comprehensive Treatise,* Vol. 1, Beator, G. H. and McHenry, E. W., Eds., Academic Press, New York, 1964, Chap. 3.
12. Winkler, A. W., Hoff, H. E., and Smith, P. K., The toxicity of orally administered potassium salts in renal insufficiency, *J. Clin. Invest.,* 20, 119, 1941.
13. Keith, N. M., Osterberg, A. E., and Burchell, H. B., Some effects of potassium salts in man, *Ann. Intern. Med.,* 16, 879, 1942.
14. Ussing, H. H., Kruhoffer, P., Thaysen, J. H., and Thorn, N. A., *The Alkali Metal Ions in Biology,* Springer-Verlag, Berlin, 1960.
15. Drescher, A. N., Talbott, N. B., Meara, P. A., Terry, M., and Crawford, J. D., A study of the effects of excessive potassium intake upon the body potassium stores, *J. Clin. Invest.,* 37, 1316, 1958.
16. Meneely, G. R., Ball, C. O. T., and Youmans, J. B., Chronic sodium chloride toxicity: the protective effect of added potassium chloride, *Ann. Intern. Med.,* 47, 263, 1957.
17. Morrison, A. B. and Sarett, H. P., The effect of deficiency of B vitamins on salt toxicity in the rat, *J. Nutr.,* 68, 231, 1959.
18. Boyd, E. M. and Shanas, M. N., The acute oral toxicity of potassium chloride, *Arch. Int. Pharmacodyn. Ther.,* 133, 275, 1961.
19. Ulrich, J. L. and Shternov, V. A., Comparative action of hypertonic solutions of chlorates and chlorides of potassium, sodium, calcium and magnesium, *J. Pharmacol. Exp. Ther.,* 35, 1, 1929.
20. Stephens, J. W., Our present knowledge of potassium in physiological and pathological processes, *Can. Med. Assoc. J.,* 66, 19, 1952.
21. Spector, W. S., Ed., *Handbook of Toxicology,* Vol. 1, W. B. Saunders, Philadelphia, 1956.

Chapter 17

IRON

Iron comprises about 5% of the earth's crust and in powder form is black to grey.[1] Normal adult men contain about 0.06 g of iron per kg body weight; 75% present in hemoglobin, 20% in ferritin and hemosiderin, and the remaining 5% in myoglobin, various enzymes, and minor compounds.[2] The concentration of iron is greatest in the red blood cells, approximating 1 g of iron per kg of red blood cells. The average daily human dietary requirement varies from about 1 mg/kg at birth, to 0.2 mg/kg at age 10, 0.1 mg/kg at age 20, and 0.03 mg/kg at age 60.[2] The need for iron is greatest during the growing period for both males and females; in adults the need of females during the reproductive period is greater than that of males of the same age. Dietary iron may consist of iron from vegetable, animal, and inorganic sources.

There are many reviews on the history of iron therapy.[3-6] The Greeks associated iron with Mars, the God of War, and believed it imparted strength to those who used it. In 1681, Thomas Sydenham introduced iron for the treatment of chlorosis or the "green sickness" which had been described some 100 years earlier and which got its name from the greenish pallor often associated with anemia.[7] During the 18th century, iron was discovered to be in blood and its concentration was found to be increased by iron therapy. In 1832 Pierre Blaud introduced his famous pill of ferrous sulfate.[8] Subsequent studies have been reviewed by Shanas.[9]

The absorption of iron varies inversely with the amount of iron stored in the cells lining the gastrointestinal tract.[10-12] It is transported by blood in combinations such as transferrin or siderophilin[13] and excess amounts are stored, for example, in the liver.[14] The amount of iron in the body is regulated largely by absorption since there are no effective mechanisms for excretion of absorbed iron.[15-17] A small amount is lost in the feces from cells sloughed off the intestinal mucosa and a small amount is excreted in bile, urine, and sweat.[18] Approximately 0.01 mg/kg body weight is lost per day by menstruation[19] and a similar amount by other mechanisms of elimination.[20] In round numbers, an average human adult excretes 1 mg of iron per day and requires 10 mg of iron in the diet per day to replace this loss since only 10 to 15% of dietary iron is absorbed.[9]

Most of the available preparations of iron appear to be equally effective in the therapy of anemia.[21-23] Total body hemoglobin contains about 2.5 g of iron and hemoglobin can be generated at the rate of about 1% per day. In anemia, therefore, about 25 mg of iron is the maximal amount needed per day. This amount of absorbed iron is provided by 2.5 g of iron powder, 1.25 g of ferric ammonium citrate, and 0.125 g of ferrous sulfate which are absorbed when given orally at the rate of 1, 2, and 20%, respectively,[24] and are equally effective hematologically.[53]

Toxicity of Iron

Most soluble salts of iron, especially ferric salts, produce irritation of the gastrointestinal tract, characterized by abdominal pain and diarrhea, when given in large doses especially on an empty stomach.[25] Solutions of iron salt taken by mouth may stain the enamel of teeth. The incidence of severe toxicity to iron increased at two historical periods when large doses were favored, one in the mid-19th century following introduction of Blaud's pill[47] and a second toward the middle of the 20th century with the introduction of many new preparations of iron such as candy coated tablets for children.[50-52] Intramuscular injections of large amounts of certain iron salts may cause necrosis of tissue at the site of injection.[16] Shanas[9] has collected data which indicate that the toxicity of iron varies as the anion with which it is combined. The toxicity of iron will be described in this volume by limiting detailed discussion to elemental iron powder together with brief reference to other forms of oral iron preparations[26-32] and to citing representative studies on parenteral iron preparations.[16]

The Acute Oral Toxicity of Powdered Iron

Powdered iron is also called reduced iron because it is prepared by the reductions of iron oxide with hydrogen at temperatures between 700 and 900°C.[33] It is an amorphous grey powder which passes freely through a No. 100 sieve.[34] It dissolves as ferrous iron in hydrochloric acid[33] and has been reported as readily absorbed as ferrous sulfate when given by mouth.[35] Reduced iron is described in the *British Pharmacopoeia* of 1932,[36] the *Pharmacopeia of the United States of America* of 1942,[37] the *Pharmacopeia of the U.S.S.R.* of 1945,[38] the *Pharmacopoeia of Japan* of 1951,[39] and in the pharmacopeias of many other countries.[40] The average individual dose recommended by U.S.P. is 0.5 g; it has been widely used in the therapy of anemia[21-23,41] in amounts up to 3 g/day or higher.[24,25,41-46]

The acute oral toxicity of powdered iron in albino rats was described by Boyd and Shanas.[27] The studies were performed on males weighing 200 to 250 g, starved overnight to empty the stomach before oral administration of Reduced Iron, N.F. IX. The doses given ranged from 50 to 200 g/kg body weight, each dose suspended in distilled water to a final volume of 75 to 100 ml/kg. Clinical signs of toxicity were recorded daily or at shorter intervals and autopsies were performed on animals that died and on survivors at two and four weeks.

The mean ± standard deviation interval to death was 62 ± 35 hr and it varied inversely with the dose administered. This relationship is illustrated in Figure 83. By contrast, the average interval to death following oral administration of ferrous sulfate solutions in distilled water is 4 hr.[47]

The regression of doses (Y axis) on percent mortality (X axis) was fitted by the equation $Y = (35.0 + 1.272 X) \pm 26.7$ from which the maximal LD_0 may be calculated to be 35.0 g/kg, the $LD_{50} \pm$ S.E. 98.6 ± 26.7 g/kg and the minimal LD_{100} 162 g/kg. Actually, a dose of 140 g/kg produced 70% mortality, doses of 170 g/kg and over produced 100% mortality, and doses less than 50 g/kg produced no deaths. A representative list of values for the acute oral LD_{50} of other preparations of iron is presented in Table 99. It may be seen that iron powder is from 50 to 400 times more safe, from the point of view of acute oral toxicity, than the other forms of iron listed in Table 99. Boyd and Shanas[27] comment, "The results indicate that reduced iron, which has gone out of fashion in iron therapy, could stand reinvestigation from the point of view of its effectiveness and low toxicity." Shanas[9] concludes that "If these various results are extrapolatable to man, they indicate that reduced iron powder

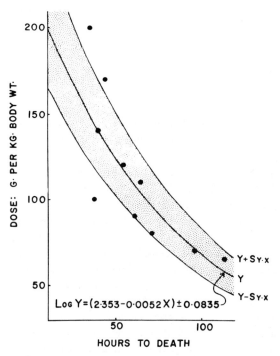

FIGURE 83. The regression of dose of elemental iron given by stomach tube to albino rats, on mean interval to death. (From Boyd and Shanas[27] with the permission of *The Canadian Medical Association Journal*.)

TABLE 99

Estimated Values for the Acute Oral LD_{50} of Iron Preparations Calculated as g Iron per kg Body Weight

Preparations	Acute oral LD_{50} (calculated as g iron per kg body weight)	Reference
Ferrous chloride	0.265	47
Ferric chloride	0.309	48
Ferrous sulfate	0.3	47
Ferrous sulfate	0.780	49
Ferrous sulfate	1.0	47
Ferrous gluconate	0.5	47
Ferrous gluconate	0.865	3
Ferrous fumarate	>2.3	3
Elemental iron	98.6	27

should be the drug of choice in the treatment of iron deficiency anemia."

Clinical Signs of Acute Toxicity to Powdered Iron

Shortly after oral administration of suspensions of iron powder in doses at the range of the acute LD_{50}, the albino rats became depressed and inactive. They were hyporeflexic in that they

TABLE 100

Clinical Measurements in Albino Rats Given Iron Powder in Doses at the Range of the Acute Oral LD$_{50}$[a]

Measurement	Days 1 to 3	Days 4 to 6	Days 7 to 9	Days 10 to 12
		Iron treated animals		
Food intake: g/kg/day	9 ± 11*	61 ± 32*	115 ± 30	119 ± 31*
Water intake: ml/kg/day	37 ± 30*	128 ± 68	158 ± 45*	158 ± 37*
Urine volume: ml/kg/day	6 ± 8*	27 ± 25*	27 ± 12*	25 ± 10*
Urine protein: mg/100 ml	65 ± 41	59 ± 32	76 ± 29	37 ± 32*
Urine glucose: g/100 ml	0.2 ± 0.2	0.2 ± 0.3	0.1 ± 0.1	0.1 ± 0.1
Urine pH	7.8 ± 0.8*	8.1 ± 0.8*	7.8 ± 0.8*	7.8 ± 0.6*
		Controls		
Food intake: g/kg/day	95 ± 29	98 ± 25	103 ± 20	98 ± 13
Water intake: ml/kg/day	138 ± 50	127 ± 45	132 ± 29	123 ± 18
Urine volume: ml/kg/day	12 ± 10	8 ± 9	6 ± 9	5 ± 5
Urine protein: mg/100 ml	49 ± 29	78 ± 40	84 ± 41	74 ± 23
Urine glucose: g/100 ml	0.1 ± 0.2	0.1 ± 0.2	0.2 ± 0.3	0.1 ± 0.1
Urine pH	7.3 ± 0.7	6.9 ± 1.1	6.9 ± 1.0	6.4 ± 0.4

[a] The results are expressed as mean ± standard deviation. Means in iron treated animals which differed at $P = 0.05$ or less from corresponding means in controls, by a t test, are indicated by an asterisk.
(From Boyd and Shanas[27] with the permission of *The Canadian Medical Association Journal.*)

failed to react to stimuli such as tapping on their cage or ruffling of their fur by air blown against its grain. More marked stimulation by prodding produced a sluggish response such as slowly moving a short distance in the cage. At 24 hr, most of the animals were hyperreflexic and active.

Most of the animals given the higher doses of iron died with impaction of iron in the gastrointestinal tract. Death occurred at 48 hr when the stomach was impacted and during the next day when impaction occurred in the intestines.

Impaction was rare at doses of iron less than 100 g/kg and the premortem signs in such animals were pallor, prostration, and dyspnea. At autopsy on the latter animals, the intestines were found to be inflamed and distended with a black fluid containing loose iron powder. Death was usually delayed to the third day or later (see Figure 83).

Clinical measurements are summarized in Table 100. The characteristic features of iron intoxication were anorexia, oligodipsia, oliguria, and alkalinuria. Anorexia was most evident during the second day when 67% of the animals ate nothing. Oligodipsia was most pronounced during the first 24 hr when 75% of the animals drank no water.

This resulted in oliguria which was most marked during the second day. In survivors, signs of recovery appeared during days 4 to 6. During the second week, survivors ate more food and drank more water than the controls. They had a diuresis during the second week. Alkalinuria persisted throughout the first two weeks.

Changes in growth of the young male rats used by Boyd and Shanas[27] are indicated in Figure 84. The changes in body weight shown in Figure 84 were not corrected for weight of iron retained in the gastrointestinal tract. Little or no iron was passed in the stool during the first 24 hr so that animals given the highest doses had actually gained weight at 24 hr, as shown in Figure 84. When the weight of administered iron was subtracted from body weight it was estimated[27] that at 24 hr the animals had lost 10% or so of their body weight during the first day. The first stools were passed toward the end of the first 24 hr; they were loose, black, and watery. Diarrhea and loss of body weight continued until death of the animals. Loss of body weight was greater the longer the interval to death but was not dose dependent within the range of doses employed.

Oral administration of lethal doses of iron

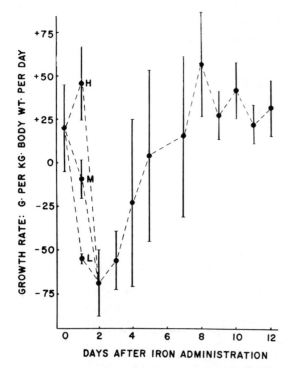

FIGURE 84. Shifts in the daily growth rate of young male albino rats, entered as means ± standard deviations, following oral administration of iron powder in doses at the range of the LD_{50} Body weight was not corrected for iron remaining in the gastrointestinal tract. This affected the results to the greatest extent during the first 24 hr when high doses (110 to 200 g/kg) are entered as H, medium doses (70 to 100 g/kg) as M, and low doses (60 to 65 g/kg) as L. (From Boyd and Shanas[27] with the permission of *The Canadian Medical Association Journal*.)

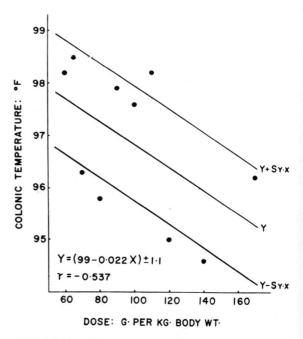

FIGURE 85. The regression of mean values for colonic temperature at 48 hr after oral administration of lethal doses of iron powder, on dose of administered iron. (From Boyd and Shanas[27] with the permission of *The Canadian Medical Association Journal*.)

powder produced a hypothermia which reached a peak at 48 hr and was dose dependent, as shown in Figure 85. Hypothermia was a premortem sign in most animals. It was marked at 48 hr in animals which received doses of iron in excess of 100 g/kg due to the fact that many rats given these doses were moribund at 48 hr. The immediate cause of death was respiratory failure.

Ferrous sulfate produces death in man at 4 to 6 hr after oral ingestion and preceded by nausea, vomiting, hematemesis, abdominal pain, diarrhea, lassitude, and collapse.[47] Death in man from ferrous sulfate may be delayed to 20 to 50 hr and follow shock. Ferrous sulfate produces similar signs of toxicity following oral administration of lethal doses to rats and dogs. Rats cannot vomit and ferrous sulfate produces death following convulsions in this species.[47]

Autopsy Findings

The gross pathological appearance of the gastrointestinal tract at death has been described above. Large doses of iron powder produced gastrointestinal obstruction and smaller doses an irritant gastroenteritis. There was an obvious stress reaction in the adrenal glands, spleen, and thymus gland and the liver had obviously lost weight, especially in delayed deaths. Residual carcass became increasingly more friable as death was prolonged.

Histological examination disclosed capillary-venous congestion of the lamina propria and submucosa of the gastrointestinal tract with varying degrees of mucosal necrosis. The sinusoids of the zona fasciculata, zona reticularis, and the medulla of the adrenal gland were congested, especially in delayed deaths. The red pulp of the spleen was contracted. The lobules and inter-lobular connective tissue of the thymus gland were congested and there was a loss of thymocytes, especially in delayed deaths. The hepatic cells were shrunken and the sinusoids distended with packed red blood cells. The kidneys were congested, especially in the region of the descending limb of Henle's loop. Congestion, venous thrombosis, and perivascular edema were found in the lungs. Minor degrees of congestion occurred in the heart and brain and there was loss of subcutaneous fat in the skin of animals which had delayed deaths. Skeletal muscle and testes appeared normal histologically.

Changes in the weight of body organs are summarized in Table 101. Loss of body weight was particularly marked in animals with delayed deaths due, at least in part, to the prolonged anorexia. There was a stressor gain in weight of the adrenal glands and loss in the spleen and thymus gland. Loss of weight was particularly marked in liver, kidneys, skin, muscle, and most parts of the gastrointestinal tract except cardiac stomach, which had undergone some hypertrophy to accommodate the large volume of administered iron powder suspension. Minor changes occurred in other organs, as listed in Table 101. There was residual loss of organ weight in survivors at two weeks, but at four weeks most weights had returned to normal.

Shifts in the water levels of body organs following oral administration of aqueous suspensions of iron powder in doses at the range of the LD_{50} are summarized in Table 102. At death, most organs were hydrated, some markedly so as in the instances of cecum, skeletal muscle, skin, and thymus gland. Loss of dry weight in these organs, therefore, was considerably greater than the loss of wet weight shown in Table 101. Hydration was particularly marked in animals with delayed deaths. In animals with early deaths, several organs were dehydrated such as brain, heart, kidneys, lungs, testes, and thymus gland. Water levels had returned to normal in survivors at two weeks after iron administration.

In summary, the LD_{50} of iron powder was approximately one tenth of body weight and the mean interval to death almost three days. The immediate cause of death was respiratory failure preceded by anorexia, oligodipsia, oliguria, alkalosis, diarrhea, loss of body weight, hypothermia, and alternating excitation and depression of the central nervous system. At death there was a marked local irritant reaction in the gastrointestinal tract and, when the dose of iron was higher than the LD_{50}, bowel obstruction from impacted metal powder. Apparently due to absorption of toxic amounts of iron, there was a widespread tissue inflammatory reaction, loss of organ weight, and, especially in delayed deaths, generalized tissue edema. In survivors, signs of toxicity were disappearing at two weeks and at four weeks measurements were normal.

The Absorption of Toxic Doses of Iron Powder

There were several aspects of the study of Boyd and Shanas,[27] cited above, which suggested that iron was absorbed when given in toxic oral doses to presumably iron saturated healthy young rats. This was theoretically possible through the inflamed lining of the gastrointestinal tract which could have destroyed in whole or in part the mucosal block which normally prevents absorption of more iron than is needed by the body.[10-12] In a subsequent study, Boyd and Shanas[28] reported that local inflammation of the gastrointestinal tract was produced by doses of 10 g/kg and over, but not under.

In 1968 Boyd and Shanas[31] reported the iron content of the carcass of albino rats at 48 hr after oral administration of a range of doses of iron powder. To avoid contamination by administered iron, the skin, head, tail, paws, and the entire gastrointestinal tract were removed prior to homogenization and iron estimation. The concentration of iron in control animals given no iron was subtracted from that in iron treated rats and the results are shown in Figure 86. It may be seen that iron was in fact absorbed and that the amount absorbed increased with increase in the toxic dose of iron administered. There was some indication that the amount absorbed would have been higher had analyses been made after 48 hr, as shown in Figure 87.

At 48 hr there was a marked increase in the iron content of blood in albino rats given toxic doses of iron powder, as shown in Figure 88. The excess iron was deposited in liver, kidney, and residual carcass. As indicated by data illustrated in Figure 89, most of the augmentation of levels of iron occurred within the first 24 hr. The regression lines in Figures 88 and 89 were calculated by solving the estimating equation $\log Y = [a + b \log (X + 1)] \pm S.E.$ For example, the estimating equation for blood in Figure 88 was found to be $\log Y = [2.34 + 0.05 \log (X + 1)] \pm 0.03$, its correlative coefficient was +0.77 and the probability (P) that the correlation coefficient is zero was 0.02. Equations for other regression lines shown in Figures 88 to 94 were tabulated by Boyd and Shanas.[28]

TABLE 101

Shifts in the Wet Weight of Body Organs of Young Male Albino Rats Following Oral Administration of Iron Powder Suspensions in Doses at the Range of the LD$_{50}$.[a]

Organ	At death		In survivors	
	Early	Delayed	At 2 weeks	At 4 weeks
Adrenal glands	+40.1*	+72.4*	+10.2	+ 2.7
Brain	− 2.3	− 4.0*	− 3.5	+ 2.9
Gastrointestinal tract				
Cardiac stomach	+13.4	+16.8	− 3.7	− 1.1
Pyloric stomach	−24.7*	−38.2*	−12.5*	+ 1.8
Small bowel	−26.2*	+ 2.7	− 9.9	− 9.1
Cecum	−26.6*	+ 3.7	− 1.8	− 3.5
Colon	−32.5*	−31.1*	− 8.1*	− 6.5
Heart	− 8.2	−18.1	−14.6*	− 1.1
Kidneys	−22.6*	−31.2*	−10.2*	+ 1.6
Liver	−41.1*	−50.4*	− 0.8	+ 6.3
Lungs	+ 3.2	+20.6	− 9.3	+33.3*
Muscle (abdominal wall)	−40.0*	−66.9*	−30.5*	−26.5
Skin	−27.5*	−39.1*	−31.9*	− 5.4
Spleen	−51.2*	−78.9*	−22.7*	+17.7
Testicles	+ 0.7	− 8.8*	−13.9*	− 7.4
Thymus gland	−57.2*	−76.3*	−28.3	−17.8
Residual carcass	−17.4	−35.0*	−22.2*	− 4.1

[a]Weight was measured as grams wet weight and the results are expressed as a mean percent change from controls given no iron, specifically as $[(\bar{X}i − \bar{X}c)/\bar{X}c] \times 100$, where $\bar{X}i$ represents the mean in the iron treated animals and $\bar{X}c$ in their corresponding controls given no iron. Differences between $\bar{X}i$ and $\bar{X}c$ which were significant at P = 0.05 or less, by a t test, are indicated by an asterisk. (From Boyd and Shanas[27] with the permission of The Canadian Medical Association Journal.)

TABLE 102

Shifts in the Water Content of Body Organs of Young Adult Male Albino Rats Following Oral Administration of an Aqueous Suspension of Iron Powder in Doses at the Range of the LD$_{50}$.[a]

Organ	At death		In survivors	
	Early	Delayed	At 2 weeks	At 4 weeks
Adrenal glands	+ 1.7	+53.8*	− 7.2	− 9.3
Brain	− 2.0*	+15.4	− 1.7	− 2.8*
Gastrointestinal tract				
Cardiac stomach	−11.2	+ 0.6	0.0	− 0.2
Pyloric stomach	+ 8.0	+16.6*	+ 2.0	+ 1.7
Small bowel	+21.1*	+40.0*	+ 4.1	+13.3*
Cecum	+16.1	+83.3*	+ 4.2	+ 2.4
Colon	− 4.2	+ 2.4	− 1.4	− 1.4
Heart	−10.6*	− 8.6	+ 1.7	− 0.9
Kidneys	− 6.0*	+ 2.8	+ 4.1	− 2.1
Liver	+ 5.3*	+13.1*	− 6.1	− 4.9
Lungs	−12.2*	+20.1*	− 1.1	+ 4.0
Muscle (abdominal wall)	+22.8*	+71.5*	+10.4	+22.3*
Skin	−20.8*	+84.5	+ 0.6	+ 8.3
Spleen	− 1.6	+ 9.3	0.0	+ 0.3
Testicles	−11.3*	− 9.4*	− 1.2	+ 0.1
Thymus gland	−13.3*	+87.9*	− 1.2	− 2.1
Residual carcass	+ 2.5	+40.6*	+ 8.6	+10.7

[a]Water levels were measured as grams water per 100 g dry weight of tissue and the results are expressed as a mean percent change from controls, specifically as $[(\bar{X}i − \bar{X}c)/\bar{X}c] \times 100$, where $\bar{X}i$ represents the mean in the iron treated animals and $\bar{X}c$ in their corresponding controls given no iron. Differences between $\bar{X}i$ and $\bar{X}c$ which were significant at P = 0.05 or less, by a t test, are indicated by an asterisk. (From Boyd and Shanas[27] with the permission of The Canadian Medical Association Journal.)

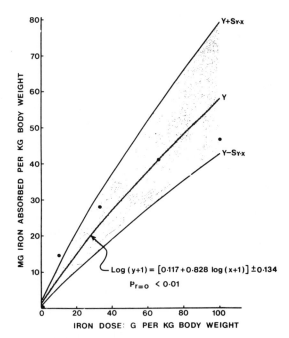

FIGURE 86. The regression of iron absorbed at 48 hr by albino rats on dose of iron powder given by stomach tube to overnight-fasted animals. (From Boyd and Shanas[31] with the permission of the *International Journal of Clinical Pharmacology, Therapy and Toxicology,* copyright © 1968, Urban and Schwarzenberg, Munich, Germany.)

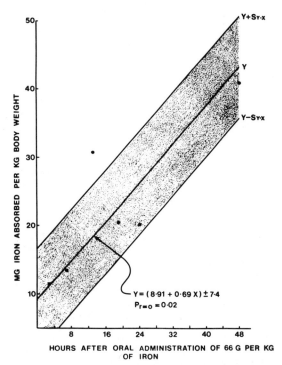

FIGURE 87. The regression of iron absorbed by albino rats on hours after oral administration of iron powder in a dose of 66 g/kg. (From Boyd and Shanas[31] with the permission of the *International Journal of Clinical Pharmacology, Therapy and Toxicology,* copyright © 1968, Urban and Schwarzenberg, Munich, Germany.)

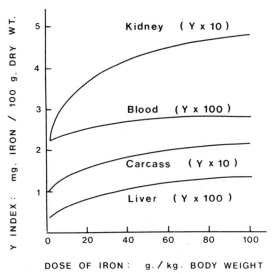

FIGURE 88. The regression, on dose of iron powder given 48 hr previously by stomach tube to albino rats, of concentration of iron in kidneys, blood, carcass, and liver. The Y index must be multiplied by the factors indicated in parentheses to obtain values for iron content. All regression lines were calculated from the equation log Y = a + b log (X + 1) and correlation coefficients were significant at P = 0.02 or less. (From Boyd and Shanas[28] with the permission of *The Canadian Medical Association Journal.*)

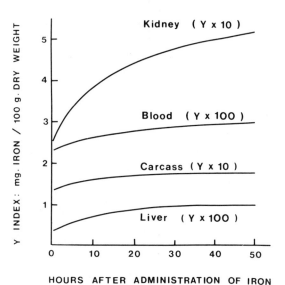

FIGURE 89. The regression, on hours after oral administration of iron powder in a dose of 66 g/kg to albino rats, of levels of iron in kidneys, blood, residual carcass, and liver. The Y index must be multiplied by the factors indicated in parentheses to obtain values for iron content. (From Boyd and Shanas[28] with the permission of *The Canadian Medical Association Journal.*)

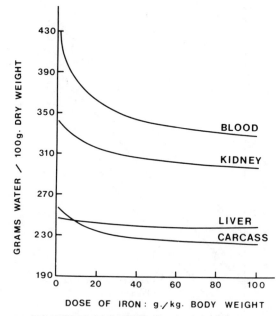

FIGURE 90. The regression, on dose of iron powder given by stomach tube 48 hr previously to albino rats, of concentration of water in the blood, kidneys, liver, and carcass. (From Boyd and Shanas[28] with the permission of *The Canadian Medical Association Journal.*)

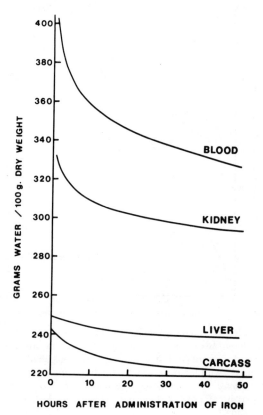

FIGURE 91. The regression, on hours after oral administration of iron powder in a dose of 66 g/kg to albino rats, of levels of water in blood, kidneys, liver, and carcass. (From Boyd and Shanas[28] with the permission of *The Canadian Medical Association Journal.*)

Accompanying the increase in levels of iron, there was a decrease in levels of water. The relationship of levels of water to dose of administered iron powder is exemplified in Figure 90 and to interval after administration in Figure 91. Estimating equations were similar to those calculated for data illustrated in Figures 88 and 89 except that each was minus, rather than plus, log (X + 1). Estimating equations were tabulated, with correlation coefficients and P values, by Boyd and Shanas.[28] All correlation coefficients were significant at P = 0.05 or less, except that of the regression for water levels of liver shown in Figure 91 which was statistically insignificant. When it was found that toxic doses of iron had produced these shifts in tissue water content, iron levels were calculated as mg per 100 g weight, as shown in Figures 88 and 89.

The inverse relationship between levels of iron and levels of water is exemplified for blood in Figure 92. These results, in turn, suggested that as levels of iron increased in blood there followed a hemoconcentration. To find if such were correct, Boyd and Shanas[28] measured the hematocrit, erythrocyte count, and blood hemoglobin levels; exemplary results are shown in Figures 93 and 94.

It may be seen that measurements of these parameters increased with increase in the concentration of iron (compare Figure 93 with Figure 89) and decreased with increase in the levels of blood water (Figure 94).

Boyd and Shanas[28] reported that increase in the concentration of blood iron, following oral administration of toxic doses of iron powder to albino rats, was not accompanied by an increase in the concentration of blood transferrin. Bothwell and Finch[54] noted that iron absorbed into the bloodstream following oral administration of toxic doses of ferrous sulfate was loosely bound to albumin and globulin. Boyd and Shanas[28] found that, at 48 hr after oral administration of an LD$_{50}$ of iron powder to albino rats, the liver contained over four times its normal amount of iron. The excess iron was seen to be diffusely deposited as ferric iron in the periportal zone of the liver.

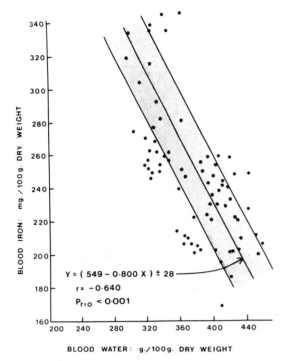

FIGURE 92. The regression, on blood water levels at 48 hr after oral administration of iron powder in a range of toxic doses to albino rats, of values for the iron content of blood in mg/100g dry weight of blood. (From Boyd and Shanas[28] with the permission of *The Canadian Medical Association Journal*.)

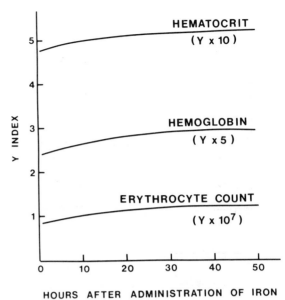

FIGURE 93. The regression, on hours after oral administration of iron powder in a dose of 66 g/kg to albino rats, of values for the hematocrit (volume of erythrocytes as percent of total blood volume), blood hemoglobin (as g/100 ml of blood), and erythrocyte count (as cells per mm³ of blood). The Y index must be multiplied by the factors indicated in parentheses to obtain the measured units of each parameter. (From Boyd and Shanas[28] with the permission of *The Canadian Medical Association Journal*.)

Deposit of iron in the liver produced hepatic congestion which accounted for some of the increase in liver iron.

While toxic doses of iron powder given by stomach tube apparently broke the mucosal barrier to absorption of iron in the gastrointestinal tract, destruction of the mucosal barrier was by no means complete. Boyd and Shanas[28] calculated that only about 0.3% of an acute oral LD$_{50}$ of iron powder was actually absorbed by albino rats. This small percentage, however, was sufficient to produce hemoconcentration and death.

It should be emphasized again that death from iron powder is produced only by huge oral doses which would never be given to man for therapeutic purposes. Boyd and Shanas[28] estimated that early signs of toxicity might be produced in man from oral administration of iron powder in a dose of 10 g/kg. This would correspond to 700 g of iron powder given at one time to an adult weighing 70 kg. As previously noted, the usual therapeutic dose is 2.5 g of iron powder per day which is equivalent to 0.04 g/kg or 0.004 of the minimal toxic dose.

These studies suggest that iron powder is by far the safest form of iron for the treatment of iron deficiency anemia.

The Toxicity of Large Amounts of Tissue Iron

The studies of Boyd and Shanas[27,28] suggest that amounts of iron of the order of 0.3 g/kg would kill 50% of albino rats when absorbed and retained in the body. Boyd, Hitsman, and Perry[16] measured the storage and elimination of a total dose of 378 mg of iron per kg body weight injected intramuscularly into albino rats over a period of 44 days. The iron was given as solutions in distilled water of either iron and ammonium citrate, U.S.P. XII, or of iron phosphogluconate (Des Bergers-Bismal Laboratories, Montreal, Quebec, Canada). Clinical signs and the output of iron in urine and feces were recorded daily or as indicated. At the end of the 44 days, the rats were autopsied and tissue iron estimated.

Almost all of the iron given intramuscularly was retained in the animals' body. A small amount of 1

197

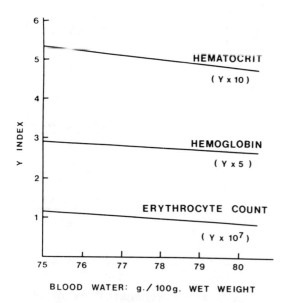

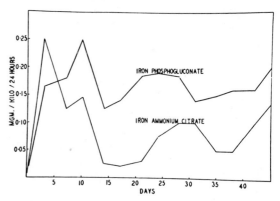

FIGURE 95. The excretion of iron in the urine of albino rats given a total of 378 mg of iron per kg body weight intramuscularly, over a period of 44 days, as either iron phosphogluconate or iron and ammonium citrate. (From Boyd et al.[16] with the permission of *Revue Canadienne de Biologie.*)

FIGURE 94. The regression, on levels of blood water in albino rats, of values for the hematocrit (volume of erythrocytes as percent of total blood volume), concentration of blood hemoglobin (g/100 ml of blood), and the erythrocyte count (cells per mm^3 of blood) after oral administration of iron powder in a dose of 66 g/kg. The Y index must be multiplied by the factor indicated in parentheses to obtain units of each parameter. (From Boyd and Shanas[28] with the permission of *The Canadian Medical Association Journal.*)

to 3% was eliminated in urine, as illustrated in Figure 95. At 44 days, 5% of the animals that had been given iron and ammonium citrate and 60% of those that received iron phosphogluconate had died. There were no deaths in the controls given

no iron. The iron phosphogluconate was soluble in water with some difficulty and it produced an extensive necrosis of tissue at the site of intramuscular injection. Necrosis at the site of injection has been reported for other iron compounds by Brownlee et al.[55] While death rates vary, these studies confirm those of Boyd and Shanas[27,28] that when iron in the body tissues of animals is retained in amounts of 0.3 to 0.4 g/kg above normal concentrations death may ensue.

The normal concentration of iron in body tissues was determined by Boyd et al.[16] and the results are summarized in Table 103. Of the tissues analyzed, the highest concentration was in liver

TABLE 103

The Mean Iron Content of the Tissues of Albino Rats Following Intramuscular Injection of 378 mg of Iron per kg Body Weight over a Period of 44 Days (as Iron and Ammonium Citrate or as Iron Phosphogluconate)

Tissue	Control	Iron ammonium citrate	Iron phosphogluconate
Liver	104.1	1,285	593
Gut	26.6	167	51.2
Injected leg	21.4	469	1,014
Skeletal muscles	18.1	42.7	40.0
Bone	10.1	48.8	28.2
Residual carcass	16.3	64.9	38.8

The results are expressed as the mean concentration of iron in mg/100 g dry weight of tissue. (From Boyd et al.[16] with the permission of *Revue Canadienne de Biologie.*)

and the lowest in bone. The total percentage of normal body iron in the liver was calculated to be 26 with 74% in the rest of the body.[16] As indicated by data in Table 104, the bulk of extra iron is concentrated in the liver. It may also be calculated from data in Table 104 that iron injected intramuscularly into albino rats in eliminated from the body at a very slow rate of about 7.5% per year.

Conclusions Regarding Iron Powder

The acute oral LD_{50} of iron powder is of the order of 10% of body weight which is much higher than that of salts of iron. Death occurs in two to four days from (a) absorption of toxic amounts of iron when given in doses below the LD_{50} or (b) from bowel obstruction due to larger amounts of administered iron powder. Soluble salts of iron produce death within a few hours.

The clinical signs of toxicity to iron powder consist of an initial depression of the central nervous system, anorexia, oligodipsia, oliguria, alkalinuria, hypothermia, and loss of body weight. When bowel obstruction was present, no stools were passed and when absent there was diarrhea. The immediate cause of death was respiratory failure following hemoconcentration.

At autopsy there was found a marked local irritant gastroenteritis with or without bowel obstruction. About 0.3% of the LD_{50} was absorbed and produced tissue inflammatory reactions with loss of weight in most body organs. Dehydration accompanied early deaths and hydration late deaths. Iron was stored in a variety of body tissues. At one and a half months 98 to 99% of the absorbed iron was still present in body tissues of survivors.

TABLE 104

A Balance Sheet of the Fate of Iron Injected Intramuscularly into Albino Rats as Iron and Ammonium Citrate

	Body weight mg/kg	Percent of total injected iron
Total iron injected	378	100%
Disposal of injected iron		
Lost in urine	3.5	0.9%
Stored in liver	222	58.8%
Stored in gut	9.0	2.4%
Stored in injected leg	63	16.6%
Stored in residual carcass	68	18.0%
Unaccounted for	12.5	3.3%
Total disposal of iron	378	100.0%

(From Boyd et al.[55] with the permission of *Revue Canadienne de Biologie*.)

REFERENCES

1. **Stecker, P. G., Windholtz, M., Leahy, D. S., Bolton, D. M., and Eaton, L. G.,** *The Merck Index. An Encyclopedia of Chemicals and Drugs,* 8th ed., Merck and Company, Rahway, N.J., 1968.
2. **Hawkins, W. W.,** Iron, copper and cobalt, in *Nutrition. A Comprehensive Treatise,* Vol. 1, Beaton, G. H. and McHenry, E. W., Eds., Academic Press, New York, 1964, Chap. 6, 309.
3. **D'Arcy, P. F. and Howard, E. M.,** Iron therapy. The history and hazards of iron medication, *Pharm. J.,* 189, 223, 1962.
4. **Read, H. C.,** Iron therapy, *Can. Med. Assoc. J.,* 92, 1219, 1965.
5. **Christian, H. A.,** A sketch of the history of the treatment of chlorosis with iron, *Med. Lib. Hist. J.,* 1, 176, 1903.
6. **Hadén, R. L.,** Historical aspects of iron therapy in anemia, *Am. Med. Assoc. J.,* 111, 1059, 1938.
7. **Greenhill, T.,** *The Works of Thomas Sydenham,* The Sydenham Society, R.G. Latham, London, 1850.
8. **Blaud, P.,** Sur les maladies chloratique, et sur un mode de traitement specifique dans ces affections, *Rev. Med. Franc. Etrang.* (Paris), 1, 337, 1832.
9. **Shanas, M. N.,** The Acute Oral Toxicity of Reduced Iron Powder, M.Sc. Thesis in Pharmacology, Douglas Library, Queen's University, Kingston, Ontario, Canada, 1968.
10. **Boyd, E. M.,** A theory of the absorption of iron, *Fed. Proc.,* 3, 60, 1944.

11. Hahn, P. F., Metabolism of iron, *Fed. Proc.,* 7, 493, 1948.
12. Charlton, R. W., Jacobs, P., Torrance, J. D., and Bothwell, T. N., The role of the intestinal mucosa in iron absorption, *J. Clin. Invest.,* 44, 543, 1965.
13. Wheby, M. S. and Jones, L. G., Role of transferrin in iron absorption, *J. Clin. Invest.,* 42, 1007, 1963.
14. Mendel, G. A., Iron metabolism and etiology of iron-storage disease, *Am. Med. Assoc. J.,* 189, 45, 1964.
15. McCance, R. A. and Widdowson, E. M., Absorption and excretion of iron, *Lancet,* 233, 680, 1937.
16. Boyd, E. M., Hitsman, J. S., and Perry, W. F., Storage and elimination of iron compounds injected intramuscularly into albino rats, *Rev. Can. Biol.,* 3, 294, 1944.
17. Darby, W. J., Iron and copper, *Am. Med. Assoc. J.,* 142, 1288, 1950.
18. Conrad, M. E., Weintraub, L. R., and Crosby, W. H., The role of the intestine in iron kinetics, *J. Clin. Invest.,* 43, 963, 1964.
19. Drabkin, D. L., Metabolism of hemin chromoproteins, *Physiol. Rev.,* 31, 345, 1951.
20. Finch, C. A., Body iron exchange in man, *J. Clin. Invest.,* 38, 392, 1959.
21. Bethel, F. H., Goldhammer, S. M., Isaacs, R., and Sturgis, C. C., The diagnosis and treatment of the iron deficiency anemia, *Am. Med. Assoc. J.,* 103, 797, 1934.
22. Strauss, M. B., The use of drugs in the treatment of anemia, *Am. Med. Assoc. J.,* 107, 1633, 1936.
23. Alstead, G., Chlorosis, *Am. J. Med. Sci.,* 201, 1, 1941.
24. Krantz, J. C., Carr, C. J., and La Du, B. N., Jr., *The Pharmacologic Principles of Medical Practice,* 7th ed., Williams and Wilkins, Baltimore, 1969.
25. Goodman, L. S. and Gilman, A., *The Pharmacological Basis of Therapeutics,* 2nd ed., Macmillan, New York, 1955.
26. Boyd, E. M. and Shanas, M. N., The acute oral toxicity of reduced iron, N. F., in the albino rat, *Pharmacologist,* 5, 231, 1963.
27. Boyd, E. M. and Shanas, M. N., The acute oral toxicity of reduced iron, *Can. Med. Assoc. J.,* 89, 171, 1963.
28. Boyd, E. M. and Shanas, M. N., Studies on the low toxicity of reduced iron, B.P. 1932, *Can. Med. Assoc. J.,* 96, 1141, 1967.
29. Boyd, E. M., Reduced Iron, B.P. 1932, *Can. Med. Assoc. J.,* 97, 1547, 1967.
30. Shanas, M. N. and Boyd, E. M., Medicinal iron powder from 1681 to 1968, *Toxicol. Appl. Pharmacol.,* 11, 292, 1968.
31. Boyd, E. M. and Shanas, M. N., Ferrum redactum, B.P. 1932, *Int. J. Clin. Pharmacol. Ther. Toxicol.,* 1, 226, 1968.
32. Shanas, M. N. and Boyd, E. M., Powdered iron from 1681 to 1968, *Clin. Toxicol.,* 2, 37, 1969.
33. Henderson, V. E. and Lucas, G. H. W., On the absorption of iron. *Am. J. Dig. Dis.,* 11, 244, 1944.
34. American Pharmaceutical Association, *The National Formulary,* 9th ed., Mack Publishing Co., Easton, Pa., 1950.
35. Moon, C. V. and Dubach, R., Metabolism and requirements of iron in the human, *J.A.M.A.,* 162, 197, 1956.
36. *British Pharmacopoeia,* General Council of Medical Education and Registration of the United Kingdom, London, 1932.
37. *The Pharmacopeia of the United States of America,* United States Pharmacopeial Convention, 1942.
38. *State Pharmacopeia of the U.S.S.R.,* 8th ed., Ministry of Public Health of the U.S.S.R., Moscow, about 1945.
39. *The Pharmacopoeia of Japan,* 6th ed., Ministry of Health and Welfare, Tokyo, 1951.
40. Martindale, W., *The Extra Pharmacopoeia,* 24th ed., The Pharmaceutical Press, London, 1958.
41. Meulengracht, E., Large doses of iron in the different kinds of anemia in a medical department, *Acta Med. Scand.,* 58, 594, 1923.
42. Martin, E. W., Cook, E. F., Leuallen, E. M., Osol, A., Tice, L. F., and Van Meter, C. T., *Remington's Practise of Pharmacy,* 12th ed., Mack Publishing Co., Easton, Pa., 1961.
43. Goth, A., *Medical Pharmacology,* 3rd ed., C.V. Mosby Co., St. Louis, Mo., 1966.
44. Salter, W. T., *A Textbook of Pharmacology,* W. B. Saunders, Philadelphia, 1952.
45. Sollman, T., *A Manual of Pharmacology,* 7th ed., W. B. Saunders, Philadelphia, 1948.
46. Grollman, A., *Pharmacology and Therapeutics,* 5th ed., Lea and Febiger, Philadelphia, 1962.
47. Hoppe, J. O., Marcelli, G. M. A., and Tainter, M. L., A review of the toxicity of iron compounds, *Am. J. Med. Sci.,* 230, 558, 1955.
48. Spector, W. S., Ed., *Handbook of Toxicology,* Vol. 1, W. B. Saunders, Philadelphia, 1956.
49. Weaver, L. C., Gardier, R. W., Robinson, V. B., and Bunde, C. A., Comparative toxicology of iron compounds, *Am. J. Med. Sci.,* 241, 296, 1961.
50. Thomson, J., Top cases of ferrous sulphate poisoning, *Br. Med. J.,* 1, 640, 1947.
51. Editorial, Acute iron poisoning in children, *Can. Med. Assoc. J.,* 66, 278, 1952.
52. Report of the Committee on Toxicology of the American Medical Association, Accidental Iron Poisoning in Children, *J. Am. Med. Assoc.,* 170, 676, 1959.
53. Gatenby, P. B., The treatment of iron deficiency, *Postgrad. Med. J.,* 35, 13, 1959.
54. Bothwell, T. H. and Finch, C. A., *Iron Metabolism,* Little, Brown and Company, Boston, 1962, 350.
55. Brownlee, G., Bainbridge, H. W., and Thorp, R. H., Pharmacology of iron in parenteral treatment, *Quart. J. Pharm. Pharmacol.,* 15, 148, 1942.

Chapter 18

SILICATES AND INSOLUBLE SALTS

Silicon is one of the most common ingredients of rocks and clay and, as such, appreciable amounts may be ingested in the diet. Silicon exists in two main forms, as silica or silicon dioxide and as silicates such as kaolin which is a hydrated aluminum silicate $(H_2Al_2Si_2O_8 \cdot H_2O)$. Silica is of interest toxicologically because of the production of pulmonary silicosis from inhalations of silica dusts.[1] Attention will be restricted in this chapter to silicates, using kaolin as an example, and to barium sulfate as an example of other insoluble salts. The acute oral toxicity of kaolin has been described by Boyd, Covert, and Shanas.[2]

Kaolin

As noted in Chapter 6, in the 16th to 19th centuries it was commonly believed that if pregnant women ate clay they would have beautiful babies.[3] Lawson and Moon[4] and Griffith[5] reported that certain tribes in South America and Africa eat clay, mostly kaolin, as part of their regular diet. Cohn et al.[6] found a silica-like granuloma in the stomach of a patient who had used large amounts of kaolin to relieve gastric pain, nausea, and vomiting. They attempted to reproduce the condition in rabbits, but were unsuccessful until they injected kaolin into the gastric mucosa. Wilson[7] fed mice a diet high in bentonite $(Al_2O_3 \cdot 4SiO_2 \cdot H_2O)$ or wilkinite, a colloidal aluminum silicate that occurs in mid-western Canada and the U.S.,[8] and found that growth was inhibited. In a later communication, Wilson[9] noted that the mice fed bentonite develop hepatomas which were found to be due, at least in part, to a choline deficiency in these animals. While excessive intake of kaolin may lead to accumulation in the intestinal tract, Sollmann[10] concluded that "serious trouble is exceptional."

Silica given orally in doses up to 2 g/kg/day has been found by Gye and Purdy[11] to have no effect on mice, rats, guinea pigs, rabbits, and monkeys. In rats, a diet high in silica has been reported to augment the silica content of liver, spleen, and testes, suggesting that at least some of the silica is absorbed.[12] On the other hand, Bertke[13]

obtained no evidence of increase in the silica content of the liver and spleen of rats fed silica-containing diatomaceous earth.

Boyd, Covert, and Shanas[2] determined the acute oral LD_{50} of kaolin in albino rats and recorded the associated clinicopathological syndrome of toxicity. When it was found that huge doses of kaolin had to be given intragastrically, small male rats, weighing 90 to 100 g, were selected for the study since their stomach is a relatively larger proportion of body weight than that of adult rats. The small animals could accommodate the large doses of kaolin better than larger animals in which gastric rupture was fairly common. Food, but not water, was withdrawn for 16 hr (overnight) before kaolin administration.

When kaolin was given through a stomach tube as large volumes of a thin suspension in distilled water, the suspension was regurgitated and aspirated into the lungs, producing death by obstructive asphyxia. Pilot studies indicated that aspiration was reduced to a minimum by concentrating the suspension. Boyd et al.[2] found that a suspension containing 100 g of kaolin in distilled water to a final volume of 100 ml was the most concentrated form in which the agent could be forced through the stomach tubes. To avoid local and systemic effects from cooling, the suspension was warmed to body temperature before intragastric administration.

The definitive doses of kaolin selected by Boyd et al.[2] extended from 100 to 210 g/kg administered slowly over an interval of 3 hr. These doses were given, therefore, with increasing amounts of distilled water because it was not possible to keep the volume constant for reasons noted above. Ferguson[14] reported that some 12 drugs were more toxic the greater the volume of water per kg body weight in which they were given orally to animals. Constantopoulos and Boyd[15] recorded a similar relationship with respect to the oral toxicity of sucrose in albino rats. Boyd[16] has reviewed other evidence and explained that augmentation of toxicity is due to a combination of the toxic effects of water with those of the agent suspended or dissolved in the distilled water. The largest volume of distilled water used in preparing the kaolin suspension was about one third the acute oral LD_{50} of distilled water reported by Boyd and Godi.[17] Death from distilled water occurs in the first few hours following oral administration. Death from bowel obstruction due to oral administration of kaolin occurred at two to three days. Some of the initial signs of toxicity, therefore, may have been due to the large volume of distilled water needed for the kaolin suspensions but the final obstructive death was probably due entirely to kaolin. Clinical signs of toxicity were recorded daily for five days and then occasionally for one month. Autopsies were performed on animals that died, and upon survivors at two weeks and one month.

Clinical Signs of Kaolin Toxicity

Animals that had mechanical deaths due to aspiration asphyxia or gastric rupture were excluded by Boyd et al.[2] in arriving at an estimate of the LD_{50} of kaolin. The calculated value of the acute oral $LD_{50} \pm$ S.E. was 148.5 ± 16.8 g of kaolin per kg body weight. The estimated LD_1 was 110 g/kg and the LD_{99} 188 g/kg. The mean $\pm$ standard deviation interval to death was 43 ± 15 hr and the interval was not dose dependent over the range of doses employed. When the suspension of kaolin was reduced to 50 g per 100 ml of distilled water, most of the animals died within a few minutes due to aspiration asphyxia. When the 100% (w/v) suspension was rapidly administered, most of the animals died at 12 to 16 hr from gastric rupture.

The initial signs of intoxication were gagging, retching, tenseness, abdominal muscular fasciculations, listlessness, hyporeflexia, and pallor.[2] These signs, particularly the muscular twitchings, appeared to be due to the marked distension of the stomach which is illustrated in Figure 96. There was 50% incidence of rats with convulsive movements during the first 5 hr after kaolin administration. Distilled water produces convulsions so that the convulsive movements were probably due, in part at least, to the large volume of distilled water given with the kaolin.

All rats were alive at 24 hr but were pale, drowsy, and listless. The paws were dry, there was a brownish incrustation about the nose and mouth, and the animals had developed a blood tinged diarrhea. When the weight of administered kaolin was subtracted from body weight, it was found that the animals had lost weight, as shown

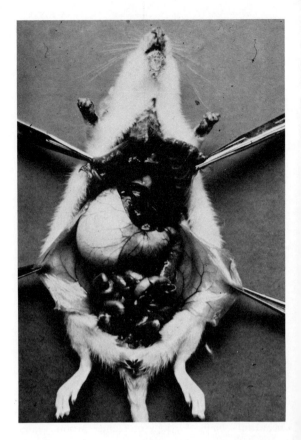

FIGURE 96. A photograph illustrating the marked distension of the stomach produced by oral administration of doses of kaolin at the range of the LD_{50} to albino rats. (From Boyd et al.[2] with the permission of *Industrial Medicine and Surgery*, copyright © 1965, Industrial Medicine Publishing Co., Miami, Fla.)

in Figure 97. Loss of weight was due in part at least to a decrease in food and water intake and was accompanied by hypothermia. As exemplified in Figure 98, there were an aciduria, oliguria, and a decreased output of urinary glucose and protein at 24 hr. At this time about one third of the administered dose of kaolin had been eliminated in the feces, as shown in Figure 99. Just before death all of these signs became marked and in addition there occurred glucosuria, proteinuria, and dyspnea. The immediate cause of death was respiratory failure.

Autopsy Observations in Kaolin Deaths

The outstanding feature seen at autopsy on rats that died from oral administration of lethal doses of kaolin was bowel obstruction. Kaoliths appeared as hard, crescent shaped masses at intervals along the small bowel, as illustrated in

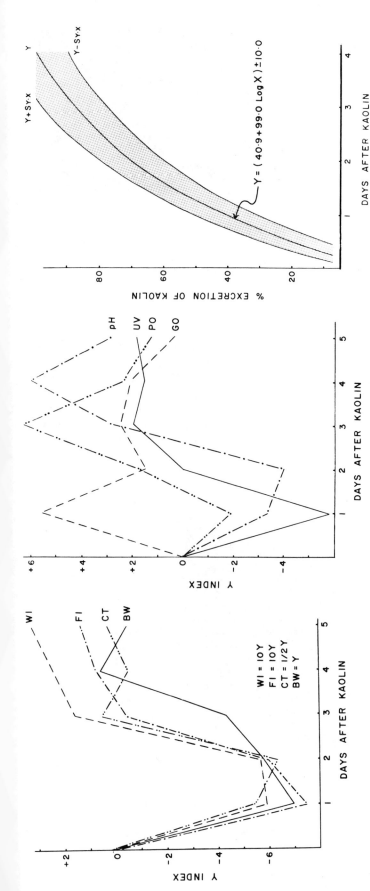

FIGURE 97. The regression, on days after oral administration of kaolin to albino rats in doses at the range of the LD_{50}, of changes in water intake (WI), food intake (FI), colonic temperature (CT), and body weight (BW). Changes were calculated as mean percentage differences from controls given no kaolin. The Y index must be multiplied by the factors indicated (e.g., WI = 10 times the Y index) to obtain the mean percentage changes. (From Boyd et al.[2] with the permission of *Industrial Medicine and Surgery*, copyright © 1965, Industrial Medicine Publishing Co., Miami, Fla.)

FIGURE 98. The regression, on days after administration of toxic doses of kaolin to albino rats, of mean percentage changes in urinary pH, volume (UV), protein output (PO), and glucose output (GO). Changes were calculated as mean percentage differences from controls given no kaolin. The Y index must be multiplied by 3 to obtain mean percentage changes in pH, by 20 for UV, by 60 for PO, and by 1,000 for GO. (From Boyd et al.[2] with the permission of *Industrial Medicine and Surgery*, copyright © 1965, Industrial Medicine Publishing Co., Miami, Fla.)

FIGURE 99. The regression, on days after administration of toxic doses of kaolin to albino rats, of percentage elimination of the agent in the feces. (From Boyd et al.[2] with the permission of *Industrial Medicine and Surgery*, copyright © 1965, Industrial Medicine Publishing Co., Miami, Fla.)

$$Y = (40 \cdot 9 + 99 \cdot 0 \log X) \pm 10 \cdot 0$$

203

Figure 100. When impaction occurred in the cecum and colon, the whole of the lumen was usually distended with a hard mass of the agent, as illustrated in Figure 101. There was a dose dependent relationship between bowel obstruction and amount of administered kaolin. The larger the dose of kaolin, the further the drug had advanced along the gastrointestinal tract and the further along the tract was bowel obstruction noted. This relationship is illustrated in Figure 102.

Other pathological signs of kaolin intoxication seen on gross observation of body organs at death included congestion and hemorrhage of all parts of the gastrointestinal tract. The adrenal glands were enlarged and congested and the spleen and thymus gland were atrophied. The liver was small and pale.

Histopathology in Kaolin Deaths

Microscopic examination of the gastrointestinal tract disclosed that the stratified squamous epithelium of the cardiac stomach was stretched and necrotic. There was a marked capillary-venous vasodilatation and leukocytic infiltration of all layers of cardiac stomach, including the subserous layer. In the pyloric or glandular stomach, there was also congestion of all layers with leukocytic infiltration. The gastric glands were relatively

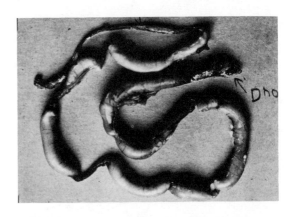

FIGURE 100. A photograph of the small intestine of an albino rat that died of bowel obstruction following oral administration of lethal doses of kaolin, showing crescent-shaped masses impacted at intervals along the gut. (From Boyd et al.[2] with the permission of *Industrial Medicine and Surgery,* copyright © 1965, Industrial Medicine Publishing Co., Miami, Fla.)

normal with an occasional ulceration. As kaolin left the stomach, healing occurred under a blanket of mucus with a few residual ulcers left in both parts of the stomach.

As the kaolin passed down the small bowel, the wall became distended and thin and the villi were tightly pressed against the remainder of the bowel

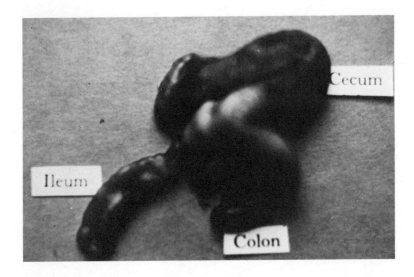

FIGURE 101. A photograph of the cecum and colon removed from an albino rat that died from oral administration of lethal doses of kaolin, showing impaction and distension of the affected parts. (From Boyd et al.[2] with the permission of *Industrial Medicine and Surgery,* copyright © 1965, Industrial Medicine Publishing Co., Miami, Fla.)

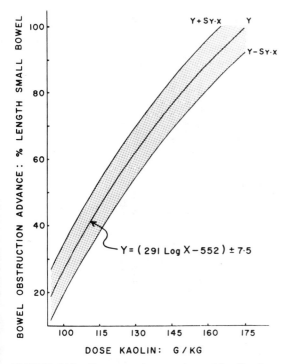

FIGURE 102. The regression, on dose of kaolin given orally to albino rats, of the advance of bowel obstruction observed at autopsy. (From Boyd et al.[2] with the permission of *Industrial Medicine and Surgery*, copyright © 1965, Industrial Medicine Publishing Co., Miami, Fla.)

tissues. Some denuding of the surface epithelium of the villi was noted. At the site of impaction, the bowel was avascular due to compression of the blood vessels by the kaolith. At each end of the kaolith, the bowel was congested and hemorrhagic. The kaolith itself acquired a coating of mucus. As it passed down the small intestine, healing occurred behind it. The mesentery was markedly congested. Passage of the kaolith through the cecum and colon was accompanied by similar reactions, although somewhat less marked, particularly in the colon.

Histopathology was of a minor nature in other body organs. The adrenal glands were enlarged and congested. The thymus gland was atrophied. The spleen was avascular and the red pulp shrunken. The cytoplasm of the hepatic cells was shrunken and there were venous stasis and thrombosis. There were areas of cloudy swelling in the renal tubules with venous thrombosis. Venous stasis and thrombosis were also present in the heart, lungs, testes, and brain.

The cause of death appeared to be respiratory failure secondary to vascular stasis and thrombosis

which in turn was due to the bowel obstruction and irritation.

Organ Weights and Water Content in Kaolin Intoxication

Data on organ wet weights are summarized in Table 105 from information provided by Boyd et al.[2] and on organ water levels in Table 106. At the time of death (data recorded as 'at 2 days' in Tables 105 and 106), there was loss of body weight due largely to loss of weight in skin and probably in muscle, although samples of skeletal muscle were not weighed at death. There was evidence of a stress reaction in the form of an increase in weight of the adrenal glands and loss of weight in spleen and thymus gland. There was an increase in weight of the cardiac stomach and small bowel due mostly to a marked increase in the water content of these organs. At two weeks and at one month after administration of kaolin, organ weights of survivors were essentially within the range of values in controls given no kaolin.

The water content of most body organs was elevated at death due to oral administration of lethal doses of kaolin. This was probably due to the large volume of distilled water administered with the kaolin. As may be seen from data exemplified in Figure 98, there was an oliguria at 24 hr with a return to normal at 48 hr in urinary volume. It would appear that this combination of events led to an increase in organ water levels. Augmentation of water content was most marked in the adrenal glands, cardiac stomach, small bowel, cecum, skin, spleen, and thymus gland. Some of the increase in wet weight of the adrenal glands must have been due to hydration of the organ. On the other hand, loss of dry weight in the spleen and thymus gland must have been greater than loss of wet weight shown in Table 105. At two weeks and at one month, the organ water levels of survivors had returned to values in the controls given no kaolin.

In summary, therefore, death from bowel obstruction was produced by the intragastric administration of kaolin at an $LD_{50} \pm S.E.$ of 149 $\pm$ 17 g/kg. The technique required that kaolin suspensions in distilled water be given slowly, to avoid gastric rupture, and at sufficient concentration that regurgitation, inhalation, and asphyxia did not occur. The mean $\pm$ standard deviation interval to death was 43 $\pm$ 15 hr. Death was due to respiratory failure following signs of depression of

TABLE 105

Shifts in the Wet Weight of Body Organs of Albino Rats Given Doses of Kaolin at the Range of the Acute Oral LD$_{50}$[a]

Organ	At 2 days	Survivors at 2 weeks	Survivors at 1 month
Adrenal glands	+19.2*	− 7.9	+ 2.3
Brain	+ 3.6	− 0.6	0.6
Gastrointestinal tract			
Cardiac stomach	+16.6*	+ 0.1	− 0.2
Pyloric stomach	+ 4.8	− 0.1	−10.5
Small bowel	+37.1**	− 4.8	+18.1
Cecum	−12.5	+10.3	− 2.0
Colon	+ 1.1	−14.0*	− 2.7
Heart	− 5.3	− 5.5	− 2.2
Kidneys	− 4.3	− 6.2	0.0
Liver	− 8.3	− 9.1	+ 8.6
Lungs	− 5.0	−15.8**	−20.0*
Muscle (ventral abdominal wall)		−17.8	+ 9.2
Skin	− 9.4**	− 0.8	+ 0.2
Spleen	−24.3*	− 6.7	−21.5*
Testes	+10.9	+ 6.0	− 8.2
Thymus gland	−28.1*	+ 2.2	+30.2*
Residual carcass	− 8.1**	− 6.4	− 5.3

[a]Weight was measured as grams wet weight. The results are expressed as a percent change from controls, specifically as $[(\bar{X}_d - \bar{X}_c)/\bar{X}_c] \times 100$, where $\bar{X}_d$ is the mean in the drug treated rats and $\bar{X}_c$ in the controls. Differences between $\bar{X}_d$ and $\bar{X}_c$ significant at $P = 0.05$ to 0.02 are indicated by one asterisk and at $P = 0.01$ or less by two asterisks.

(From Boyd et al.[2] with the permission of *Industrial Medicine and Surgery*, copyright © 1965, Industrial Medicine Publishing Co., Miami, Fla.)

TABLE 106

Shifts in the Water Content of Body Organs of Albino Rats Given Doses cf Kaolin in the Range of the Acute Oral LD$_{50}$[a]

Organ	At 2 days	at 2 weeks	at 1 month
Adrenal glands	+33.3**	+ 0.4	+ 0.4
Brain	+ 0.8	− 1.1	+ 1.4
Gastrointestinal tract			
Cardiac stomach	+17.6**	− 0.1	+ 0.1
Pyloric stomach	+ 6.3	+ 3.8	− 4.3
Small bowel	+29.2**	+ 3.7	+ 3.6
Cecum	+ 9.2**	+ 3.7	+ 2.7
Colon	+12.9	− 3.6	− 6.8
Heart	+ 0.8	+ 0.8	− 0.3
Kidneys	− 0.3	+ 0.6	+ 5.7
Liver	+ 8.9	+10.8*	+ 2.4
Lungs	+ 1.9	+ 1.9	− 0.8
Muscle (ventral abdominal wall)	+ 7.2	+18.8*	− 7.8
Skin	+17.8**	− 5.9	− 4.7
Spleen	+14.3**	+ 0.1	+ 3.4
Testes	+ 0.8	− 1.9	− 3.5
Thymus gland	+20.2**	+ 6.2	+ 0.6
Residual carcass	− 2.8	+ 6.2	+11.7*

[a]Water levels were measured as grams water per 100 g dry weight of tissue. The results are expressed as a percent change from controls, specifically as $[(\bar{X}_d - \bar{X}_c)\bar{X}_c] \times 100$, where $\bar{X}_d$ is the mean in the drug treated rats and $\bar{X}_c$ in the controls. Differences between $\bar{X}_d$ and $\bar{X}_c$ significant at $P = 0.05$ to 0.02 are indicated by one asterisk and at $P = 0.01$ or less by two asterisks.

(From Boyd et al.[2] with the permission of *Industrial Medicine ard Surgery*, copyright © 1965, Industrial Medicine Publishing Co., Miami, Fla.)

the central nervous system, perinasobuccal incrustations, anorexia, hypothermia, and signs of renal and metabolic failure. At autopsy, death was found to be due to bowel obstruction associated with venous stasis and thrombosis. Survivors recovered in two to four weeks.

Other Salts

Davis[18] has reviewed the toxicity of minerals which may be found in the diet. He notes that man is one of the end points of the food chain and as such benefits from toxicity that may have killed his food precursors, from food plants to food animals. Deficiencies of essential minerals may likewise have eliminated food precursors. In considering salt toxicity from food, therefore, we must confine evidence to plant foods in the instance of vegetarian animals and to animal foods for meat eaters.

Davis[18] states that naturally occurring dietary calcium rarely exceeds 1% of the diet and larger amounts are usually due to addition of substances such as bonemeal. Gershoff, Legg, and Hegsted,[19] Hollinger and Pattee,[20] Migicovsky and Jamieson,[21] and others reviewed by Davis[22] had shown that man and other animals can adapt to excess calcium intake through variations in absorption and utilization. The main problem associated with excess dietary calcium is impeded absorption of other elements such as phosphorus (which can be overcome by adding vitamin D[23]), zinc (deficiency of which produces parakeratosis in pigs[24]), magnesium, manganese, iodine, and iron.[18]

Davis[18] has reviewed evidence indicating that poisoning from excess dietary copper, iron, manganese, cobalt, zinc, and magnesium is extremely unlikely in man due to the various control mechanisms of the body. An excess of one of these elements tends to interfere with the availability of others as in the case of calcium. The toxicity of other salts will be limited in this volume to a review of the toxicity of barium sulfate.

Barium Sulfate Toxicity

Boyd and Abel[25] studied the toxicity of barium sulfate given orally to albino rats as a 150% (w/v) suspension in distilled water. This particular study was part of an investigation of deaths produced in Canada following use of the tannic acid-barium sulfate radiodiagnostic enema.[26]

Spector[27] lists the acute LD_{50} values of five barium salts but did not include barium sulfate and the publication of Boyd and Abel[25] appears to be the first on the acute oral toxicity of barium sulfate. Barium sulfate or $BaSO_4$ is soluble in water to less than 2 ppm, is used medically as an x-ray contrast medium, and is fairly widely used in industry for such purposes as making artificial ivory and cellophane, as a filler for linoleum and oilcloth, and as a size for pigmentation.[8] Boyd and Abel[25] found that the killing dose in albino rats was of the order of 40% of body weight and the main cause of death was bowel obstruction.

Regurgitation and pulmonary aspiration were produced when barium sulfate was given as a thin suspension. This was largely prevented by administering a suspension containing 150 g of barium sulfate in distilled water to a final volume of 100 ml, which was the most concentrated suspension that could be forced through an intragastric cannula. Following pilot studies, barium sulfate was given in a range of doses of from 188 to 375 g/kg. If these large volumes were given rapidly, gastric rupture followed. The barium sulfate was, therefore, administered as 40% of the total dose at first, followed by 35% in 3 hr and 25% after a further 3 hr.

Following administration of barium sulfate, the animal was sedated and had difficulty walking due to its protruding stomach, as illustrated in Figure 103. Clinical signs of toxicity are summarized in Table 107. The outstanding measurements of toxicity are indicated in Figures 104 and 105. The immediate cause of death was respiratory failure following convulsions or deep cyanosis. The interval to death due to bowel obstruction was not significantly dose dependent but, as illustrated in Figure 106, that of death due to stomach rupture decreased with increase in orally administered dose of barium sulfate. The mean ± standard deviation interval to death from bowel obstruction was 40 ± 12 hr. The acute oral LD_{50} ± S.E. of barium sulfate was 364 ± 41 g/kg, the maximal LD_0 was 163 g/kg, and the minimal LD_{100} 564 g/kg in the case of death due to bowel obstruction.[25]

At autopsy, the outstanding feature was bowel obstruction and hemorrhage along the gastrointestinal tract (see Table 107). Hemorrhage in the intestinal lumen had apparently stimulated blood clotting in the rest of the body since arteriovenous thrombosis was seen in all body organs. Along with thrombosis there were congestion of the heart,

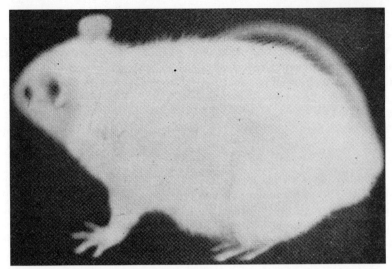

FIGURE 103. The appearance of an albino rat following oral administration of barium sulfate in a dose of 338 g/kg. Note protruding abdomen and piloerection. (From Boyd and Abel[25] with the permission of *The Canadian Medical Association Journal.*)

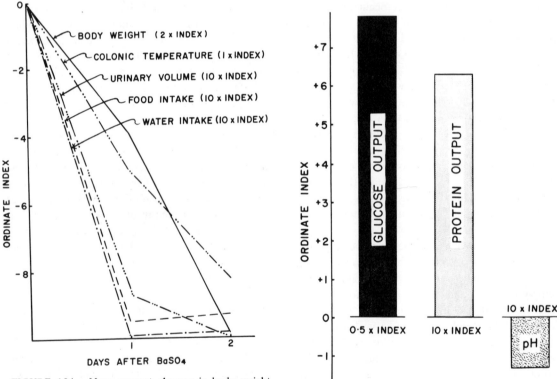

FIGURE 104. Mean percent changes in body weight, colonic temperature, urinary volume, food intake, and water intake of albino rats following oral administration of barium sulfate in doses at the range of the LD_{50}. The ordinate index must be multiplied by 2 to obtain percentage changes in body weight calculated in g, by 1 to obtain percentage changes in colonic temperature measured as °F, by 10 for changes in urinary volume and water intake calculated as ml/kg/24 hr, and by 10 for food intake measured as g/kg/day. (From Boyd and Abel[25] with the permission of *The Canadian Medical Association Journal.*)

FIGURE 105. The effect of lethal oral doses of barium sulfate upon urinary measurements in albino rats. The ordinate index must be multiplied by 0.5 to obtain values for urinary glucose output calculated as mg/kg/24 hr, by 10 for protein output measured as mg/kg/24 hr, and by 10 for the pH of 24-hr samples of urine, the latter two parameters being expressed as mean percentage changes from controls. (From Boyd and Abel[25] with the permission of *The Canadian Medical Association Journal.*)

TABLE 107

The Clinical and Gross Pathological Signs of Toxicity to Barium Sulfate in Doses
that Produced Death due to Bowel Obstruction in Albino Rats

Sign	Units	Bowel obstruction (N = 15)	Survivors (N = 49)
First appearance of drug in stool	Hours	1 to 16	3 to 23
Disappearance of drug in stool	Hours	–	27 to 48
Constipation (24+ hr)	% incidence	100	50
Duration of drowsiness	Hours	34 to 39	0 to 29
Duration of piloerection	Hours	20 to 34	0 to 29
Deficient righting reflex	% incidence	20	6
Rolling on floor	% incidence	15	6
Dragging dependent abdomen	% incidence	33	16
Cyanosis	% incidence	47	6
Convulsions	% incidence	27	0
Respiratory failure	% incidence of observed deaths	100	–
Impaction in small bowel	% incidence	100	Not available
Additional impaction in colon	% incidence	73	Not available
Hemorrhages in			
anterior gastric wall	% incidence	80	Not available
pyloric stomach	% incidence	67	Not available
cardiac stomach	% incidence	67	Not available
major gastric curvature	% incidence	67	Not available
posterior gastric wall	% incidence	60	Not available
minor gastric curvature	% incidence	53	Not available

(From Boyd and Abel[25] with the permission of the *Canadian Medical Association Journal.*)

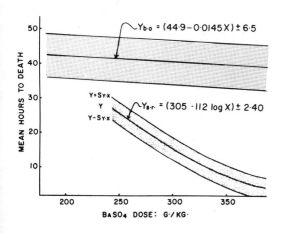

FIGURE 106. The regression, on dose of barium sulfate given orally to albino rats, of mean hours to death due to bowel obstruction (Y_{BO}) and to stomach rupture (Y_{SR}). (From Boyd and Abel[25] with the permission of *The Canadian Medical Association Journal.*)

kidneys, and testes and fatty degeneration of the renal tubules. Most organs had lost weight (Table 108) and many were dehydrated (Table 109). Clinical signs of toxicity disappeared in survivors at 72 hr and at two weeks and especially at one month, organ weights (Table 108) and water levels (Table 109) were essentially within normal limits.

In brief, barium sulfate produced death by bowel obstruction and the syndrome was similar to that produced by kaolin. Barium sulfate caused the appearance of multiple hemorrhages along the gastrointestinal tract, which produced augmentation of blood clotting and extensive arteriovenous thrombosis in body organs. This was associated with dehydration and loss of organ weight, congestion, and some degenerative changes such as renal fatty degeneration.

Conclusions Regarding Silicates and Insoluble Salts

Insoluble salts such as kaolin and barium sulfate

TABLE 108

Changes in the Wet Weight of Body Organs of Albino Rats Given Barium Sulfate in Doses at the Range of the Acute Oral LD$_{50}$ [a]

Organ	At death due to bowel obstruction (N = 6 plus 21 controls)	Fortnight survivors (N = 16 plus 16 controls)	Month survivors (N = 16 plus 13 controls)
Adrenal glands	+31.2**	− 8.4	− 4.0
Brain	+ 4.6	− 1.8	− 1.1
Gastrointestinal tract			
Cardiac stomach	+21.9**	− 3.1	+13.4
Pyloric stomach	− 6.5	− 0.4	+ 5.1
Small bowel	−42.9**	+ 4.4	+ 5.5
Cecum	−36.9**	+ 5.4	− 3.6
Colon	−33.0**	+ 0.7	+ 2.3
Heart	−18.9*	+ 1.5	− 4.9
Kidneys	−31.8**	+ 8.5*	−10.9*
Liver	−39.2**	+ 8.2*	− 3.8
Lungs	−19.1*	−12.4	+ 1.6
Muscle (anterior abdominal wall)	−46.9**	+ 8.4	− 6.0
Skin	−34.1**	− 3.3	− 3.0
Spleen	−52.8**	+15.3	− 8.0
Testes	−11.1*	+11.3*	− 4.0
Thymus gland	−61.2**	+26.2**	− 4.6
Residual carcass	−23.5**	− 1.9	− 0.5

[a]The results are expressed as % change from controls, specifically as $[(\bar{X}_d - \bar{X}_c)/\bar{X}_c] \times 100$, where $\bar{X}_d$ is the mean in the drug treated animal and $\bar{X}_c$ in the controls. Mean differences significant at P = 0.05 to P = 0.02 are indicated by one asterisk and at P<0.02 by two asterisks.

(From Boyd and Abel[25] with the permission of *The Canadian Medical Association Journal*.)

TABLE 109

Changes in the Water Content of Body Organs of Albino Rats Given Barium Sulfate in Doses at the Range of the Acute Oral LD$_{50}$ [a]

Organ	At death due to bowel obstruction (N = 6 plus 21 controls)	Fortnight survivors (N = 16 plus 16 controls)	Month survivors (N = 16 plus 13 controls)
Adrenal glands	− 8.4**	− 3.4	− 4.1
Brain	− 3.2	+ 1.7	− 1.1
Gastrointestinal tract			
Cardiac stomach	+23.1**	− 2.7	+ 4.2
Pyloric stomach	+22.0**	+ 2.4	+ 1.5
Small bowel	−17.2**	+ 3.4	− 1.1
Cecum	− 4.9	+ 3.7	+ 1.2
Colon	− 9.7*	+ 2.4	+ 4.2
Heart	− 6.6*	+ 0.3	+ 0.7
Kidneys	− 7.2*	+ 2.5	0.0
Liver	+13.2**	+ 0.8	+ 0.4
Lungs	− 3.0	− 0.8	+ 0.9
Muscle (anterior abdominal wall)	+40.5**	+ 0.1	− 2.9
Skin	− 8.7	+ 8.3	+ 3.1
Spleen	+ 0.3	+ 6.1	− 0.3
Testes	− 5.4*	+ 1.1	+ 0.3
Thymus gland	−18.4**	+ 0.8	− 3.0
Residual carcass	+ 0.8	+ 2.3	+ 0.7

[a] Water levels were measured as grams water/100 g dry weight of tissue. The results are expressed as per cent change from controls, specifically as $[(\bar{X}_d - \bar{X}_c)/\bar{X}_c] \times 100$, where $\bar{X}_d$ is the mean in the drug-treated group and $\bar{X}_c$ in the controls. Mean differences significant at P = 0.05 to P = 0.02 are indicated by one asterisk and at P < 0.02 by two asterisks.

(From Boyd and Abel[25] with the permission of *The Canadian Medical Association Journal*.)

produce death due to bowel obstruction from oral administration of doses in the range of one sixth to one third of body weight. Those agents have to be given slowly to avoid stomach rupture and as highly concentrated suspensions in water to avoid regurgitation, aspiration into the lungs, and death due to asphyxia.

Death from bowel obstructions is delayed to the second or third day following oral administration of the agent. It is preceded by respiratory failure following a period of depression of the central nervous system, anorexia, loss of body weight, and evidence of renal and metabolic disturbances. Bowel obstruction is associated with hemorrhage in the gastrointestinal tract which augments blood clotting and produces thrombosis in body organs. Other signs of systemic toxicity include congestion of body organs, some degenerative changes, and dehydration or hydration. Survivors recover rapidly over a period of two to four weeks.

It is unlikely that this complete syndrome would occur in man because of the huge dose of the agents required to produce it. Variants from smaller amounts could happen in man.

REFERENCES

1. Heppleston, A. G., The fibrogenic action of silica, *Br. Med. Bull.*, 25, 282, 1969.
2. Boyd, E. M., Covert, E. L., and Shanas, M. N., Death from bowel obstruction due to intragastrically administered kaolin, *Ind. Med. Surg.*, 34, 874, 1965.
3. Boyd, E. M. and Liu, S.-J., Toxicity of starch administered by mouth, *Can. Med. Assoc. J.*, 98, 492, 1968.
4. Lawson, A. and Moon, H. P., A clay adjunct to potato dietary, *Nature,* 141, 40, 1938.
5. Griffith, G., Clay in a vegetable diet, *Nature,* 141, 793, 1938.
6. Cohn, A. L., White, A. S., and Wehrauch, H. B., Kaolin granuloma of the stomach, *J.A.M.A.*, 117, 2225, 1941.
7. Wilson, W. J., Nutritional deficiency produced in the mouse by feeding bentonite, *J. Natl. Cancer Inst.*, 14, 57, 1953.
8. Sticher, P. G., Windholz, M., Leahy, D. S., Bolton, D. M., and Eaton, L. G., *The Merck Index. An Encyclopedia of Chemicals and Drugs,* 8th ed., Merck and Company, Rahway, N. J., 1968.
9. Wilson, W. J., Hepatomas in mice on a diet containing bentonite, *J. Natl. Cancer Inst.*, 14, 65, 1953.
10. Sollmann, T., *A Manual of Pharmacology,* 8th ed., W. B. Saunders, Philadelphia, 1957.
11. Gye, W. E. and Purdy, W. J., The poisonous properties of colloidal silica. III., *Br. J. Exp. Pathol.*, 5, 238, 1924.
12. Webb, J. L., Selle, R. M., and Thienes, C. H., Absorption, accumulation and excretion of ingested silica, *J. Ind. Hyg. Toxicol.*, 24, 43, 1942.
13. Bertke, E. M., The effect of ingestion of diatomaceous earth in white rats: a subacute toxicity test, *Toxicol. Appl. Pharmacol.*, 6, 284, 1964.
14. Ferguson, H. C., Dilution of dose and acute oral toxicity, *Toxicol. Appl. Pharmacol.*, 4, 759, 1962.
15. Constantopoulos, G. and Boyd, E. M., Factors affecting sucrose toxicity, *Int. J. Clin. Pharmacol. Ther. Toxicol.*, 1, 539, 1968.
16. Boyd, E. M., *Predictive Toxicometrics,* Scientechnica (Publishers) Ltd., Bristol, England, 1972.
17. Boyd, E. M. and Godi, I., Acute oral toxicity of distilled water in albino rats, *Ind. Med. Surg.*, 36, 609, 1967.
18. Davis, G. K., Toxicity of the essential minerals, in *Toxicants Occurring Naturally in Foods,* Publication 1354, The National Academy of Sciences and the National Research Council, Washington, D.C., 1966, 229.
19. Gershoff, S. N., Legg, M. A., and Hegsted, D. W., Adaptation to different calcium intakes in dogs, *J. Nutr.*, 64, 303, 1958.
20. Hollinger, H. Z. and Pattee, C. J., A review of abnormal calcium and phosphorus metabolism, *Can. Med. Assoc. J.*, 74, 912, 1956.
21. Migicovsky, B. B. and Jamieson, J. W. S., Calcium absorption and vitamin D, *Can. J. Biochem. Physiol.*, 33, 202, 1955.
22. Davis, G. K., *Transfer of Calcium and Strontium Across Biological Membranes,* Academic Press, New York, 1963.
23. Schohl, A. T. and Farber, S., Effect of A.T.10 (dihydrotachysterol) on rickets in rats produced by high-calcium low-phosphorus diets, *J. Nutr.*, 21, 147, 1941.
24. Tucker, H. F. and Salmon, W. D., Parakeratosis or zinc-deficiency disease in the pig, *Proc. Soc. Exp. Biol. Med.*, 88, 613, 1955.
25. Boyd, E. M. and Abel, W., The acute toxicity of barium sulfate administered intragastrically, *Can. Med. Assoc. J.*, 94, 849, 1966.
26. Singh, J., The acute toxicity of tannic acid and other drugs administered rectally to albino rats, Ph.D. thesis in Pharmacology, Douglas Library, Queen's University, Kingston, Ontario, Canada, 1967.
27. Spector, W. S., Ed., *Handbook of Toxicology,* Vol. 1, W. B. Saunders, Philadelphia, 1956.

FOOD TOXICANTS AND CAFFEINE

In addition to pure carbohydrates, fats, proteins, salts, and water, the diet of man and of animals contains many other substances which collectively have been termed food adjuvants or substances that may affect the quality of food and the lives of men and animals eating such food. The original selection of food by man was based upon availability of food, its taste, and absence of obvious toxic effects. Obvious toxic effects were those that could be seen within a few hours of the eating of a particular food. In other words, elimination of a poisonous food was based largely upon its acute toxicity. Chronic toxicity or effects of food that did not appear for months or years were not as obviously due to food in the observation of early man, especially if all his neighbours had the same effects. Such chronic effects have been gradually discovered through research.

Coon[1] has noted that research to date has barely touched the surface of information on toxicants which occur naturally in foods. He concludes: "Our ultimate goal is to achieve a knowledge not only of what, under various circumstances, constitutes the optimum in the nutritional content, but also of what involves the minimum of long-range toxicologic hazard in the diet." Toxicants that may occur naturally or be added to foods will be discussed briefly in this chapter mainly by reference to reviews and books in which the subject is described in detail. The main purpose of this book is to describe the toxicity of pure foods and discussion of food adjuvants will be limited to such common substances as caffeine and tannic acid which occur in the caffeine beverages and to atropine which is common in the diet of herbivora.

Natural Food Toxicants

Practically all foods may naturally contain poisonous substances, sometimes in amounts that may produce toxic effects but usually at ineffective levels. Potatoes may contain solanine alkaloids,[2] tomato juice may contain lycopene,[3] prunes may contain derivatives of hydroxyphenylisatin, a gastrointestinal irritant,[4] wheat may contain toxins,[5] and honey may contain cardiotoxic glycosides,[6] to name a few.

Seafood

Puffer fish and newts contain tetrodotoxins[7-9] which interfere with the passage of sodium ions in many excitable membranes,[10] thus lessening or eliminating action potentials.[11] Ciguatera fish contain ciguatoxin[12] which has an action on membranes somewhat like that of tetrodotoxin.[13] Sea cucumbers and starfish contain saponins which blockade the neuromuscular junction.[14] Wills[15] notes that seafood poisoning is particularly prevalent in Japan where seafood comprises 10% of the diet and seafood poisoning 60 to 70% of all food poisonings.

Fungi and Bacteria

The technology of fungi as food has been reviewed by Gray.[16] A moisture content of 10 to 20% predisposes dry food to attack by potentially toxic fungi[17-21] such as ergot, certain strains of aspergillus[22] which may contain aflatoxins,[21] of penicillia which may contain citrinin and other poisons,[21] and of various other fungi reviewed briefly by Wilson.[21] The toxicity of bacterial and viral contaminants in food has been reviewed by Gell and Coombs,[23] Landy and Braun,[24] and by Smith.[25] Rašková[26] has prepared a general review of naturally occurring toxins.

Pharmacological Agents in Foods

The National Academy of Sciences and the National Research Council of the United States of America have assembled data on pharmacological and toxicological agents in a wide variety of foods.[27] These include goitrogens, estrogens, carcinogens, lathyrogens, hemagglutinins, stimulants, depressants, antigens, pressor amines, antivitamins, enzyme inhibitors, and radioactive elements.[27] There are also chapters on unusual foods, vitamins, essential amino acids, essential minerals, and other salts.[27] Phosphates are reviewed by Ellinger,[28] and soybeans by Wolf and Cowan.[29]

Toxicants Added to Foods
Food Additives

While the term "additive" is literally all inclusive, it is restricted by Furia[30] to certain groups of chemical agents. These include coloring agents, enzymes, amino acids, vitamins, certain antimicrobial agents, antioxidants, acidulants, sequestrants, gums, starch, surfactants, polyhydric alcohols, flavors, flavor potentiators, and sweetening agents. Certain solvents may be allowed as food additives at amounts not above a specified maximum, e.g., 30 ppm for acetone and 30 ppm for ethylene dichloride.[31] The toxicity of mercury in the environment has been reviewed by Friberg and Vostal[32] and of cadmium by Friberg et al.[33] Food flavors is the subject of a review by Furia and Bellanca.[34]

Pesticides and Pollutants

There are several recent reviews on the toxicity of pesticides as contaminants of food. Edwards[35] has discussed the source, fate, and control of pesticides in the environment. Boyd[36] has reviewed evidence demonstrating that the toxicity of certain pesticides is markedly augmented when the diet is low in protein, as in many underdeveloped countries of the world. Cavanagh[37] has discussed degenerative changes in the central nervous system produced by organic phosphorus compounds and certain other chemical groups. The toxicity of gases, vapors, mists, and dusts in ambient air is described by Linch,[38] odor pollution by Summer,[39] and methods of control by Nonhebel.[40] Information on noise pollution is reviewed by Goodfriend.[41]

The Toxicity of Caffeine
Acute Oral Toxicity

The acute oral toxicity of caffeine in dogs and albino rats was described by Boyd,[42] who also described that in guinea pigs.[43] In female rats, starved overnight to empty the stomach, the acute oral $LD_{50} \pm$ S.E. was reported to be 192 ± 18 mg/kg by Boyd.[42] Spector[44] lists the LD_{50} in a variety of species at between 100 and 360 mg/kg and Gemmill[45] estimated the LD_{50} in man to be over 140 mg/kg. Death in rats occurs at 30.0 ± 9.6 hr after caffeine administration.[42]

During the first hour or two after caffeine dosing, albino rats were weak, tense, withdrawn, ataxic, and exhibited catalepsy and phonation on being moved.[42] At 6 to 24 hr the animals had loose stools or mild diarrhea, eye infections, tremors, pallor, and excitement. Similar signs were recorded in rats by Maloney,[46] and Holck,[47] in mice by Fühner[48] and in other species by Salant,[49] Salant and Rieger,[50] and Sollmann and Pilcher.[51] Clinical measurements are summarized in Table 110. The immediate cause of death was respiratory failure following tetanic convulsions or cardiac collapse.

At autopsy there was a fulminating inflammation of the gastrointestinal tract with an occasional intussusception of the ileum. The liver was congested and the hepatic cells pale-stained. The kidneys were congested, especially in the region of Henle's loop, and the convoluted tubules were edematous and necrotic. The heart and lungs were congested. Degenerative changes were present in the pancreas, spleen, and thymus gland. Changes in organ wet weights and water contents are summarized in Table 111. Recovery was rapid in survivors, as indicated by exemplary measurements shown in Figure 107.

In brief, caffeine produced death in 20 to 40 hr at an acute oral LD_{50} of 192 ± 18 mg/kg in female albino rats. The alkaloid produced signs of excitation and depression of the central nervous system, blepharitis, diarrhea, hypothermia, anorexia, and loss of weight. Autopsy disclosed a marked gastroenteritis, inflammation of several body organs, some degenerative changes, dehydration, and a stress reaction. Recovery of survivors was rapid.

Multiposal Oral Toxicity

The toxicity of caffeine in doses at the range of the oral $LD_{50 \, (100 \, days)}$ has been reported in female albino rats by Boyd et al.[52] who reviewed the literature on the chronic toxicity of caffeine. Caffeine was given daily for 100 days to unstarved animals in a range of doses. The daily dose that killed 50% of animals was calculated at weekly intervals and the results are shown in Figure 108. From data listed in Figure 108, the $LD_{50 \, (100 \, days)} \pm$ S.E. may be calculated to be 150 ± 3.1 mg/kg/24 hr. In a similar manner, the maximal $LD_{0 \, (100 \, days)}$ was found to be $110 \pm$

TABLE 110

Clinical Measurements in Female Albino Rats Following Oral Administration of Caffeine in Doses at the Range of the LD_{50}[a]

Group	No. of animals	Days after caffeine		
		1	2	3
Body weight: grams increase (+) or decrease (−)				
Controls	20	+13 ± 4	+14 ± 5	+13 ± 6
Survivors	19	− 7 ± 9	− 8 ± 12	+ 1 ± 14
Nonsurvivors	21	−16 ± 5	−22 ± 5	—
Food intake: grams chow per kilogram body weight per 24 hr				
Controls	20	93 ± 23	93 ± 24	82 ± 24
Survivors	19	16 ± 20	46 ± 28	79 ± 26
Nonsurvivors	21	0 ± 0	0 ± 0	—
Water intake: milliliters per kilogram body weight per 24 hr				
Controls	20	183 ± 51	127 ± 32	124 ± 25
Survivors	19	59 ± 67	138 ± 60	183 ± 74
Nonsurvivors	21	0 ± 0	0 ± 0	—
Urine output: milliliters per kilogram body weight per 24 hr				
Controls	20	39 ± 31	38 ± 18	37 ± 15
Survivors	19	26 ± 23	65 ± 28	82 ± 43
Nonsurvivors	21	10 ± 9	1 ± 3	—
Colonic temperature: °F				
Controls	20	98.9 ± 0.8	99.1 ± 0.9	99.6 ± 1.1
Survivors	19	98.1 ± 2.8	99.9 ± 1.1	100.0 ± 1.5
Nonsurvivors	21	93.7 ± 3.2	94.9 ± 4.0	—

[a]The results are expressed as mean ± standard deviation.

(From Boyd[42] with the permission of *Toxicology and Applied Pharmacology*, copyright © 1959, Academic Press, New York.)

TABLE 111

Changes[a] in the Wet Weight[b] and Water Content[c] of Body Organs of Albino Rats at Death Due to Oral Administration of Caffeine in Doses at the Range of the LD_{50}

Organ or tissue	Wet weight		Water level	
Spleen	−58.0	(<0.001)	+ 3.1	(0.05)
Liver	−43.0	(<0.001)	− 6.4	(0.02)
Jejunum	−27.3	(<0.001)	+ 4.5	(0.6)
Colon	−26.3	(<0.001)	−12.6	(<0.001)
Submaxillary glands	−25.3	(<0.001)	−21.5	(0.001)
Pyloric stomach	−24.4	(<0.001)	+ 2.2	(0.4)
Ileum	−21.9	(0.02)	+ 8.3	(0.1)
Cecum	−15.8	(0.02)	− 1.7	(0.8)
Duodenum	−15.3	(0.2)	− 2.6	(0.4)
Thymus gland	−14.6	(0.2)	− 2.5	(0.6)
Kidneys	− 3.2	(0.6)	− 3.5	(0.4)
Cardiac stomach	− 1.4	(0.8)	− 3.1	(0.3)
Mesentery-omentum	− 1.2	(0.9)	−27.2	(0.01)
Skin	+ 0.5	(0.9)	−20.1	(<0.001)
Brain	+ 6.5	(0.1)	0.0	(1.0)
Abdominal wall muscle	+ 6.6	(0.1)	− 8.8	(0.025)
Residual carcass	+10.3	(<0.001)	− 9.4	(0.02)
Ovaries	+16.7	(0.025)	−15.4	(0.005)
Heart	+20.1	(0.001)	− 2.9	(0.1)
Lungs	+47.4	(0.005)	−11.8	(<0.001)
Adrenal glands	+67.9	(0.001)	+11.9	(0.005)

[a]Expressed as a mean percentage change from the controls, specifically as $[(\bar{X}_d - \bar{X}_c)/\bar{X}_c] \times 100$, where $\bar{X}_d$ is the mean of the drug treated animals and $\bar{X}_c$ is the mean of the controls. In parentheses is the probability (P) that $\bar{X}_d - \bar{X}_c$ equals zero by a t test.

[b]Calculated as a percentage of body weight at autopsy.

[c]Calculated as grams water per 100 g dry weight of tissue.

(From Boyd[42] with the permission of *Toxicology and Applied Pharmacology*, copyright © 1959, Academic Press, New York.)

215

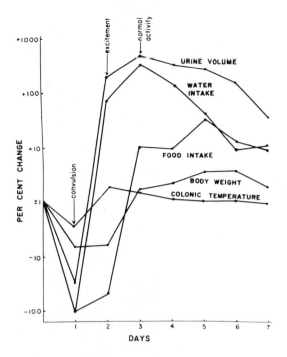

FIGURE 107. Mean percentage changes from controls in representative clinical measurements on albino rats that survived oral administration of caffeine in doses at the range of the LD_{50}. (From Boyd[42] with the permission of *Toxicology and Applied Pharmacology,* copyright © 1959, Academic Press, New York.)

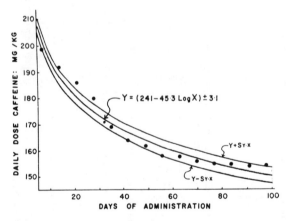

FIGURE 108. The regression, on days of repeated oral administration, of daily dose of caffeine which killed 50% of young female albino rats. (From Boyd et al.[52] with the permission of the *Canadian Journal of Physiology and Pharmacology,* copyright © 1965, the National Research Council of Canada, Ottawa.)

2.5 mg/kg/24 hr and the minimal $LD_{100 (100 \, days)}$ 191 ± 5.7 mg/kg/24 hr.

In doses at the range of the maximal

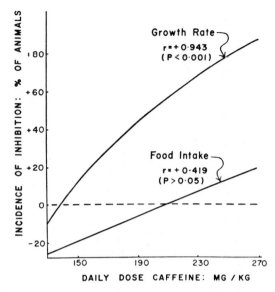

FIGURE 109. The regression, on daily oral dose of caffeine given to albino rats, of percentage incidences of inhibition of growth and of food intake. (From Boyd et al.[52] with the permission of the *Canadian Journal of Physiology and Pharmacology,* copyright © 1965, the National Research Council of Canada, Ottawa.)

$LD_0 (100 \, days)$ to the $LD_{50} (100 \, days)$ the animals appeared and acted normal most of the time. At the end of the first month of daily administration of caffeine, self aggression and automutilation appeared in segregated animals and fighting when the rats were aggregated. Caffeine-induced automutilation has been described in detail by Peters.[53] During the last month of drug administration there appeared varying degrees of alopecia and dermatitis. As shown in Figure 109, growth rate and food intake were not reduced until the daily dose approached the minimal $LD_{100 (100 \, days)}$ at which dose the clinical signs of toxicity were similar to those seen at the acute oral $LD_{50} (1 \, dose)$. Also increasing with increase in daily dose of caffeine were water intake and urinary volume (Figure 110) and the degree of proteinuria, glycosuria, aciduria, and hypothermia (Figure 111).

Histopathological signs of toxicity seen at death due to daily oral administration of caffeine are summarized in Table 112. At the $LD_{50} (100 \, days)$ and lower doses, caffeine administration produced a hypertrophy of the gastrointestinal mucosa presumably due to the bulk of the daily aqueous solution (20 ml/kg/day). At these doses, some body organs were mildly congested, there was a

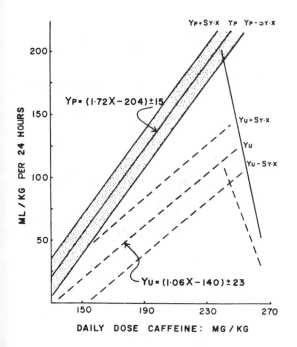

FIGURE 110. The regression, on daily oral dose of caffeine given to albino rats, of changes in polydipsic water intake (Y_p) and urinary volume (Y_u). Declining regression lines shown to the right include many pre-mortal decreases in water intake and urinary volume. (From Boyd et al.[52] with the permission of the *Canadian Journal of Physiology and Pharmacology,* copyright © 1965, the National Research Council of Canada, Ottawa.)

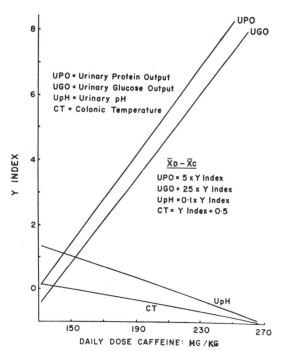

FIGURE 111. The regression, on daily oral dose of caffeine given to albino rats, of changes in the composition of urine and changes in colonic temperature. The Y index must be multiplied by 5 to calculate urinary protein output as mg/kg/day, by 25 for urinary glucose output as mg/kg/day, and by 0.1 for the pH of 24-hr samples of urine. To determine changes in colonic temperature, measured in °F, add 0.5 to the Y index. (From Boyd et al.[52] with the permission of the *Canadian Journal of Physiology and Pharmacology,* copyright © 1965, the National Research Council of Canada, Ottawa.)

stress reaction, degenerative reactions appeared in a few organs, and the main cause of death was bronchopneumonia. As the daily dose was increased, the microscopic findings began to approximate those seen at death from an acute oral $LD_{50\ (1\ dose)}$ of caffeine.

Loss of weight of body organs was particularly marked at high daily doses of caffeine.[52] At the $LD_{50\ (100\ days)}$ loss of weight was present only in spleen and thymus gland. There were no significant changes in organ water contents until the daily oral dose of caffeine approached the maximal $LD_{100\ (100\ days)}$, as shown by data summarized in Table 113. Large doses produced hydration of body organs, presumably due to loss of body fat from such doses.

Application to Man

From available data Boyd et al.[52] calculated that the average consumption of caffeine as coffee was about 4 mg/kg/24 hr in the U.S. during the year 1962. This is about the amount of caffeine present in one cup of coffee (150 mg). Ten cups of coffee per day would be about 40 mg/kg/24 hr and 20 cups 80 mg/kg/24 hr. The intake of caffeine would vary with body weight and would tend to be higher per kg body weight in women and children than in men from drinking the same amount of coffee. Caffeine may also be taken in the form of other caffeine beverages such as tea and various soft drinks and in caffeine-containing analgesic tablets. It is obvious, therefore, that the human daily intake of caffeine can closely approximate the maximal $LD_{0\ (100\ days)}$ in albino rats.

Boyd et al.[52] also reviewed evidence on clinical signs of caffeine intoxication in man in relation to daily dose of caffeine. They note that cerebral reactions of heavy coffee drinkers are less satisfactory than those of moderate coffee drinkers and that caffeine produces cerebral hyperemia and excitant effects in doses near the

TABLE 112

Histopathological Signs of Toxicity Seen at Death of Albino Rats from Daily Oral Administration of Caffeine in Doses at the Range of the $LD_{50 (100 days)}$

Organ	Daily dose of caffeine (mg/kg)		
	136 and 142	158 and 165	181 and 238
Adrenal glands	Cortical hypertrophy	Cortical hypertrophy	Sinusoids congested
Brain	Mild hyperemia	Mild hyperemia	Meningeal congestion
Gastrointestinal tract			
Cardiac stomach	Mucosal hypertrophy	Normal	Normal
Pyloric stomach	Mucosal hypertrophy Occasional small ulcer	Capillary congestion Occasional small ulcer	Mild inflammation
Small bowel	Mucosal hypertrophy	Mild hyperemia	Moderate inflammation
Cecum	Mucosal hypertrophy	Mild hyperemia	Moderate inflammation
Colon	Mucosal hypertrophy	Normal	Mild inflammation
Heart	Mild hyperemia	Mild capillary congestion	Marked capillary congestion
Kidneys	Mild edema and congestion	Edema and congestion, occasional venous thrombosis and thrombophlebitis	Marked edema and congestion
Liver	Normal	Mild sinusoidal congestion	Cloudy swelling and congestion
Lungs	Bronchopneumonia	Congestion, edema, thrombosis	Congestion, edema, hemorrhage
Muscle (ventral abdominal)	Normal	Weak cross striation	Weak cross striation
Ovaries	Deficiency primary follicles	Mild congestion	Mild congestion
Salivary gland (submaxillary)	Normal	Normal	Mild hyperemia
Skin	Normal	Occasional dermatitis	Normal
Spleen	Mild loss red pulp	Moderate loss red pulp	Marked loss red pulp
Thymus gland	Moderate atrophy	Marked atrophy	Marked atrophy
Thyroid gland	Colloid deficiency	Mild congestion	

(From Boyd et al.[52] with the permission of the *Canadian Journal of Physiology and Pharmacology,* copyright © 1965, the National Research Council of Canada, Ottawa.)

maximal $LD_0 (100 days)$ in rats. At this daily dose caffeine produced gastric ulcers in rats and gonadal inhibition. Boyd et al.[52] note that no gonadal inhibition occurs from daily doses approximately one half the maximal $LD_0 (100 days)$. Peters and Boyd[54] found that caffeine was relatively more toxic to old than to young rats and, on a mg/kg/day basis, more toxic to males than to females. Other factors affecting the toxic response to caffeine have been reviewed by Peters.[55-57]

Conclusions Regarding Food Toxicants and Caffeine

Food toxicants may be classified into (a) natural substances such as toxins in everyday foods, seafood, fungi, bacteria, and various pharmacologically active substances in ordinary foods and (b) toxicants added to foods such as food additives, pesticides, and pollutants. These are discussed mainly by references to reviews and books.

Caffeine is a common adjuvant to the human diet in the form of caffeine beverages and caffeine-containing analgesic drugs. The daily intake of caffeine by a person consuming large amounts of these sources of caffeine approaches the maximal $LD_0 (100 days)$ and may even approach the acute oral LD_{50} of caffeine, which is 192 ± 18 mg/kg in albino rats. Toxicity from caffeine can, therefore, contribute to the toxicity of the diet in man.

TABLE 113

The Effect of Daily Oral Administration of Caffeine to Albino Rats on the Water Content of Body Organs[a]

Organ	Less than minimal LD_{100} (0.1L) (N = 27 plus 28 controls)	LD_{100} (0.1L) and greater (N = 11 plus 11 controls)
Adrenal glands	− 2.4	+24.3**
Brain	− 0.7	+ 1.0
Gastrointestinal tract		
Cardiac stomach	+ 5.9*	+ 3.2
Pyloric stomach	+ 2.8	+14.6*
Small bowel	+ 6.3*	+10.8*
Cecum	+ 9.0*	+ 0.3
Colon	+ 4.2	+ 3.0
Heart	+ 8.6	+ 3.4
Kidneys	+ 2.7	+ 0.2
Liver	+ 3.5	+12.9*
Lungs	+ 5.2	− 1.8
Muscle (ventral abdominal wall)	− 0.8	+ 9.0*
Ovaries	+11.1*	− 0.7
Salivary glands (submaxillary)	− 1.1	− 8.6
Skin	+26.4*	+18.6**
Spleen	+ 2.0	+ 4.3
Thymus gland	+11.1	− 1.2
Residual carcass	+10.8	+12.1*

[a]Water levels were measured as grams water per 100 g dry weight of tissue. The results are expressed as percentage change from controls, specifically as $[(\overline{X}_d - \overline{X}_c)/\overline{X}_c] \times 100$, where $\overline{X}_d$ is the mean in the drug treated rats and $\overline{X}_c$ the mean in the controls. Differences significant at P = 0.05 to 0.02 are indicated by one asterisk, and at P = 0.01 or less by two asterisks.

(From Boyd et al.[52] with the permission of the *Canadian Journal of Physiology and Pharmacology,* copyright © 1965, the National Research Council of Canada, Ottawa.)

REFERENCES

1. **Coon, J. M.,** *Discussion of Toxicants Occurring Naturally in Foods,* Publication 1354, The National Academy of Sciences and the National Research Council, Washington, D.C., 1966.
2. **Talburt, W. F. and Smith, O.,** *Potato Processing,* The Avi Publishing Co., Westport, Conn., 1959.
3. **Reich, P., Schwachman, H., and Craig, J. M.,** Lycopenemia: a variant of carotenemia, *N. Engl. J. Med.,* 262, 263, 1960.
4. **Emerson, G. A.,** The laxative principle in prunes, *Proc. Soc. Exp. Biol. Med.,* 31, 278, 1933.
5. **Frazer, A. C.,** Deleterious effects due to wheat gluten, *Food Cosmet. Toxicol.,* 2, 670, 1964.
6. **Carey, F. M., Lewis, J. J., MacGregor, J. L., and Martins-Smith, M.,** Pharmacological and chemical observations on some toxic nectars, *J. Pharm. Pharmacol.,* 11, 269T, 1959.
7. **Halstead, B. W.,** *Poisonous and Venomous Marine Animals of the World, Vol. 1, Invertebrates,* U.S. Govt. Print. Off., Washington, D.C., 1965.
8. **Halstead, B. W.,** *Poisonous and Venomous Marine Animals of the World, Vol. 2, Vertebrates,* U.S. Govt. Print. Off., Washington, D.C., 1967.
9. **Halstead, B. W.,** *Poisonous and Venomous Marine Animals of the World,* Vol. 3, U.S. Govt. Print. Off., Washington, D.C., 1970.
10. **Kao, C. Y.,** Pharmacology of tetrodotoxin and saxitoxin, *Fed. Proc.,* 31, 1117, 1972.
11. **Narahashi, T.,** Mechanism of action of tetrodotoxin and saxitoxin on excitable membranes, *Fed. Proc.,* 31, 1124, 1972.
12. **Halstead, B. W.,** *Dangerous Marine Animals,* Cornell Maritime Press, Cambridge, Md., 1959.
13. **Rayner, M. D.,** Mode of action of ciguatoxin, *Fed. Proc.,* 31, 1139, 1972.
14. **Friess, S. L.,** Mode of action of marine saponins in neuromuscular tissues, *Fed. Proc.,* 31, 1146, 1972.
15. **Wills, J. H., Jr.,** Seafood toxins, in *Toxicants Occurring Naturally in Foods,* Publication 1354, The National Academy of Sciences and the National Research Council, Washington, D.C., 1966.

16. **Gray, W. D.,** Fungi as food and in food processing, in *C.R.C. Critical Reviews in Food Technology,* Furia, T. E., Ed., The Chemical Rubber Co., Cleveland, 1972.

17. **Kingsberry, J. M.,** *Poisonous Plants of the United States and Canada,* Prentice-Hall, Englewood Cliffs, N.J., 1964.

18. **Gajdusek, D. C.,** *Acute Infectious Hemorrhagic Fevers and Mycotoxicoses in the Union of Socialist Soviet Republics,* Med. Sci. Publication No. 2, Army Med. Ser. Grad. School, Walter Reed Army Med. Center, Washington, D. C., 1953.

19. **Bilay, V. I.,** Ed., *Mycotoxicoses of Man and Agricultural Animals,* Office of Tech. Ser., U.S. Dept. of Commerce, Washington, D.C., 1960.

20. **Barger, G.,** *Ergot and Ergotism,* Gurney and Jackson, Ltd., London, 1931.

21. **Wilson, B. J.,** Fungal toxins, in *Toxicants Occurring Naturally in Foods,* Publication 1354, The National Academy of Sciences and the National Research Council, Washington, D.C., 1966.

22. **Thom, C. and Church, M. B.,** *The Aspergilli,* Williams and Wilkins, Baltimore, Md., 1926.

23. **Gell, P. G. H. and Coombs, R. R. A.,** Eds., *Clinical Aspects of Immunology,* 2nd ed., Blackwell Scientific Publications, Oxford, 1968.

24. **Landy, M. and Braun, W.,** Eds., *Bacterial Endotoxins,* Rutgers University Press, New Brunswick, N.J., 1964.

25. **Smith, H.,** Toxic activities of microbes, *Br. Med. Bull.,* 25, 288, 1969.

26. **Rásková, H.,** Ed., *Pharmacology and Toxicology of Naturally Occurring Toxins,* Vol. 1, 1971 and Vol. 2, 1972, Pergamon Press, Toronto.

27. **National Academy of Sciences and National Research Council,** *Toxicants Occurring Naturally in Foods,* Publication 1354, The National Academy of Sciences and the National Research Council, Washington, D.C., 1966.

28. **Ellinger, R. H.,** *Phosphates as Food Ingredients,* The Chemical Rubber Co., Cleveland, 1972.

29. **Wolf, W. J. and Cowan, J. C.,** *Soybeans as a Food Source,* The Chemical Rubber Co., Cleveland, 1971.

30. **Furia, T. E.,** Ed., *Handbook of Food Additives,* The Chemical Rubber Co., Cleveland, 1968.

31. **FDD,** Solvent Use in Food Production and Processing, T.I.L. No. 367, the Food and Drug Directorate, Department of National Health and Welfare, Ottawa, 1972.

32. **Friberg, L. T. and Vostal, J. J.,** *Mercury in the Environment,* The Chemical Rubber Co., Cleveland, 1972.

33. **Friberg, L. T., Piscator, M., and Nordberg, G. F.,** *Cadmium in the Environment,* The Chemical Rubber Co., Cleveland, 1971.

34. **Furia, T. E. and Bellanca, N.,** Eds., *Fenaroli's Handbook of Flavor Ingredients,* The Chemical Rubber Co., Cleveland, 1971.

35. **Edwards, C. E.,** *Persistent Pesticides in the Environment,* The Chemical Rubber Co., Cleveland, 1971.

36. **Boyd, E. M.,** *Protein Deficiency and Pesticide Toxicity,* Charles C Thomas, Springfield, Ill., 1972.

37. **Cavanagh, J. B.,** Toxic substances and the nervous system, *Br. Med. Bull.,* 25, 268, 1969.

38. **Linch, A. L.,** *Evaluation of Ambient Air Quality by Personnel Monitoring,* The Chemical Rubber Co., Cleveland, 1973.

39. **Summer, W.,** *Odor Pollution of Air,* The Chemical Rubber Co., Cleveland, 1972.

40. **Nonhebel, G.,** *Processes for Air Pollution Control,* The Chemical Rubber Co., Cleveland, 1971.

41. **Goodfriend, L. S.,** *Noise Pollution,* The Chemical Rubber Co., Cleveland, 1972.

42. **Boyd, E. M.,** The acute oral toxicity of caffeine, *Toxicol. Appl. Pharmacol.,* 1, 250, 1959.

43. **Boyd, E. M.,** The acute oral toxicity in guinea pigs of acetylsalicylic acid, phenacetin, and caffeine, alone and combined, *Toxicol. Appl. Pharmacol.,* 2, 23, 1960.

44. **Spector, W. S.,** Ed., *Handbook of Toxicology,* Vol. 1, W. B. Saunders, Philadelphia, 1956.

45. **Gemmill, C. L.,** The xanthines, in *Pharmacology in Medicine,* 2nd ed., Drill, V. A., Ed., McGraw-Hill, New York, 1958.

46. **Maloney, A. H.,** Contradictory actions of caffeine, coramine and metrazol, *Quart. J. Exper. Physiol.,* 25, 155, 1935.

47. **Holck, H. G. O.,** Dosage of drugs for rats, in *The Rat in Laboratory Investigation,* Farris, E. J. and Griffith, J. Q., Eds., J. P. Lippincott, Philadelphia, 1949.

48. **Fühner, H.,** Beitrag zur Vergleichenden Pharmakologie. 1. Die Giftigen und Tödlichen Gaben einiger Substanzen für Frösche und Mäuse, *Arch. Exp. Pathol. Pharmakol. Naunyn-Schmiedeberg's,* 166, 437, 1932.

49. **Salant, W.,** The effect of caffeine on the circulation, *J. Pharmacol. Exp. Ther.,* 3, 468, 1911.

50. **Salant, W. and Rieger, J. B.,** The toxicity of caffeine, *J. Pharmacol. Exp. Ther.,* 1, 572, 1909.

51. **Sollmann, T. and Pilcher, J. D.,** The action of caffeine on the mammalian circulation. 1. The persistent effects of caffeine on the circulation, *J. Pharmacol. Exp. Ther.,* 3, 19, 1911.

52. **Boyd, E. M., Dolman, M., Knight, L. M., and Sheppard, E. P.,** The chronic oral toxicity of caffeine, *Can. J. Physiol. Pharmacol.,* 43, 995, 1965.

53. **Peters, J. M.,** Caffeine-induced hemorrhagic automutilation, *Arch. Int. Pharmacodyn. Ther.,* 169, 139, 1967.

54. **Peters, J. M. and Boyd, E. M.,** The influence of sex and age in albino rats given a daily dose of caffeine at a high dose level, *Can. J. Physiol. Pharmacol.,* 45, 305, 1967.

55. **Peters, J. M.,** Factors affecting caffeine toxicity. A review of the literature, *J. Clin. Pharmacol.,* 7, 131, 1967.

56. **Peters, J. M.,** Caffeine Toxicity in Rats on a Protein Deficient Diet, M.Sc. Thesis in Pharmacology, Douglas Library, Queen's University, Kingston, Ontario, Canada, 1964.

57. **Peters, J. M.,** Factors in Caffeine Toxicity, Ph.D. Thesis in Pharmacology, Douglas Library, Queen's University, Kingston, Ontario, Canada, 1966.

Chapter 20

TANNIC ACID

Tannic acid is the name given to esters of a sugar, usually glucose with gallic acid or 3,4,5-trihydroxybenzoic acid.[1] It occurs in the bark, fruit, and leaves of plants, including tea leaves and coffee beans; the medicinal product is obtained from nutgalls. Tannic acid is a light brown amorphous powder which is readily soluble in water and the solution darkens on standing. It is used medically as an astringent and styptic and is widely employed in the tanning and other industries.[2]

Tannic acid is readily absorbed from the gastrointestinal tract and metabolites are excreted in urine.[3] Apart from its local action as an astringent, the effects of tannic acid on the body are mainly toxic.[4] While studying local coagulants for burns, Davidson in 1925[5] proposed use of tannic acid for the local therapy of burns and reviewed early information on the agent. Tannic acid proved itself an extremely useful local agent for burns and was extensively so employed. Following introduction of this therapeutic procedure, reports of liver necrosis in patients dying from burns began to appear.[6-8] Allen and Koch[9] reported no liver necrosis; they had not used tannic acid. Wells, Humphrey, and Coll in 1942[10] finally demonstrated that tannic acid was the cause of liver necrosis in burn therapy.

Meanwhile the addition of tannic acid to barium sulfate radiodiagnostic enemas had been found to clarify the x-ray picture.[11] By 1963, it was estimated that tannic acid was added to 600,000 barium sulfate enemas per year in the U.S., apparently without toxic effects.[12] In the same year, liver necrosis was reported from Canada[13] and from the U.S.[14] in patients who had received barium sulfate enemas containing large amounts of tannic acid. In 1964, the Food and Drug Administration considered withdrawal of approval of the use of tannic acid in barium sulfate enemas.[15] In 1965 Boyd et al.[16] concluded that variation in appearance of toxicity was probably related to the amount of tannic acid added to the diagnostic enema. This led to an extensive study of the toxicity of tannic acid by Boyd and associates.[4,16-23]

The Acute Oral Toxicity of Tannic Acid

Boyd et al.[16] reviewed evidence indicating that in the decade from 1940 to 1950 it was believed that tannic acid was poorly absorbed from the gastrointestinal tract. In 1951, Korpassy and co-workers[3] demonstrated that tannic acid was readily absorbed when given orally. They found that normal urine contains metabolites of tannic acid, presumably derived from tannic acid in tea, coffee, and certain astringent wines. Boyd et al.[16] quoted reports indicating that the acute oral LD_{50} of tannic acid is of the order of 3.5 g/kg in mice and 5.0 g/kg in rabbits.

Boyd et al.[16] used young male albino rats housed one per metabolism cage and starved overnight to empty the stomach. Tannic acid was employed as 3-galloyl gallic acid dissolved in distilled water and given through a stomach tube in a volume of 20 ml/kg. The LD_{50} ± S.E. was found to be 2.26 ± 0.083 g/kg. The mean interval to death was 38 hr and varied inversely with the dose of tannic acid, as shown in Figure 112. The common clinical signs of intoxication were drowsiness, pallor, cyanosis, and diarrhea. The degree of these signs was dose dependent and the relation of degree of the signs to time after giving tannic acid is shown in Figure 113 and for clinical measurements in Figure 114. The degree of inhibition of growth, food intake, and water intake increased with increase in the dose of tannic acid. This dose response relationship in the instance of food intake is illustrated in Figure 115. The regression equation shown in Figure 115 is a linear one; actually the data were also well fitted by the equation

$$Y = (91-330 \log X) \pm 8.5.$$

Statistically significant changes in urine produced by oral administration of tannic acid, in doses at the range of the LD_{50}, are indicated in Figure 116. The degrees of diuresis and alkalinuria were dose dependent. The range of doses of tannic

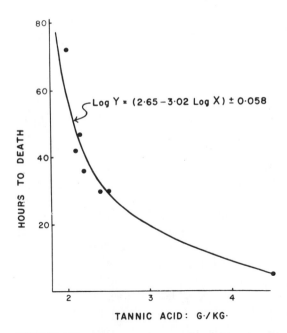

FIGURE 112. The regression, on dose of tannic acid given orally to young male albino rats, of mean hours to death. (From Boyd et al.[16] with the permission of the *Canadian Medical Association Journal.*)

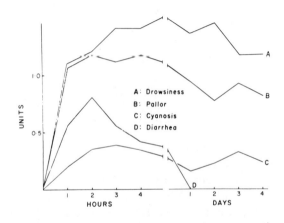

FIGURE 113. The relation of intensity of clinical signs of intoxication to tannic acid, in doses at the range of the acute oral LD_{50}, to time after administration to albino rats. (From Boyd et al.[16] with the permission of the *Canadian Medical Association Journal.*)

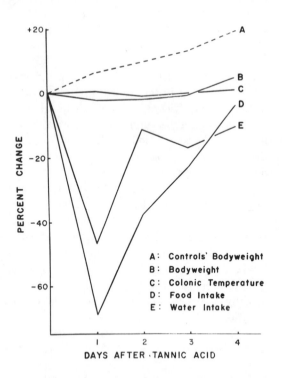

FIGURE 114. Percentage changes in clinical measurements from those of the day before administration of tannic acid to albino rats, in doses at the range of the acute oral LD_{50}. (From Boyd et al.[16] with the permission of the *Canadian Medical Association Journal.*)

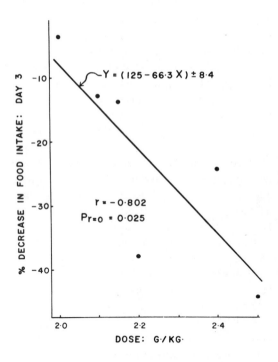

FIGURE 115. The regression, on dose of tannic acid given orally to albino rats, of percentage decreases in food intake, from values in controls given no tannic acid, on the third day following drug administration. (From Boyd et al.[16] with the permission of the *Canadian Medical Association Journal.*)

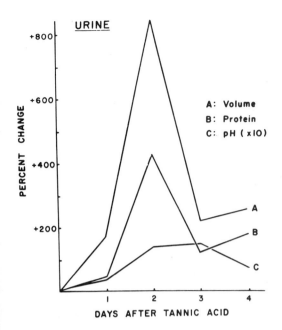

FIGURE 116. Percentage changes, from values during the day before oral administration of tannic acid (in doses at the range of the LD_{50}) in the urinary volume (measured as ml/kg/day), urinary protein output (calculated as mg/kg/day), and 10X the changes in the pH of 24-hr samples of urine of albino rats. (From Boyd et al.[16] with the permission of the *Canadian Medical Association Journal*.)

acid was not quite wide enough to prove that the proteinuria was dose dependent. The toxicity syndrome involved no significant changes in urinary glucose output.

When death occurred early from large doses of tannic acid (4.5 to 8.0 g/kg), the premortem signs included diarrhea, pallor, cyanosis, prostration, tremors, convulsions, and respiratory failure. At the acute oral LD_{50}, the premortem signs were marked anorexia, oligodipsia, loss of body weight, hypothermia, pallor, cyanosis, tremors, and respiratory failure.

Histologically, there was a fulminating gastroenteritis in early deaths but this gradually disappeared when death was delayed to 48 and particularly to 72 hr. Hepatic necrosis became evident at 24 hr and reached a peak at 48 to 72 hr when hemorrhage into the necrotic area produced an almost complete loss of hepatic microscopic structure. At 96 hr, fibrosis (cirrhosis) began to appear. Associated lesions included necrosis of the renal convoluted tubules and, curiously, a stimulation of spermatogenesis in the testes. There were a

stress reaction in the adrenal glands, spleen, and thymus gland and congestion of some organs such as the lungs.

Shifts in organ wet weight are summarized in Table 114. Tannic acid had produced loss of weight in many organs, especially in the small and large bowel, kidneys, liver, skin, and thymus gland. The weight of the adrenal glands was increased due in part to an increase in water content, as shown by data on water levels assembled in Table 115. The significant change in water levels at death was hydration so that loss of dry weight must have been even more marked than loss of wet weight shown in Table 114. In survivors, organ weights and water levels were largely within the range of values in controls at a fortnight and one month after administration of tannic acid.

In discussing their results, Boyd et al.[16] noted that tannins apparently serve to protect plants from invasion by viruses and fungi. They employed a chemically pure form of tannic acid and noted that results could be different if other forms of tannic acid were used. Tannin extracts had been employed in ancient times to control diarrhea in oral doses less than those which produced nausea and vomiting. Boyd et al.[16] quoted literature showing that the clinicopathological syndrome of intoxication to tannic acid given orally to albino rats is similar to that reported in human beings who died from liver necrosis following use of the tannic acid-barium sulfate radiodiagnostic enema.

The Acute Rectal Toxicity of Tannic Acid

Jarzylo et al.[19] made preliminary studies on the toxicity of tannic acid given rectally to young male albino rats. The tannic acid was added to a suspension of barium sulfate. X-ray studies revealed that when such suspensions were given rectally in a volume of 20 ml/kg, the upward passage of the enema was not beyond the ileocecal valve; when the volume was increased to 70 ml/kg, the suspension passed upward into a large portion of the small bowel. From these results, a volume of 20 ml/kg was selected for further studies. This volume corresponds to a barium sulfate enema of 500 ml given to a child weighing 25 kg.

Man is able to retain a barium sulfate radiodiagnostic enema for about 2 min. The relation of retention time to the toxic effects of tannic acid given rectally to albino rats is illustrated in Figure 117. A dose of 8 g/kg produced 50% deaths when

TABLE 115

Changes in the Water Content of Body Organs of Albino Rats Following Oral Administration of Tannic Acid in Doses at the Range of the LD_{50} [a]

Organ	At death	Fortnight survivors	Month survivors
Adrenal glands	+30.6**	-46.7**	-13.3
Brain	- 0.8	- 2.5	+ 0.3
Gastrointestinal tract			
Cardiac stomach	+18.6**	- 1.2	+ 0.3
Pyloric stomach	+21.1**	+ 0.6	+ 3.0
Small bowel	+11.4*	- 3.8	+ 7.1
Cecum	+13.7**	- 1.0	- 6.5
Colon	- 3.6	+ 5.9	+ 4.6
Heart	+ 9.5	+ 1.2	- 3.6
Kidneys	+ 3.7	+ 0.9	+ 1.8
Liver	+13.1**	+ 8.2*	+ 4.9
Lungs	- 8.1**	- 3.0	+ 1.1
Muscle (ventral abdominal wall)	- 2.7	+ 5.8	+ 4.3
Salivary glands (submaxillary)	-14.0**	+ 1.5	+10.6
Skin	+ 7.0	- 6.8	+11.8
Spleen	+ 0.3	+ 3.2	+ 5.1
Testes	- 6.6**	+ 0.8	+ 2.7
Thymus gland	- 3.0	- 4.0	- 2.3
Residual carcass	- 5.2	+ 5.0	+ 0.5

[a]Water levels were measured as grams water per 100 g dry weight of tissue. The results are expressed as percent change from controls given no tannic acid, specifically as $[(\bar{X}_d - \bar{X}_c)/\bar{X}_c] \times 100$, where $\bar{X}_d$ is the mean in the drug treated group and $\bar{X}_c$ in its control group. One asterisk indicates that the probability (P) that $\bar{X}_d - \bar{X}_c$ is zero, is between 0.05 and 0.02; and two asterisks, that it is 0.01 or less. (From Boyd et al.[16] with the permission of the Canadian Medical Association Journal.)

TABLE 114

Changes in the Fresh Wet Weight of Body Organs of Albino Rats Following Oral Administration of Tannic Acid in Doses at the Range of the LD_{50} [a]

Organ	At death	Fortnight survivors	Month survivors
Adrenal glands	+41.2**	-11.4	-20.5**
Brain	- 1.1	+ 7.1	5.7
Gastrointestinal tract			
Cardiac stomach	+ 4.2	- 4.9	- 0.3
Pyloric stomach	- 3.9	- 4.2	-11.7**
Small bowel	-18.7**	- 1.0	- 3.5
Cecum	-22.4**	+ 5.0	+ 2.0
Colon	-15.3**	-11.1*	+ 6.0
Heart	- 2.9	+ 7.5	+10.7
Kidneys	-13.4*	+ 2.6	+ 5.9
Liver	-21.3***	- 9.9*	+ 1.9
Lungs	+22.1	+ 3.3	+15.6
Muscle (abdominal wall)	-13.2	- 3.2	-14.8
Salivary glands (submaxillary)	+ 1.1	+ 4.8	0.0
Skin	-13.4*	-11.4**	-11.7*
Spleen	-11.5	+37.5*	+27.0
Testes	- 3.5	+14.1*	+ 3.9
Thymus gland	-35.1*	-12.4	-19.0
Residual carcass	-11.0*	- 7.0	5.6

[a]The results are expressed as percent change from controls given no tannic acid, specifically as $[(\bar{X}_d - \bar{X}_c)/\bar{X}_c] \times 100$, where $\bar{X}_d$ is the mean weight in g of the drug treated group, and $\bar{X}_c$ the mean in its control group. One asterisk indicates that the probability (P) that $\bar{X}_d - \bar{X}_c$ is zero, is between 0.05 and 0.02; and two asterisks, that it is 0.01 or less.

(From Boyd et al.[16] with the permission of the Canadian Medical Association Journal.)

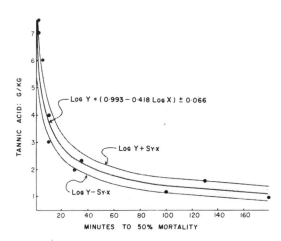

$$\text{Log } Y = (0.993 - 0.418 \text{ Log } X) \pm 0.066$$

Log Y + Sy·x

Log Y − Sy·x

FIGURE 117. The regression of the dose of tannic acid, given rectally to albino rats, on the numbers of minutes of retention in the rectum and colon required to produce 50% mortality. (From Singh and Boyd[22] with the permission of the authors and of the *Journal of the Canadian Association of Radiologists.*)

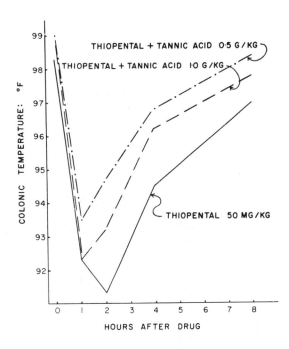

THIOPENTAL + TANNIC ACID 0·5 G/KG

THIOPENTAL + TANNIC ACID 1·0 G/KG

THIOPENTAL 50 MG/KG

FIGURE 118. Changes in the colonic temperature of albino rats following administration of thiopental sodium intraperitoneally with and without rectal administration of tannic acid. (From Singh and Boyd[21] with the permission of the authors and the *Canadian Medical Association Journal.*)

retained for 2 min.[18] As retention time was increased to 1 to 4 hr, the toxicity of tannic acid was markedly increased. Singh and Boyd[22] decided to use a retention time of 4 hr in further studies of the toxicity of tannic acid given rectally to albino rats, although an interval of 1 hr would probably have sufficed, as indicated in Figure 117.

To retain tannic acid solutions for this interval in the rectum of an albino rat, it was necessary to anesthetize the animal and apply a bulldog clamp to the anus after giving the enema. Singh and Boyd[21] found that thiopental sodium given intraperitoneally in a dose of 50 mg/kg produced anesthesia lasting 2 hr in controls given no tannic acid and up to 4 hr or more in animals given tannic acid rectally in doses at the range of the acute rectal LD_{50}. Prolongation of anesthesia appeared to be due to impaired oxidation of thiopental in tannic acid treated animals since prolongation varied directly with the dose of tannic acid. On the other hand, thiopental lowered body temperature (see Figure 118). The hypothermic effect was particularly marked in animals which were ataxic and drowsy at 5 hr after giving thiopental and tannic acid, as shown in Figure 119, and just before death from liver necrosis, as illustrated in Figure 120.

Using a rectal retention time of 4 hr, Singh and Boyd[22] found that the regression of dose of tannic acid on percent mortality was linear for rectal doses between 1.0 and 1.4 g/kg, as

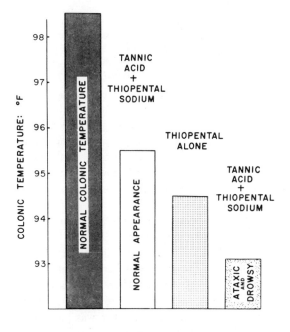

TANNIC ACID + THIOPENTAL SODIUM

THIOPENTAL ALONE

TANNIC ACID + THIOPENTAL SODIUM

NORMAL COLONIC TEMPERATURE

NORMAL APPEARANCE

ATAXIC AND DROWSY

FIGURE 119. Colonic temperature at 5 hr after giving tannic acid rectally in a dose of 0.8 g/kg and thiopental sodium intraperitoneally in a dose of 50 mg/kg. (From Singh and Boyd[21] with the permission of the authors and the *Canadian Medical Association Journal.*)

TABLE 116

The Interval to Death Following Rectal Administration of Tannic Acid to Albino Rats

Dose of tannic acid (g/kg)	Hours to death (mean ± S.D.)	Dose of tannic acid (g/kg)	Hours to death (mean ± S.D.)
1.0	72 ± 12	1.2	41 ± 18
1.1	53 ± 21	1.3	48 ± 22
1.15	41 ± 20	1.4	31 ± 21

(From Singh and Boyd[22] with the permission of the authors and of the *Journal of the Canadian Association of Radiologists.*)

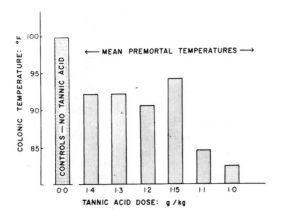

FIGURE 120.   Mean colonic temperatures in albino rats just before death from liver necrosis produced by tannic acid. Note absence of dose response effect. (From Singh and Boyd[21] with the permission of the authors and of the *Canadian Medical Association Journal.*)

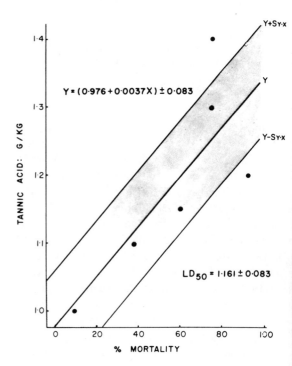

FIGURE 121.   The regression of dose of tannic acid retained rectally by albino rats, on percent mortality. (From Singh and Boyd[22] with the permission of the authors and of the *Journal of the Canadian Association of Radiologists.*)

illustrated in Figure 121. The acute rectal $LD_{50} \pm$ S.E. was found to be 1.161 ± 0.083 g/kg, the maximal LD_0 was 0.976 g/kg, and the minimal LD_{100} was 1.35 g/kg. The acute rectal LD_{50} of tannic acid was significantly lower than the acute oral LD_{50} under the conditions of this comparison.

Data on interval to death are summarized in Table 116. At the acute rectal LD_{50}, the mean ± standard deviation hours to death was 41 ± 20 which was insignificantly different from 38 hr at the acute oral LD_{50}. There was an inverse relationship between interval to death and dose of tannic acid, a relationship that was also present following oral administration.

The clinical signs of intoxication to tannic acid given rectally included drowsiness, pallor, ataxia, hyporeflexia, slow and labored respiration, sluggish reflexes (corneal), diarrhea, and prostra-

tion. The degree of these signs was dose dependent, as illustrated for loss of righting reflex in Figure 122. At 24 hr, there were inhibition of growth, anorexia, oligodipsia, hypothermia, and diuresis. These signs persisted in survivors to 48 hr and, from large doses, to 72 hr. At 48 and 72 hr there appeared proteinuria, hematuria, and either aciduria or alkalinuria. The premortal signs were hypopnea, absent reflexes, and coma.

A summary of lesions observed on gross

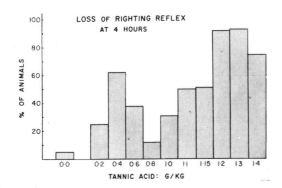

FIGURE 122. The percentage of animals which had not regained their righting reflex at the end of 4 hr of rectal retention of tannic acid. (From Singh and Boyd[22] with the permission of the authors and of the *Journal of the Canadian Association of Radiologists.*)

examination of body organs at autopsy following death due to rectal administration of tannic acid is presented in Table 117. Local pathology in the colon and cecum was roughly dose dependent. Gross pathology in the testes and urinary bladder was somewhat less dependent on dose of tannic acid.

Histopathologically, there was a marked local necrotic inflammatory reaction in the colon and cecum followed by localized hemorrhagic ulcer formation at one to three days. Healing was almost complete in survivors at a fortnight and at one month there was no residual pathology in the colon and cecum.

Systemically, liver necrosis took the form of congestion of the hepatic sinusoids at 6 to 8 hr and of extensive centrilobular necrosis at 72 hr. In survivors at two weeks there was some residual hepatic fatty degeneration but at one month the liver appeared normal microscopically. There were congestion with edema in the kidneys and congestion with ulcer formations in the lining of the urinary bladder. The testes were hyperemic, but spermatogenesis was not impaired and at and after the third day there appeared augmented production of sperm.

Shifts in the fresh wet weight of body organs are shown in Table 118. At death due to rectal administration of tannic acid, there was a loss of body weight due to loss of weight in several organs and to the fact that the lumen of the gastrointestinal tract was almost empty from failure of the animals to eat. Loss of weight was marked in small bowel, cecum, liver, salivary glands, and thymus gland. There was a stressor gain in weight of the adrenal glands. The colon was congested with red and white blood cells and it too had gained wet weight.

Changes in the water content of body organs are summarized in Table 119. There was a considerable hydration of the adrenal glands at death, which accounted for most of the increase in wet weight shown in Table 118. The liver was hydrated, indicating that loss of dry weight was even more marked than loss of wet weight shown

TABLE 117

A Quantitation of Gross Pathology at Death due to Rectal Administration of Tannic Acid to Albino Rats[a]

Dose of tannic acid (g/kg)	Ulcers		Hemorrhages		Hemorrhagic inflammation	
	Colon	Cecum	Colon	Cecum	Testes	Urinary bladder
0.6	0.0 ± 0.0	0.0 ± 0.0	0.0 ± 0.0	0.0 ± 0.0	0.0 ± 0.0	0.0 ± 0.0
0.8	0.0 ± 0.0	0.0 ± 0.0	0.0 ± 0.0	0.0 ± 0.0	0.0 ± 0.0	0.0 ± 0.0
1.1	1.2 ± 0.4	0.6 ± 0.2	0.3 ± 0.1	0.2 ± 0.1	0.0 ± 0.0	0.3 ± 0.3
1.15	0.6 ± 0.2	0.7 ± 0.2	0.7 ± 0.2	0.8 ± 0.2	2.5 ± 0.8	0.7 ± 0.4
1.2	1.0 ± 0.2	0.9 ± 0.2	0.0 ± 0.0	0.0 ± 0.0	0.4 ± 0.3	0.2 ± 0.3
1.3	1.1 ± 0.4	0.9 ± 0.4	0.7 ± 0.3	0.7 ± 0.3	0.8 ± 0.4	0.1 ± 0.1
1.4	2.0 ± 0.4	1.6 ± 0.3	1.4 ± 0.3	1.3 ± 0.3	0.7 ± 0.3	0.0 ± 0.0

[a]Gross pathology was quantitated a 1 (minor) to 4 (marked) upon 6 to 11 animals per dosage group. The results are expressed as mean ± standard error. (From Singh and Boyd[22] with the permission of the authors and of the *Journal of the Canadian Association of Radiologists.*)

TABLE 118

The Fresh Wet Weight of Body Organs of Albino Rats Following Rectal Administration of Tannic Acid in Doses at the Range of the LD_{50}[a]

Organ	At death (N = 7 + 7 controls)	Fortnight survivors (N = 15 + 9 controls)	Month survivors (N = 29 + 13 controls)
Adrenal glands	+20.9*	− 3.8	− 2.9
Brain	− 8.6	− 1.3	− 0.4
Gastrointestinal tract			
Cardiac stomach	− 4.4	− 6.3	− 3.9
Pyloric stomach	− 3.3	− 4.0	− 2.8
Small bowel	−34.1**	− 7.5	− 1.6
Cecum	−17.2**	− 9.3	− 6.4
Colon	+41.8**	− 2.3	− 3.1
Heart	+ 2.0	+ 3.2	+ 1.7
Kidneys	+ 1.2	− 8.4	+ 0.2
Liver	−25.0**	− 9.3	+ 3.8
Lungs	+ 4.5	− 4.4	+ 3.5
Muscle (ventral abdominal wall)	+ 7.0	− 0.3	− 5.3
Salivary glands (submaxillary)	−10.9*	+ 6.5	− 6.0
Skin	− 4.9	+ 7.2	− 6.4
Spleen	− 0.1	−21.7*	− 2.5
Testes	+ 9.5	− 4.6	− 7.8
Thymus gland	−42.3**	+ 4.6	+10.5
Residual carcass	− 2.5	+ 1.9	− 4.1
Body weight at autopsy	− 7.8	− 3.0	− 5.5

[a]Wet weight was measured in grams. The results are expressed as percent change from respective controls given no tannic acid, specifically as $[(\bar{X}_d - \bar{X}_c)/\bar{X}_c]$ x 100, where $\bar{X}_d$ is the mean in the tannic acid (drug) treated animals and $\bar{X}_c$ the mean in the controls. Mean differences $(\bar{X}_d - \bar{X}_c)$ significant at P = 0.05 to 0.02 are indicated by one asterisk and at P = 0.01 or less by two asterisks. (From Singh and Boyd[22] with the permission of the authors and of the *Journal of the Canadian Association of Radiologists.*)

in Table 118. At two weeks and at one month, the weight and water content of body organs of survivors were mostly within the range of values in controls given no tannic acid.

Conclusions Regarding Tannic Acid

Tannic acids are glycosides of gallic acid found in the leafy and woody parts of plants where their presence affords some protection to the plant from parasitic infestation. They are present in various dietary items such as tea, coffee, and astringent wines.

The acute LD_{50} given orally to albino rats was 2.26 g/kg and rectally 1.16 g/kg. The mean interval to death varied inversely with the dose administered and at the LD_{50} was 38 hr following oral and 41 hr following rectal administration.

The clinical signs of intoxication were dominated by those reflecting depression of the central nervous system such as drowsiness, prostra-tion, ataxia, anorexia, and dyspnea. These in turn produced loss of body weight and hypothermia. Associated signs were pallor, diuresis, and proteinuria. Death occurred in deep hypothermic coma.

Histopathologically, death from tannic acid was associated with a marked local inflammatory reaction, either mostly in the upper alimentary tract following oral administration or in the colon and cecum following rectal dosing. This was followed by necrosis of the liver, degenerative changes in the kidneys and, in survivors, a stimula-tion of spermatogenesis.

Death was accompanied by loss of dry weight and hydration of many body organs with a stress reaction. Survivors began to recover in three to seven days and at two weeks and especially at one month measurements were essentially within the range of those in controls given no tannic acid.

TABLE 119

The Water Content of Body Organs of Albino Rats Following Rectal Administration of Tannic Acid in Doses at the Range of the LD_{50} [a]

Organ	At death (N = 7 + 7 controls)	Fortnight survivors (N = 12 + 9 controls)	Month survivors (N = 27 + 13 controls)
Adrenal glands	+44.9**	− 8.2	+11.2
Brain	+ 0.6	+ 3.0	− 3.7
Gastrointestinal tract			
Cardiac stomach	+ 0.5	+ 0.8	+ 0.6
Pyloric stomach	+ 2.5	+ 5.7	+12.8
Small bowel	− 9.8*	+11.0	− 0.7
Cecum	+ 4.9	− 1.3	− 1.8
Colon	+ 1.2	− 1.3	+ 7.4
Heart	+ 9.0	+ 2.3	+ 2.0
Kidneys	− 3.4	− 8.1	+ 0.8
Liver	+22.5**	+ 3.2	+ 5.5
Lungs	− 9.7*	− 1.0	− 3.7
Muscle (ventral abdominal wall)	+ 0.4	− 3.4	− 2.7
Salivary glands (submaxillary)	+ 1.0	+ 1.0	− 3.1
Skin	−14.0	− 3.8	− 6.1
Spleen	− 1.6	+ 1.6	+ 0.1
Testes	− 3.4	− 4.4	− 0.4
Thymus gland	−13.0	0.0	− 0.7
Residual carcass	+ 6.9	+ 2.1	− 9.0

[a]Water content was measured as grams water per 100 g dry weight of tissue. The results are expressed as percent change from respective controls given no tannic acid, specifically as$[(\overline{X}_d - \overline{X}_c)/\overline{X}_c] \times 100$, where $\overline{X}_d$ is the mean in the tannic acid (drug) treated animals and $\overline{X}_c$ the mean in the controls. Mean differences $(\overline{X}_d - \overline{X}_c)$ significant at P = 0.05 to 0.02 are indicated by one asterisk and at P = 0.01 or less by two asterisks. (From Singh and Boyd[22] with the permission of the authors and of the *Journal of the Canadian Association of Radiologists*.)

While some signs of tannic acid poisoning could occur in human beings consuming, for example, huge amounts of black tea, it is doubtful if enough tannic acid could be retained in the gastrointestinal tract to produce deaths. Deaths have occurred in man from use of excessive amounts of tannic acid applied locally to burns or added to barium sulfate radiodiagnostic enemas.

REFERENCES

1. Symposium on the Chemistry of Vegetable Tannins, Soc. Leather Trades Chemists, Croydon, 1956.
2. **Sticher, P. G., Windholz, M., Leahy, D. S., Bolton, D. M., and Eaton, I. G.,** *The Merck Index. An Encyclopedia of Chemicals and Drugs,* Merck and Company, Rahway, N.J., 1968.
3. **Korpassy, S., Horvai, R., and Koltay, M.,** On the absorption of tannic acid from the gastrointestinal tract, *Arch. Int. Pharmacodyn. Ther.,* 88, 368, 1951.
4. **Singh, J.,** The Acute Toxicity of Tannic Acid and Other Drugs Administered Rectally to Albino Rats, Ph.D. Thesis in Pharmacology, Douglas Library, Queen's University, Kingston, Ontario, Canada, 1967.
5. **Davidson, E. C.,** Tannic acid in the treatment of burns, *Surg. Gynecol. Obstet.,* 41, 202, 1925.
6. **Wilson, W. C., MacGregor, A. R., and Stewart, C. P.,** The clinical course and pathology of burns and scalds under modern methods of treatment, *Br. J. Surg.,* 25, 826, 1938.
7. **McClure, P. D.,** The treatment of patients with severe burns, *J.A.M.A.,* 113, 1808, 1939.
8. **Brins, L. J. and Hartman, F. W.,** Histopathology of the liver following burns, *Am. J. Clin. Pathol.,* 11, 275, 1941.
9. **Allen, H. S. and Koch, S. L.,** The treatment of patients with severe burns, *Surg. Gynecol. Obstet.,* 74, 914, 1942.
10. **Wells, D. B., Humphrey, H. D., and Coll, J. J.,** The relationship of tannic acid to the liver necrosis occurring in burns, *N. Engl. J. Med.,* 226, 629, 1942.
11. **Hamilton, J. B.,** The use of tannic acid in barium enemas, *Am. J. Roentgenol.,* 56, 101, 1946.
12. **Janower, M. L., Robins, L. L., Tomchik, F. S., and Weylman, W. T.,** Tannic acid and barium enemas, *Radiology,* 85, 887, 1965.
13. **Lucke, H. H., Hodge, K. E., and Patt, N. L.,** Fatal damage after barium enemas containing tannic acid, *Can. Med. Assoc. J.,* 89, 1111, 1963.
14. **McAlister, W. H., Anderson, M. S., Bloomberg, G. R., and Margulis, A. R.,** Lethal effects of tannic acid in the barium enema, *Radiology,* 80, 765, 1963.
15. United States Department of Health, Education, and Welfare, Food and Drug Administration, Docket No. FDC-D-80, Federal Register, Superintendent of Documents, Govt. Print. Off., Washington D.C., March 31, 1964.
16. **Boyd, E. M., Bereczky, K., and Godi, I.,** The acute toxicity of tannic acid administered intragastrically, *Can. Med. Assoc. J.,* 92, 1292, 1965.
17. **Boyd, E. M.,** An estimation in animals of the toxicity of the tannic acid-barium sulfate diagnostic enema, 40th Anniversary Pan American Medical Association Congress, Miami Beach, Fla., April 29–May 2, 1965.
18. **Singh, J. and Boyd, E. M.,** Retention time and toxicity of rectally administered tannic acid, *Proc. Can. Fed. Biol. Soc.,* 8, 17, 1965.
19. **Jarzylo, S. V., Boyd, E. M., and Fransman, S. L.,** Experimental toxicity of tannic acid with barium sulfate enemas, Annual Meeting, Canadian Association of Radiologists, Montreal, March, 1966.
20. **Singh, J. and Boyd, E. M.,** Hypothermia from rectal tannic acid, *Proc. Can. Fed. Biol. Soc.,* 9, 22, 1966.
21. **Singh, J. and Boyd, E. M.,** Thiopental anesthesia and tannic acid diagnostic enemas, *Can. Med. Assoc. J.,* 95, 558, 1966.
22. **Singh, J. and Boyd, E. M.,** The acute toxicity of tannic acid in the tannic acid-barium sulfate radiodiagnostic enema, *J. Can. Assoc. Radiol.,* 17, 124, 1966.
23. **Singh, J. and Boyd, E. M.,** Thiopental anesthesia and tannic acid diagnostic enemas, *Invest. Radiol.,* 3, 134, 1968.

Chapter 21

ATROPINE AND PILOCARPINE

Atropine or dl-hyoscyamine is the tropic acid ester of tropine, an alkaloid found in *Atropa belladonna L., Datura stramonium L.,* and other *Solanaceae.* In plants it is present in the levorotatory form, which is partially racemized during extraction and completely racemized by heating in chloroform solution or by treatment with dilute alkaline solutions.[1] In the studies of Boyd and Boyd on the acute[2] and chronic[3] toxicity of atropine, the alkaloid was employed as the sulfate salt. While atropine base is soluble in water to only 0.2%, atropine sulfate is soluble to about 2.5%. Atropine is widely used as an anticholinergic drug in human and veterinary medicine. Toxic effects include a dry mouth and dilated pupils.

Acute Toxicity of Atropine Sulfate

The acute oral LD_{50} of atropine sulfate given orally has been reported to be 400 to 795 mg/kg in mice,[4-8] 750 mg/kg in rats,[4] 1,100 mg/kg in guinea pigs,[4] and 1,400 to 1,500 in rabbits.[7] Corresponding values for the subcutaneous LD_{50} are 400 to 900 mg/kg in mice,[4-8] 2,000 mg/kg in rats,[4] 250 to 700 mg/kg in rabbits,[7] and 181 mg/kg in dogs.[9] Boyd and Jarzylo[9] reported that the LD_{50} ± S.E. of atropine base dissolved in olive oil and given subcutaneously was 125 ± 5 mg/kg in dogs and 108 ± 10 mg/kg in cats. When atropine sulfate was dissolved in distilled water and given subcutaneously, the LD_{50} ± S.E. was 181 ± 12 mg/kg in dogs. Free atropine killed the dogs in 38 ± 12 hr and atropine sulfate in 11 ± 9 hr. The minimal lethal dose in man has been estimated at 1 to 2 mg/kg.[10] Herbivora such as rabbits are able to tolerate large doses of atropine due to the presence in their blood of an atropine-splitting enzyme[11] and not due to differences in the rate of urinary elimination.[12] Boyd and Boyd[2] reported a detailed study of the acute toxicity of atropine sulfate given intramuscularly to rabbits; their work will be cited in exemplification.

Boyd and Boyd[2] gave atropine sulfate intramuscularly to young male rabbits in single doses between 300 and 900 mg/kg and then placed the animals singly in metabolism cages with a weighed excess of food (Purina rabbit pellets) and a measured excess of drinking water. There were two types of death: (a) an initial convulsive death and (b) a delayed anorectic death at one to three weeks.

Convulsive Death

This was an early death occurring in 25 ± 11 (mean ± S.D.) min. The LD_{50} ± S.E. was 588 ± 85 mg/kg. The clinical signs of intoxication were those of cholinergic inhibition (such as mydriasis) plus convulsions followed by prostration, hypothermia, cyanosis, pallor, and respiratory failure. There were no significant microscopic changes at autopsy. This type of death has been recorded in mice,[5] dogs,[9] and man[13] from much smaller doses of atropine.

Delayed Anorectic Death

All rabbits that survived initial convulsive deaths appeared normal by the third or fourth day when clinical measurements were normal, as shown by data summarized in Table 120. At seven days following administration of atropine, one quarter of the survivors had subnormal food intake (see Figure 123) and began to lose weight (see Figure 124). They exhibited oligodipsia, oliguria, and gangrene at the site of atropine injection (gluteal muscles of the left leg). Death occurred at 15 ± 8 (mean ± S.D.) days and at an LD_{50} ± S.E. of 414 ± 169 mg/kg. Anorexia and oligodipsia have been reported as signs of delayed atropine poisoning in rats[14] and dogs.[9] At death, body weight was about one third less than in the controls given no atropine.

Endarteritis Obliterans in Survivors

Rabbits that survived both types of death were eating (see Figure 123) and growing (see Figure 124) as well as the controls at four weeks. Some 10% of the survivors developed a gangrenous sloughing of the tissues of the left atropine-injected leg, which was observed for six months when such animals were killed and autopsied. At six months, the animals with sloughed left legs had lost a slight amount of body weight, the stump of the left leg was covered by scar tissue, there were

TABLE 120

Clinical Measurements, Expressed as Mean ± Standard Deviation, in Rabbits that Survived Initial Convulsive Deaths due to Intramuscular Injections of Atropine Sulfate

Group	N	Day 1	Day 2	Day 3	Day 4
Body weight: g gain (+) or loss (−)					
Controls	14	+28 ± 7	+21 ± 15	+23 ± 9	+33 ± 22
Survivors	28	−66 ± 67	−51 ± 117	−13 ± 91	+25 ± 92
Delayed deaths	10	−17 ± 66	+ 7 ± 59	+38 ± 112	+53 ± 119
Food intake: g chow/kg/24 hr					
Controls	14	72 ± 6	84 ± 10	77 ± 9	85 ± 5
Survivors	28	34 ± 22	62 ± 18	64 ± 13	75 ± 18
Delayed deaths	10	22 ± 11	74 ± 39	65 ± 48	57 ± 41
Water intake: ml/kg/24 hr					
Controls	14	153 ± 16	190 ± 5	206 ± 13	177 ± 27
Survivors	28	84 ± 55	134 ± 42	143 ± 45	143 ± 55
Delayed deaths	10	63 ± 16	248 ± 66	150 ± 44	126 ± 53
Urine output: ml/kg/24 hr					
Controls	14	46 ± 10	67 ± 17	53 ± 14	63 ± 13
Survivors	28	41 ± 19	42 ± 17	39 ± 32	42 ± 31
Delayed deaths	10	30 ± 23	50 ± 17	32 ± 5	23 ± 6
Colonic temperature: °F					
Controls	14	103.6 ± 0.6	103.5 ± 0.6	103.3 ± 0.4	103.0 ± 0.4
Survivors	28	103.0 ± 0.4	103.2 ± 0.7	103.3 ± 0.5	103.3 ± 0.4
Delayed deaths	10	102.7 ± 0.5	103.4 ± 0.5	103.7 ± 0.6	103.5 ± 0.6

(From Boyd and Boyd[2] with the permission of the *Canadian Medical Association Journal.*)

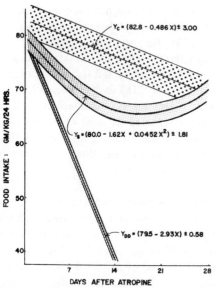

FIGURE 123. The regression of food intake on days after administration of toxic doses of atropine to rabbits, in controls given no atropine (Y_C), in animals which ultimately survived (Y_S), and in animals with a delayed death (Y_{DD}). (From Boyd and Boyd[2] with the permission of the *Canadian Medical Association Journal.*)

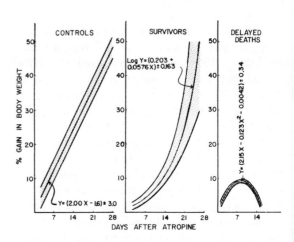

FIGURE 124. The regression of gain in body weight of rabbits on days after administration of lethal doses of atropine. (From Boyd and Boyd[2] with the permission of the *Canadian Medical Association Journal.*)

minor skin lesions about the head, the right heart was dilated, and the lungs were pale.

Microscopic examination disclosed the presence of endarteritis obliterans in arteries of the gastrocnemius muscle of the left leg into which atropine had been injected (see Figure 125) and in which sloughing had occurred. Muscle of the leg was atrophied and replaced by fibrous tissue and infiltrating leukocytes. The skin lesions consisted of thinning of the epidermis and leukocytic infiltration of the dermis and subcutaneous tissue. Cardiac muscle was edematous and granular and there were areas of edema and venous thrombosis in the lungs.

The Chronic Toxicity of Atropine
Rabbits

Boyd and Boyd[3] injected atropine sulfate intramuscularly in doses of 44 to 118 mg/kg/day for 100 days. Since these daily doses of atropine inhibited food intake, two groups of controls were employed, one fed ad libitum and the other pair-fed to atropine-treated rabbits. Results on a series of clinical measurements are summarized in Table 121. Loss of appetite accounted for some but not all of the loss of body weight, as indicated by results shown in Table 122. The $LD_{50 \, (100 \, days)}$ was 78 ± 5 mg/kg/day which is 13.2% (= 100-day LD_{50} index) of the acute $LD_{50 \, (1 \, dose)}$. The regression of the maximal daily dose producing no deaths on days of administration is shown in Figure 126. Since one out of ten rabbits died on the day following the entry in Figure 126, the estimates shown in Figure 126 approximate daily doses producing 10% mortality.

There was a decrease in the concentration of blood hemoglobin at 9 to 12 weeks, as illustrated in Figure 127. At this time there was impaired flexion of the left hind limb, but no sloughing

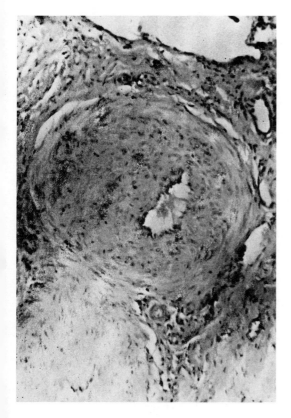

FIGURE 125. A photomicrograph of an artery adjacent to the gastrocnemius muscle of the left leg of a rabbit which had been given atropine into the same region six months earlier. Note hypertrophy of the subendothelium, almost complete loss of the internal elastic lamina, and a normal media and externa. (From Boyd and Boyd[2] with the permission of the *Canadian Medical Association Journal*.)

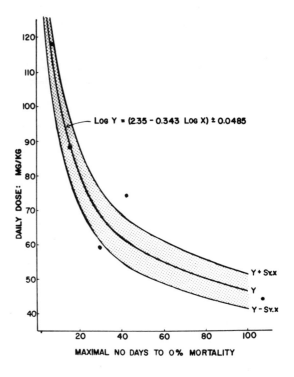

FIGURE 126. The regression, on maximal number of days of daily intramuscular injection, of the maximal daily dose which produced no deaths in rabbits. (From Boyd and Boyd[3] with the permission of *Toxicology and Applied Pharmacology*, copyright © 1962, Academic Press, New York.)

TABLE 121

Daily Intramuscular Doses of Atropine Sulfate that Produced Certain Clinical Signs of Toxicity in 50% of Rabbits[a]

Days of administration	Inhibition of growth	Inhibition of water intake	Inhibition of urine output	Augmentation of colonic temperature	Death
10	86 ± 4	73 ± 10	91 ± 14	–	127 ± 9
20	83 ± 4	71 ± 10	87 ± 14	–	110 ± 8
30	80 ± 4	69 ± 10	84 ± 14	–	101 ± 7
40	77 ± 4	67 ± 10	80 ± 14	80 ± 20	95 ± 6
50	74 ± 4	65 ± 10	76 ± 14	75 ± 20	90 ± 6
60	72 ± 4	63 ± 10	73 ± 14	69 ± 20	87 ± 6
70	69 ± 4	61 ± 10	69 ± 14	63 ± 20	84 ± 6
80	66 ± 4	59 ± 10	66 ± 14	58 ± 20	82 ± 5
90	63 ± 4	57 ± 10	62 ± 14	52 ± 20	79 ± 5
100	60 ± 4	55 ± 10	57 ± 14	46 ± 20	78 ± 5

[a]Doses are expressed as mean ± S.E. mg/kg/day.

The results were derived by comparison with measurements in pair-fed controls. (From Boyd and Boyd[3] with the permission of *Toxicology and Applied Pharmacology,* copyright © 1962, Academic Press, New York.)

TABLE 122

Mean Percentage Changes,[a] from Pair-fed and Ad Libitum-fed Controls, in Rabbits Surviving at the Time when 50% Had Died from Daily Dosing with Atropine Sulfate

Measurement	Control for comparison	Daily dose of atropine sulfate (mg/kg) 44[b]	59	74	88	118
Body weight	Ad lib-fed	– 6	–29[c]	–35[c]	–41[c]	–33
	Pair-fed	–10	–19[c]	–26[c]	–30[c]	–14
Food intake	Ad lib-fed	– 9	– 5	+ 8	+ 6	–45[c]
Water intake	Ad lib-fed	–33	–18	–56[c]	–46[c]	–31[c]
	Pair-fed	–18	–21	–55[c]	–35[c]	–42[c]
Urine output	Ad lib-fed	–68[c]	–24	–63[c]	–64[c]	–47[c]
	Pair-fed	–46[c]	–47[c]	–57[c]	–67[c]	–31
Colonic temperature	Ad lib-fed	– 0.39	+ 0.097	– 0.19	– 0.096	– 0.097
	Pair-fed	+ 0.53[c]	+ 0.73[c]	+ 0.58	+ 0.81[c]	– 0.39

[a]Calculated as $[(\bar{X}_d - \bar{X}_c)/\bar{X}_c] \times 100$, where $\bar{X}_d$ is the mean in the atropine treated animals and $\bar{X}_c$ is the mean in the indicated controls.
[b]Calculations in this column were made from measurements recorded after 98 days of drug administration when no rabbits had died.
[c]Significant at $P = 0.05$ or less.

(From Boyd and Boyd[3] with the permission of *Toxicology and Applied Pharmacology,* copyright © 1962, Academic Press, New York.)

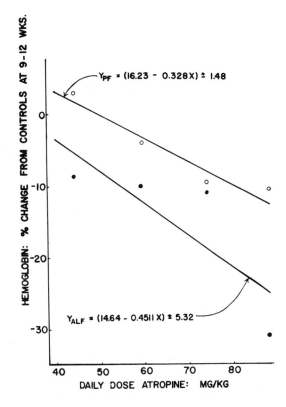

$$Y_{PF} = (16.23 - 0.328X) \pm 1.48$$

$$Y_{ALF} = (14.64 - 0.4511X) \pm 5.32$$

FIGURE 127. Percentage changes from pair-fed controls (Y_{PF}) and ad libitum-fed controls (Y_{ALF}) in the concentration of blood hemoglobin of rabbits after 9 to 12 weeks of daily intramuscular injection of atropine sulfate. (From Boyd and Boyd[3] with the permission of *Toxicology and Applied Pharmacology*, copyright © 1962, Academic Press, New York.)

occurred. The main cause of death was respiratory failure following convulsions. Ability of animals to survive was related to ability to maintain food intake.

Histopathological lesions found at death included fibrosis in the muscles of the left hind limb with local hemorrhage and leukocytic infiltration. There were varying degrees of endarteritis obliterans similar to that shown in Figure 125, although with less blockage of the arterial lumen. There was central fatty degeneration or cirrhosis of the liver, venous thrombosis in the lungs, a deficiency of zymogenic granules in the acinar glands of the pancreas, inhibition of spermatogenesis, and a stress reaction.

Changes in the wet weight of body organs of survivors are summarized in Table 123. With increasing daily doses of atropine, there was loss of fresh weight in most body organs, especially salivary glands, liver, kidneys, heart, and total

body. Corresponding shifts in water content of body organs of survivors are shown in Table 124. The most common change was hydration in organs such as the esophagus, gallbladder, trachea, and thymus gland.

Dogs

Boyd and Jarzylo[9] gave atropine subcutaneously daily to young dogs in a dose of 16 mg/kg/day. The daily dose was about one eighth of the subcutaneous LD_{50} and at three weeks three fourths of the animals were dead. The signs of intoxication included vomiting, excitement, diarrhea, chronic infection, signs of vagal inhibition, loss of organ weight with hydration, and degeneration in some organs.

Acute Toxicity of Pilocarpine

The clinical signs of toxicity to pilocarpine nitrate given orally to albino rats were described by Covert and Boyd[15] and the pathological signs by Jarzylo and Boyd.[16] Boyd and Fulford[17] studied the acute toxicity of pilocarpine hydrochloride given subcutaneously to albino rats. Earlier studies were reviewed by Boyd and Fulford.[17]

Single lethal doses of pilocarpine produced two types of death, an initial muscarinic convulsive reaction and a delayed catatonic psychotic reaction. The $LD_{50} \pm$ S.E. of the initial reaction was 911 ± 111 mg/kg when given orally and 642 ± 90 mg/kg given subcutaneously. The mean $\pm$ standard deviation interval to death in the initial reaction was 54 ± 30 min given orally and 34 ± 20 min given subcutaneously. When pilocarpine was given orally, there were two types of delayed death, one at one to three days with an $LD_{50} \pm$ S.E. of 730 ± 164 mg/kg, and another at three to seven days with an $LD_{50} \pm$ S.E. of 570 ± 138 mg/kg.[15] When given subcutaneously, delayed deaths occurred at 4.4 ± 2.5 (mean $\pm$ S.D.) days and at an $LD_{50} \pm$ S.E. of 430 ± 126 mg/kg.[17] An exemplification of the double distribution of deaths is presented in Figure 128.

A summary of the clinical signs of intoxication to pilocarpine is given in Table 125. It will be noted that convulsions and signs of cholinergic stimulation were confined to the first day. The signs that appeared on the second to seventh days included listlessness, ataxia, an upright stance, anal discharge, and spatial disorientation. Survivors

TABLE 123

Changes in the Fresh Wet Weight of Body Organs of Rabbits Surviving Daily Intramuscular Injections of Atropine Sulfate[a]

Organ	Daily dose of atropine sulfate (mg/kg)			
	44.2	58.8	73.7	88.3
Submaxillary salivary glands	+17.0	− 4.4	−12.8	−24.9*
Esophagus	− 4.1	−14.9	−21.1*	− 0.1
Stomach	+ 2.9	−17.8	−26.3*	− 7.3
Duodenum	+ 0.5	− 5.9	−23.0	−29.3
Jejunum	−19.6	− 1.4	−24.4	−28.2
Ileum	−13.7	−19.7*	−22.5	−21.7
Cecum	+ 5.1	−16.0*	−24.5	+ 6.4
Appendix	− 8.6	−23.7	−41.0*	−42.6
Colon	+ 7.4	− 8.1	− 3.7	0.0
Liver	−18.4	−23.7*	−37.2*	−36.4*
Gallbladder	+ 1.1	+ 6.8	− 4.3	+15.3
Kidneys	−12.0	−14.3	−26.5*	−26.5*
Heart	−14.3	−29.7*	−35.2*	−31.9*
Trachea	− 2.1	−19.7*	−38.6*	− 2.8
Lungs	+ 1.1	−21.4*	−36.8*	−16.1
Spleen	− 0.3	+11.0	−41.9*	−35.5
Adrenal glands	+21.0	− 7.3	+ 5.7	+ 6.5
Testicles	− 1.8	− 0.8	−32.5*	−11.9
Thymus gland	−15.7	−18.2	−54.1*	−28.3
Brain	—	−28.0*	− 5.7	—
Autopsy body weight	− 9.8	−18.7*	−26.7*	−28.9*

[a]Calculated as the mean difference from pair-fed controls and expressed as a percentage of the mean of these controls. An asterisk indicates that the mean difference was significant at P ± 0.05 by a t test. (From Boyd and Boyd[3] with the permission of *Toxicology and Applied Pharmacology*, copyright © 1962, Academic Press, New York.)

TABLE 124

Changes[a] in the Water Levels[b] of Body Organs of Rabbits Surviving Daily Intramuscular Injections of Atropine Sulfate

Organ	Daily dose of atropine sulfate (mg/kg)			
	44.2	58.8	73.7	88.3
Submaxillary salivary glands	0.0	+ 7.6	+ 2.8	+ 13.4
Esophagus	− 3.2	+ 9.5	+ 5.7	+ 15.4*
Cardiac stomach	− 7.9	−21.3*	− 9.5*	+ 40.6*
Pyloric stomach	+ 8.7*	− 1.2	− 0.7	+ 9.6*
Duodenum	− 7.2	− 1.7	+13.8*	− 2.0
Jejunum	+15.1*	− 1.5	+10.1	+ 3.5
Ileum	− 0.7	+17.5*	+15.3	+ 22.2
Cecum	+ 9.1	+19.9*	+ 0.9	− 3.8
Appendix	+ 1.4	+ 5.8	0.0	+ 3.4
Colon	+ 9.0	+18.1	+ 1.3	+ 13.3
Liver	+ 3.0	+ 5.0	− 2.6	+ 2.4
Gallbladder	+23.8*	+21.8*	− 9.4	+ 30.6*
Kidneys	+ 6.9	+ 5.5	− 4.3	− 15.1*
Heart	+ 1.0	+ 2.3	+ 1.2	+ 11.6*
Trachea	+ 7.3	+16.5*	+46.9*	+ 50.0*
Lungs	+17.4*	+11.0	− 0.8	+ 2.2
Spleen	− 1.1	+ 2.4	+ 0.6	+ 1.9
Adrenal glands	−11.0	+ 3.8	− 8.5	+ 5.6
Testicles	− 0.6	+ 1.2	− 4.8	+ 0.8
Thymus gland	+56.5*	+13.2	− 2.5	+138.5*
Cerebrum	—	+ 1.3	+ 0.9	—
Cerebellum	—	+ 6.5	+19.4	—
Muscle	—	+14.1*	+11.8	—
Skin	− 0.6	+ 2.8	+17.1	+ 12.1*

[a]Calculated as the mean difference from pair-fed controls and expressed as a percentage of the mean of these controls. An asterisk indicates that the mean difference was significant at P ≤ 0.05 by a t test.
[b]Water levels were measured as grams water per 100 g dry weight of organ.

(From Boyd and Boyd[3] with the permission of *Toxicology and Applied Pharmacology*, copyright © 1962, Academic Press, New York.)

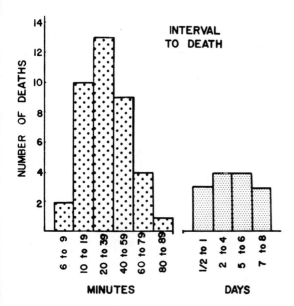

INTERVAL
TO DEATH

NUMBER OF DEATHS

MINUTES   DAYS

FIGURE 128. The frequency distribution of deaths in albino rats following subcutaneous injection of pilocarpine hydrochloride in doses of from 200 to 1,000 mg/kg. Note variation in the time scale of the abscissa. (From Boyd and Fulford[17] with the permission of the *Canadian Journal of Biochemistry and Physiology,* copyright © 1961, the National Research Council of Canada, Ottawa.)

exhibited signs noted in Table 125 during the first week. They were then excited for a few days before returning to normal. A summary of clinical measurements is presented in Table 126. It will be noted that survivors developed a voracious appetite and a slight fever toward the end of the first week after being given pilocarpine.

The outstanding feature seen at autopsy on animals that died within a few hours of administration of pilocarpine was congestion of many body organs, sometimes associated with hemorrhage or thromboses. Some of the congestion was still present in animals with delayed psychotic deaths who also had hepatic necrosis, nephritis, pulmonary congestion, a stress reaction, and inhibition of spermatogenesis. Most published accounts of the toxicology of pilocarpine confine description to the initial muscarinic reaction and fail to mention the delayed psychotic reaction.[17,18]

Chronic Toxicity of Pilocarpine

A study of the chronic toxicity of pilocarpine nitrate given orally daily to young male albino rats was reported by Boyd and Jarzylo,[19] who

TABLE 125

The Percentage Incidence of Clinical Signs of Intoxication to Pilocarpine Hydrochloride Given Subcutaneously to Albino Rats in Doses at the Range of the LD_{50}

Clinical sign	Immediate deaths	Delayed deaths		Survivors	
		1st day	2nd−7th days	1st day	2nd−7th days
Sialorrhea	100	100	0	100	0
Mucous diarrhea	100	100	0	100	0
Clonic convulsions	100	85	0	100	0
Listlessness	69	54	75	33	0
Chromodacryorrhea	18	46	0	67	0
Impaired righting reflex	18	69	0	12	0
Nystagmus	10	0	0	0	0
Ataxia	−	−	25	−	0
Upright stance	0	0	25	4	14
Muscular twitching	−	−	0	−	14
Anal discharge	−	−	50	−	29
Spacial disorientation	−	−	25	−	43
Normal	0	0	0	0	43
Irritability	−	−	0	−	57

(From Boyd and Fulford[17] with the permission of the *Canadian Journal of Biochemistry and Physiology,* copyright © 1961, the National Research Council of Canada, Ottawa.)

TABLE 126

Clinical Measurements in Albino Rats Following Subcutaneous Injection of
Pilocarpine Hydrochloride in Doses at the Range of the LD_{50}

		Days after pilocarpine		
Group	N	1	3	5
Body wt (g increase (+) or decrease (−))				
Nonsurvivors	53	− 35.2 ± 13.0	− 51.8 ± 29.6	− 65.4 ± 36.0
Survivors	27	− 24.5 ± 18.2	− 25.1 ± 33.6	− 17.8 ± 41.2
Controls	31	+ 2.0 ± 4.6	+ 4.9 ± 5.3	+ 8.0 ± 6.8
Food intake (g chow/kg body wt/24 hr)				
Nonsurvivors	53	17.4 ± 33.2	36.2 ± 58.7	32.4 ± 40.6
Survivors	27	65.2 ± 58.8	94.1 ± 79.4	123.3 ± 81.1
Controls	31	80.3 ± 11.4	70.8 ± 8.5	71.0 ± 7.7
Water intake (ml/kg body wt/24 hr)				
Nonsurvivors	53	48.2 ± 63.6	56.2 ± 89.1	45.8 ± 51.0
Survivors	27	111.5 ± 97.1	156.0 ± 83.9	214.3 ± 83.0
Controls	31	104.8 ± 18.2	89.0 ± 13.8	88.7 ± 19.6
Urine volume (ml/kg body wt/24 hr)				
Nonsurvivors	53	8.8 ± 4.4	9.6 ± 11.8	3.8 ± 5.2
Survivors	27	12.5 ± 8.3	7.6 ± 5.0	31.5 ± 44.8
Controls	31	23.3 ± 6.9	28.9 ± 7.2	35.1 ± 9.0
Colonic temperature (°F)				
Nonsurvivors	53	99.4 ± 1.0	96.4 ± 1.9	94.1 ± 6.0
Survivors	27	99.2 ± 1.6 ·	97.9 ± 2.5	100.1 ± 0.7
Controls	31	99.3 ± 0.7	99.2 ± 0.7	99.2 ± 0.5

(From Boyd and Fulford[17] with the permission of the *Canadian Journal of
Biochemistry and Physiology,* copyright © 1961, the National Research Council
of Canada, Ottawa.)

reviewed the literature on the subject. As indicated
in Figure 129, the $LD_{50\ (100\ days)}$ ± S.E. was
found to be 156 ± 20 mg/kg/day. The maximal
$LD_0\ (100\ days)$ was similarly estimated to be 1.4
± 4.8 mg/kg/day and the minimal
$LD_{100}\ (100\ days)$ to be 298 ± 27 mg/kg/day.

The main clinical signs of intoxication consisted
of diarrhea, sialorrhea, hemodacryorrhea, fur
soiling, irritability, and convulsions. The first three
cholinergic signs appeared only during a period of
about 2 hr following pilocarpine administration, as
indicated in Table 127. None of the animals
exhibited the cachectic psychoses seen in delayed
acute pilocarpine intoxication.

The relationship of daily dosage of pilocarpine
to changes in clinical measurements is exemplified
in Figures 130 and 131. At the maximal
$LD_0\ (100\ days)$ there was no significant inhibition
of growth; at the $LD_{50\ (100\ days)}$ there was a

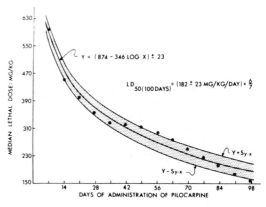

FIGURE 129. The regression on days of daily oral
administration to albino rats, of the dose of pilocarpine
nitrate which killed 50% of animals. Since the drug was
given daily for 6 days a week, the results must be
multiplied by 6/7 to obtain the dose given daily for 7
days a week. (From Boyd and Jarzylo[19] with the
permission of the *Archives Internationales de Pharmacodynamie et de Therapie.*)

TABLE 127

The Intensity of the Main Clinical Signs of Intoxication to Pilocarpine Nitrate Given Orally Daily to Albino Rats[a]

Daily dose (mg/kg)	Immediate diarrhea	Immediate sialorrhea	Immediate hemodacryorrhea	Soiling of fur	Irritability	Convulsions
0.39	0.0	0.0	0.0	0.0	0.0	0.0
0.78	0.0	0.0	0.0	0.0	0.0	0.0
1.95	0.0	0.0	0.0	0.0	0.0	0.0
7.8	0.0	0.1	0.0	0.0	0.0	0.0
19.5	0.0	0.3*	0.0	0.0	0.0	0.0
39.0	0.4*	1.0**	0.2	0.3**	0.1	0.0
78.0	2.0**	1.0**	0.1	0.9**	0.1	0.0
156	1.8**	0.9**	0.4*	2.1**	0.1	0.1
234	3.0**	1.0**	0.2	1.8**	0.1	0.0
312	3.0**	0.8**	0.4*	1.9**	0.1	0.1
390	2.8**	1.0**	1.0**	1.6**	0.1	0.1*
468	3.1**	1.0**	0.4*	2.3**	0.1	0.1
546	3.3**	1.0**	0.5*	3.0**	0.3	0.3*
624	2.9**	1.0**	1.0**	3.0**	0.4*	0.3*
702	3.0**	0.9**	0.8**	2.8**	0.5*	0.8**
781	2.9**	0.9**	0.9**	2.0**	0.5*	0.7**

[a]The signs were semiquantitated in clinical units of 1 to 4 and are expressed as the mean intensity over the interval of administration. One asterisk indicates that the mean intensity was significantly different from zero at $P = 0.05$ to 0.02 and two asterisks at $P = 0.01$ or less. (From Boyd and Jarzylo[19] with the permission of the *Archives Internationales de Pharmacodynamie et de Therapie.*)

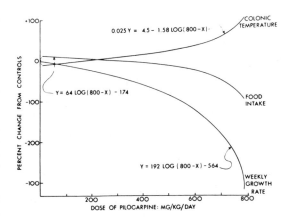

FIGURE 130. The regression, on daily dose of pilocarpine administered orally to albino rats, of mean percent change, from values in controls given no pilocarpine, in weekly growth rate (measured in g), food intake (measured as g/kg/day), and colonic temperature (measured as °C). (From Boyd and Jarzylo[19] with the permission of the *Archives Internationales de Pharmacodynamie et de Therapie.*)

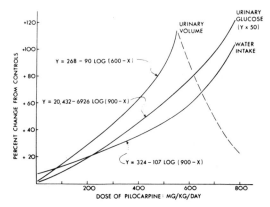

FIGURE 131. The regression, on daily dose of pilocarpine given orally to albino rats, of mean percent change, from controls given no pilocarpine, in urinary volume (measured as ml/kg/day), urinary glucose output (measured as mg/kg/day), and water intake (measured as ml/kg/day). Note that the ordinate values for glucose output must be multiplied by 50 to obtain mean percentage changes from controls. (From Boyd and Jarzylo[19] with the permission of the *Archives Internationales de Pharmacodynamie et de Therapie.*)

significant inhibition of 38% and at the minimal LD_{100} (100 days) and over, growth was increasingly depressed, as shown in Figure 130. Inhibition of growth was not due to a decrease in food intake except at the highest doses shown in Figure 130. Doses below the LD_{50} (100 days) produced a slight but significant hypothermia and higher doses produced a fever. There were no significant changes in urinary volume, pH, glucose, protein, acetone, or blood at the maximal LD_0 (100 days). At and above the LD_{50} (100 days) there occurred a significant diuresis, glycosuria, and polydipsia, as shown in Figure 131. Radiologically, a barium sulfate meal was found to be propelled rapidly along the gastrointestinal tract during the first half hour after pilocarpine administration and thereafter more slowly than in controls.

Autopsy findings at death due to pilocarpine intoxication are summarized in Table 128. Doses up to 19.5 mg/kg/day had no histological effect apart from some renal congestion. Larger daily doses produced widespread capillary-venous congestion, pneumonitis, nephritis, hepatitis, a stress reaction, and inhibition of spermatogenesis.

Changes in organ weights of survivors at 100 days are indicated in Table 129 and in water content in Table 130. Apart from a stressor increase in the weight of adrenal glands, most

TABLE 128

The Effect of Daily Oral Administration of Pilocarpine Nitrate on the Histological Appearance of Body Organs of Albino Rats

Organ	Daily doses 0.39 to 19.5 mg/kg	Daily doses 39 to 780 mg/kg
Adrenal glands	Normal appearance	Lipoid droplets prominent in cortical layers
Brain	Normal appearance	Occasional meningeal congestion
Gastrointestinal tract		
Cardiac stomach	Normal appearance	Normal appearance
Pyloric stomach	Normal appearance	Normal appearance; occasionally hypertrophied
Small bowel	Normal appearance	Normal appearance
Cecum	Normal appearance	Normal appearance
Colon	Normal appearance	Normal appearance
Heart	Normal appearance	Occasional areas of capillary congestion
Kidneys	Occasionally capillary-venous congestion	Congestion and occasionally areas of tubular necrosis and leukocytic infiltration
Liver	Normal appearance	Centrilobular pale-staining with occasionally minor fatty degeneration or necrosis
Lungs	Normal appearance	Capillary-venous congestion; pneumonitis
Muscle (ventral abdominal wall)	Normal appearance	Normal appearance
Pancreas	Normal appearance	Normal appearance
Salivary (submaxillary glands)	Normal appearance	Minor loss of zymogenic granules in the serous glands
Skin	Normal appearance	Normal appearance
Spleen	Normal appearance	Contracted red pulp
Testes	Normal appearance	Varying degrees of deficiency of sperm
Thymus gland	Normal appearance	Loss of thymocytes

(From Boyd and Jarzylo[19] with the permission of the *Archives Internationales de Pharmacodynamie et de Therapie.*)

TABLE 129

The Effect of Daily Oral Administration of Pilocarpine Nitrate on the Fresh Wet Weight of Body Organs in Surviving Albino Rats[a]

Organ	Daily doses 0.39 to 19.5 mg/kg (N = 39 + 25 controls)	Daily doses 39 to 312 mg/kg (N = 25 + 25 controls)	Daily doses 390 to 780 mg/kg (N = 30 + 30 controls)
Adrenal glands	– 2.8	+72.3**	+26.1*
Brain	– 1.6	+ 0.1	+ 1.9
Gastrointestinal tract			
Cardiac stomach	–13.4**	–10.4**	– 4.6
Pyloric stomach	–10.6**	+ 4.1	+ 8.0*
Small bowel	– 3.4	+ 2.1	– 4.6
Cecum	+ 3.1	+ 3.2	+ 4.2
Colon	– 7.1*	+ 1.0	0.0
Heart	– 7.5**	–12.8**	+ 1.3
Kidneys	– 9.1**	– 4.9	– 4.2
Liver	–12.1**	– 9.3*	– 3.1
Lungs	– 4.5	– 3.9	– 7.3
Muscle (ventral abdominal wall)	– 9.2*	–22.4**	– 6.2
Pancreas	–13.5*	– 6.6	– 1.8
Salivary (submaxillary glands)	+ 1.1	– 4.1	+ 3.4
Skin	–14.2**	–27.8**	– 7.7
Spleen	– 5.2	–18.1**	–24.4**
Testes	– 3.8	–11.9**	– 5.2
Thymus gland	–10.6*	– 9.1	–33.9**
Residual carcass	–11.6**	–13.9**	– 1.7
Autopsy body weight	– 9.7**	–13.8**	– 4.1

[a]Wet weight was measured in grams. The results are expressed as mean percent change from controls given no pilocarpine, specifically as $[(\bar{X}_d - \bar{X}_c)/\bar{X}_c] \times 100$, where $\bar{X}_d$ is the mean in the drug treated rats and $\bar{X}_c$ in their controls. One asterisk indicates that $\bar{X}_d - \bar{X}_c$ is significant at P = 0.05 to 0.02 and two asterisks at P = 0.01 or less. (From Boyd and Jarzylo[19] with the permission of the *Archives Internationales de Pharmacodynamie et de Therapie.*)

organs lost weight. Loss of wet weight was marked in cardiac stomach, heart, liver, muscle, skin, spleen, testes, thymus gland, and residual carcass. Loss of weight was less marked in the survivors of large daily doses. As noted in Table 130, changes in the water content of body organs were of a minor nature and mainly of hydration.

Abrupt withdrawal of pilocarpine administration at 100 days disclosed no evidence of physical dependence. Locomotor activity (measured in Wahman activity wheels) declined over a period of 33 days of withdrawal from high values toward the end of the 100 days of daily drug administration. Other signs of intoxication gradually disappeared during the month of withdrawal of pilocarpine administration.

Conclusions Regarding Atropine and Pilocarpine

Single intramuscular lethal doses of atropine produced an early convulsive anticholinergic death in less than 1 hr after administration. Some of the survivors died in the following weeks following an anorectic cachexia, while others developed a non-lethal endarteritis obliterans of the injected leg.

Single lethal oral doses of pilocarpine produced an early muscarinic convulsive death within the first hour of administration. Some survivors developed a lethal cachectic psychosis and died within one week.

The $LD_{50 \ (100 \ days)}$ of both atropine and pilocarpine was some 10 to 20% of the $LD_{50 \ (1 \ dose)}$. The clinical signs of intoxication included those on the autonomic nervous system

TABLE 130

The Effect of Daily Oral Administration of Pilocarpine Nitrate on the Water Content of Body Organs of Surviving Albino Rats[a]

Organ	Daily doses 0.39 to 19.5 mg/kg (N = 39 + 25 controls)	Daily doses 39 to 312 mg/kg (N = 25 + 25 controls)	Daily doses 390 to 780 mg/kg (N = 30 + 30 controls)
Adrenal glands	+9.9*	+ 6.3	+ 0.5
Brain	+0.2	+ 1.4	+ 0.6
Gastrointestinal tract			
Cardiac stomach	+2.4	+ 0.4	− 0.5
Pyloric stomach	+1.3	+ 2.6	− 2.8
Small bowel	+1.9	+ 4.9	+ 3.2
Cecum	+7.0*	+ 8.7*	+ 0.2
Colon	−1.2	+ 0.7	+ 2.2
Heart	+2.1	+ 0.8	− 0.6
Kidneys	−1.8	+ 3.4	− 5.1*
Liver	+8.2*	+ 8.4*	− 2.8
Lungs	+3.4	− 1.1	− 2.2
Muscle (ventral abdominal wall)	+4.1	+ 2.2	+ 2.1
Pancreas	+5.3	+13.6*	+ 5.8
Salivary (submaxillary glands)	+1.2	+ 7.4*	+ 2.6
Skin	+1.4	+ 0.3	+12.8*
Spleen	−0.2	+ 0.3	− 2.2
Testes	+3.8	− 5.4	− 0.6
Thymus gland	+0.9	− 3.1	− 4.2
Residual carcass	+4.8*	+10.4**	− 0.4

[a]Water content was measured as grams water per 100 g dry weight of tissue. The results are expressed as mean percent change from controls given no pilocarpine, specifically as $[(\bar{X}_d - \bar{X}_c)/\bar{X}_c] \times 100$, where $\bar{X}_d$ is the mean in the drug treated rats and $\bar{X}_c$ in their controls. One asterisk indicates that $\bar{X}_d - \bar{X}_c$ is significant at P = 0.05 to 0.02 and two asterisks at P = 0.01 or less. (From Boyd and Jarzylo[19] with the permission of the *Archives Internationales de Pharmacodynamie et de Therapie*.)

plus convulsions and inhibition of growth. Histological signs at death were similar in the two types of chronic intoxication and included a stress reaction, inhibition of spermatogenesis, and degenerative changes in the kidneys and liver. Both drugs produced loss of organ wet weight and some degree of organ hydration.

Apart from opposite pharmacological effects on the autonomic nervous system the acute and chronic toxicity of pilocarpine was similar to that of atropine.

REFERENCES

1. Stecker, P. G., Windholz, M., Leahy, D. S., Bolton, D. M., and Eaton, L. G., *The Merck Index. An Encyclopedia of Chemicals and Drugs,* 8th ed., Merck and Company, Rahway, N.J., 1968.
2. Boyd, C. E. and Boyd, E. M., The acute toxicity of atropine sulfate, *Can. Med. Assoc. J.,* 85, 1241, 1961.
3. Boyd, C. E. and Boyd, E. M., The chronic toxicity of atropine administered intramuscularly to rabbits, *Toxicol. Appl. Pharmacol.,* 4, 457, 1962.
4. Cahen, R. L. and Tvede, K., Homatropine methylbromide: pharmacological reevaluation, *J. Pharmacol. Exp. Ther.,* 105, 166, 1952.
5. Cazort, R. J., Atropine-like action of alpha, alpha-diphenyl-gamma-dimethylaminovaleramide HCl (BL 139), *J. Pharmacol. Exp. Ther.,* 100, 325, 1950.
6. Ing, H. R., Dawes, G. S., and Wajda, I., Synthetic substitutes for atropine, *J. Pharmacol. Exp. Ther.,* 85, 85, 1945.
7. Spector, W. S., Ed., *Handbook of Toxicology,* Vol. 1, W. B. Saunders, Philadelphia, 1956.
8. Stoll, H. C., Pharmacodynamic considerations of atropine and related compounds, *Am. J. Med. Sci.,* 215, 577, 1948.
9. Boyd, E. M. and Jarzylo, S., Chronic atropinization and fibrocystic disease of the pancreas, *Can. Med. Assoc. J.,* 82, 821, 1960.
10. Gordon, A. S. and Frye, C. W., Large doses of atropine: low toxicity and effectiveness in anticholinesterase intoxication, *J.A.M.A.,* 159, 1181, 1955.
11. Godeaux, J. and Tonnesen, M., Investigations into atropine metabolism in animal organism, *Acta Pharmacol. Toxicol.,* 5, 95, 1949.
12. Tønnesen, M., The excretion of atropine and allied alkaloids in urine, *Acta Pharmacol. Toxicol.,* 6, 147, 1950.
13. Joos, H. A. and Frye, C. W., Atropine intoxication in infancy, *Am. J. Dis. Child.,* 79, 855, 1950.
14. Schmidt, H., Jr., Moak, S. J., and Van Meter, W. G., Atropine depression of food and water intake in the rat, *Am. J. Physiol.,* 192, 543, 1958.
15. Covert, E. L. and Boyd, E. M., The acute oral toxicity of pilocarpine. I. Clinical observations, *Pharmacologist,* 4, 176, 1962.
16. Jarzylo, S. and Boyd, E. M., The acute oral toxicity of pilocarpine. II. Pathological observations, *Pharmacologist,* 4, 176, 1962.
17. Boyd, E. M. and Fulford, R. A., Pilocarpine-induced convulsions and delayed psychotic-like reaction, *Can. J. Biochem. Physiol.,* 39, 1287, 1961.
18. Carrier, O., Jr., *Pharmacology of the Peripheral Autonomic Nervous System,* Year Book Medical Publishers, Chicago, 1972.
19. Boyd, E. M. and Jarzylo, S. V., Daily oral doses of pilocarpine tolerated by albino rats, *Arch. Int. Pharmacodyn. Ther.,* 175, 84, 1968.

INDEX

Encephalitis, 175
Enzymes, 214
Epistaxis, 29, 59, 64, 73, 74, 82, 152
Erythrocyte count, 196
Erythrocytes, 2, 83, 84, 124, 148, 149, 189
  concentration of iron in, 189
  lipid content of, 2
Ether, 107
  extraction with, 107
Extracellular fluid, 167, 170

F

Fasting, 2
  blood lipids in, 1
  prolonged, 2
Fat depots, 3, 4, 5
  genital, 3
  mesenteric, 3
  omental, 3
  perirenal, 3
  physiological activity in, 5
  skinfold, 3
Fat, 121
Fatty acids, 71, 103
  classification of, 71
  unsaturated, 103
    oxidation of, 103
Fatty degeneration, 41, 42, 64, 83, 90, 115, 119, 122,
    124, 136, 170, 227, 235, 240
Feces, 197, 202
  elimination of kaolin in, 202
  ouput of iron in, 197
Fermentation (green skin) death, 58, 64
Ferritin, 189
Ferrous chloride, 190
Ferrous fumarate, 190
Ferrous gluconate, 190
Ferrous sulfate, 189, 190, 192, 196
Fever, 10, 29, 64, 72, 86, 89, 114, 117, 124, 132, 163,
    174, 184, 237, 240
Fibroblast infiltration, 26, 175
Fibrosis, 235
Flavor potentiators, 214
Flavors, 214
Food adjuvants, 213
  toxicity of, 213
Food contaminants, 1
Food intake, 10, 17, 40, 46, 73, 85, 104, 105, 108, 118,
    126, 130, 136, 152–157, 159, 167, 168, 172, 173,
    191, 202, 215, 216, 221, 222, 231–233, 235, 239,
    240
  changes in albino rats fed laboratory chow, 104
  changes in albino rats fed a rancid biotin deficient diet,
    104
Foods, 35
  the 100-day LD_{50} index of, 35
Food toxicants, 213, 214, 218
    fungi and bacteria, 213
    honey, glycosides in, 213
    potatoes, solanine in, 213

    prunes, hydroxyphenylisatin in, 213
    seafood, 213
    tomato juice, lycopene in, 213
    wheat, toxins in, 213
  toxicants added to foods, 214
    food additives, 214
    pesticides and pollutants, 214
  conclusions regarding, 218
  natural food toxicants, 213
Fox chow (see Laboratory chow)
Free cholesterol, 6
  in the tissues and organs of albino rats, 6
Fresh biotin deficient diet, 110
Fructose, 29, 39
Fruits, 23

G

Galactose, 39, 45
Gangrene, 231
  at the site of atropine injection, 231
Gases, 214
Gastric distension syndrome, 58, 59, 62
Gastric rupture, 48, 58, 61, 65, 121, 122, 147, 148, 201,
    207
Gastric tube insertions, 52, 65, 152
  effects of, 65, 152
  organ weights and water levels in albino rats following,
    52
Gastroenteritis, 24, 25, 27, 30, 163, 167, 184, 192, 223
Gastrointestinal hypertrophy, 64
Gastrointestinal impaction, 97
Gastrointestinal inflammation, 24
Gastrointestinal obstruction, 192
Gastrointestinal tract (see individual agents)
Globulin, 196
Glucose, 18, 29, 39–43, 57, 72, 119, 133, 183, 221
  acute oral toxicity of, 39
  autopsy findings at the acute oral LD_{50}, 40
  conclusions regarding, 43
  effect on body weight, 40
  effect on food intake, 40
  effect on water intake, 40
  effect on urinary blood, 40
  effect on urinary glucose, 40
  effect on urinary pH, 40
  effect on urinary protein, 40
  effect on urinary volume, 40
  histopathological findings in albino rats, 41
  oral LD_{50} of, 119
  organ water levels in albino rats at the range of the
    acute oral LD_{50}, 43
  organ weights in albino rats at the range of the acute
    oral LD_{50}, 42
  transport of, 183
Glycosuria, 25, 27, 29, 40, 46, 47, 86, 141, 150, 202,
    216, 240
Goblet cells, 75, 83
Growth, 5, 12, 18, 73, 85–87, 97, 108, 117, 122, 129–
    131, 134, 137, 153, 155, 170, 172, 173, 221, 226
  inhibition of, 12, 73, 85, 86, 97, 117, 122, 129, 130,
    137, 153, 155, 170, 172, 173, 221, 226

intestinal synthesis of, 18
supplementation of, 18
Growth rate, 14, 130, 140, 152, 170, 216, 239
decline in, 14
Guinea pigs, 9, 163, 201, 214, 231
Gum tragacanth, 45–57
acute oral toxicity of, 45
clinical signs of intoxication, 46
conclusions regarding, 56
death rates during the initial reaction, 47
effect on colonic temperature, 47, 52
effect on food intake, 47, 52
effect on urine blood, 47, 52
effect on urine glucose, 47, 52
effect on urine pH, 47, 52
effect on urine protein, 47, 52
effect on urine volume, 47, 52
effect on water intake, 47, 52
gross and microscopic pathology at death, 47, 48
histopathological lesions in albino rats after, 55
histopathological lesions seen at autopsy on albino
rats, 49
illustration of congestion of the renal capillaries, 50
illustration of effects on the cardiac stomach, 48
illustration of necrosis of the acinar glands, 51
illustration of the effect on the cecum, 53
inhibition of hepatic enzyme induction by, 45
organ weights and water levels in albino rats after, 54
pathological changes seen in albino rats due to oral
administration of a lethal dose of, 48
post-toxicity tolerance, 50
tolerance to, 46

H

Heart (see individual agents)
Hematuria, 16, 29, 40, 46, 47, 60, 72, 157, 226
Hemoconcentration, 106, 107, 123, 196, 197
Hemodacryorrhea, 29, 74, 238, 239
Hemoglobin, 2, 10, 107, 123, 140, 186, 196, 233
Hemorrhage, 2, 26, 31, 47–49, 61, 64, 74, 75, 83, 84,
87–90, 124, 176, 184, 235, 237
Hemosiderin, 189
Henle's loop, 26, 50, 55, 88–90, 92, 193, 214
Hepatic diseases, 2
plasma lipids in, 2
Hepatic enzymes, 39
Hepatitis, 175
Hepatomegaly, 103, 108, 109
Hereditary fructose intolerance, 39
High egg white biotin deficient diet, 103
Hydration, 86, 91, 100, 105, 138, 148–150, 156, 177,
193, 217, 223, 227, 235, 241
Hydrogenated cottonseed oil, 88
Hydrogenated vegetable oils, 71, 135
Hydroperoxides, 103
Hypercalcemia, 170
Hypercholesterolemia, 170
Hyperemia, 25, 26, 47, 55, 83, 84, 90, 115, 135, 157,
217, 218
Hyperkalemia, 183

Hyperpnea, 71
Hyperreflexia, 46, 135
Hypersensitivity reactions, 58
Hypertension, 163, 170, 183
administration of cortisone, 170
growth of arterial branch pads as the primary lesion in,
170
induced by renal artery compression, 170
induced by vasoactive drugs, 170
relationship of intake of sodium chloride to, 170
toxic effects of sodium chloride in, 163
Hypertonic contraction, 167, 170
Hypertonic expansion, 167
Hypertrophy, 30, 53, 55, 58, 61, 86, 90, 110, 129, 136,
157, 159, 175–177, 193, 216, 218, 240
Hypokalemia, 183
Hypokinesia, 24, 27, 59, 60, 152
Hyporeflexia, 29, 59, 64, 114, 118, 135, 153, 154, 190,
202, 226
Hypothermia, 11, 12, 46, 47, 82, 97, 104, 117, 122, 130,
136, 137, 138, 152, 175, 192, 193, 202, 214, 216,
223, 226, 231, 240
Hypothermic coma, 39, 175
Hypotonic contraction, 167
Hypotonic expansion, 167

I

Infections, 132, 163, 175, 235
sodium chloride in, 163
Inflammation, 30, 41, 42, 47, 56, 74, 87, 90, 122, 123,
214, 218
Inflammatory reaction, 12, 27, 41, 84, 87, 99, 115, 117,
122, 123, 165, 175, 193, 227
Intestinal flora, 15, 18
changes produced by antibiotics, 18
changes produced by benzylpenicillin, 15
Intestines, 191
impaction by iron, 191
Intracellular fluid, 167, 183
potassium as the main cation of, 183
Iodine, 57, 207
Iron, 189, 190, 192, 193, 197–199, 207
acute oral toxicity of powdered iron, 192, 193
autopsy findings, 192
delayed deaths in, 192, 193
early deaths in, 193
adsorption and elimination of, 189
balance sheet of the fate of iron injected intramuscularly
into albino rats, 199
content of the tissues of albino rats following
intramuscular injection, 198
history of therapy with, 189
toxicity in man, 189
toxicity of large amounts of tissue iron, 197
Iron and ammonium citrate, 197, 198
Iron deficiency anemia, 58, 197
iron powder in, 197
Iron phosphogluconate, 197, 198
Iron powder, 153, 189, 190, 191, 193–196, 199
absorption of toxic doses of, 193

organ weights and water levels in albino rats receiving 20 ml/kg/day, 156

organ weights in albino rats given varying amounts of, 158

organ weights in albino rats receiving amounts in the range of the acute LD_{50}, 151

total amounts of given by stomach tube to adult male albino rats, 147

withdrawal syndrome to, 156

Water intake, 10, 17, 18, 29, 40, 46, 59, 73, 85, 86, 97, 105, 118, 122, 126, 131, 136, 138, 150, 152–157, 159, 167, 168, 170, 172, 173, 191, 202, 215, 216, 221, 222, 232, 239

  decrease in, 138

Water intoxication, 147

  in man, 147

  in obstetric patients, 147

Water requirements, 129

Weight, 12, 14, 24, 32, 40, 42, 50, 53, 66, 119, 134, 135, 156, 159, 165, 177, 185, 193, 202, 214, 217, 231, 241

  loss of, 12, 14, 24, 32, 40, 42, 50, 53, 66, 119, 134–135, 156, 159, 165, 177, 185, 193, 202, 214, 217, 231, 241

Weight gain, 46, 76, 82

Weight loss, 46, 62, 65, 73, 74, 76, 77, 82, 84, 86, 89, 91, 99, 104–106, 108, 113, 115

X

Xylose, 45

Z

Zinc, 207

Zona fasciculata, 42, 136, 192

Zona glomerulosa, 99, 167

Zona reticularis, 136, 192

Zymogens, 25

Zymorgenic granules, 32, 49, 55, 74, 75, 138, 235, 240

  deficiency of, 138, 235

  loss of, 240